Religion at the Service of Nationalism

To the many unknown Prabhu Dayals,
who kept hope alive by asserting their
instinctive humanity at the darkest
moments of our national history.

Religion at the Service of Nationalism and Other Essays

Madhu Kishwar

DELHI
OXFORD UNIVERSITY PRESS
CALCUTTA   CHENNAI   MUMBAI
1998

Oxford University Press, Great Clarendon Street, Oxford OX2 6DP

Oxford   New York
Athens   Auckland   Bangkok   Calcutta
Cape Town   Chennai   Dar es Salaam   Delhi
Florence   Hong Kong   Istanbul   Karachi
Kuala Lumpur   Madrid   Melbourne   Mexico City
Mumbai   Nairobi   Paris   Singapore
Taipei   Tokyo   Toronto

and associates in

Berlin   Ibadan

ISBN 0 19 564161 2

Typeset by Eleven Arts, Keshav Puram, Delhi 110 035
Printed at Pauls Press, New Delhi 110 020
and published by Manzar Khan, Oxford University Press
YMCA Library Building, Jai Singh Road, New Delhi 110 001

Contents

Introduction

This volume contains a collection of my essays written between 1984 and 1996 in response to specific situations of ethnic violence and conflict. Most of them were published in *Manushi*. Except for slight editorial corrections, I have neither revised nor rewritten any of them. All were written contemporaneously with the events they describe and analyse, in response to moments of grave crisis. Based on firsthand accounts, they try to dispel popular misconceptions about what was happening. But they are not pieces written only for the moment. They combine some of the characteristics of investigative journalism with some aspects of more systematic research and political analysis. While they would read somewhat differently were I to write them today, the issues they raise and the framework of analysis that developed out of them over these years remain relevant because the types of problem they describe remain very much with us. This kind of writing is made possible because there is a courageous community of human rights activists in India whose work, commitment and writings have inspired and encouraged me in my small efforts over the years.

Prior to the November 1984 massacre of the Sikhs in Delhi and at other places in north India, I used to concentrate my attention primarily on problems of poverty, a variety of human rights issues, and the special problems of women. After the events of 1984, finding ways to combat the spread of ethnic violence and the closely related criminalization of our polity became one of my highest priorities. Each one of the essays represents an important stage in my attempts to understand why communal massacres take place, why they are becoming a regular feature of our polity, why almost all those who were responsible for these murders remain free and powerful, how these brutal acts were legitimated, and what could be done to prevent them from happening again.

The massacre of the Sikhs in north India following Mrs Gandhi's assassination was projected as a Hindu–Sikh riot by the mainstream media, our political leaders and their government. My own investigations that came out of our work in relief camps under the aegis of Nagrik Ekta Manch, as well as the contemporaneous report of the People's Union for Civil Liberties–PUCL-PUDR People's Union for Democratic Rights entitled *Who are the Guilty?* demonstrate beyond doubt that this was a politically engineered attack on the Sikhs, led and organized by the national-level leaders of the Congress party, along with their local cohorts in various cities and towns. In addition, my account tries to understand why the sexual atrocities inflicted on Sikh women had not been acknowledged in any of the other reports written at that time.

At a time when the media was calling it a Hindu–Sikh riot, a 'spontaneous outburst of anger' by the Hindu community, I deliberately chose to term it a 'massacre of the Sikhs'. The killer brigades organized by the Congress leaders did not face any interference from the police; indeed, they often received open support from them and the administrative machinery. The killings were a one-sided affair. Thousands of Sikhs were murdered but there was hardly any loss of life or property among Hindus. It took several years of unrelenting campaigning by a handful of human rights activists and Sikh community leaders before most people understood that this was a massacre, not a riot, and the lies were exposed.

The article 'This is the Guru's House' was written after a visit to the trouble-torn Punjab of the mid-1980s. It reflects my surprise at finding out how different Sant Longowal and his close associates were from the way they were projected in the national mass-media, and how effective had been the deliberate misinformation campaign launched by the Congress party and its government. Not only had the Congress been able to hide and bury the evidence of their previous covert support to Sikh terrorists that was one of the main reasons for the widening of the Hindu–Sikh divide both in and outside Punjab, they had even been able to get away with shifting much of the blame for the violence onto the Akali Dal leadership.

The 1984 massacre proved that the Indian state was incompetent and incapable of performing the most basic task of governance—

providing a safe and secure environment so that ordinary people from all ethnic groups can live safely and work without fear. The lack of accountability in-built into our machinery of governance lets those in positions of power get away with murder, loot and plunder. In broad daylight, in the heart of our capital city, the ruling party leaders were brazen enough to instigate violence against thousands of people belonging to a well-regarded minority. More than a decade after the massacre not one top leader or official who was known to have taken part in it has yet been convicted. The trials of a few of the killers have begun but continue only fitfully.

The newspaper coverage of these events provided a disturbing example of the failures of our supposedly free press. Habituated to publishing government hand-outs as news, the press too often fails to rise to the occasion even when a grave crisis threatens to tear the country asunder. Our national press was unable or unwilling to provide accurate information on events taking place right under its nose in the nation's capital, let alone what was happening in distant towns and remote areas. It willingly allowed itself to be blinded by nationalist rhetoric and to be cowed down by the media's own fears of standing up to our lawless rulers. It was obvious that what was happening was a carefully co-ordinated large-scale butchering of innocent citizens led by the ruling party. Seeing the vast discrepancy between what actually happened and what our free press reported, I vowed to myself that I would never write on any important event basing myself primarily on newspaper reports. Countering government's misinformation campaigns with honest and accurate information has to become an essential political responsibility of those concerned with building democracy and defending human rights in our country.

'Changing the Rules of the Political Game' was another attempt to dispel some of the misleading stereotypes about Sikh community politics by sharing with *Manushi's* readers the threats and problems we faced in our small attempt to make a contribution towards bridging the Hindu–Sikh divide. It shows how and why, even at the most local level, party politicians use a variety of devious tactics to thwart ordinary citizens from taking political initiatives—even on non-controversial issues like communal harmony—thus leading to a dangerous kind of depoliticization of the citizenry. Democracy is thereby reduced to the single ritual of casting votes whenever called upon to do so To be politically active in such a society usually only means becoming a link in the chain of vote-gatherers in return for the patronage of some powerful party leader.

Some of these essays on Punjab politics and on the Sikh community were translated into Punjabi by various groups and individuals. These were widely circulated in Punjab and among the overseas Sikh community, which emerged as the main financial and ideological support base of Khalistani politics. As a result of its in-depth reporting, *Manushi* gained the trust of a wide spectrum of politically active Sikhs, and was able to act as one of the few small communication lines at a time when relations between Hindus and Sikhs had suffered a serious breakdown.

By the mid-1980s the guns of Sikh terrorists had succeeded in silencing many dissenting voices within the Sikh community. Nevertheless, I was invited to address numerous gurudwara *sangats* in various parts of the Sikh diaspora and was able to challenge the destructive politics of those who had taken to terrorism. The essay 'Need to Re-establish Links' reports on the heated, honest and intense discussions I had with members of the Sikh community in North America and my attempt to get them to understand that the 1984 massacre of the Sikhs was part of a larger pattern of human rights abuses in India. Rather than build their politics on the mistaken belief that they were singled out for attack because the Indian government was innately anti-Sikh, I tried to communicate that the basic conflict in India was not based on religion but was rather a fight between those who support accountable democratic decentralization and the loot and plunder beneficiaries of our corrupt authoritarian centralism.

The essays in the second half of the book deal with Hindu–Muslim relations. Hindu–Muslim conflict is a special case; it is more problematic than all other majority–minority relations in India. It is the central problem that still remains unresolved since the days of the freedom movement. Given the long history of Hindu–Muslim problems in India and the legacy of the 1947 Partition, it is easy to use available rhetorical stereotypes to target Muslims and claim they are an anti-national community. The essays in this section attempt to break down these stereotypes.

'In Defence of our Dharma' analyses the Ram Mandir campaign primarily in terms of the harm done to the Hindu community by the Sangh Parivar politicians who promote *adharma* in the name of religion and nationalism and thereby destroy the self-confidence of the Hindu community, making it behave like a phobic minority. In this essay my own attraction to Gandhi's approach and the legacy of the Bhakti movement leads me to seek solutions in the realm of improving intercommunity relations rather than relying mainly or exclusively on government intervention.

Baba Lal Das, the official *pujari* of the Ramjanambhoomi temple who was forcibly deposed during the Ram Mandir take-over by the Sangh Parivar, was later murdered along with Rama Chandra Acharya, *mahant* of another temple in Ayodhya. My interview with him and the essay 'Criminalization of Politics' shows how the take-over of temples by political thugs is destroying the sanctity and autonomy of religious spaces and converting them into the lairs of criminals. Once again the mainstream media failed to give coverage to these important developments. The murder of Baba Lal Das, who paid with his life for opposing the demolition of Babri Masjid, received only cursory acknowledgement in our national press.

My investigation into the 1992 Bombay riots once again showed how, despite their political rivalry, the Congress, Shiv Sena and other components of the Sangh Parivar, though involved in deadly power struggles among themselves, find it easy to come together when it comes to participating in anti-Muslim massacres. This study revealed some disturbing new developments:

• many leftist trade-union leaders joined the rioting Hindu mobs.
• women are beginning to play an active role in killings, looting and arson attacks.
• riots are no longer merely due to intra-party rivalries but are also engineered to settle political scores between rival politicians of the same party (a former and the then serving Chief minister—both from the Congress, in this case.)

The essay 'Pro-Women or Anti-Muslim?' was written in response to the Shah Bano controversy. It similarly tries to combat the misleading impression conveyed by those who campaigned against the Muslim personal law, that the reformed Hindu law had been secularized in the 1950s and was equivalent to the provisions of a uniform civil code. They claimed that Hindu women had better rights in every respect as compared to Muslim women, and that the Muslim community's defence of their personal law was proof of their anti-national bias. At that time secularists, leftists, rightists, communalists, rationalists and feminists were all enamoured with the idea of imposing an as yet undefined form of a uniform civil code on an unwilling Muslim majority. As a consequence of this campaign that was ostensibly launched to protect Muslim women, the Hindu–Muslim divide grew sharper and anti-Muslim sentiment acquired more respectability. It took several years and much discussion before sections of the women's movement, leftists and secularists realized that forcing reform through high-handed statist measures was the wrong stand to take.

The Shah Bano essay was widely disseminated in the Urdu press. It opened many channels of communication for me with different sections of the Muslim community. The feedback I received provided valuable insights into the dilemmas they face. It provided guidelines for suggesting strategies that might help strengthen the inner urge of the Muslim community for improvement of the status of women rather than proposing policies that may thwart and kill that urge by making the whole community feel insecure as targets of hate campaigns from outside the community. The essays 'Breaking the Stalemate' and 'Stimulating Reform, Not Forcing It' build on this theme.

My work on minority rights issues taught me an important lesson. If you take up issues of social reform, especially those relating to women's rights, in the spirit of an attacking outsider, most of the time a community thus targeted will turn hostile and see you as an enemy. The women of that community are likely to shun efforts at such reform—even those meant to be for their benefit. This is especially true of insecure minority communities who are already vulnerable because of widespread prejudice against them. In order to be effective in intervening to enlarge women's rights, you have to have a proven track record of standing by that community in times of crisis and attack. For instance, if you remain silent when Muslims are being attacked and killed by Hindu nationalists or targeted by a communalized police, your interventions on women's rights issues, however well-meaning, are likely to be received with mistrust and hostility. Women's rights work cannot be carried out effectively by trying to drive a wedge between the men and women of any community.

A workable long-range strategy also requires a simultaneous balancing of support provided to minority rights and women's rights. Too many of those involved with minority rights issues end up taking positions which justify even cruel and unreasonable acts of the minority community towards its women, just as some feminists, in their single-minded pursuit of women's rights, turn a blind eye to the injustices suffered by the men of that community. Similarly, many human rights activists often end up being soft on violations of human rights by terrorists in their attempt to focus on abuses by the government and the ruling elites, thereby severely reducing their own effectiveness and risking their credibility.

The article 'Religion at the Service of Nationalism' marks the beginnings of a more pragmatic approach to suggesting strategies to help resolve the Hindu–Muslim conflict in India. It contains a comprehensive statement of the political framework and perspective that emerged out of my long involvement with issues of ethnic conflict. Even though I continue to be influenced by the Mahatma's complex and multilayered position on the place of nationalism in political life, I am now closer in my thinking to Tagore, who emphasized throughout most of his life that the European poison of nationalism was the source of much of the violence and hatred that has brought so many disasters to the Indian people.

Hindu–Muslim relations have been put through their severest test by the secessionist movement in Kashmir, just as it has acted as a harsh litmus test for the human rights activists in India. A small section of them went overboard and began to justify terrorist killings because of their commitment to opposing state terrorism. A much larger section turned nationalistic and declared that human rights discourse is irrelevant when dealing with a secessionist movement. Even though my essay report 'Voices from Kashmir' does not adequately cover the predicament of Hindu refugees from Kashmir, it incorporates the viewpoint of more responsible voices within that community. It also points out that much of the responsibility for the outbreak of a secessionist movement and of terrorism in Kashmir is a consequence of the corruption and high-handedness of the central government and the consequent political subversion of even the limited amount of federalism enshrined in our Constitution—all for the short-term interests of politicians who wish to rule India from the Delhi durbar. At the same time it takes a strong stand against terrorist politics and the insensitivity of Kashmiri Muslim leaders to the aspirations of ethnic minorities and regions within the state of Jammu and Kashmir.

Most of the essays reach a common conclusion—the biggest threat to the well-being of our society and inter-community relations comes from those who rule us, with their lack of concern about the awful consequences of their greed and callousness. What distinguishes ethnic hostilities in India from those of Europe is that, left on their own, our traditional communities have worked out eminently feasible norms for co-existence, including evolving common cultural symbols and spaces, and sharing in each other's rituals and festivities. There is nothing in Indian history comparable to the unremitting and vast blood-letting, torture and hostility Christians unleashed against Jews in Europe or the centuries-long bloody denominational wars between Protestants and Catholics. In India mutual antagonisms among various sects and communities did not begin to conceive of mass murder as ethnic cleansing until some ambitious political leaders imported the notion of ethnic nationalism from Europe and combined it with a vulgar but convenient idea of democracy as the rule of the majority community.

One of the hallmarks of democracy is the notion of rule by majority vote of all adults—men and women, rich and poor. However, some deify head-counting in an attempt to create monolithic majorities as the sole criterion of democracy rather than use the principle for decision-making on appropriate issues. Combined with the idea of membership in a nation on the basis of an arbitrary and supposedly objective marker such as religion, language, colour or caste, this ideology has produced many disasters for many societies in the twentieth century. In this incarnation, confusions about democratic principles easily lend a false legitimacy to majoritarianism, that is, an attempt by the self-proclaimed leaders of the 'majority' ethnic grouping to assume total control over the fate of the 'minority' by forcing the latter to live solely according to the terms dictated by those who claim to rule in the name of the ethnic 'majority'. A leader of a ruling group claims supremacy in a particular area by attempting to demonstrate he/she represents such a majority 'identity'. Such rulers have escalated ethnic conflicts to unprecedented levels of bloody slaughter of crores of people in this century, especially in Europe, the birthplace of nationalism.

Most traditional micro-societies, by contrast, worked out rules of co-existence through a consensual process. Decisions were made on the basis of customary practices which kept evolving over time to meet with changing situations. Those who possessed the patience and skills to conciliate or manipulate local groups to elicit consensus among them about a mutually agreed upon course of action were the most effective and sought-after leaders. The diverse communities inhabiting the Indian subcontinent were able to evolve fairly sophisticated and workable norms for co-existence because, unlike in Europe, there was no central religious authority mobilizing sections of the population under its umbrella against those professing a different faith. Moreover, local communities remained largely independent of the political rulers at the top, just as the secular and the religious domains remained somewhat independent of one another. Therefore, local differences in almost all cases had to be settled locally without help or interference from outside political or religious authorities. The local people understood that failure to work out such ground rules leads directly to basic insecurity for all concerned. Hostilities and attacks on others at a local level have to be carried out at personal risk and expense.

However, the emergence of the imported modern ideology and practices of nation-states changed all that. In most cases the leaders who could claim to speak for the majority identity, real or engineered, acquired control over the state machinery with its advanced technology for the use of organized violence. They could, therefore, use its coercive and repressive power against the minorities, without themselves or their followers among the majority incurring much personal risk in doing so.

Definitions of majority and minority frequently change, with power-hungry leaders identifying ever new markers of who is in the majority and who should be targeted as a minority. If we look around the world today we find that the original idea of democracy by majority vote is working well only in those societies which have:

(a) small, homogeneous populations where there is a broad consensus regarding the basic organizational principles of that society as, for example, in Sweden and Denmark; or

(b) multicultural, multi-ethnic populations where over long periods of time the common acceptance of certain workable political rules of decision-making have more or less allowed for their evolution into functioning polities (e.g. Switzerland, Canada, USA).

But even in the most well-functioning Western democracies a certain equilibrium between the majority and minority populations has been arrived at by setting definite limits to majority and minority rights. To begin with, the ethnic minorities, in theory at least, are assured basic rights to participate in important political decisions, including those regarding raising and allocating public resources. However, the possibility of political separation is not normally on the agenda. The minorities in these societies are now beginning to be given somewhat more political and cultural space for the expression and assertion of their identity with some autonomy in the context of majority defined cultures. But they do not have the right to challenge or veto the basic principles of governance. They cannot call into question certain basic rights of all citizens or seek parallel governance by subjugating individual members of their group in ways that conflict with the individual rights of citizens. They can live as distinct communities but do not ordinarily have the right to declare themselves as separate nationalities. Since they have come to believe that their right to life, to liberty, and the freedom to pursue a livelihood is guaranteed by the nation-state, minorities in these democracies are rarely likely to challenge the nation-state itself. We must, however, recognize that Europe began to have a stable political context which allows majority rule in just a few mutually agreed upon areas of political functioning only recently, after tens of millions of Europeans were killed in all out wars or were exterminated or forced to migrate. Democracies of European settlers, such as those in the US, Canada and Australia, were built while the indigenous populations were either wiped out or confined to reservations and peripheral areas. And now that Europe is once again forced to confront non-European peoples on its soil who were originally asked to come as 'guest workers' to provide temporary cheap labour, there is a fresh resurgence of violent and murderous forms of racism. In addition, the outbreak of another genocidal conflict, this time in the former Yugoslavia after the collapse of communism, and the ethnic conflicts that have broken out in other areas of eastern Europe, are examples that show that Europe has not fully learned as yet how to evolve genuine democracies within a framework of ethnic diversity.

By contrast, India is a striking example of a multi-ethnic society with a long established tradition of mutual accommodation and respect for diversity among communities. Much of our political mess has arisen out of our uncritical acceptance of many of the continental European national ideologies that make the mechanical equivalency of ethnic and national identities the keystone of nation-building and head-counts of ethnic majorities a licence to carry out all sorts of genocidal acts. Implementing such an ideology is totally unworkable in India because of its complex heterogeneity. But some political leaders will not stop trying to create this cleavage.

While the principle of majority vote may have proved facilitative in areas where there has been basic agreement about the ruling principles of state functioning, it has created disastrous consequences when it is applied to making fundamental choices regarding the character and guiding principles of the nation-state, especially regarding the critical choice of who is to have which basic rights and who is not to have those rights. Significant populations in nation-states have been 'constitutionally' disenfranchised, expelled, annihilated, or treated as subhuman through use of this majoritarian principle.

The notion that an arbitrarily defined majority and minority could and should claim sovereign rights over different parts of the newly emerging and yet undefined subcontinent in the places where they were in a majority led to the disastrous Partition of 1947. Pakistan was justified on the ground that the sole spokesman for a majority of those resident in certain provinces could claim sovereignty for those who had been born into the same faith. This sovereignty, in turn, was supposed to give him the right to push out many millions of people from their homes merely because they were not of the same faith despite the fact that the two communities had lived together for centuries, sharing common territory, languages and culture.

Manto's powerful story 'Toba Tek Singh' describes the bewilderment of the 'mad' hero who resists being forcibly moved to a new state of which he is a 'national' while he has no right to live where his family had lived for centuries. He finally collapses on the imaginary line called the 'Indo-Pakistan border'. This ending brings out the tragedy and the absurdity behind the notion of carving out nation-states on the basis of a politically manipulated majority vote based on identities.

The dominant political leadership in India was determined not to go the way of Pakistan and identify the state with any particular religion. But despite this, the legacy of the Partition and the fact that two breakaway territories have adopted majoritarian and theocratic polities, have distorted the political agenda in India. The additional disability of a dysfunctional, incompetent and lawless government easy to hijack for personal benefit or sectarian ends by any group who manages to capture the levers of power, has vitiated inter-community relations in dangerous ways. Most of the essays in this book grope for approaches to a solution to this problem.

Even though my own thinking is deeply influenced by our traditional heritage of working out inter-community relations and Gandhi's approach which relied on reviving some of the traditional bonds and norms of co-existence worked out among our different ethnic communities, in recent years I have come to realize that the solution to contemporary ethnic conflicts cannot lie in hearkening back to that past and making futile attempts to revive that spirit. Even the Mahatma failed in this effort despite the epic grandeur of his experiment. Gandhi tried to forge Hindu–Muslim unity by insisting on the oneness of all religions. What Balraj Puri describes as the 'Ram–Rahim approach' was drawn from the Bhakti–Sufi tradition and emphasized the shared common heritage and bonds between the two communities.

The Ram–Rahim approach historically evolved in attempts at resolving theological conflicts between Islam and Hindu religious beliefs in pre-British times, when the rulers were mostly distant figures and had little influence on the day-to-day lives of ordinary people who were free to work out mutually agreed upon arrangements for co-existence. The modern nation-state does not allow for that kind of autonomy, for it encroaches upon every aspect of a citizen's life and insists on more or less direct relations with each household. Therefore, influence or control over the state machinery becomes a do-or-die issue for every community, especially their leaders. Whoever controls the state machinery can 'lawfully' subjugate others. And since acquiring this control is seen as legitimate if you can claim to objectively represent a majority, modern politics brings many of the ingredients of warfare into the electoral arena.

Successful democracies are those which are able to establish civilized rules and norms that provide explicitly for the rights of minorities during this battle, rather than rely on moral sermons to make people rise above mundane conflicts over power and privileges. They also ensure institutional safeguards against outright abuse of power by whichever group comes to control or dominate the government. For example, many democracies are currently experimenting with different schemes of proportional representation in their parliament.

In most parts of the world, majority–minority relations are soured by the majority insisting on the inferiority and 'otherness' of the minority and proclaiming their own 'superiority'. In India, the situation is the reverse. Here the problem is created due to the insistence of the Hindu majority that the Muslims, Buddhists, Sikhs and Jains are not really different from the Hindus, that the term Hindu includes all the people of Hindustan and is not a religious marker. They bolster this argument by pointing out that most of those professing other religions in India are converts from various Hindu sects and castes and the term Hindu was originally used to denote people living in the land beyond the Sindhu river. The minorities fear this assimilative tendency of Hinduism perhaps more than its aggressive attacks. An essential component of the political demands of the minorities is the recognition of their separate identity or special rights based on their separateness. The *dohas* of Kabir and the verses of Tukaram or Guru Nanak cannot provide us meaningful answers to these vexed questions.

Today we need to figure out more workable political solutions. When any group arrives at a point where its primary urge is to seek recognition of its separate identity with a view to demanding a share in political and economic power, emphasis on oneness can only act as an irritant. A polity that fails to provide a legitimate space for identity assertion of various types along with well-worked-out rules for deciding which issues are to be decided by majority vote and which should be left out of the public arena of polling and be worked out through some sort of agreement that keeps the minorities from feeling overwhelmed, is one that is heading for civil war or worse.

The future of democracy in India is integrally tied to our ability to work out a satisfactory solution to majority–minority relations that goes beyond temporary palliatives and moral appeals. Instead, we have to devise functional institutional arrangements for power-sharing among the different groups that contain mutually agreed upon compacts between different communities. However, that can happen only after we find ways of making our government behave lawfully and adhere to well-defined and effective rules for monitoring its conduct. Observing these rules of procedure makes it harder for politicians to play divisive games that become an excuse for the government to usurp some of the essential functions and responsibilities of a civil society and disempower its citizens.

Gangster Rule:
The Massacre of the Sikhs

T he communal riots that followed Indira Gandhi's tragic death
on 31 October 1984 were like the sudden eruption of a gigantic
volcano. The ferocity of the explosion took by surprise both
the victimized community as well as the community in whose name
the vicious campaign of looting, arson, killing, burning, rape and
molestation took place.

Most observers agree that the violence began as random attacks
on individual Sikh men who were pounced upon in public places,
on public transport and on the streets on 31 October. Some people
attempted to pass off the day's events as a reactive outburst of anger
at the assassination of Indira Gandhi by two Sikh members of her
security guard. But what happened over the next three days makes
it impossible to dismiss those events as spontaneous expressions of
outrage.

The series of attacks on Sikh homes, gurudwaras and commercial
establishments which began on 1 November seems to have been
the work of organized hoodlums who collected large mobs for
systematic looting and killing. Broadly speaking, the attacks can be
placed in three categories:

(a) Looting and killing in middle and upper middle-class localities,
such as Lajpat Nagar, Jangpura, Defence Colony, Friends Colony,
Maharani Bagh, Patel Nagar, Safdarjung Enclave, and Punjabi
Bagh. Here, houses, gurudwaras and shops were looted and
burnt, and a large number of vehicles, including buses, trucks,
cars and scooters, were set ablaze. Some people were injured
and others killed. But, on the whole, relatively fewer lives were
lost in middle and upper class colonies.

First published in *Manushi* No. 25 (Nov–Dec 1984).

(b) Systematic slaughter and rape that accompanied looting, arson and burning in the resettlement colonies, slums and villages around the city. Most of the deaths occurred in areas like Trilokpuri, Kalyanpuri, Mangolpuri, Sultanpuri, Nand Nagri, Palam village, Shakurpur and Gamri. Rows of houses and huts were burnt down and hundreds of men and young boys were beaten, stabbed and burnt to death. Many women were abducted and raped. A large number of persons are still reported missing by their families. Houses and gurudwaras were looted and burnt down.

(c) Attacks on Sikh men and boys in the streets, trains, buses, markets and workplaces. Many of them were brutally murdered. Some were burnt alive or thrown out of trains. Others escaped with injuries of a more or less serious kind. This kind of attack seems to have been done at random—any man who looked like a Sikh was made a target.

Most of my observations are based on tape-recorded interviews with men and women from some trans-Yamuna colonies, especially Trilokpuri. These were among the worst-hit areas in Delhi. Some other observations are based on what I saw happening in our neighbourhood, Lajpat Nagar, and on conversations with our neighbours, as well as with friends living in different middle-class colonies in the city. The pattern of murder and arson was similar in most parts of Delhi, in as far-flung places as Palam village, Mangolpuri, Kalyanpuri, and Bhogal. However, the intensity of violence was far more severe in poorer resettlement colonies than in middle-class areas.

Trilokpuri is one of those resettlement colonies which were brought into existence during the Emergency, when Sanjay Gandhi spearheaded slum-clearance drives in Delhi. Thousands of families were forcibly evicted from slums and unauthorized colonies in the city. They were transported to areas several miles away from the city proper, and were resettled there. Each evicted family was supposed to be given a small plot measuring 25 square yards, and also, in some cases, a loan to build a house. Thus were founded these colonies of the city poor who had been evicted from the inner city slums and pavement dwellings where they lived earlier.

Even though, at that time, many people saw the evictions as cruelty inflicted on the city poor, the Congress (I) was able to convert the resettlement colonies into solid support bases and vote banks, because the evicted families slowly began to feel that their status had been considerably boosted since each of them now owned a piece of land and a *pukka* house, instead of living as formerly in unauthorized structures in slums. Many of the riot victims interviewed—people who were the original recipients of land—mentioned that they were very grateful to Indira Gandhi and to her party for this favour. However, many of these people sold off their allotments because the resettlement colonies are very far away from the city proper. Many lower middle-class families bought plots of land from the original allottees. Thus, today, the social composition of these colonies provides a rich mixture. For instance, one finds north Indians and south Indians, Hindus, Christians and Sikhs living side by side in a typical settlement colony like Trilokpuri.

The residents of these colonies have wide ranging occupations such as petty shopkeeping, business, domestic service, low-level government employment, Rickshaw-pulling, scooter-driving, peddling and artisanry. In normal times, there seems to be a good amount of intermingling and friendly feeling between neighbours of different communities, even among those who speak different languages. Yet the innate feelings about relative status are also pronounced.

There are significant variations among the Trilokpuri Sikhs. A large number of them, especially those most severely affected by the riots, are known as Labana Sikhs. These are not Punjabi Sikhs. They are migrants from Sikligarh in Sind, now part of Pakistan. They speak either Hindi or their own dialect, a language which is distinctly different from Punjabi. The traditional occupation of the community is weaving string cots and pounding rice. Few of the men still perform these jobs. Most of them have switched over to other occupations. A number of them drive scooters or pull cycle-rickshaws. Some work as porters at different railway stations. Others have taken to working as mechanics, carpenters and construction workers. A few have been to Gulf countries as skilled labourers.

Even though they do not call themselves Mazhabi Sikhs, they are considered low caste by other Sikhs. Makhan Bai of Trilokpuri summed up the distinction aptly. Referring to urban-based Sikhs, most of whom are involved in commerce, she said: 'Punjabi Sikhs are Seths. We Labana Sikhs are labourers. Traditionally, we are *charpai* (string bed) makers.' Differences are also visible even amongst the Labana Sikhs in this colony. Those who have entered some of the newer occupations such as scooter-driving or mechanical repair work are relatively better off. They have pukka houses and their own plots of land. They are an upwardly-mobile community. Many of them own television sets, tape-recorders and other such consumer goods. However, those who were not able to move into these new occupations are much poorer. Some of them live in illegally constructed huts in open spaces which are meant to be parks.

Labana Sikhs live together in clusters in blocks 30 and 32 of Trilokpuri. There are also some families scattered in other blocks. Labana Sikhs have a separate small gurudwara of their own. There is also a big gurudwara adjoining the main road in Trilokpuri. The Labana Sikh community seems to have very little connection with Punjab politics. Many of them are traditional Congress (I) supporters. That is one reason why they, like most Sikhs in Delhi, were totally surprised by the attack.

More than 400 people were murdered in Trilokpuri alone. The largest member of deaths has so far been reported from the two blocks of Trilokpuri where the Labana Sikhs were concentrated. This is how Gulzar Singh, a resident of block 30 in Trilokpuri, describes the events of 1 November:

My house was the first to be burnt in Trilokpuri. I work for a tailor's shop. I bring the material from the shop every morning and stitch the garments at home. On 31 October, when I was on my way back from the shop, I heard rumours that Indira Gandhi had died. But no one stopped me or tried to hurt me. I never imagined that such a thing could happen to me. None of us were really prepared for what happened the next day.

At about 10 a.m. on 1 November, we heard a lot of noise and shouting. We climbed on the roofs of our houses to see what was happening. We saw smoke rising from Noida colony and then we smelt human flesh burning. In the meantime, we heard people say that the mob, having set fire to the main gurudwara, was now coming to burn our Labana Sikh gurudwara. So we rushed and got together whatever weapons we had, and tried to save the gurudwara. But even when the gurudwara was attacked, we thought there would be fighting for a short while, and then the police would come and stop it. We never thought things would go so far. There has been no atmosphere of conflict between Hindus and Sikhs in Trilokpuri.

Several men from our block went and hid in other lanes nearby. So we were not more than 500 men left to defend the whole block as well as the gurudwara. About 50 of us stood on each side of the streets in our block. The attackers came in a mob of about 4,000 strong, and began to attack the gurudwara. They were armed with lathis. They began throwing bricks and stones at us. We also stoned them. See, my fingers are cut with throwing bricks. Many of us got hurt. Heads were split open. The attackers far outnumbered us. Gradually, we had to give up. They advanced and we began to retreat into our houses. They set fire to the gurudwara.

Then they began to attack our houses. We ran from one house to another, trying to save ourselves. They broke into each house and carried away all our possessions on *thelas*. There were about four policemen watching this looting campaign. They told us to put down our swords and not to worry. They said: 'Nothing will happen to you.' Then they went away and left us to be killed.

Sajan Singh from block 32 adds that the attackers had three guns. The police kept telling the Sikhs to go into their houses, assuring them that peace would be restored. 'We believed the police and we went in. That is how they got us killed.' He accuses the SHO of the area, one Tyagi, of having actively encouraged the attackers. Many others of the area also testify that they heard Tyagi tell the attackers: 'You have three days to kill them. Do your job well. Do not leave a single man alive, otherwise I will have to suffer.'

Once the attempt at group defence broke down, the Sikhs were in a much more vulnerable position. Each man ran desperately to find for himself a hiding place from the mob. Gulzar Singh continues his narrative:

By the evening of 1 November, some peace was restored. The attackers left. They threatened that they would return the next day and would take away the women. Several men died that day. About half a dozen died in my presence. The attackers hit them with lathis and *khurpis*. They also managed to snatch some of our *kirpans* and stabbed some of us with them. When they were looting and burning my house, they caught hold of me. They burnt part of my hair and cut part of it before I managed to break free.

I saved myself by hiding in my brother's house which is in a Hindu street. For one day and two nights, my brother and I hid under a double bed. On 2 November, a group of men came and began to search each house for Sardars. My wife says three men were caught and killed in the neighbouring house. The attackers turned everyone out of the house and searched it. We were hiding behind boxes and bags under the bed. They kicked the boxes and thought there was no one there. Another minute and we would have been finished.

On 3 November, the military came and my wife told them to rescue us. That is how we reached the relief camp. One of my brothers was found by the attackers and killed the previous day. They threw him down from the roof of his house and broke his spine. Then they burnt him alive. Many women were molested and abducted. I saw a jeep-load of women being carried away to village Chilla.

Most others who survived had been through similar experiences. The attackers would kill every Sikh male in sight, then would leave for a while, but would return again to search Sikh houses and neighbours' houses to finish off those men who were still in hiding.

Sajan Singh, who works as a porter at Nizamuddin railway station, and lives in block 32 Trilokpuri, saved himself by hiding in his house. He took refuge in a small aperture where cow-dung cakes were stored for fuel. The attackers came in repeated waves into his house and looted everything they could find. He says he had Rs 12,000 in cash, a television set, a radio, a tape-recorder, utensils, eight quilts, blankets and other household goods, many of which were being stored up as dowries for his four daughters. At night, the attackers came with torches to search for men who were still hiding. Sajan got his children to bring him a pair of scissors and a stick. He cut off his long hair and beard while he was hiding under the cow-dung cakes. Then, he says:

When the next wave came, I picked up a stick and mingled with the mob. All night, I shouted anti-Sikh slogans like 'Kill the Sardars ' That is how I saved myself. At 6 a.m., I somehow managed to slip away and came to Nizamuddin railway station. There, the other porters gave me shelter and consoled me. I did not know what had befallen my family. On 6 November, I came to Farash Bazar relief camp and found them there. My sister had been raped; the other women and children were safe.

Many others were less fortunate. One old man, Gurcharan Singh, also from block 32, lost all the three young men of his family. He had only one son, aged about 17, and two nephews, aged 20 and 22. All four men stayed in hiding for two days and one night. Finally, the door of the house was broken open. The four men had already clipped their beards and cut off their long hair. They came out and pleaded to be spared now that they were like Hindus. But the rioters caught hold of the three young men, threw them on their own string beds, covered them with mattresses and quilts, then poured kerosene over them and set them on fire in Gurcharan Singh's presence. Gurcharan Singh was beaten up. He and his aged wife, who is a TB patient, are in the relief camp, despairing over the loss of their three sons, and rendered destitute.

Many of these one-sided battles continued for hours on end.

The woman neighbour of a victimized family in Shakurpur described the attack:

The mob came here on the night of 31 October, and the fighting continued until 2 November. The attackers began by stopping vehicles-to check if there were Sikhs in them. Electricity failed in this area, in the houses as well as on the streets. The extreme darkness at night heightened the terror. The attacks on houses and gurudwaras started around 9.30 a.m. on 1 November. They came and started stoning the house of our neighbour, Santokh Singh. The family stayed quiet. The attackers were hesitant to enter the house because they were afraid of possible resistance. People are generally afraid of Sikhs, you know. Finally, one of the men tried to break into the house. The men of the family hit him with a sword and his hand got slightly cut. This frightened the crowd and they retreated for a while. Then they slowly collected more men and returned. Now there were about 1000 men. They dragged some furniture and wood that was lying in Santokh Singh's courtyard, piled it up around the house, and set the house on fire. Then, the four men of the family came out with swords in their hands. The attackers immediately ran away. They did not want to take any risk. They were armed only with lathis and kerosene. But they soon advanced again and started stoning the house from all sides. The house was now burning. The four men of the family ran for their lives. One went to the house of a neighbour who cut his hair, gave him shelter and later smuggled him out of the colony. The youngest son was pounced upon on the road, hit with lathis and burnt to death. Another son is missing. We do not know what happened to him. Most probably, he was murdered by the same group. After some time the police came and took away the old father and the women to a camp. They have not yet arrested anyone.

So murderous were the attacks throughout the city that most of the men who fell into the hands of the mobs did not survive. The number of injured men was very small in comparison to the numbers killed.

Most people in Trilokpuri said that though their immediate neighbours were not amongst the attackers, a fair number of rioters were from other parts of the same colony. They identified these men as Chamars, Sansis, Musalmans and Gujjars. They said the last named had been specially brought in for the attack that morning from Chilla, an adjoining village. Many eyewitnesses confirm that the attackers were not so much a frenzied mob as a set of men who had a task to perform and went about it in an unhurried manner. They behaved as if certain that they need not fear intervention by the police or anyone else. When their initial attacks were repulsed, they retired temporarily but returned again and again in waves until they had done exactly what they meant to do—killed the men and boys, raped women, looted property and burnt houses.

This is noteworthy because in ordinary, more spontaneous riots, the number of people injured is usually observed to be far higher than the number killed. The nature of the attack confirms that there was a deliberate plan to kill as many Sikh men as possible; hence nothing was left to chance. That also explains why the victims were first hit or stabbed and then doused with kerosene or petrol and burnt. This left no possibility of their survival.

According to careful unofficial estimates, more than 2500 men were murdered in different parts of Delhi between 31 October and 3 November.*

There were few cases of women being killed except when they got trapped in houses which were set on fire. Almost all the women interviewed described how men and young boys were the targets of the violence. They were dragged out of the houses, attacked with stones and rods, and set on fire. In Trilokpuri, many women said that the attackers did not allow any woman to remain inside her own home once the attack on individual homes started. The attackers wanted to prevent the women from helping the men to hide or from providing assistance to those who were in hiding. Throughout this period, many of the women were on the streets.

When women tried to protect the men of their families, they were given a few blows and forcibly separated from the men. Even when they clung to these men, trying to save them, they were hardly ever attacked the way men were. I have not yet heard of a case of any woman being assaulted and then burnt to death by the mob. However, many women were injured when they tried to intervene and protect men, or when they were molested and raped. A number of women and girls also died when the gangs burnt down their houses while they remained inside.

The instances described above are somewhat unusual. For instance, when Dalit bastis and homes in villages are burnt and attacked, women are prominent among the victims. When I asked why the killing was so selective, I got a uniform answer from most

* Initially the government gave a figure of 650 for those killed but later admitted that 3000 Sikhs were murdered in those three days in Delhi alone.

people interviewed: 'They wanted to wipe out the men so that families would be left without earning members. Also, now they need not fear retaliation even if we have to go back and live in the same colony.' Though this may not provide a complete explanation, the effect has been exactly that which the women describe.

In many cases, families tried to save male adolescents and little boys by dressing them up as girls and tying their hair in loose hanging plaits. Sometimes neighbours pointed out these disguised boys to the attackers. When such boys were caught, they were pounced upon by the crowd and set on fire. However, a few, especially very young ones, did manage to escape death by assuming this guise.

Fifteen-year-old Sukhpal Singh is one of the few older boys of Trilokpuri who was able to escape by dressing as a girl. His family lives in block 19 but on that fateful morning, his parents sent him to his sister's house in block 30 because they felt he would be safer in the latter area where Sikhs lived together in a larger cluster. Sukhpal's brother-in-law sought shelter in a Sikh house but he was turned out. The mob caught him on the second floor of a house, threw him down and burnt him alive. Sukhpal Singh's sister dressed him up in girl's clothes and braided his long hair. Somehow, he managed to escape attention and discovery.

In most camps, there is a disproportionately large number of women and children. Among boys, most of those who managed to escape were little ones. According to figures collected by the Nagrik Ekta Manch volunteer Jaya Jaitley, out of about 539 families housed in Farash Bazar camp, there are 210 widows. Families which have lost all adult male members are the ones most afraid of going back to the colonies where they formerly lived. Most do not want to go back even to reclaim their plots of land, and would rather be settled elsewhere.

Even though women were seldom killed, they were subjected to other forms of torture, terror and humiliation. This part of the story also makes familiar reading for anyone who has gone through accounts of riots, communal clashes and wars. Gurdip Kaur, a 45-year-old woman from block 32, Trilokpuri, told a typical story. Her husband and three sons were brutally murdered in front of her. Her husband used to run a small shop in the locality. Her eldest son, Bhajan Singh, worked in the railway station, the second in a radio repair shop and the third as a scooter driver. She says:

On the morning of 1 November, when Indira Mata's body was brought to Teen Murti, everyone was watching television. Since 8 a.m. they had been showing the homage being paid to her dead body. At about noon, my children said: 'Mother, please make some food. We are hungry.' I had not cooked that day and I told them: 'Son, everyone is mourning. She was our mother, too. She helped us to settle here. So I don't feel like lighting the fire today.' Soon after this the attack started. Three of the men ran out and were set on fire. My youngest son stayed in the house with me. He shaved off his beard and cut his hair. But they came into the house. Those young boys, 14 and 16 years old, began to drag my son out even though he was hiding behind me. They tore my clothes and stripped me naked in front of my son. When these young boys began to rape me, my son began to cry and said: 'Elder brothers, don't do this. She is like your mother just as she is my mother.' But they raped me right there, in front of my son, in my house. They were young boys, maybe eight of them. When one of them raped me, I said: 'My child, never mind. Do what you like. But remember, I have given birth to children. This child came into the world by this same path.'

After they had taken my honour, they left. I took my son out with me and made him sit among the women but they came and dragged him away. They took him to the street corner, hit him with lathis, sprinkled kerosene over him, and burnt him alive. I tried to save him but they struck me with knives and broke my arm. At that time, I was completely naked. I somehow managed to get hold of an old sheet which I had wrapped around myself. But that could easily be pulled away unless I held on tight to it with my arms. It inhibited my physical movements. If I had had even one piece of clothing on my body, I would have gone and thrown myself over my son and tried to save him. I would have done anything to save at least one young man of my family. Not one of the four is left.

According to Gurdip Kaur, hardly any woman in her neighbourhood was spared the humiliation she underwent. She said even nine- and ten-year-old girls were raped. She was an eyewitness to many such rapes. The attackers first emptied the houses of men who were burnt alive. After that, they dragged the women inside the ransacked houses and gang-raped them. Not many women would openly admit this fact because, as Gurdip Kaur says: 'The unmarried girls will have to stay unmarried all their lives if they admit that they have been dishonoured. No one would marry such a girl.' Therefore, most families do not openly acknowledge the rapes.

I asked Gurdip Kaur why she had come forward to narrate her experience. I also asked her whether she wanted me to publish her statement. She categorically said she wanted her statement to be published: 'Those women in whose homes there are one or more surviving men cannot make a public statement because they will be dishonouring those men. I have no one [no male member of the family] left. My daughter has also been widowed. She has two children. My daughter-in-law, who has three children, has also been widowed. Another daughter-in-law was married only one and a half months ago and has also been widowed. I have nothing left. That is why I want to give my statement.'

In fact, many other families whose adult men had all been killed similarly felt that there was 'no one left in the family'. At times, when people said that all their children (*bacchey*) had been killed, they were actually referring only to their sons. I had specifically to enquire about surviving daughters, whose lives did not count in the same way.

Indra Bai narrates:

At about 4 p.m., after they had murdered all the Sikh men they could get hold of in our block, they asked the women to come out of the houses. They said: 'Now your men are dead. Come out and sit together or else we will kill you, too.'

We women all huddled together and they offered us some water. As we were drinking water, they began dragging off whichever girl they liked. Each girl was taken away by a gang of 10 or 12 boys, many of them in their teens. They would take her to the nearby masjid, gang-rape her, and send her back after a few hours. Some never returned. Those who did were in a pitiable condition and without a stitch of clothing. One young girl said 15 men climbed on her.

Gurdip Kaur and many other women from Trilokpuri whom I interviewed at Balasaheb gurudwara and at Farash Bazar camp also talked about several women who had been abducted by gangsters and taken to Chilla village which is dominated by Gujjars, some of whom were supposed to have led the attacking gangs. On 3 November, the military brought some of these women back from Chilla. But many of them were untraceable at the time I interviewed these families. They were very worried that these women had either been murdered or were still being held captive.

Rajjo Bai, another old woman from the same neighbourhood, who had sought shelter in Balasaheb gurudwara in Ashram, had a similar story to tell. Two of her sons were killed in her presence. One who was hiding in a hut is still missing. All three sons were rickshaw pullers. She got separated from her two daughters-in-law who were probably abducted. The daughters-in-law were found much later at the Farash Bazar camp but Rajjo's 24-year-old daughter, who had had to be left behind in the house because she was disabled, could not be traced. Nanki Bai, also from Trilokpuri, was distraught when she asked us to look for her daughter, Koshala Bai, who had been snatched away from her. She says:

All night, the attacks continued. My husband was hiding in a trunk. They dragged him out and cut him to pieces. Another 16-year-old boy was killed in front of my eyes. He was carrying a small child in his arms. They killed the child, too.

We women were forced to come out of our houses and sit in a group outside. I was trying to hide my daughter. I put a child in her lap and dishevelled her hair so that she would look older. But finally one of our own neighbours pointed her out to these men. They began to drag her away. We tried to save her. I pleaded with them. My son came in the way and they hit him with a sword. He lost his finger. I could not look at his hand. I just wrapped it in my veil.

They took Koshala to the masjid. I don't know what happened to her. At about 4 a.m., when we were driven out of the colony, she called out to me from the roof of the masjid. She was screaming to me: 'Mummy, mujhe le chal, mujhe le chal, Mummy' [take me with you]. But how could Mummy take her? They beat her because she called to me. I don't know where she is now.

Later, I met Koshala in the Farash Bazar camp and told her that her mother was in Balasaheb gurudwara. She confirmed her mother's account and added that her father's eyes had been gouged out before he was killed. But she did not say that she had been raped. She merely said: 'They slapped me and beat me and struck me with a knife. They tore up my clothes.'

The rapists made no distinction between old and young women. In Nand Nagri, an 80-year-old woman informed a social worker that she had been raped. In Trilokpuri, several cases were reported of old women who were gang-raped in front of their family members. As in all such situations, the major purpose of these rapes seems to have been to inflict humiliation and to destroy the victims' morale altogether. Mancha Devi, about 55, says she was gang-raped. Four men of her family, including her son-in-law and her nephew, were murdered.

When I tried to intervene to save the children, several of those men grabbed me. Some tore my clothes, some climbed on top of me. What can I tell you, sister? Some raped me, some bit me all over my body, and some tore off my clothes. All this happened around 11 p.m. in my own house. I don't know how many men there were. The whole house was full of them. About a dozen raped me. After that, they caught hold of some young girls outside. My old husband and one nine-year-old son are the only ones left in my family. Whom shall I depend on in my old age? What can this nine-year-old do?

Most of these rapes took place while the bodies of husbands, sons or brothers of these women were still smouldering in their presence, and their homes had thus been converted into cremation grounds. Baby Bai, a young bride, aged around 20, was also gang-raped. She was married barely a year ago. Her husband was a rick-shaw puller, and sometimes worked as a scooter driver. She says:

There were six members in our family. The three men, my husband and my two brothers-in-law, were murdered. Now only three women are left. My house was attacked at about 4 p.m. and the fighting continued until next morning. My husband was first beaten and then burnt to death. I was sitting and crying when a big group of men came and dragged me away. They took me to the nearby huts in front of block 32, and raped me. They tore off all my clothes. They bit and scratched me. They took me at 10 p.m. and released me at about 3 a.m. When I came back, I was absolutely naked, just as one is when one comes out of the mother's womb. They took away all my jewellery—earrings, a gold chain, bangles, nose ring and anklets. They left without giving me anything to cover myself. On the road, I found someone's old sheet. I wrapped myself in it and walked up to Chilla village. There, I borrowed some clothes from my relatives.

Pyari Bai, aged about 70, has also lost all the male members of her family—three sons, a grandson, two sons-in-law and two nephews. Most of the men in her family used to weave string beds for a living and one was a rickshaw puller. Her daughter-in-law, who is several months pregnant, was dragged inside the house and raped. Pyari Bai too says that not even old women or little girls were spared.

Even though it was widely known that these attacks had been going on unabated since 1 November, the government neither provided the victims with any physical protection nor made any arrangements for them to be evacuated until the worst was over.

Most of the women, especially those who had some surviving male members in their family, were not willing to say they had been raped although most of them did talk about the abduction and rape of women in general. They were pressurized into staying silent about their personal experience not only by the threat of social ostracism within their own community, such as being abandoned by husbands or not finding husbands if unmarried; other outside pressures played an important role, too.

Gurdip Kaur narrated how the raped women in Farash Bazar camp were prevented from getting even a routine medical examination and registering a complaint. A few women did come forward to get their cases registered. Some of the doctors of the medical relief team also confirmed that several such women had come to them, but since rape cases are considered medico-legal cases for which special evidentiary procedures have to be followed, the women had to be referred to a hospital by the government doctor who was posted at the camp. This, however, did not happen. Gurdip Kaur said: 'Most of the women who went to register a case were young, unmarried women. Four of them were sent into the doctor's room. I was asked to wait outside. The women who went inside were intimidated by those in charge and were warned not to undergo the medical examination. They were told that hands would be shoved up their vaginas and much else would be done to them. They, being young and inexperienced, got frightened, and did not insist on a medical examination. Hence no case was registered.' Gurdip Kaur regrets that she was not allowed to be with them to encourage them. She says she heard that H.K.L. Bhagat was coming to Farash Bazar camp. She tried to give him her statement but could not meet him.

The physical violence that these women experienced is going to be buried in their hearts as their own 'shame'. Several men of their community who were staying in the camp talked to me of these 'dishonoured' women, who had been forced to do a 'wrong action' and whose lives were now worthless. Thus, it seems very unlikely that these women will be treated even by their own community with any measure of the sympathy and understanding that the male victims of violence received.

In Trilokpuri very few Sikh women work for a wage. Thus, the families who are left with no male members are also without wage-earners. Widowed women constitute the most vulnerable group amongst the surviving victims of the carnage. Many of them are illiterate or barely literate. Few have any skills at all. Very few have ever worked outside the house. Most of the women have several young children so that going out of the house for long hours to earn a living may not be feasible.

Thakari Bai, who is in her early twenties, is a typical example. Her husband worked as a coolie at the railway station and earned more than Rs 50 a day. She has three daughters, aged seven years, three years, and two months respectively. One of them is disabled and retarded. In tears, she told us that three of her brothers-in-law, who managed to survive by cutting their hair and hiding, do not wish to support her now. Already, they and their families have begun to ill-treat and quarrel with her, because they fear that she and her daughters will become a burden on them. She says her widowed mother, who lives in a Rajasthan village, is very poor. Her mother works as a labourer and often has not enough to eat. So Thakari Bai does not know where she will go if the relief camp forces her out without providing her with some means of livelihood and accommodation.

Several relief workers reported that fierce conflicts were erupting between daughters-in-law and mothers-in-law over the question of who should receive the Rs 10,000 promised by the government as compensation for a dead man who was the son of one woman and husband of the other. Given the fact that neither wives nor mothers have any independent sources of income and can only look forward to destitution, the conflict appears to be inevitable.

Much has been made of the so-called provocation offered by the Sikhs who came out with swords and kirpans, as at the Trilokpuri gurudwara. But all available eyewitness accounts confirm that swords were used, if at all, as a desperate measure of self-defence when no other help was available. Either the police were not present or, if present, were playing the role of passive onlookers or active abettors.

We would also do well to remember that the Indian Penal Code gives citizens the right to use weapons in private self-defence of their lives and property against illegal attack. Specifically, it lays down that if in the course of such defence, even innocent people happen to get killed, the persons engaged in self-defence are not culpable for the deaths. Moreover, in many places, no defence whatsoever was offered, yet gurudwaras and homes did not escape destruction.

For instance, Vasan Singh of East Vinod Nagar, another trans-

Yamuna colony, described how his neighbourhood was attacked. He said that on 1 November, at about 10 a.m., truckloads of men from nearby villages were on their way to Delhi. They were shouting anti-Sikh slogans. Some of them came down the highway and set on fire the gurudwara which is near the main road. None of the Sikhs in the colony dared go to the defence of the gurudwara. The police were present at this time, but remained inactive. The mob next went to the house of Niranjan Singh, a postmaster. They beat up the family, burnt the house and several members of the family, including children. Vasan Singh goes on: 'We went and hid in the house of a Hindu neighbour. Every Sikh ran and sought shelter in Hindu homes but very few could save their lives.'

Despite all the rumours that have been set afloat, ever since Bhindranwale's terrorist squads shot into prominence, about the 'enormous supplies' of arms that have been accumulated by the Sikh community, the facts that came to light from the accounts of the four days of violence are quite contrary to popular prejudice. Very few Sikhs had any arms to speak of. Even the major gurudwaras in Delhi which were strongly suspected of being storehouses for weapons and arsenals, had to give in to the attackers without much of a fight. There were hardly any non-Sikhs among those killed.

An explanation frequently offered for the massacres is that anger and resentment against the Sikhs had been brewing ever since Bhindranwale's gang began the indiscriminate murder of Hindus in Punjab, in pursuance of their demand for Khalistan, a separate nation-state for Sikhs, which might involve a forcible mass exodus of Hindus from Punjab, similar to that which look place from various areas when Pakistan came into existence. There is no denying that the manner in which the demand for Khalistan was being pursued in the previous two years or so had created a good deal of resentment against Bhindranwale among Hindus both in Punjab and outside. But the fact that one small gang of terrorists who happened to be Sikhs killed some Hindus and Sikhs in Punjab is no justification for the massacre of thousands of innocent Sikhs all over India—who had no connection with Punjab politics.

Today, there seems to be a widespread belief, based on the desire to justify the recent riots, that Bhindranwale and his men killed only Hindus. But the fact, which ought to be well-known, is that Bhindranwale's men killed Sikhs who opposed them with even greater fervour than they did Hindus. In fact, Bhindranwale began, as do most terrorist groups, by hitting out at those members of his own community who opposed him. This was done with the intention of terrorizing his own community into silent submission. Yet this fact is meticulously ignored because it does not help fan the fires of communalism.

Further, the sudden eruption of violence against Sikhs seems quite out of proportion to the extent of anger amongst Hindus. It is noteworthy that throughout the period when Sikhs, Nirankaris and Hindus were being killed in Punjab, there had been no retaliation whatsoever against Sikhs in Delhi or in other states. Even when some sections of the Akalis organized fairly aggressive processions in Delhi, no political group or set of Hindu militants reacted with violence or even as much as tried to obstruct the processions and rallies. The only clashes that occurred were with the police and the administrative machinery. There were no attacks on gurudwaras or on the homes of prominent Sikh or Akali leaders. It is even more noteworthy that in Punjab, apart from select killings by small organized gangs of terrorists, there were no communal riots throughout the Bhindranwale period.

Hindus and Sikhs do not have a long history or tradition of conflict. The two communities not only share a common past and a common culture but even today, most Sikh families have Hindu relatives because it used to be a common practice for some Hindu parents in certain areas of Punjab to dedicate one son to the guru. Even today, marriages between Sikhs and Hindus are considered a normal practice. Many Hindus routinely visit gurudwaras and read the Granth Saheb with much devotion. The fact that all Punjabis use the word *mona* to indicate either a Hindu or a clean shaven Sikh shows that no rigid distinctions have been set up by the people of the two communties between themselves.

Many have tried to justify the violence by asserting that Sikhs 'provoked' an attack on themselves by celebrating Indira Gandhi's killing. They are supposed to have distributed sweets at home and champagne abroad as soon as they got the news. During these days, I have met hundreds of people who talk authoritatively about the distribution of sweets by Sikhs in celebration of Indira Gandhi's killing, but when questioned, not one of them could say that he or she saw this happen.

There is very little evidence that, barring a few stray cases, Sikhs in general 'rejoiced' at Mrs Gandhi's death. For instance, the reality behind the rumour that Sikh students of Khalsa College, Delhi University, danced the *bhangra* is a fairly typical example of how facts are distorted beyond recognition. These students had been practising bhangra every day on their college lawn for over a month prior to Mrs Gandhi's death. They were preparing the dance as an item for the forthcoming winter festivals that are held in every college. On 31 October, they were practising as usual and stopped as soon as they got the news.

A friend tried to investigate the source of another rumour that a wealthy Sikh family in Janakpuri had distributed sweets and dry fruit soon after Mrs Gandhi's death. They discovered that there had indeed been some distribution of sweets. This was done in honour of the coming Gurpurab. Traditionally, about 10 days before Guru Nanak's birthday, which fell on 8 November in 1984, *prabhat pheris* are organized in each area, and it is customary for families to entertain the pheri participants with sweets and other refreshments. However, the most important point we need to remember is what Dharma Kumar said in her article in the *Times of India*: 'If all the sweets in India had been distributed—that would not have justified the burning alive of one single Sikh.'

Surely, it was not only Sikhs who could be accused of not cancelling a routine ritual celebration such as this one after they heard of Mrs Gandhi's death on the night of 31 October, when I was walking down the main road in our locality, I saw a wedding procession marching along in full pomp and show, complete with band music, dancing and lights. Nobody showed any concern that this Hindu wedding procession was going through the normal ritual.

In our own neighbourhood, where at least half the families are Sikhs, I saw no sign of celebrations or distributions of sweets. In fact, even on the morning of 31 October, when the news of the assassination came, I was really surprised to see everyone, both Hindu and Sikh, going about their business without any apparent sign of grief or frenzy. No one I talked to broke down when discussing the news even through most people felt sad that Mrs Gandhi's life had ended so tragically.

Other rumourmongers point to the fact that many Sikhs did not celebrate Diwali in 1984 because they were mourning the army operation and the killing of Bhindranwale and other Sikhs in the Golden Temple in June. This is cited as proof that they are 'anti-national' and hence it is assumed that they must have rejoiced at Mrs Gandhi's death.

First, it is not true that no Sikh celebrated Diwali. Some of the victims mentioned that new clothes and utensils bought by them for Diwali were destroyed in the attacks on their homes. Further, the argument itself is based on a bizarre logic of the kind that the government very often uses. Anyone who does not support every action and policy of the government automatically becomes an enemy of the nation. This way of thinking is based on an authoritarian ideology which seeks to deny the people the right to differ with the rulers and the right to mourn the tragic consequences of the rulers' actions.

Another thing that is held against the Sikhs is that they felt outraged at the entry of the army into the Golden Temple. To say that all those who grieved at the desecration of the Temple were desirous of Indira Gandhi's assassination is a bizarre falsehood. Many of those who were attacked, beaten and murdered were long-standing supporters of the Congress (I). Many men in relief camps talked about how they had worked for the Congress (I) party in previous elections. I saw pictures of Indira Gandhi still hanging on the walls of some burnt houses. Her pictures also adorn the walls of many Sikh homes in our neighbourhood, and continue to do so even after the riots. More important is the fact that the group of Sikhs who bore the main brunt of violence were those living in resettlement colonies. This group had very little connection with Punjab extremist politics. In fact, many of them have no connection at all with Punjab.

The most popular of all justifications offered is that the violence was the spontaneous result of public fury at the brutal assassination of India's foremost leader at the hands of two Sikhs. One would have been compelled to take this explanation seriously had the riots remained sporadic, unorganized and spontaneous. From the information so far available in Delhi, one is left in no doubt that the whole affair was masterminded and well-organized, and that the killers and looters seemed to be quite confident that no harm would come to them. They seemed to be in no hurry. They came, went back, and came again and again. Each time, they returned with reinforcements.

Those who saw the mobs did not get the impression that they were a group of angry or anguished people. Rather, they seemed to be a bunch of hoodlums who seemed to be having a good time. On 1 November, I confronted one mob in Lajpat Nagar. Around noon, when we heard that the local gurudwara had been set on fire, three of us rushed to the spot and tried to persuade the neighbours to help extinguish the fire. At once, we were surrounded by hostile men while the women jeered at and abused us from a distance. One or two women even came up and called us names for being so shameless as to argue with men on the streets. At the same time, a crowd of about 200 men came, shouting slogans about revenge. Looking at them laughing, jeering, catcalling, one did not get the impression of any grief whatsoever. All one saw was some hoodlums delight in demonstrating their power. The jeering mob told us that if we did not keep quiet and go away, they would throw us into the fire.

The fact that all over the city the attacks started simultaneously, with identical patterns of violence, indicates that these were not spontaneous outbursts. Victims from different parts of the city say that the first organized attacks in residential areas began between 9 and 10 a.m. on 1 November. Almost everywhere, the attackers came armed with lathis, a few knives and kerosene. There seem to have been few instances of the use of revolvers to kill. Almost everywhere, males were singled out and slaughtered. A fairly standard method of killing was adopted all over the city and in fact, in almost all the towns where riots took place. The victim would be stunned with lathi blows or stabbed. Kerosene or petrol or diesel would then be poured over him and he would be set on fire while he was still alive. Very few of the burn victims seem to have survived.

An eyewitness account of some of the happenings outside the All India Institute of Medical Science (AIIMS) gives us a clue about the genesis of the murderous slogan, 'Khoon ka badla khoon se lenge' (We will avenge blood with blood), that was chanted by the groups of killers throughout Delhi.

I was outside AIIMS between 1.30 and 5 p.m. on 31 October. There was a large crowd gathered there but it had no resemblance to a frenzied mob. At about 2 p.m., two truckloads of men from neighbouring villages were brought to the AIIMS. They dismounted from the trucks in a calm and orderly fashion. They behaved like soldiers waiting for orders.

The trucks were followed by a tempo full of lathis and iron rods. There were no men in the tempo other than the driver. At about 3 p.m., a Congress corporator from the trans-Yamuna area addressed the gathering. Later information has confirmed that he is one of those who masterminded the riots in the trans-Yamuna area. He gave a fiery speech. There was a lot of drama and slogan-shouting during his speech. He was the first to raise the slogan: 'Khoon ka badla khoon se lenge.' From that moment, it became a popular chant. The first victim of their wrath was a Sikh SHO from Vinay

Nagar police station who came to the hospital on his motorbike. He was attacked with rods and was rescued with difficulty by senior police officers. This, in my view, was the first attack on a Sikh in Delhi, and it was instigated when the mob took their cue from the Congress leader. From AIIMS this gang soon went in different directions—towards Naoroji Nagar, INA Market, Yusuf Sarai and South Extension. They began to stop all vehicles driven by Sikhs. They beat up the Sikhs and burnt the vehicles. Some Sikhs were burnt to death. Sikh shops in these areas were looted and burnt.

A vast number of investigative reports in newspapers and victims' accounts have pointed out that high officials of the Congress (I) masterminded the whole operation. They rounded up anti-social elements from their constituencies. These elements routinely receive Congress(I) patronage. On this occasion, they were incited to kill, rape, loot and burn, and were assured that no one would interfere with them.

The populous resettlement colonies and the UP and Haryana villages around Delhi have been meticulously cultivated as vote banks and political bases by the Congress (I) throughout the last decade. It is from these areas that truckloads of men are routinely mobilized for Congress (I) rallies and processions. These professional processionists have become accustomed to hiring out their services to the ruling party. The gang leaders are on the regular payroll of the party. That is how Congress(I) leaders could, in a matter of hours, mobilize thousands of hoodlums for the orgy of violence which they organized. Among the most active participants in the gangs were young boys, many in their early teens.

It is significant that reports confirm that Jats, Gujjars, scheduled-caste men and poor Muslims constituted the bulk of the attacking mobs. This identical pattern has been reported from areas of Delhi that are many kilometres apart.

Many victims have alleged that Congress (I) men used voters' lists and ration shop records to supply the attackers with addresses of Sikh families in each locality. So pre-planned was the whole operation that the attackers not only had prior knowledge of which houses and shops belonged to Sikhs but also seem to have known which Sikh house owners had Hindu tenants and vice versa. Such houses were handled differently from those inhabited by Sikhs only. Instead of the whole house being burnt, only the Sikhs were killed and their possessions looted so that the Hindus in the house were left unscathed.

Many prominent leaders have been named in several newspapers as having instigated riots. Many victims have been given testimonies implicating H.K.L. Bhagat, Minister of State for Information and Broadcasting as one of those who personally supervised and led the attacks; Sajjan Kumar, Congress (I) MP from Mangolpuri, is alleged to have paid Rs 100 and a bottle of liquor to each man involved in the killing; Lalit Maken, Congress (I) trade-union leader and metropolitan councillor, is also alleged to have paid Rs 100 and a bottle of liquor to rioters. Many testified that they saw him actively instigating arsonists; Dharam Das Shastri, Congress (I) MP from Karol Bagh; Jagdish Tytler, Congress (I) MP; Dr Ashok Kumar, member of the municipal corporation, Kalyanpuri; Jagdish Chandra Tokas, member of the municipal corporation; Ishwar Singh, corporator; Faiz Mohammad and Satbir Singh of the Youth Congress (I), and many others, along with the lower-level local Congress (I) ruffians and hoodlums, have been accused of having led many of the mobs.*

In Naoroji Nagar market, an eyewitness saw the Youth Congress (I) office-bearer, Pravin Sharma, stand in front of a Sikh shop and personally direct the looting operation. Young boys from the nearby hutments were invited to take whatever they wanted from the shop. This distribution continued for at least an hour. Perhaps this is the Congress(I) way of implementing their version of socialism. In fact, some Trilokpuri residents reported that they were invited to join the looting operations which were christened the 'Garibi Hatao' (Remove poverty) campaign.

The way party stalwarts chose to pay tribute to Mrs Gandhi and mourn her death during those four days blatantly brought out what the ruling party has been reduced to. Many of the leaders behaved as though they were gang leaders rather than prominent members of a national political party. It was as though their chief gang leader had been killed and they wanted to terrorize those who they imagined constituted a threatening rival gang. Since there was really no rival gang at hand, they substituted for it all Sikhs with long hair and beards. These men, they decided, were a threat to their being considered the top gangsters; terrorizing them would therefore show who still had the real power. A popular explanation of prominent Congressmen's involvement that we heard was 'Takat azma rahe thay' (They were testing and proving their strength).

*Some of these leaders have subsequently been brought to trial for the above mentioned crimes. The cases are still going on.

One of the most positive things that happened during those dark days in Delhi was the spontaneous emergence of defence and peace committees in most colonies and marketplaces. At a time when the government machinery voluntarily chose to become defunct; Hindus, Muslims, Sikhs and other communities jointly organized security measures to defend their neighbourhoods from attack by outsiders. In many colonies, potential trouble-makers were chased away and active resistance was offered to the mobs who tried to enter the areas. Men barricaded the streets and patrolled the neighbourhoods all night. During the days and nights when government machinery voluntarily chose to become defunct people organized themselves irrespective of caste or religion. These committees seem to have been more effective in areas inhabited by relatively better off and more organized communities who had resources at their command. In the very poor areas, where people have been dumped together in appalling conditions, and the communities are not as well organized internally, the inhabitants could not put together effective self-defence measures.

In all areas, however, there were numerous instances of immediate neighbours, who were not Sikhs, sheltering Sikhs. For instance, Surinder Kaur of Trilokpuri described how her family was saved by Hindu neighbours. She locked her son inside the house and came out with her daughter. Despite the fact that the attackers bombarded her house with bricks; neighbours came to her aid. One neighbour stood in front of the door to prevent the house being broken open.

In most places where the residents were predominantly non-Sikhs with a small sprinkling of Sikh houses, after the initial surprise attack on the first day, Hindus and Muslims did get together to protect the Sikhs. Many families narrated how they were given shelter by neighbours who took great risks in doing so. Even in Trilokpuri, the damage to Sikh life and property was much greater where they were concentrated together, as in blocks 30 and 32, than where they lived interspersed with people of other communities.

Shan Kaur of Shahdara was given shelter by Muslims who escorted her and her children to a place of safety. A Hindu family in Shakurpur saved three families by hiding them, masking their identity and helping them to escape in rickshaws. In many cases, after Sikh men were killed or forced to flee to save their lives, women and children continued to stay with their neighbours.

A Sikh family which had recently shifted to a middle-class colony, Dilshad Garden, beyond the Yamuna, said that even though there were many acts of killing, burning and looting all around, they were kept in a protective cocoon by their neighbours who brought them everything they needed so as to save them from having to step out of the house. When the city was facing a severe shortage of milk, they had more than enough. Many Hindu families also kept in safe custody the cash and valuables such as cars, jewellery, videos and other expensive items belonging to their Sikh friends and neighbours.

Mahinder Kaur narrates how some of the Muslim neighbours from her mother's locality came to rescue her and her brother's family from another colony. She herself lives in Nand Nagri with her husband and three children but had gone to visit her brother at Yamuna Vihar. There were three men, two women and five children in the house at about 9 a.m. on 1 November when a mob of about 500 came and began to stone their house. The family locked themselves inside. Their neighbours, in an attempt to save them, told the mob that the house was empty since the Sikh family had escaped the previous night. Even these helpful neighbours were not willing to shelter Sikh men in their homes because that could jeopardise their own safety. The mob went ahead and burnt the nearby gurudwara as well as dozens of Sikh homes in the locality. Some of their neighbours advised Mahinder Kaur's family to escape since the mob had gone away for a while. But they were afraid to travel along the roads while the mob was still on the rampage and decided to stay hidden together in their house. At 3 p.m., however, a group of Muslim men came to their house to rescue them. These were neighbours of Mahinder Kaur's mother who lives in Jafrabad, a trans-Yamuna village which has a predominantly Muslim population. These men had brought several *burkas* with them. The three Sikh men and the two boys were dressed in women's clothes, covered with burkas and taken to Jafrabad where they remained safely till the relief camps came into existence. Had they not been rescued at that juncture it would have meant certain death because the mob returned at 5 p.m., broke open the door and searched the house to see if anyone was hiding. They looted some of the stuff but were dissuaded by the neighbours from setting fire to the house. Mahinder Kaur says the Muslims of that locality had similarly rescued dozens of Sikh men and kept them in their houses for several days.

However, in many cases, the neighbours were not willing to take the risk involved. In many cases, the families initially gave shelter, but as soon as the mob began to approach, the Sikhs, especially the men, were asked to leave on the plea that the sheltering family would otherwise be placed in danger. This amounted to handing over these men to the murderous mobs because once they came out, there was no possibility of escape.

The fact that people of different communities did come to the rescue of Sikh neighbours was perhaps the only hopeful sign in an otherwise grim situation. Yet the help offered was not enough. While many helped neighbours to hide and escape surreptitiously, the mob fury was hardly ever resisted in an organized way.

There is evidence that wherever some determined individuals came forward, they were able to stop even big mobs from running amok. For instance, in Yusuf Sarai market, which is only about a furlong away from AIIMS, the local shopkeepers organized very brave resistance efforts on 31 October. A mob came and set fire to the gurudwara. They were about to attack Sikh shops next. The Hindu shopkeepers came and lay down in front of the shops and told the mob they would have to burn them before they burnt the shops. Not a single shop was burnt or looted in this area, then or afterwards.

Similarly, a friend went and rescued a Sikh colleague from his house in a riot-affected neighbourhood in broad daylight on 1 November, and brought him to his own house. Some of the neighbours threw stones at them but went no further when this failed to intimidate the rescuer. Even in a highly disturbed area like Punjabi Bagh, an old woman and my 70-year-old father successfully prevented a mob from setting fire to a house. A couple of rioters threw petrol balls into the house but the rescuers mobilized help from the locality to extinguish the fire, and persuaded the mob to leave.

In rare cases, those non-Sikhs who tried to come forward and remonstrate with the mob did get beaten up. A few were even killed. But on the whole, those who stood their ground were able to save that particular situation.

Many neighbours allowed Sikh women to seek refuge but refused to shelter men. Somti Bai of Trilokpuri says she and her family hid in the house of a local political leader. While he kept assuring her that her three sons were safe in the house, he subsequently turned them out of the house, which was as good as handing them over to the rampaging mob. All three sons were killed. Somti's sister-in-law was raped. Her two sisters were kidnapped and released only after three days.

Another horrifying but typical example of callous cowardliness of neighbours was reported by an eyewitness in Shankar Garden, a middle-class colony newly established in West Delhi. A mob attacked a Sikh house, pulled out an old man and set his clothes on fire. He ran into the house of a neighbour who helped him to get the clothes off and extinguish the fire. But the mob soon began to pelt this house with stones. The family begged the elderly Sikh neighbour to leave by the back door because they were not ready to risk further attack. As soon as the Sikh emerged, the mob encircled him. They seemed to be in no hurry for they spent about 20 minutes collecting stones. They then formed a circle round him and began stoning him to death. At this, his young son came running out of the house to save his father, who was by then half dead. The mob immediately pounced on the son, tied his arms and legs, poured kerosene on him and burnt him to death.

This entire incident, from beginning to end, was watched by hundreds of neighbours standing in their courtyards or on roof-tops, yet no one had the courage or humanity to intervene. The old man was crying for water but no one came forward because the attackers stood around in threatening postures.

Several such instances have been reported where determined intervention by neighbours and onlookers could have averted killings. Not only did people fail to intervene, but they seem to have watched the violence with a mixture of fascination and repulsion as though they were watching a violent film.

Unfortunately, an overwhelming majority of people in Delhi seem to feel that all the killings and arson were, in some way, justifiable. They believe this not just because they are possessed by the desire for revenge for the murder of Indira Gandhi but because they have been convinced by years of vicious chauvinist propaganda that a purging operation was necessary in order to 'save the nation' and 'keep the nation united'. The ruling party has made itself the arch symbol of a so-called united nation. Its opponents are invariably accused of 'weakening the nation' in the face of the dangers of the 'foreign hand'. Once such a chauvinist, nationalist fever infects the brains of people there is little hope that rationality or humanity or logic will prevail. This nightmarish vision of a nation begins to act as a monster devouring its own people.

The amazing thing is that many of those who were a witness to senseless murders and who feel sorry about their neighbours' and friends' deaths, still continue to assert with unabated vigour that the Sikhs had to be 'taught a lesson'. The bizarre logic or rather illogic behind this sentiment is most difficult to challenge. Many felt that Sikhs who were their personal friends should be protected from these regrettable attacks. But the moment they began to think of themselves as members of the Hindu community or as nationalist and patriotic Indians (these two were usually seen as synonymous), their ability to see Sikhs as fellow human beings seemed to vanish. The transition from 'Santokh Singh, our neighbour and friend' to 'those Sikhs' was remarkably sudden, drastic and violent. Sikhs as Sikhs were 'they' pitted against 'us.' They became another species altogether, who needed to be sternly dealt with, perhaps even exterminated, for their 'otherness'.

Amongst the majority of Hindus, who did not join the violent mobs, there unfortunately seems to be a distinct feeling of pride that the Hindus have finally put fear in the hearts of a supposedly aggressive community. At the same time, nobody wants to face the responsibility for the horrific deeds that were done in the name of teaching this lesson. This is especially so amongst middle-class people. After asserting that the Sikhs had to be given a fitting reply, people at once seek shelter behind the comforting reflection that it was 'these lower caste' poor people who did it, conveniently forgetting that the leaders who incited the mobs are from their own class. They are also quick to cite instances of how, in their own way, they tried to help their neighbours. Thus they betray a curious blend of pride in the mob actions which were done in the name of avenging Hindus, while shrinking from taking individual responsibility for the carnage.

In middle-class colonies, other factors than mere undiluted concern for neighbours seem to have influenced an effort to offer help. In affluent colonies, almost none of the local residents were key participants in the mob activity. Almost always, the attackers descended on the colony from outside and were perceived as belonging to the lower castes and classes, who were making use of the opportunity to loot and plunder. Many people perceived it as some sort of class war.

Those middle- and upper-class colonies which adjoined villages and resettlement colonies seem to have been the worst affected.

The residents fell prey to the fear that the selective looting of Sikh houses could spread to other houses. I heard residents of some of the affluent colonies say that the '*neech jatis*' had been eyeing the growing prosperity of the rich with increasing resentment. They had grabbed this occasion to acquire objects that they could not hope to purchase in their lifetime. The fear that if an adjoining house was burnt, the fire might spread or that the attackers might lose their sense of discrimination and loot non-Sikh houses as well, seems to have spurred many more people into organizing mutual defence.

Sadly, there are also cases reported of neighbours having helped the attacking mob to identify Sikh homes. A woman from Babarpur alleges:

A local ration shop owner brought the attackers to our house. We know him very well. We always had good relations with him. But he and his brother betrayed us. The killers were men from the interior alleys of our locality. They came around noon on 1 November. My son had been told to cut off his hair and had done so the night before. He had kept vigil all night with the other men of the neighbourhood. But the ration shop owner recognized him though his hair was cut and pointed him out, saying: 'He is a Sardar. Kill him.' The killers poured kerosene on him and on my husband and burnt them both to death.

Yet it remains true that in most areas, immediate neighbours, on the whole, offered help, or at the very least, did not join the attackers. When local men joined the mob, or rejoiced with it, they were usually not immediate neighbours of the victims but were residents of a nearby block or street in the same locality.

Even while people helped their neighbours and friends, vicious rumours were set afloat to discourage people from offering such help. In Trilokpuri, as well as in other areas, several families who had given shelter to Sikh women told me obnoxious and unbelievable stories about Sikhs who were given shelter in Hindu homes butchering their benefactors. There was also the absurd story of a barber who cut the hair of a Sikh at the latter's request but received sword blows on his ears and in his stomach as a parting gift. Such rumours were rife in every locality, from the affluent to the poverty-stricken.

Unfortunately, this kind of rumour-mongering goes on unabated even after the Sikhs have been subjected to such violence and terrorization. During and after the carnage, rumours were rife of how Sikhs had retaliated or were planning to retaliate, in and outside Punjab. The stories about water poisoning and train loads of massacred Hindus have been proved utterly baseless. But stories of how Sikhs are planning to avenge themselves are still doing incalculable damage. For instance, a domestic servant in our locality told us that the army had to be called into her colony because the residents were convinced that the Hindus were in imminent danger of an attack by the Sikhs who had sought shelter in Balasaheb gurudwara nearby. It was rumoured that 9000 armed Sikhs had gathered in the gurudwara and were ready to attack. However, the reality was that about 1500 people, most of them women and children, were living in the gurudwara relief camp in a pitiable condition. The rumour also gave rise to a disgusting demand that the relief camp in the gurudwara be disbanded because Sikhs were congregated in large numbers there.

Thus these rumours have become not only a way of justifying the monstrous happenings which have no real justification, but also a deadly weapon against the victims.

All acts of killing, looting and burning were organized by men. In some cases, after the initial attack was over, women and children also joined in picking up whatever they could lay hands on by way of loot. At Punjabi Bagh, for instance, men, women and children from J.J. Colony, Madipur, came in swarms to claim their share of the booty from the gurudwara and from some houses. But the attacking mob was exclusively composed of men.

The organized efforts at defence and peace-keeping were also confined almost exclusively to men. Women were meticulously kept out of these efforts in most areas. On television, when residents were interviewed, some women said the role they played was that of serving tea to the men who kept vigil all night.

In our neighbourhood, Lajpat Nagar, the first initiative to call a meeting of the residents was taken by the Residents' Association of the block, which is not a very active body in normal times. In this association, as in all such bodies, women are never approached to become even nominal members if there are any men in the household. A widow without grown sons may be asked to pay a membership fee in her own name, but will not be expected to attend meetings or to take an active interest in the doings or non-doings of the association. Since I happen to be one of the few women who have no male 'head of the household', I was enrolled as a member in my own right.

Yet, though I approached the office bearers to find out if a meeting was being called and to ensure that I was informed so that I could attend, neither I nor any other woman was allowed to be part of the neighbourhood meetings and deliberations. Men took it for granted that it was their job to defend the area. Women were expected to run inside their homes if an attack occurred.

At night, young men patrolled the streets, and made rather aggressive enquiries about the women they saw walking around at a late hour. They were on the ready with lathis, iron bars and other weapons. The way they went about their business, it was difficult to distinguish these night patrollers from trouble-makers. In fact, in a few places, including parts of Lajpat Nagar, different patrolling parties clashed with each other, mistaking each other for hoodlums.

For many young men this seemed an exciting opportunity to prove their *filmi* heroism. Some of them seemed to have a good time creating false alarms, spreading rumours, running around with sticks and rods at the slightest provocation—real or imagined. Observing the aggressive behaviour of some of the young men in our locality, I had the uneasy feeling that their very presence on the road was likely to spark off a clash, with or without reason.

Women in our locality and in most other areas of the city, acted merely as carriers of rumours that their sons, husbands and brothers brought in from outside. None of the men thought it necessary to involve women in the effort at self-defence nor were there any instances of women taking the initiative to organize their own meetings to discuss what they should do in case of an emergency. In contrast, most of the outside chores had to be performed by women in Sikh households. This was necessary because of the danger to men's lives. Within most homes, of course, women did participate in discussions as to what the family should do if something went wrong. But this was not allowed to happen at the community level.

Women were, however, active in relief work. Students and teachers of women's colleges in Delhi were particularly active in organizing relief teams. Even here, however, authorities in some colleges tried to put hurdles in the students' way. For instance, in Miranda House and University Hostel for Women, rules regulating visitors' entry into the premises were made more stringent. Thus, women students had even less freedom than in ordinary times to go out of the premises and this restricted their ability to be active in relief work. Girls were repeatedly warned against the supposed dangers of relief work. Residents of the University Hostel were even forbidden to join the Delhi University peace marches on the campus.

The experience of these days confirmed the fact that people's preconceptions seem to determine and influence their thinking much more than the reality of the situation and of their experience. For instance, whenever communities were attacked, men seemed quite incapable of defending their homes all by themselves. In most cases, women did come forward to protect not only their homes and children but also the lives of men. Most of the men seem to have been forced to flee to save their lives, leaving women to take care of the children, the old and their home. This has been the standard experience everywhere—in Assam, in Bihar tribal movements, during the Partition, during various riots, and so on. Yet the myth holds powerful sway that men alone are the defenders of the community and that women are incapable of performing this task. The powerful hold of this myth prevents women from acquiring any say in key decision-making processes, even in those areas which affect their lives as profoundly as they do those of men.

The entire government machinery seems to have lived up to its usual motto: 'Do not move or do anything until there is a push and a kick from above. If you do something you are more likely to annoy someone in power than if you do nothing.'

This is summed up very aptly by N.K. Saxena, a senior police officer quoted in the 25 November issue of *Express Magazine*: 'I have no doubt that a good few police officers make dangerous compromises because, according to their calculations, the risk of their dismissal for failure is not more than one per cent, while their being disgraced for doing their duty seriously is over 50 per cent.'

A striking example of the inaction of the government was the way All India Radio handled the news of Mrs Gandhi's death. They were the last to announce her death, and kept playing their routine jazz and film music hours after BBC and several other foreign radio stations had announced the news and started broadcasting condolence messages from different world leaders. It was a typical display of mindless servility and slavish self-censorship, characteristic of the government-owned media in India.

While the city burned, many senior politicians, bureaucrats and police officers seem to have spent most of their time dancing attendance at Teen Murti house where Mrs Gandhi's body lay. They were also preparing to receive foreign dignitaries for the grand funeral. Others were busy helping to coordinate the murder, rape and plunder.

Almost everywhere in the city, the police too seem to have performed a well-rehearsed role. Either they were absent from the scene and failed to make their appearance despite repeated appeals from the affected and concerned citizens or, if they were present, they behaved at best like amused spectators. In many cases, they actively abetted the criminal acts, and in some cases, even participated in them.

A friend who witnessed the burning of the Yusuf Sarai gurudwara described the role of the police:

Between 3 and 4 p.m., on 1 November, a local hoodlum came to the policeman on duty and said, 'Please go away from here. We want to burn the gurudwara.' The policeman good-humouredly replied: 'Wait for a while till I go off duty. Then you can burn it. In fact, you should burn it.' He assured him that between his going off duty and the next man's coming to replace him, there would be an interval of at least 15 minutes, in which the job could be done. However, the 'leader' was not convinced and said: 'Look, we have the men now. We can't wait. Besides, we know you. Who knows who the next fellow may be?' So saying, he put his arm around the policeman and walked him down the road for a few hundred yards, during which time the rest of the miscreants set the gurudwara ablaze.

The PUCL–PUDR report describes similar experiences:

On 1 November, when we toured the Lajpat Nagar area, we found the police conspicuous by their absence, while Sikh shops were being set on fire and looted. Young people armed with swords, daggers, spears, steel *trishuls* and iron rods were ruling the roads. The only sign of police presence was a police jeep, which obstructed a peace procession brought out by a few concerned citizens. When the procession was on its way to the Lajpat Nagar main market, a police inspector from the van stopped the procession and warned it not to proceed, reminding its members that the city was under curfew and Section 144 had been imposed. When leaders of the procession wanted to know why the arsonists and rioters were not being dispersed if curfew was on, he gave no reply and warned instead that the processionists could go to Lajpat Nagar market at their own risk.

Even in our own locality, after the gurudwara was set on fire, the policemen looked on indulgently and did nothing to stop the arsonists. When we tried to persuade local residents that we should try to put out the fire, the policemen accused us of creating a 'disturbance' and tried to push us away. Elsewhere, too, the same story was repeated.

Even for those who wish to believe that there were no explicit orders to this effect, the role that the policemen at the lower levels played would still need to be explained. The least one could say is that since the policemen knew that several Congress (I) men were fomenting the riots, they did not want to take the responsibility of stopping them lest they incur the wrath of their senior officers and the ruling party bosses. Hence they may have decided to adopt a safer course and do nothing obstructive.

However, since traditionally there is a close link up between the politician-cum-ruffian and the local police, the two are likely to have acted in unison. And since there was promise of loot and plunder, the arsonists found ready allies among the police. Several people have alleged that a substantial portion of the looted property was cornered by policemen. Sardar Santokh Singh, who lives in Shivpuri Extension, says: 'No police came to our rescue when we were attacked on 2 November, even though the place where we live is a stone's throw from the police station.' No first information report had been registered even though they, along with many others, came and sought shelter in the police station after it was converted into a relief camp by the government.

Several of the families I interviewed had been denied protection and shelter after they had somehow managed to reach a police station. For instance, Shan Kaur and her daughter managed to reach the Seelampur police station after the male members of their family were murdered. But she says that the police threw them out and they then sought refuge in the house of Hindu relatives. She says that in her colony some murders took place right in front of the police station.

Sardar Mahinder Singh of Shanker Nagar, who works as a *granthi* in a gurudwara, describes how his family fared:

On 3 November, at about 4.30 p.m., the military came and asked if people wanted to be taken to relief camps. All those who were in hiding came out. One truckload left for the camp. Just as the others were preparing to get into the next truck, the military drove it away, saying: 'We have some urgent work nearby, so we will come back for you.' No sooner had the military left than the mob fired on the families who were now standing exposed on the street. One Sardar died. There was a stampede, with people rushing to hide and being pursued. My brother-in-law and my young son ran into our house and tried to hide. The attackers pursued them and broke down the door. The two of them climbed on the roof of a Hindu neighbour's house but they were dragged down and hit with lathis and bricks. Immediately, petrol was poured on them and they were burnt alive. My wife tried to save them and got badly burnt. Everything in our house was looted though the neighbours somehow managed to save the house from being burnt.

In Krishna Nagar, 12 members of a family were burnt alive in their own house without any intervention by the police even though the police station is just a few yards away. One of the men tried to escape but was hit with iron rods and thrown back into the burning house. A woman too tried to escape but was already so badly burnt that she died, soon after, in hospital.

There were instances, however, of the police coming to disarm Sikhs who tried to resist attackers, using whatever arms they had. Thus the police deprived them of their legal right to private self-defence. These actions to disarm Sikhs were among the very few active interventions by the police, ostensibly to preserve law and order. More Sikhs died as a consequence of this type of police intervention than they would have, had the police just kept away.

Bindo from Kalyanpuri says that the SHO of the area ordered the police to loot Sikh houses. Those who resisted were arrested. Police raided the Sikh houses instead of protecting them. In other blocks in this colony, people allege that the SHO had accompanied the attacking mob and provided them with diesel from police jeeps for burning Sikh men alive.

Several cases have been reported of Hindus who had sheltered Sikhs having gone to seek help from the police and having been told to hand over the Sikhs to the mob. An eyewitness in Shakurpur says a Sikh man, who was being pursued by a mob, attempted to save his life by climbing into a police jeep. He was thrown by the police to the mob who killed him on the spot.

An additional reason for police inaction in this instance is believed to be that Sikh policemen were deliberately immobilized. One version is that the Delhi police were officially informed of Mrs Gandhi's death only at 5 p.m. even though she had died much before noon. The two DIGs spent the whole night disarming that large proportion of the Delhi police force who are Sikhs. They were taken off duty. Even in the army, some Sikh soldiers are said to have been disarmed.

Thus, not only was precious time lost which should have been spent keeping the criminals in check, but also, Sikh policemen, who could have helped keep the situation somewhat under control, were got rid of. Thus, the murderers, looters and arsonists had a free hand and could act with greater assurance born of the knowledge that no one would block their way.

The press, All India Radio and Doordarshan reported that shoot-at-sight orders had been issued and the army had been called in to enforce the curfew on 1 November. But even following large-scale violence, the troops in the field were not given firm and clear instructions to move independently to crush the rioters. The police and the civil administration failed to provide accurate information to the troops deployed in the city, especially during the crucial first few days.

The first few days saw very few instances of the army firing on mobs of attackers or coming to the rescue of the victims while they were under attack. Many officers in the field seemed unsure of what was expected of them and were chary of ordering their troops into action without the concurrence of the police and civil authorities, both of whom seemed reluctant to cede authority to act to the military. There seems to have been a deliberate plan to keep the army ineffective until the murderers, looters and arsonists had done their job.

The advent of the army was welcomed by almost everyone. Many openly declared that they wanted military rule. This is indeed a sad comment on the state of our society. People themselves are demanding more and more military interventions in the mistaken hope that the army is 'above politics' and hence will clean up the corrupt administration.

The conduct of our politicians and bureaucrats is such that democracy has unfortunately become synonymous with corruption and ruffianism. Hence, too frequently, the desire for a well-ordered society seeks expression, tragically, in the desire for army rule. Is this because people see army rule as rule by a caste apart from the rest of the people? Are they really as incorruptible as some of us hope?

We have the examples of such close neighbours as Pakistan and Bangladesh. Both countries have had long spells of army rule, and they are, perhaps, worse off in matters of corruption and disorder.

Yet the myth persists that the army can best perform the task of governance. The brutal face of army rule is visible in certain border areas in India, where, for a long time, the army has been doing exactly what the police is notorious for doing in most other parts of the country.

As things began to calm down from 4 November onwards, the army was assigned the task of keeping peace in the city. People who had been rendered homeless or felt too insecure in their own neighbourhoods moved into relief camps set up in different parts of the city. Some of these camps were started by the government, but most were set up by gurudwaras. As usual, the government was slow and callous in meeting the demands of the situation.

Even though it is well-known that key members of the Congress(I) party led and instigated the riots and much of the governmental machinery slavishly collaborated with the rioters, the same crew have entrusted themselves with the task of doing relief and rehabilitation work. The attitude displayed was that of pious bountifulness toward the poor helpless victims of a natural disaster.

It is tragic, indeed, that several petitions and memoranda have had to be submitted by concerned citizens and organizations to the very same authorities who are directly or indirectly responsible for the massacre. For instance, a letter signed by several organizations was sent to Rajiv Gandhi asking that special relief be made available for widows, and women who have lost all the male members of their families. There have been similar requests for enhancing the compensation money for each death. The whole tone of such letters is one of asking a favour.

In the early days, people were dumped in police stations, colleges and school buildings that had been hastily converted into relief centres. Food and medical or other relief, such as blankets and clothing were not provided by the government. For the first few days, people from neighbouring areas, both Hindus and Sikhs, brought food for the victims. For instance, in Farash Bazar camp, people from Jhilmil Colony organized a *langar* for the victim families because the government had not made any food arrangements. Many of the victims had not eaten for the days they had been in hiding.

Even when the government did begin to send in food and other supplies, it sent them only to the 10 camps which the Delhi administration chose to 'recognize'. About 20 other camps, most of them set up in gurudwaras, were not recognized by the government and therefore received scarcely any material help from it. The Sikh community, with help from voluntary organizations, arranged food and other supplies for these camps. Even in the 10 recognized camps, government food supplies are so poorly distributed and inadequate that voluntary organizations have had to continue supplying food, clothing and other necessities such as blankets, soap, utensils, and buckets on a regular basis.

Several voluntary organizations such as the Nagrik Ekta Manch, which was formed specifically in response to this mayhem, tried their best to fill the gap. They collected donations, food supplies, old clothes, medicines and other items. A few doctors joined these relief teams. In some camps, government machinery began to put obstacles in the path of voluntary organizations and insisted on issuing identity cards to people before letting them enter the camps. However, this plan could not be implemented. Even as the voluntary organizations began to assess and grasp the magnitude of the problem, the government announced its plans to fold up the camps on the plea that the situation had returned to 'normal'. The government insisted that people return to their 'homes' so that the process of 'rehabilitation' could be expedited. Many people whose houses had been completely destroyed were similarly packed into buses and sent off. Mahinder Kaur, whose flat in Nand Nagri had been completely looted and damaged, was left with no source of income. Her husband's tea-shop and her knitting machine were both destroyed, yet she was forced out of the camp in Shyamlal College, Shahdara. She says that on 11 November, a day before the university opened, inmates of this camp, which was one of the largest in Delhi, were forced out. When they manifested reluctance, they were told: 'dhakke mar ke nikalenge' (If you do not go, you will be thrown out). In Kalyanpuri and Shakurpur people are living in the open near their wrecked homes.

It was around 6 November that the government declared its intention of winding up the camps. This was the time when people were still coming into the camps and most of those who were there categorically stated that they would rather die than return to the areas where they had seen their relatives slaughtered and where degradation had been heaped upon them. The common feeling is: 'That place has become a cremation ground for us.' Those who lived in somewhat safer localities returned on their own without any prodding from the government. It is primarily the poorer families from resettlement colonies where even local people and some neighbours had joined in the looting and killing, who are not prepared to go back.

In order to pre-empt any government move to throw out vulnerable and shelterless people onto the streets, Nagrik Ekta Manch was forced to approach the High Court and demand that the government be disallowed from closing down the camps until satisfactory arrangements were made for the safety of the affected families. The High Court granted a stay order on 16 November, and on 19 November made the government give an assurance that no further evacuation would take place against the will of the evacuees. However, by then, almost all the government-run camps, except for the Farash Bazar one, had been emptied.

The political considerations behind the desire to evacuate people are obvious. First, as long as people stay together in the camps, they remain visible as victims of riots and of the collusion and failure of the government machinery during this period. This is obviously too big an embarrassment with the elections round the corner. Second, as long as people live together, they inevitably have a certain measure of solidarity. This gives them a relatively stronger bargaining position in demanding compensation and relief. Third, it is easier for voluntary agencies and concerned individuals to monitor the compensation process and to make sure that the money actually reaches those for whom it is meant and is not misappropriated by the disbursement agents or local leaders and hoodlums. Those families who were evacuated from the camps are now scattered and completely at the mercy of a callous governmental machinery. The Congress hoodlums are also playing an active role in distributing compensation money.

Fourth, those families who were compelled to go back will be forced to make their homes habitable by removing the wreckage. They will, thus, be made to destroy the evidence of the carnage and loot. The government has not yet taken the trouble to begin collecting evidence on a systematic basis or even assessing the total economic damage caused to individual families. Nor is there any hope of such a process commencing.

Fifth, once people are back in their colonies, they are likely to be intimidated into silence so that they do not follow up criminal charges or give witness against the attackers. The problem is most acute for the relatively poorer section of victims from resettlement colonies. The bulk of the people who stayed in refugee camps came from these colonies. The more wealthy people took shelter with friends, relatives, or in privately arranged places. Had there been any attempt by the government to record the statements of the victims while they were still in camps, it would have been far easier to get testimony, as these people have been freely talking to press reporters and other investigators. When I interviewed people in the camps, except for some women who had been gang-raped, not one person showed any unwillingness to tell his or her story. They were willing to be tape-recorded, photographed, and also to identify all those whom they knew to be abettors and perpetrators of crimes, however high up or powerful these people were. Once forced to go back to the areas where murderers and looters still roam around freely, the victims are not likely to be able to testify openly. Not that any effort to record statements is likely to be made by the government at any point since the carnage was mostly the government's own doing.

Very little has been done to curb the elements which were behind the riots. It has been reported that even when the police have been forced to make some arrests, people are charged with petty crimes which do not carry any serious penalty. A majority of arrests were made under Section 107 of the penal code. A person apprehended under this Section can at most be ordered to execute a bond for keeping peace and public tranquillity for a period not exceeding one year.

Moreover, since Congress (I) leaders are alleged to have instigated the rioters, the hoodlums behaved as though they were assured of political protection. In some cases, Congress(I) leaders are alleged to have actually gone to the police stations and insisted on their followers being immediately released. The best known example is that of Congress(I) leader, Dharam Das Shastri, who was reported to have openly intimidated the SHO who had ordered the arrest of some criminal rioters. Many other leaders are known to be doing the same, some of them through less visible pressures. Even the few rioters who were arrested have been released on bail within a day or two and are known to be openly intimidating the victimized families in their areas.

Despite pressure from large sections of the public, the government has not ordered a full enquiry into the origin of the riots. In fact, the government is making a shameless attempt to dismiss the violence as an inevitable outburst of people's natural frustration, grief and anger. The Congress (I) party has come back to fight the next election, posing as the arch defender of national unity. This has led several prominent citizens to appoint an independent enquiry commission to go into the causes of the riots. But the question is: how does a commission lacking any enforcement authority put the government and the ruling party on public trial for its criminal conduct?

The amount of relief and compensation promised is so low as to be absurd. The government has announced a Rs 10,000 compensation for each person killed. Since most of those killed were main bread-winners of their families, the money promised is ridiculously inadequate. When people have tried to point out the inadequacy, government representatives declare that any larger amount would set a 'bad precedent', since victims of floods and other natural disasters are given much smaller amounts. The procedures for getting even this meagre sum are so cumbersome that most people, particularly the illiterate and the poor, have no hope of ever obtaining it. The most problematic procedure is that a death has to be 'proved'. Considering the circumstances under which people were murdered, burnt to ashes and their remains lost amidst the wreckage, this is a cruel demand indeed.

The official figure for deaths in Delhi is set at about 600 whereas the actual number of deaths is likely to be much over 2500. The government is trying its utmost not to pay compensation for all the deaths. If it acknowledges more claims, this would amount to admitting the extent of the tragedy and of its own hypocrisy and negligence.

The government is paying about Rs 1000 for damages to a house. The upper limit of compensation for property is Rs 10,000. Even those who had their life's earnings, home and vehicles destroyed cannot get more than this. Even this meagre payment is being made in the most dishonest manner and many of the disbursement agents are taking bribes. Very, very few of those who filled out claim forms have been given the full amount of Rs 10,000.

For instance, in Farash Bazar camp, where people from Trilokpuri had sought shelter, there were 243 death claims, 515 house and property claims and 113 injury claims. On 19 November, government officials brought only 31 cheques to be disbursed. Out of these, one was for Rs 10,000, one for Rs 5000 and 29 were for Rs 1000 each. The people were so angry that no one accepted the cheques and the officer was asked to go back. Similar or worse things have been happening in other areas. Government inactivity has compelled some voluntary organizations and private business houses to undertake the task of repairing and rebuilding houses in some of the poorer areas, a task which the government should have undertaken as a priority.

When families were made to leave the camps, they were supposed to be given Rs 50 and a week's rations. Many did not get even this paltry amount. In some cases, people were so angry with the government for its role in instigating the riots that when they reached the camps they refused to touch food supplied by the ruling party. They would only accept help from gurudwaras, voluntary agencies or local residents who had spontaneously organized relief. Thus, even though on paper several lakhs of rupees will be shown to have been spent in providing relief and rehabilitation, very little even of this pitifully inadequate amount is likely to reach the people. This will provide another opportunity to the bureaucracy and the Congress party to bungle and misappropriate funds.

Ever since relief camps have been disbanded, voluntary agencies have found it more difficult to provide support and relief because the victims are scattered. Relief workers have found that because the colonies where most of the victims live are places where the city poor are concentrated, the job of relief becomes more difficult. Many poor families flock to the volunteers and ask for help, even though they are not riot victims. If they are denied what they ask, fresh grounds for resentment and hostility against the survivors are created.

Most people feel that the little that is being done or promised by way of relief and rehabilitation by the government is essentially a way of creating a favourable atmosphere for the ruling party in the forthcoming elections, and that as soon as the elections are over, all aid to the victimized families will terminate. Considering the government's past record, this apprehension is by no means unjustified.

One's first response to the enormity of what has happened is to feel a sense of absolute loss and despair. Even though the political instigation from within the ruling party played a very crucial role, we cannot escape facing the fact that the poison that erupted flows in the very bloodstream of our social and political life. This has frightful implications. The most significant is that we are being ruled by a deadly alliance of goondas and politicians, and all other groups have abdicated responsibility. Equally frightening is the passivity with which even the supposedly most enlightened and educated of our citizens have accepted the massacre as a minor aberration in normal life. As the election fever heightens, those terrible events are fast receding from everyone's awareness.

However, if we do not learn and act on a few of the basic lessons that emerge so clearly from these tragic events, we will not be able to avert still larger catastrophes. We must realize that what was done to the Sikhs can at any moment be done to any group of people. All it needs is a bunch of powerful politicians who, for some vested interest or other, decide to make a scapegoat of any identifiable group in the country. This has been done to Muslims for decades.

In rural areas, lower caste and so-called untouchable people have repeatedly been made victims of mass murder, rape and arson. The pace of such attacks has escalated in recent years. Such attacks by upper-caste landlords and their hirelings, with the complicity of the police, have not aroused much public outrage. Violence seems to have become so much a part of 'normal' life that people's sensibilities have been benumbed towards it.

Similarly, there is an old history of dubbing every radical opposition to the government as 'Naxalite' or 'anti-national' and thus justifying extermination drives against political opponents by the state machinery and its hired hoodlums. This time, the Sikhs came to be chosen as special targets. Next, it could be virtually anyone.

In this connection, *Manushi* filed a public interest litigation in the Supreme Court of India against the Indian state, the Home Minister and Home Secretary. Also included as respondents were the Delhi administration through the Lieutenant Governor, the Metropolitan Council through the Executive Councillor, the Delhi Police through the Commissioner, the Congress (I) party through its President and General Secretaries, the Chief Congress (I) officials of the Union Territory of Delhi, including the Congress (I) Lok Sabha members from Delhi, the members of the DPCC (I) and its ward leaders in various parts of Delhi.

Manushi's argument was that the crimes were violations of a whole community's fundamental and constitutional rights. For example, Article 21 of the Constitution which says that no person shall be deprived of his life or personal liberty except according to procedure established by law. This was violated with impunity by those controlling the government machinery.

We also argued that though the Police Commissioner has since instituted an enquiry into the functioning of the police during the riots, the entire responsibility for the complete paralysis of the police force for many days in the capital city, cannot be ascribed to a dereliction of duty by individual policemen or even by the police force alone.

Individual policemen could not have acted in such unison in their dereliction of duty unless they had received orders and instructions from their superiors in the force. Further, the police force could not have acted as it did or remained as totally inactive as it did, for such a length of time, without the complicity of higher levels of the state, government and administrative machinery. As such, while the police enquiry might identify some derelict policemen, the intent and purpose of that enquiry is to pre-empt the identification of the initiators of the conspiracy, by establishing that the guilty were merely some policemen and not the senior officers of the government or the ruling party. An enquiry conducted by the police into its own malfunctioning cannot be expected to uncover the truth.

We challenged the government policy of offering some of the survivors a lump sum of Rs. 10,000 as compensation for life lost. It seeks to equate the situation of these victims with that of victims of natural disasters and thus can be viewed as part of the cover up operations undertaken by the respondents. We demanded that the Supreme Court should levy punitive damages of a sufficient amount to be paid from the personal assets of those found guilty of perpetrating this massacre to deter those responsible for the riots from repeating these heinous acts.

This should be arranged in conjunction with the provision of pensions similar to those given to the families of members of the armed forces, who lose their lives during war. Government jobs should be provided to surviving members of victims' families which will give them an income equal to that earned by the deceased.

Manushi had appealed to the court to:

- Order an interim suspension from office of those who are accused of leading or instigating the massacre and the subsequent cover up operation;
- Pending the court's decision, freeze all assets of those organizations and individuals including that of the Congress party and its senior leaders, involved in the massacre and those who were under enquiry.

This petition was not only dismissed very peremptorily by the court but we were also threatened with action against us for Contempt of Court by Justice Ranganathan Mishra, when we tried arguing that such a cursory, high-handed dismissal of the petition was absurd considering the seriousness of the crime.

However, even though we failed in getting a proper hearing from the court, *Manushi* campaigned indefatigably for years along with other human rights organizations to bring the guilty to book. We need to demand that:

1. All those who are responsible for the carnage be dealt with appropriately. A public trial of the Congress (I) party and its chief office bearers who fomented violence and led the killings should be held. Additionally, they should be made to pay reparations both from the party funds and from their individual wealth, for the heavy looting and damage to homes and other property of Sikh families. They should also pay heavy punitive fines for their criminal conduct, though of course no fines can ever be a recompense for murder, rape, maiming and the other forms of terror that they unleashed.

2. The functioning of the various arms of the state machinery which actively connived with the arsonists or by their criminal neglect let the arsonists have a free hand for more than four days should also be subject to an independent inquest. This includes the police and the civil administration.

   Equally important is the long-term need to devise ways whereby the police and the administration can be made accountable directly to each local community for what they do or fail to do.

3. Apart from curbing the arbitrary powers of the police and administration, in which abuse is inherent, we need to learn from the strength that lies in each community organizing itself for its own defence and self-determination. It has been widely acknowledged that more than the police or the army, it was the citizens' self-defence efforts that sprang up during those days of crisis which succeeded in preventing the violence from spreading on a still larger scale. In many neighbourhoods Hindus, Muslims and Sikhs patrolled together and kept hoodlums at bay, even at the height of the incitements to communal massacre. We need to have the courage to learn the appropriate lesson from this experience—namely, that this form of self-organization has a much greater potential for giving genuine protection to citizens than the police has ever had.

   We need to recognize the urgent need for the people to take back for the community the power that has been appropriated by the ruffian-politician combine. It is futile to expect protection from the 'higher' authorities because this only ends up rendering us powerless and servile.

We need to rebuild the institutions of local self-government at every level so that we do not have to live with a crippling sense of dependence on a highly corrupt, authoritarian and centralized state machinery.

4. It is equally important that women be actively involved in this process in substantial numbers. The active presence of women in community life has several advantages, one being that because of their relatively lesser capacity for, and lack of a tradition of, committing organized violence, the active presence of women on such committees will make the atmosphere far less conducive to violence.

5. These riots have highlighted with great urgency the role that wrong, bad and dishonest information plays in breeding hatred, violence and injustice. This has been true not only for these but for all communal riots. In the absence of factual information, people become vulnerable to rumours repeated a hundred times with vigour and apparent authority.

Thus it becomes crucial to make honest information easily available and accessible on a very large scale. This task cannot be left to the government. It has to be undertaken by those who feel the need to build a more humane society. Prejudices feed on ignorance. We have to make a much greater and more concerted effort to collect systematically accurate and honest information, and to distribute it effectively in times of crisis and on a day-to-day basis.

6. These and other murderous campaigns such as anti-Muslim riots in many parts of India, the ongoing repression in areas such as Assam and Nagaland, the chronic massacres and terrorization of Harijans, also highlight the inherent dangers in the kind of thinking that puts abstract 'isms' above human life. The killing of Sikhs has been justified in the name of national unity just as Bhindranwale justified killing of people—Sikhs and Hindus—in the name of Sikhism or Sikh nationhood. Any 'ism', whether it is socialism, nationalism, Hinduism, or feminism, if it teaches us to kill, terrorize and subjugate human beings for some larger cause or 'ism', is a virtual death trap.

It also shows the danger of abstractions which hide human reality. People are often willing to stand by their neighbours because they see them as individual human beings but the moment people are seen as Sikhs or Muslims or Hindus, stereotyped prejudices about communities take over and destroy the possibility of human relationships.

7. We need to combat the authoritarian thinking which permeates every aspect of our social and political life—from the family to the government. Any differences of opinion are seen as signs of rebellion and are sought to be put down with a heavy hand. We need to build a culture of tolerance and respect for differences of opinion, and an institutional framework wherein mutual cooperation is produced by common interest rather than by military and police coercion or appeals to a mysterious idol called the nation.

A key aspect of relying on authoritarian thinking is the desire for simplistic, dogmatic solutions to all social problems. For example, there is a demand for more and more police and army intervention as one violent episode follows another. We need to remember that at no time in history and in no part of the world has the police or the army ever been able to inculcate a sense of fellow feeling or respect for other members of society. It is mostly in authoritarian and unjust regimes that the police play a very active, dominant role and have excessive powers. Therefore, we need to find other non-authoritarian ways of dealing with violence, crime and differences of opinion amongst our people.

8. Even the hired murderous gangs were aware that if the Hindus had but said, 'We won't allow you to go ahead with it', they would have had to stop. Many Hindus did resist the murderers even at tremendous personal risk. By doing this they not only saved Sikh lives but also saved and asserted their own humanity.

However, at the height of the massacres, this impulse remained largely limited to some neighbours and immediate friends of the attacked minority, acting as individuals or as a family. This impulse has to spread so that our concern does not remain confined to our neighbourhood, family and friends. It has to gather strength from a common purpose and effort to see to it that these massacres are not repeated.

'This is the Guru's House...':
A Day in the Longowal Gurudwara

I n mid June this year (1985), I went on a visit to Punjab to see for myself how far the situation in the state matched with its portrayal in the press. In this connection, I also visited the gurudwara at Longowal village where Sant Longowal lived.

On my return I was really surprised to find that my visit to the Longowal gurudwara provoked bizarre reactions from most of my Hindu friends and acquaintances. They seemed to be as shocked as if I had come back alive from a sojourn in a lion's den. My own experience of that place was so dramatically different from what people imagined that I feel compelled to write about it in some detail.

For the last few months, Sant Longowal had been consistently demanding an enquiry not only into the anti-Sikh riots in North India but also into the genesis of terrorist violence in Punjab. Time and again he asserted that, if the government ordered such an enquiry, the Akalis would provide evidence that much of the violence that was being attributed to extremist Akalis was in fact instigated by the Congress (I) factions in Punjab. Prior to this trip, I had discussed the issue with some civil liberties activists in Delhi. We had come to the conclusion that even if the government did not agree to institute an enquiry, a group of independent citizens could be called upon to do the job. One of the questions I wanted to explore with Sant Longowal was whether he and his party would assist such a citizens' enquiry team.

I was accompanied on this trip by a woman friend, who had so far not been involved in Punjab politics. Before leaving for Punjab, we tried to contact Longowal's party office in Amritsar in order to

First published in *Manushi* No. 30 (Sep–Oct 1985).

fix up an appointment but did not succeed. His partymen in Amritsar could not say for sure when and where we could meet him in Amritsar. He was constantly travelling from one place to another, addressing meetings in rural areas and small towns of Punjab.

We were told he might be coming towards Amritsar on a particular date. We decided to begin our trip with Amritsar. On reaching Amritsar, we found that Longowal's plans had changed and he was not likely to be anywhere near Amritsar for the next couple of days. It was impossible to get through on the telephone to his headquarters in village Longowal. So we were advised to take a chance and go there, without bothering about prior intimation or appointment. We were informed that since he used the gurudwara near Longowal as his base, he was likely to be there sooner than at Amritsar, even if he was constantly on the move.

We took the early morning train to Ludhiana, from there a bus to Sangrur, where we had to wait several hours to get a connecting bus to village Longowal. We reached there at about 2.30 pm, in the blistering heat. To our dismay, we found that the gurudwara was at least three kilometres away from where we had alighted. While we were waiting for some form of transport, some men standing near the bus stop got into a conversation with us. They were curious to know where we were from. When we said we were from Delhi, they assumed we were journalists. However, two of them asked me if I was from the Congress (I). I was alarmed that I should be so mistaken and wondered what had caused it. It was apparently my white khadi kurta and salwar which created this impression. Since it was not possible for me to change clothes at this point, I became a little apprehensive about giving a wrong impression to the people in the gurudwara me. As it was, we were very hesitant about how we would be received because we were arriving without any prior intimation. I also had apprehensions that we might not be taken seriously as we were women. We had no impressive press cards or any letter of introduction. Even in normal times, it is difficult to approach important political leaders without the help of intermediaries. Sant Longowal faced grave danger both from Sikh terrorists and from certain Congress (I) elements in Punjab. We expected that he would not be easily accessible.

Anyway, it was too late for such doubts. We hired a tempo and proceeded to the gurudwara. The road went through dry, parched countryside. When our tempo reached the gurudwara, the driver stopped the vehicle near two young men posted as guards, who were sitting on a charpai. They made no attempt to stop or interrogate us as to the purpose of our visit. They offered us some water and asked us to go inside.

I had expected that a man as endangered as Sant Longowal would be living under heavy protection in a fortress-like place surrounded by multitudes of armed guards. Nothing could have been less like a fortress than the building in front of us. It looked like a secondary school building in an ordinary village. It had boundary walls made of brick on two sides. On the other two sides, it was surrounded by open fields dotted with a few low bushes and eucalyptus trees which certainly did not constitute a protective wall. Even the two brick walls had no gate nor anything resembling one. On the right hand corner of the premises the two boundary walls had a big opening which acts as the main entrance. We walked to the inner compound.

We saw a small group of men of differing ages sitting and talking to each other, in soft, quiet tones under the shade of a tree. On seeing us, no one rushed towards us. They continued chatting. We looked around for something that looked like an office. There was nothing of the kind. All we saw was a row of about ten rooms with a corridor in front just as in school buildings. The doors of the rooms opened into the corridor and they faced the inner compound. The compound had two handpumps and several trees and shrubs, many of them in an early stage of growth. The compound and the plants looked well tended.

We walked to the men sitting under the tree and asked if we could talk to the person in charge of the gurudwara. 'Everyone is in charge here', one of them replied, 'Talk to anyone you like.' In the meantime, two young men came out of a room and offered us water. We told them we had come to meet Sant Longowal. 'Santji is not in at the moment. He will come back sometime in the evening.' We asked: 'Can we wait for him here?' The young man replied in a friendly voice: 'This is the Guru's house. Everyone is welcome here at any time.' They asked us no questions whatsoever as to who we were or why we wanted to meet the Sant. One of the young men led us to a room, set up two big string beds for us and asked us if we would like to have lunch. We assured him we had eaten on the way. He offered to make some tea for us.

There was something very unusual in the way we were accepted in the gurudwara. These young men whom we talked to, simply offered us this room in which they said we could stay. They did not seem to need anyone's permission or approval.

We were tired and lay down on the beds. The room we were in was like all the other rooms, absolutely bare in its simplicity. As far as I can remember, the brick walls were not whitewashed. They were covered with grey cement plaster. Apart from the beds, there were a few hooks on the walls on which hung some clothes, and a few open cement shelves holding some odd things—the sparse belongings of the *sewadars*. The only noticeable things on those shelves were the two *Gurbani Gutkas* wrapped in satin, according to the custom.

The room, like all the others, had an electric bulb and a ceiling fan, and large windows. The whole place had an air of rustic simplicity without any ostentation. The effortless austerity of the place seemed to be geared to ensure that the inhabitants did not suffer any needless discomfort. There seemed to be no fetishising of austerity of the kind that is often witnessed in monastic communities.

As we lay down to rest, there was a soft knock on the door and an elderly man came in to take his clothes hanging on the hooks. I mumbled an apology: 'Sorry, we have inconvenienced you by occupying your room.' His voice was gentle: 'Why do you call it my room? It belongs to the Guru just as everything here does.' He talked to us briefly but asked us no questions, displayed no curiosity or suspicion.

Tea was brought in by another young man in his early twenties. He was polite, shy and soft-spoken like the first one. He asked if we were comfortable and whether we needed anything. He indicated the location of the toilets, brought a new bar of soap for us, and cleaned the room used for bathing, even though everything seemed already clean. Once again, there were no probing questions or suspicious looks. This was very unlike what one usually confronts travelling anywhere in the country, especially in the countryside.

Instead I was the one who expected my curiosity to be satisfied and insistently asked the young man endless questions such as how long he had lived in the gurudwara, what the nature of his job was, how many men lived there as Sewadars and so on. Every question was answered without any uneasiness or any attempt to be cautious. He told me that about 15 Sewadars lived in the gurudwara. All of them belonged to neighbouring villages. The younger men were educated, most of them in village schools and colleges. Some had studied up to matriculation, a couple of them were graduates. One of them had a master's degree. This was the one who had first brought us to the room and set up the beds for us.

He said that at an early age he had decided to devote his life to the Guru, but had continued studying even after he joined the gurudwara as a Sewadar. Apart from helping in the general running of the gurudwara, he also took care of Sant Longowal's needs and acted as his guard. What about their Santji? What kind of schedules did he keep? What was the nature of Sant Longowal's current political activity in Punjab? Again, the answers were clear and informative. He explained how, for the last few months, Santji was constantly travelling from one part of Punjab to another, in an attempt to conduct an intensive mass contact campaign. He went wherever he was invited—not just to gurudwaras but also to temples. He spoke not only to Sikh gatherings but also to Hindu gatherings in Punjab. Many of these meetings were scheduled and fixed in advance in which case the people at this gurudwara knew of his programme and his movements. But he often made unscheduled stops and addressed gatherings without prior arrangements. Often, people collected around him after a meeting, and sometimes, they would insist that he visit a particular village or make a stopover at someone's house. He often yielded to such requests, especially if he had no fixed programme during those few hours.

Did not all this pose a big risk to his life? The young man replied that it was indeed very risky but then so was the work that Sant Longowal had chosen to do. He felt there was no escaping that work. Had the government provided him with adequate security? The young man replied that Santji had consistently refused government security but the government insisted on sending a whole trail of guards wherever he went. In addition, a few of his young followers stayed with him night and day, acting as his guards. Why did Santji refuse the security provided by the government? The young man replied in the same soft tone: 'Santji does not want to inhibit his movements and restrict his work because of the risk to his life. He wants to remain fully accessible to people and the presence of government security men does come in his way.' And then, without any agitation or bitterness, he went on: 'Moreover, who can trust the government? He faces greater danger from them than from anyone else.'

I was reminded of the time when Sant Longowal paid his first public visit to Delhi after the November riots at the end of April. Apart from addressing a series of public meetings at Delhi, he made it a point to have a quiet private gathering with individuals and organizations such as PUCL, PUDR and Nagrik Ekta Manch who had played a leading role in organizing relief for riot victims. They had also helped to expose the real nature of the anti-Sikh violence through their writings. He made no fiery political speech at that meeting, but with folded hands, in a very quiet and modest way, expressed his thanks to all those who had helped Sikhs in their time of crisis.

After tea, we both had a bath. The washrooms were at the farthest end of the buildings. There were some men sitting in a group in the corridor, having a quiet conversation. As we walked up and down the corridor, no one gave us more than a casual look. It was not as if any of them was making a deliberate effort to ignore our presence. They took our presence as matter of factly as if we were part of the regular establishment.

Their ease was puzzling. As we found out later, no woman lived or worked in the gurudwara. Women and men from neighbouring villages did come to the gurudwara to perform *sewa*, pay homage or to have *darshan* of Santji. It was unlikely that the gurudwara had many women visitors like us who had not come for a religious purpose. Young women travelling unescorted in rural or even urban areas usually excite a lot of curiosity. Even in places where the presence of unescorted women is not unusual, women are usually subjected to curious stares, and often have to answer a number of personal queries. I remembered the time some years ago, when I, with two women friends of my age, had gone to Varanasi. We went to a *sarai* looking for a place to stay. These sarais are religious charitable establishments and are supposed to provide subsidized accommodation to pilgrims and other visitors to the holy city. We were given a thorough grilling before the man in charge of the sarai allowed us the use of a room. He questioned us regarding our marital status and asked why we had come unescorted. He also enquired what time we would return in the evening if he gave us the room, and so on. In this gurudwara, no one had even asked us for our names so far, let alone any questions about our marital status—a question women can scarcely ever avoid in any part of India.

Even more impressive was the fact that we were not asked any questions about our religion. At first, I thought this might be because they assumed that we both must be Sikhs. To dispel any doubts they might have, I made sure to tell my name to the men with whom I talked. Even ordinarily, people are puzzled by my surname. The first name indicates that I am from a Hindu family but the second name comes from a Persian word. So I have often been questioned regarding the combination. But throughout our stay in Longowal gurudwara, neither I nor my friend faced a single query about our religious, communal or political identity.

They treated us like honoured guests even though they had no idea who we were. Even when I said I wanted to interview Sant Longowal no one asked me which newspaper or magazine I represented. Their open-heartedness was very surprising, considering the dangers these men were facing.

It was about 4 p.m. by the time we finished bathing. I decided to walk round the temple compound. Not far away from the row of rooms on the left side of the compound was a small room used as the gurudwara. Next to it stood a beautiful exotic tree of a type I had never seen before. Under a tree at the other end of the compound, sat a group of elderly men drinking tea which they had prepared on an improvised brick stove. One of them asked me if I would like to have some tea. I accepted the offer and went and sat among them on the string bed. The person who had offered me tea and had answered most of my queries offered to show me around the gurudwara. He told me he was a former army man who had travelled widely all over the country during his service days. After retirement, a couple of years ago, he came back to his village which was not far from this gurudwara, and decided to devote the rest of his life to the service of the gurudwara as a Sewadar (one who serves). He also told me the story of how this gurudwara came into existence.

It is named after Bhai Mani Singh, said to have died a martyr's death at the hands of one of the Mughal rulers. The spot of his martyrdom is the site of the present gurudwara, which was constructed about 10 years ago. Ever since then, it has also been Sant Longowal's abode. This place had belonged to a zamindar and the *sthan* or location of the holy tree which stands next to the gurudwara was used as *pashu sthan* or a place to tie animals. The Zamindar donated the land for the building of a gurudwara because of its historical and religious significance. My guide told me that just as Bhai Mani Singh stood against the tyrannical power of the central authority at Delhi which tried to subjugate people in different parts of the country, so Sant Longowal was fighting against the authoritarian politics of the Centre and its attempts to enslave the states. Few people today remember that Sant Longowal was among the first to oppose the imposition of the Emergency in 1975. Throughout the Emergency, the Akali Dal sent groups of volunteers almost every day from the Golden Temple to court arrest in protest against the repressive policies of the government. It seems Indira Gandhi's special aversion to the Akalis dates back to this period.

The actual gurudwara is a small room about 10 feet by 10 feet. The *Granth Sahib* is kept in the centre of the room and a few oil paintings depicting scenes from Bhai Mani Singh's life adorn the walls. The room has some shelf space covered by wooden panels. The structure is as plain as possible.

After showing me the gurudwara, the retired armyman accompanied me so that I could have a look at the fields surrounding the building. We passed an area where a large room was being constructed. He explained that it would be the room for *langar* or free meals. Right now, *din da prasad* or the noonday meal comes from the neighbouring villages and *rat da prasad* or the night meal is cooked by the sewadars in the gurudwara. The work is shared by all of them. On the left side, the compound merges with the part of the gurudwara land used for cultivation. This small piece of land is used to grow food for their own consumption. He explained about the different crops grown there, the problems with irrigation and so on. We briefly discussed Punjab politics. He talked about the indiscriminate arrests of innocent people all over the state in the name of curbing terrorism and how even children were not spared. He described how men from Punjab were afraid to travel in buses outside their village, especially in Haryana, because anyone could be hauled in by the police or army without even an explanation. There was no anger or bitterness in his tone. His voice remained soft and gentle, and the words he used to express his sentiments were calm and peaceful.

Such a man would be considered exceptionally soft-spoken and genuinely courteous in any part of the world. But he seemed to merge quietly in the overall atmosphere of the gurudwara. It is not rare to come across gentle, soft-spoken and open-hearted people, but one usually meets them as stray individuals. The unusual thing about the whole place was that all those living there seemed to have imbibed this quality. The soft tones did not seem the product of rigid discipline. The gentleness was not the artificially acquired quality that one comes across by way of gentlemanliness in some public school products. There were no hushed whispers or secretive silences. They were communicative without being pushy or inquisitive.

Throughout our stay, I did not hear anyone speak in a loud

voice either in discussion or in any other routine forms of communication. For instance, it is fairly common for people in India to give instructions to someone from a distance or to call out loudly if a person is some yards away: 'O Banta Singh, go and feed the animals' or 'Ram Sharan, where is the axe kept?' Not once did we hear any of these men shout to another from a distance or speak in agitated tones.

Moreover, we did not see any visible signs of hierarchy or seeking permission. This is quite uncharacteristic of most religious institutions. Since there is a long history of Akali politics being plagued by conflicts over the control of gurudwaras, the functioning of this gurudwara seemed rather extraordinary. To the end, I could not say who the more senior or powerful personages at the gurudwara were.

Since Sant Longowal had not yet returned, my friend and I decided to take a walk in the nearby fields. On our way, we saw two young men posted as guards, sitting on a charpai near the outer edge of the gurudwara land. They were smiling as they read aloud from a Punjabi newspaper. I stopped and asked what was making them so happy. 'We were reading an account of Santji's speech at a public meeting yesterday.' We lingered for a while and continued to talk. They were among the personal bodyguards of Santji, young men in their early twenties, belonging to neighbouring villages, living their life as sewadars in the gurudwara.

Their shyness and soft-spokenness looked at variance with the weapons they had on their persons. I happened to remark that we had come from Delhi to meet Santji but since we had not made an appointment, I was apprehensive that he might not have time for us. They replied with confidence: 'Why won't he talk to you? Santji never refuses time to anyone who comes to talk to him.'

They spoke of their Santji with the affection, reverence and loyalty usually felt for beloved elderly people in the family, rather than the heads of religious or political organizations. Even though they had the alertness required to fulfil their task, they seemed relaxed and cheerful, and seemed to feel a deep sense of pride in being called upon to protect a man they loved. These and other young sewadars of the gurudwara seemed to form a magic circle of love and reverence around Sant Longowal. These were men who did not manifest any violent impulses or any great pride in their weapons but seemed ready to risk their lives in the defence of their Santji.

At about 6 p.m., we saw Sant Longowal returning, in a white Fiat car, along with some other men, probably his bodyguards. He was followed by a jeep full of armed police guards provided by the government. Considering that he had been out on dusty village roads since morning in the dry heat of June, he looked remarkably cool and fresh, and his clothes were a spotless white. As soon as he arrived, the various sewadars slowly gravitated towards his room although no one seemed in a nervous rush or flurry. Within 10 minutes of his arrival, he sent for us to come to him in his room. He could not even have had time for a wash or a few minutes of rest because some other people waiting for him were already in his room.

The room he used was no different from the others, except that it was smaller and more neat and orderly. It had a wooden divan-like structure which he used as a bed at night and as a seat in the daytime. There were also two plain wooden chairs for visitors, a simple centre table and a small portable room cooler which, we were told, was sent by a well-wisher in Delhi. This room had a small attached bathroom for his personal use. The door to his room was constantly open. I do not remember seeing it closed for 10 minutes during the entire length of our stay. It stayed open until late at night when we went to sleep and was open in the morning when we woke up. People walked in and out without as much as a knock at the door. I did not see anyone asking for permission to enter the room or going through any elaborate ritual greetings. That one small room, neat and orderly, functioned as his bedroom, office and a place for receiving visitors and holding small meetings.

As we walked in, he greeted us with his eyes and a quiet smile and gestured towards the two chairs as if to say: 'Please be seated.' He waited quietly for us to say what we wanted. My friend introduced herself as the sister of someone known to Sant Longowal. He did not say a word in response but just gave us that steady, kindly look which put one at ease in his presence, while at the same time discouraging one from taking unnecessary liberties with him. It was surprising that he made no attempt to be more familiar with her because of previous acquaintance with her family. Before reaching Longowal, I had assumed that I would depend on my friend to act as a link so that I was not received with mistrust at the gurudwara. But within a few moments of reaching there, I realized how unnecessary that approach was. Here was a place where no one needed any introduction to prove their credentials. Everyone received pretty much the same treatment. When I introduced myself, he remained similarly benign and detached. I told him I would like to talk to him whenever he was relatively free so that we could talk uninterrupted for a while. He did not ask me what it was I wanted to talk about but merely requested us to give him a little time to attend to the others who had been waiting for him. His face had a strange half smile. It could well be mistaken for a complacent look but seemed to me to be a reflection of an inner calm.

About an hour later, he called us and sat down to talk to us in the open courtyard, not far from his room. He was as soft-spoken as all the other men we had met and talked to in the gurudawara. My own voice sounded unduly agitated to me in contrast to his calm monotone. There was no drama in his voice nor the rhetoric that flows so easily from the tongues of most political leaders. He spoke in measured tones and did not labour to produce any particular effect or impression. The voice stayed at the same pitch and so did his courtesy and temper.

I questioned him on a range of issues and he gave simple lucid answers to each question, even to those which must have been thrown at him dozens of times every day.* Soon after we began talking, a young man and woman from a neighbouring village walked up to Santji and stood with folded hands. The woman stepped forward and put a ten-rupee note in his lap, folded her hands again and stood quietly looking at him for a few minutes with reverence and love. Santji looked at them, nodded quietly with something resembling a smile on his face, but did not say a word. After a few minutes, they went away as quietly as they had come and Santji resumed his conversation with us. In the meantime, he had gestured to a sewadar who was walking nearby and handed the note to him. He had not given any blessings to the couple nor had they shown any visible sign of obeisance. Looking on, it struck me that I had seen him use words only when he had to answer a question or had something definite to say. He did not make any unnecessary conversation.

While we were talking to Sant Longowal, not one of his security guards or members of his staff hung around us. In the beginning, a young man sat some distance from us, but he too quietly moved away after a few minutes. Even though some other people were waiting for Santji, he did not try to rush through or answer abruptly although most of his answers were brief. It was I who cut short the conversation at the end of one and a half hours, realizing that he

*The interview is reproduced at the end of this chapter.

had to attend to other business. He did not ask me whether I was interviewing him for a particular newspaper or magazine, even though I tape-recorded a substantial part of our conversation. If he had asked me, I would not have known what to say because I had not gone with the intention of recording a formal interview for a newspaper.

The trustful openness in the atmosphere of the place urged me to ask something of him that I had not originally intended: would he be willing to come and preside over a function which *Manushi* was planning to hold in honour of Shri Prabhu Dayal who died in November 1984 while trying to rescue three Sikh women who were trapped in a house set on fire by a riotous mob? He agreed without a moment's hesitation, and said he would be happy even to make a special trip for such a mission.

He asked if we knew other such cases because he would like to visit the families and offer his gratitude and homage to them. I gave him a copy of *Manushi* in which we had written about the heroic sacrifice of Shri Prabhu Dayal, and left him to attend to the others who were waiting for him.

Soon after, the two young men who had brought us tea served us dinner. The food was from the gurudwara langar or community kitchen. It consisted of plain *roti*, unfried *dal* and some raw onions. This seemed to be their normal diet. They served us with the tender care one usually associates with women. They stood by and chatted with us while we ate so that it did not feel as if they were attending upon us.

After dinner, they spread bright coloured cotton sheets for us on the string beds. Sant Longowal was sitting in the courtyard and talking to a group of men, some of whom seemed to have come from neighbouring areas. It was a fairly large group of men but the conversation was a quiet one, conducted in the same soft tones one had got used to hearing.

Our beds were inside the room and the room was very hot. We wanted to take the beds out into the open but hesitated to do so, because we did not want to disturb their meeting. So we waited for the meeting to finish, and in the meantime, I began to stroll in the corridor. Two of the younger men sensed that we were in need of something and came up to us to find out. We explained that we would like to sleep out in the open but that we could wait for the meeting to conclude before we took the beds out. Before we knew it, they had picked up the beds and taken them outside, assuring us that we would be no disturbance to anyone. We were somewhat uneasy, especially since the place they set the beds was not far away from the place where the men were talking to Santji. Moreover, we also wondered whether the men of the gurudwara who slept in the open might feel uneasy with two strange women sleeping not far away from them. But they were so matter-of-fact and graceful about our presence that I felt foolish at having gone through the initial hesitance.

In the morning, we received our glass of tea from the same shy, smiling young man. I wanted to take a few photographs of the place and the gurudwara. Not being in the habit of always wearing a *dupatta*, I walked into the gurudwara without remembering to cover my head, and stayed there for about 25 minutes. No one came to chide me or even politely remind me to cover my head as is the practice for both men and women when they approach the Granth Sahib. Sant Longowal joined me in the room for a few minutes, and explained the history of the gurudwara, but he too seemed wholly unperturbed at my not having covered my head. This lack of dogmatism in not fetishising rituals made me feel a much greater sense of reverence for the place than I would have if I had been snubbed into displaying reverence through an obsessively enforced ritual. As I was taking photographs of the place and of the men living and working there, no one asked me why or what use I would put them to. One young man who was cooking *paranthas* for our breakfast felt somewhat shy and tried to hide when I approached him with a camera. Some others came around, laughed at his shyness and coaxed him into coming forward for the photograph.

I walked into Sant Longowal's room and found him listening as one of the members of staff translated the write-up on Prabhu Dayal in *Manushi* from English into Punjabi since he read and wrote only in Punjabi. He had a letter ready for Delhi Akali Dal in charge, Sardar Ajaib Singh. This letter explained that he had agreed to attend the function to be organized by *Manushi* and that we should coordinate and fix a date around 25 June. During the course of a brief conversation, he reminded me twice that we must not leave without having prasad, or breakfast. We were to leave by the 9 a.m. bus.

My friend went to bathe and Sant Longowal saw me waiting for her to finish. He at once insisted that I use the bathroom attached to his room to make sure that we were not delayed. The suggestion was made without any self-consciousness.

Even in normal life, rules of male–female segregation are fairly strict in Punjab. Religious institutions, especially those that admit only men, tend to become even more fetishistic. The naturalness with which the gurudwara people accepted our presence even though normally no women stay there, the total effortlessness behind the courtesy extended to us, the warmth and hospitality and the lack of mistrust in the atmosphere, all combined to make that one day a very memorable experience.

I cannot remember another place in all my travels where I have felt better treated than in that village gurudwara. Even while taking full care of our needs, these men allowed us enough personal space and privacy although the gurudwara represents public space. If we cared to have a conversation, they would stop by and talk but no one pushed himself on us. With such people around, it was not difficult to lose the awareness that we were two women in a strange place, surrounded by men. It was a rare experience of human beings dealing with fellow human beings rather than the tension and conflict that usually underlies most male–female interactions. And the beauty of it is that these people were not aware of doing something extraordinary.

Before we left, I gave the sewadars a couple of copies of *Manushi*. They were not aware of the magazine's existence and requested that if I wrote anything about Santji, I should send them a clipping. My friend caught a bus back to Delhi but I decided to spend a few more days in Punjab and proceeded towards Jalandhar where I have several friends.

Throughout my stay in Punjab and even afterwards, in Delhi, most people who heard that I had been to visit Sant Longowal at his village gurudwara reacted with horror, amazement and mistrust. This came as a real shock to me. A typical conversation would go as follows:

'What ! You went alone!'

'No, I went with another woman but I could easily have gone alone.'

'You mean you went without police escort?'

'I didn't think it was needed.'

'But did you at least inform the police that you were going there?'

'No. Why should I inform the police before I go to a gurudwara?'

'But don't you know they stock arms in gurudwaras? See what Bhindranwala had done in the Golden Temple.'

'But everyone knows that Bhindranwala had been propped up

by the Congress (I) to cut at the political base of the Akali Dal in Punjab.'

'That was only in the beginning. Afterwards, he turned against them and thought he had become a big power by himself.'

'How can Akalis be blamed for that, considering he had been propped up to destroy them?'

'But he was a Sikh and he did it in the name of Sikhism.'

'He killed as many Sikhs as he did Hindus.'

'Well, did you ask Longowal why they did not try to stop Bhindranwala?'

'I will, if you first get an answer from Congress (I) as to why they propped up such a murderer.'

'No, no, you are politicizing the issue unnecessarily. They are dangerous people. You should watch out for your safety.'

And that is how most conversations would come to a dead end. I was surprised to find that this ignorance and prejudice was much more pronounced among educated, urban Hindus. In the cities of Punjab where Hindus are in a majority they seem more paranoid than the Hindus living in villages where they constitute a small minority of the population. Communication and interaction amongst Hindus and Sikhs in the villages of Punjab seems fairly easy and spontaneous, while in cities people are full of mistrust.

Until a generation ago, Hindus and Sikhs could only be distinguished with an effort. It was common for one son to be dedicated to the Guru, and to become a Sikh, while another son remained a Hindu. Inter-marriages were fairly common. In a matter of a few years, how could they grow so far apart as to know each other only through prejudice and misleading political propaganda?

The reality of my experience of that gurudwara seemed more incomprehensible to many people within Punjab and in Delhi than would have been the case if I had described exploits in some strange distant land. That is why, after I came back and repeatedly confronted the same expression of shock and disbelief, I felt compelled to jot down my impressions of that visit, lest, after a while, I too begin to doubt my own experience, surrounded as we all are by a sea of prejudice. These jottings would probably have remained a private affair, had it not been for the untimely and tragic death of Sant Longowal at the hands of some madmen. I write this in the hope that sharing the tranquillity, kindness and honesty I experienced that day will be of some help in allowing more of us to understand who he was and what he stood for.

An additional reason for telling this story is that it helps to contradict the popularly held notions about the character of Sikhs in general and Jat Sikhs in particular. I have shared some of these prejudices myself. People have come to associate them with aggressiveness, a martial tradition, rugged manners, rough tones and behaviour, and blatantly anti-woman attitudes. Yet everything I saw, heard and experienced, revealed a very different aspect of Sikh life and culture. I am fully aware that it was far from a representative gurudwara. Yet it was not as atypical as many people would like to believe.

The assassination of Sant Longowal came as a severe setback to all those people in India who seek a peaceful settlement in Punjab. But it did not come as a surprise to anyone who observed the difficult, risky path he had chosen. Not very long ago, he was just another name in Akali politics and was hardly known outside Punjab. Even in Punjab, he was known more as a religious leader as the title Sant implies, rather than a political figure. In less than a year, he emerged as a major political leader and assumed importance for the future of the entire country. He entered the political arena reluctantly and with hesitation. He was a simple man who did not try to make any grand or dramatic gestures to draw public attention. Yet he has left behind an important political legacy.

The most significant feature of this political legacy lies in the fact that he dared to avow the politics of settlement by fair compromise between the Central Government and the Sikh community. He did this at a time when few people were willing to make such a commitment. He pursued this course in a principled way with rare detachment even though he knew that he was endangering his life by doing so. He knew that the hostility of communalists and statists made the likelihood of political rewards very dim. Sant Longowal came into prominence in the months after the country was engulfed by a corrosive wave of communalism. The Sikhs felt besieged because of the massacres that took place in many parts of North India after Indira Gandhi's assassination. They also faced continued political repression following Operation Bluestar. The understandable anger and resentment amongst the Sikhs could well have taken a more disastrous communal turn. Sant Longowal came to play a crucial role by making common cause with those who understood that this was an engineered communal conflict.

From then onwards, he began a crusade, travelling to different parts of Punjab and of the country, explaining that neither the Akalis nor the Sikhs had any real conflict with Hindus and that their real fight was against the Congress Party. He made no demagogic speeches but in a quite determined way went on demanding an enquiry into the riots and the punishment of the guilty. At the same time he asserted that his party would stand against Hindu–Sikh violence in Punjab in a determined fashion. This stand did not endear him to all those with a vested interest in strife and bloodshed. Sant Longowal paid for his stand with his life. He was fully aware of the dangers to which his politics exposed him, and also aware that the Akalis had been terribly isolated from potential support throughout the country because of misleading propaganda against them, and could not count on many friends.

His greatest disadvantage lay in the fact that he and his party were held accountable not just for their own actions, but also for the actions of their opponents. It has been reported that Bhindranwale and his crew were propped up by certain Congress (I) factions in order to undercut the Akali political base in Punjab. It is also well known, though not acknowledged, that a major part of terrorist violence was directed at moderate Akalis in order to terrorize the party into submission. Longowal and his colleagues lived under constant threat of murder at the hands of extremist elements even before Operation Bluestar.

Yet Longowal and his colleagues had to answer for the doings of Bhindranwale and his followers. This was not only before Operation Bluestar, when the dividing lines within the Sikh community were not as clearly visible to most people, but even after a clear split had taken place and Longowal had publicly disowned terrorist politics and also constantly pointed at the Congress (I) link-up with it. He had time and again demanded an enquiry into the entire history of terrorist activity in Punjab. It is unfortunate that except for a few small civil liberties groups, few others, including the major opposition parties, paid little attention to this important demand.

Whatever the other merits or demerits of Akali politics, there is no denying that Longowal and his Akali party suffered because they stood for a more decentralized political system which would involve greater political decision-making for the states. They stood for a genuinely federal structure as envisaged by our Constitution. Given the vast diversity of India, most perceptive people acknowledge that this is the only effective way of keeping the country together. But, confronted with a ruling party at the Centre which was not only unwilling to allow any meaningful autonomy to the states but was also constantly engaged in installing puppet governments at the state level, this power struggle assumed bloody dimensions for the Sikhs in general and for Akalis in particular. It was in such a time of crisis that Sant Longowal rose above narrow political considerations of electoral power politics and tried to free the Akali politics from the dangerous trap into which it had fallen. During this brief period many people had begun to look on him as a symbol of hope and principled politics. In an atmosphere charged with mistrust and hatred, he stood by his religious and political beliefs with rare courage and foresight.

Many avowedly secular politicians view religious leaders with mistrust and see them as representatives of conservative right wing communal politics. However, religious leaders at certain times have become the force behind powerful, progressive impulses in society. In Punjab, the Congress (I) came to play an outright and bloody communal role despite its secular pretensions. This was visible not only during the anti-Sikh riots and during the Lok Sabha election, but also in the way the conflict over the economic and political demands of the Akalis was manipulated into a Hindu–Sikh conflict in Punjab. On the other hand, an avowedly religious leader, Sant Longowal, came to act as an important bridge between the Hindus and Sikhs at a time of acute estrangement from each other. He played a crucial role in preventing Sikh politics from falling into the trap of Hindu–Sikh confrontation after the November 1984 riots, when Sikhs were being pushed more and more in that direction. In this effort, he sought for and joined hands with all those who genuinely stood for Hindu–Sikh amity.

Sant Longowal's meteoric rise reveals another important facet of political life in India. He was from a rural background and was trained for a religious life. Most politicians, even when they originate in rural areas, tend to gravitate towards cities as they move up in the political hierarchy. They usually maintain only a nominal contact with their own people and their native environment. To the end, Sant Longowal continued to operate from a humble gurudwara in an ordinary village of Punjab. Even when he reluctantly contested elections at the behest of his party soon after the Emergency, he refused to have a house in Chandigarh. Though he had to spend relatively more time in the state capital, his home remained his village gurudwara. He preferred to continue using it as his base. This is one indication that he stayed in close contact with the lives and concerns of ordinary people. He continued to strengthen that contact even though it endangered his life.

For many people, Akali politics is synonymous with bitter factional struggles over the control of gurudwara management boards and terrible infighting over vast financial resources. It is of great significance that most sections of the Akali party chose a man like Sant Longowal to lead them in their hour of crisis. He lived a near ascetic life, had renounced worldly pursuits, and owned no wealth or property. He quietly demonstrated the courage to work for peace even when guns were pointed at him. The majority of Sikhs rallied around him. It is a sign of the inner vitality of the Sikh community that they grasped the significance of his efforts and lent strength to him in isolating and exposing those Sikhs and Hindus who stood for communal strife and violence.

The manner in which Sant Longowal and his fellow sewadars ran the gurudwara also explodes another myth. Cynics often contend that gurudwaras only serve the political purpose of harnessing money resources for the Akalis and hence are basically hotbeds of corruption and power struggle. The gurudwara in Longowal seemed to act as a spiritual repository for people in Punjab. Part of Longowal's success in mobilizing his people for a struggle for peace may well lie in the fact that he could draw on the spiritual resources of his people.

Now that Sant Longowal is dead there is inevitably a sense of despair. An able and courageous leader has gone before he could finish his task. But the outcome of recent elections in Punjab is one indication that he did not die in vain. Yet there is much that needs to be and can be done by all of us. The Punjab crisis has taught important lessons and we can ignore them only at great cost not just for Sikhs but for all other communities as well.

1. The most important lesson is that we should not blindly and gullibly accept all that is told us by those in power. We should make the effort to seek more accurate information and should not become gullible victims of biased propaganda.

2. Communal violence and warfare are not just the creations of bloodthirsty criminals who go around killing in the name of their religion, their nation or some other ideology. Those who passively acquiesce in that ideology of hatred begin to see Hindus, Sikhs and Muslims as monolithic blocks rather than each group consisting of widely differing ordinary human beings no better or worse than any others—and become accomplices in violence and bloodshed. For a long time, Hindus failed to distinguish between a Bhindranwale and a Longowal, merely because both happened to be Sikhs. What is worse, people have been taught

to justify violence and injustice inflicted on any member of the Sikh community, simply because of the actions of a small number of men who also happen to be Sikhs. If a bomb suspected to be planted by terrorists explodes in Delhi, innocent Sikhs hundreds of miles away from that city begin to fear for their lives. This is a matter of great shame for any society and spells disaster not only for the victim community but for the entire society.

3. The Hindus, including those who see themselves as secular-minded, need to do some rethinking about their role in fomenting communal conflicts. Being the majority community, it is very easy for them to identify their sectarian interests, prejudices and mistrust of other communities as 'national' interests. This attitude has contributed to communal tension much more than the doings of a Bhindranwale have. Instead of confronting this reality, many avowedly secular Hindus began to use a Bhindranwale to justify their moving towards anti-Sikh or anti-Muslim positions, all in the name of national unity. This attitude can only encourage more bloodshed and a nation of people with such ideas is not likely to be able to stay together.

4. Those who focus obsessively on individual acts of violence and terrorism obscure our understanding of the more crucial issues around which the conflicts are being waged. Newspapers choose to report on spectacular violent events rather than on the ways that most Sikhs and Hindus in Punjab have actively combated and resisted the spread of terrorism.

5. Most acts of terrorism are meant as provocations. If we learn not to be stampeded by them and to base our political reactions on the overall situation rather than on such provocations, these acts of terrorism will not succeed in destroying hopes of reconciliation.

6. Sant Longowal and others have tried in their own way to press for the truth about the genesis of terrorist violence in Punjab as well as the anti-Sikh riots in north India. The government has conceded a probe into the Delhi riots after much dilly-dallying. But even that probe has not made much headway yet. The real story behind terrorism in Punjab has been told in small bits and pieces through stray newspaper reports; the government has so far successfully resisted any proper enquiry. Small groups of civil liberties activists have tried to undertake the job such as those who prepared the recent *Report to The Nation: Oppression in Punjab* released by Citizens For Democracy. The way the ruling party and the government reacted to this report indicates that

they have a vested interest in not letting the truth be told. We should press for an immediate lifting of the ban on the Citizens For Democracy report, and withdrawal of the charge of sedition levelled against its authors. The wilful suppression of such vital information has grave consequences for any society which aspires to function as a democracy. Therefore, we need to put more effort and energy into pressing for a proper investigation and demanding that the information be made openly available. If the government refuses to concede this demand, independent groups of citizens can undertake this job on their own, however modest their resources.

7. Sant Longowal displayed great courage in signing an agreement with the central government in an attempt to end the Punjab crisis. In working for such an agreement he demonstrated that Hindu–Sikh conflict is not inherent in the situation. Once the Central Government conceded the Akali demands, it strengthened the Akalis in combating elements in both communities who were fomenting communal clashes. Operation Bluestar and the November riots made many in Longowal's community and party mistrustful of the Congress government. He knew that they were going to accuse him of selling out to the Congress (I). But he also realized that this was a viable settlement. If the conflict was allowed to go any further, it would surely spell disaster for both Sikhs and Hindus. So even at the risk of being accused as a traitor or having the rug pulled from under his feet if the Congress (I) backed out, he actively promoted this settlement so that the conflict might be resolved. We need to ensure that the agreement is honoured and implemented, and not allow a small group of hoodlums to sabotage it.

8. The lesson that has the greatest bearing on India's contemporary politics is that any attempt to run this country directly from the Delhi throne can only lead to disaster. Indira Gandhi has left a harmful legacy in this regard. She tried to run the country as a private kingdom, and was extremely intolerant of non-Congress (I) governments in the states, even if they came into power by majority vote. Even with Congress (I) governments, she would hand-pick chief ministers and try to install puppet ministries. In Bengal, Andhra Pradesh, Kerala, Kashmir, Karnataka, and Punjab, when the Congress(I) lost power to opposition parties, she spared no stratagem to throw elected governments out of power. The present Punjab crisis owes its genesis to precisely this kind of

politics of the Centre. The demands of the Akali Dal could have been resolved in a few hours had that been the intention. Instead Indira Gandhi followed a disastrous policy. The entire country has paid a heavy price for her Bhindranwale ploy. We need to become more vigilant against such power games indulged in by our rulers. An important aspect of that vigilance is a struggle to ensure greater local autonomy and a more decentralized politics while ensuring that the interests of the more vulnerable groups at the local level are protected. For example, while we should press for greater autonomy for state governments and protection of the Sikh community's rights as a minority community, we should likewise resist any attempt by some of the Akalis to take away the legal rights of Sikh women by imposing a discriminatory version of personal law.

9. Finally, we need to understand that the unity and integrity of the country is not identical with the unity and integrity of a centralist state machinery. We can perhaps best safeguard the unity of India by encouraging its diversity to be reflected in popular regional forces in power in different states. Pressing for an artificial unity through an all-India party threatens to impose a highly authoritarian, centrist form of government.

'We Appeal To Honest People To Come And See For Themselves...'

An Interview With Sant Longowal

You have been repeatedly asking for an enquiry into events in the Punjab. If an enquiry is held, what facts do you think will come out?

When an enquiry takes place, all the doings of those who are behind the terrorists will be exposed. We will let people know everything. This will be possible only if honest people conduct the enquiry. We can go to them and present the facts before them.

Why does the Akali Dal not collect these facts and publish its own report?

Firstly, the Akali Dal has very little time or energy to spare from the struggle. We have to fight the cases of thousands of men, women and children who have been unjustly accused. Further, even if we do conduct an enquiry, none of our opponents will believe in its truth. The enquiry has to be conducted by impartial people as the

PUCL-PUDR enquiry was conducted into the Delhi riots. If Sikhs had conducted the Delhi enquiry it would have had no value. It was honest and impartial Hindus who played a big role in conducting that enquiry. That is why it is such a strong piece of evidence

So if organizations like the PUCL-PUDR send a team to conduct an enquiry, will you be able to give them the facts?

Yes, the facts are available in the villages. How people in villages have been looted, robbed, how their homes have been raided by the police. For instance, in Bhatinda there was a dacoit in a village. One woman managed to catch hold of one dacoit. While he was struggling to be free, in the scuffle, she bit him hard. The next day, the villagers went to the police station to file a report. The SHO asked whether they could recognize the dacoit. They said they could. Just then, the ASI came in. The woman said · 'There he is.' The SHO said 'This is our ASI. How can he be the person?' The woman said 'Ask him to remove his shirt and see.' And they found the marks of her teeth on his body.

Similarly, when some Nirkanaris were killed in 1982, the police brought dogs to trace the murderers. The dogs first climbed into the SDM's car. Then they went through Talwandi village to the rented house of a particular policeman and caught hold of his shirt. The police then got another team of dogs. Those dogs too climbed into the SDM' car and next went through Talwandi village to the policeman's house and caught hold of his hand. The people said: 'The dogs have caught the murderers. Arrest them.' But the DSP said: 'If dogs are to catch thieves then what is the use of keeping policemen?' The people said: 'Then what is the use of keeping dogs?'

What do you think was behind the murder of the editor of Preetlari?

I think the Congress hand was behind that murder too. It was done just to frighten the Hindus. He was not a Hindu nor was he a Sikh. He was a man of progressive ideas. He was anti-Congress. What quarrel did the Akalis have with him?

They say he used to write against terrorism in his paper and that is why extremists killed him?

The Congress is the *janamdnta*, the mother of terrorists. The Congress gave birth to terrorism so as to defame Sikhs. It will take a long time for people to understand this fact.

What about the murder of Chaudhri Balbir Singh in Hoshiarpur?

We have always supported Chaudhri Balbir Singh. The Akali Dal had no conflict with him because he was a leader of the Janata Party which has had an alliance with the Akali Dal. Janata Party leader Chandrashekhar supports our present struggle too. So Chaudhri Balbir Singh's conflict was with the Congress. The conflict was over the control of DAV colleges in that area. There had been many quarrels over those colleges. It was a power struggle in which there were only two contestants—the Congress and Chaudhri Balbir Singh. Chaudhri Balbir Singh defeated the Congress several times because he had the Hindu votes as well as the Sikh votes. He was a Hindu Saini but Sikhs in that area are also Sainis. He was well-respected among the Sikhs. The Congress killed two birds with one stone—got rid of the Chaudhri and also defamed Sikhs and got their shops burnt.

As soon as the Chaudhri was murdered, a curfew was declared. Thus. Sikhs from villages were prevented from coming into town for the cremation of Chaudhri Balbir Singh. The Sikhs in the town being in a minority got isolated. Then rioters came and looted Sikh shops, in the presence of the police. If the SSP had not been standing there, perhaps so much looting could not have taken place. People would have defended themselves but the presence of the police rendered them helpless. Afterwards, the police killed one man, Gurmair Singh, and also arrested those whose shops had been looted. They were accused of having fought with the rioters. They are still in jail. But those who looted the shops have been set free even though the property was recovered from their houses.

The Akali Dal told the people in Hoshiarpur to remain peaceful since our fight is not with Hindus but with the Congress. We want the murderers of Chaudhri Balbir Singh to be caught. They can be caught only from the house of the Congress. If government really wants to catch the murderers, the first suspects should naturally be those who were his traditional enemies, with whom he had a quarrel—the Congress.

Could you speak about the death of Gurinder Singh in PGI hospital, Chandigarh, who was arrested by the police as a suspected terrorist'

I don't know any more than you do because he was killed soon after he confessed he was a Congressman. He was Santokh Singh Randhawa's and Darbara Singh's man. He lived with them in the MLA's hostel, in their rooms. He attended Congress sessions which only chosen people attend. He was at Santokh Singh's son's wedding. He was a Congressman, used to defame Sikhs and terrify Hindus.

I say and I have said at Delhi too, that if the Congress government remains, neither India's unity nor India's integrity can remain. The Congress has broken India's unity. Consider this—if there is a revolt of PAC soldiers in UP, Sikh regiments are sent there to suppress it. Why? Why should Sikh soldiers be sent? Why not a mixed battalion of Hindus, Sikhs and Muslims? When Muslims are to be killed, Sikhs are sent, as has happened in UP, and in Bihar. If they sent Hindus, Sikhs and Muslims together, every incident would not become a communal one.

Many people complain that although nowadays you condemn such killings, before you never used to issue any statement when killings took place.

Why don't you just look back at old newspapers? When Lala Jagat Narain was killed, we asked for an enquiry into his death. We pointed out that the accused in that case had been arrested on the 5th of that month and had not been released. On the 9th, the Lala was killed. How could those men have committed a murder when they were in the control of police, unless they were brought from the police station in a jeep to commit the murder and were taken back to the police station afterwards?

If Sikh communalists had been behind these killings, they would have killed only Hindus. You can look at the record—more than half of those killed so far are Sikhs.

This could be said to be due to the inner power struggle?

There was no such inner struggle in the Akali Dal. The Akali Dal has made one lakh twenty five thousand of its members take a vow before the Akal Takht that they will follow the Akali Dal policy which is to conduct a peaceful struggle. Those who take this vow are called *marjivras*, that is, those who are ready to die for their rights. They will not kill anyone else but they will die themselves. We did this because we know that the government always attempts to discredit peaceful movements by infiltrating them with terrorists. We swore that if the government attacks us with *lathis*, we will bear the *lathis*, if the government attacks us with bullets, we will not reply with bullets. We will remain peaceful and will die as martyrs.

Two lakh thirty five thousand of our members have been to jail at different times but it could not proved against any one of them that they had raised a wrong slogan or harmed anyone. One incident came before us. A group of Akali Dal members were arrested and taken in a bus to Ferozepur. On the way, the bus stopped at Hari ke

Patan and the driver began to drink tea. The Singhs were hungry. They saw a shop selling *sev*. They took the *sev* and ate it. The shopkeeper dared not protest because the police were with them.

The arrested men said: 'Take the payment from the police. We are under arrest and the police have not fed us. So let them pay.' The next day, our workers brought the shopkeeper to us and told us the story. We asked him how much he had to be paid. He said: 'Rs. 500'. We gave him Rs. 550. After that, we have special instructions to all our members that whenever they ate or drank anything, they were to pay for it from their own pocket. We have kept full control over our workers. It cannot be proved that any one of them is a terrorist.

I have heard that you have evidence of the hand behind the random killings in buses too. Would you like to talk about that?

When the government conducts an enquiry, we will present the proof. At that stage, people will testify. At this stage, if we expose those who can give evidence, the enquiry cannot be held later. The events of Delhi can be repeated here. Just as in Delhi, now, people are intimidated by bomb blasts, so people here too can be finished off. Because the government is completely given over to ruffianism (*gundpane te utri hai*). People are fighting for their constitutional rights. At present, I can say this much—the Congress hand is behind this terrorism. The Congress hand is behind the killing of Hindus in Punjab. Conduct an enquiry and the guilty will be exposed.

Today, we are blamed for the concept of Khalistan. In 1979, in the *Gurudwara* Prabandhak Committee elections, the government set up a team called Dal Khalsa, against us, against the Akali Dal. Those who contested the election against us were Santa Singh Buda Dal, Jagjit Singh Chauhan Dal, Master Tara Singh Dal and Sant Bhindranwale group. Giani Zail Singh gave the slogan of Khalistan, Sanjay Gandhi provided the money and Indira Gandhi helped them. They had Congress backing and they fought the election on the Khalistan slogan. They told the people that if they were elected, they would create Khalistan out of the land that lies between Shyam Singh Atari's *samadhi* and Jarnail Singh's *samadhi*. Their plank was that they would give Khalistan to the people. The Akali Dal said: 'How can you give Khalistan to anyone? Where will your strength come from? This is *gurudwara* election. You are to serve and look after the *gurudwara*. Here, you can give more or less *kadah prasad* to someone. But how can you possibly give Khalistan to anyone? Kindly explain this to us.'

Well, they lost and forfeited their deposits. One Congressman won, one of Sant Jarnail Singh's men won, two independents won, and 136 Akalis won. They fought on the Khalistan slogan, Akali Dal fought against that slogan, and Akali Dal won. And today they accuse us of demanding Khalistan. We say: 'Good people, you raised this slogan, you set up a Dal Khalsa, you fought elections against us, you spent lakhs of rupees. Akali Dal won, the people stood with Akali Dal, you lost. And now you call us terrorists and separatists.'

Could you say something about the Akali Dal's demands?

The Sikhs fought very bravely against the British, they participated in the freedom struggle and made many sacrifices. First, we fought to free the country. Now our fight is to free the states—how long can the centre treat the states as slaves? The states should have the freedom to solve their problems themselves—such as unemployment.

The states should be able to decide the export prices of their own products. Our wheat is taken over by Delhi and exported to Russia at Rs. 240 but the farmer gets only Rs. 155. Is this not cheating the farmer? Why should we not conduct our trade ourselves? The Anandpur Sahib resolution framed by a committee headed by Sardar Surjit Singh Barnala in 1973 has four parts—religious, political, economic and ethical. The first three are addressed to the central government. Akali Dal demands are legitimate and not confrontationist. They do not conflict with anyone's interests.

One demand which has been disturbing supporters of women's rights in the country is the demand for a Sikh personal law which seems to have an adverse effect on women's matrimonial and property rights. Could you talk about that?

We want a law according to which, as soon as a woman gets married, her husband's property will automatically be divided, and she will have an equal share in it. So, if a man has two sons, then his land will be divided into four parts, and will be owned by the two sons and the two daughters-in-law. This is for the good of all concerned. If she inherits her father's land she cannot cultivate it because she goes to live in her husband's house. She will have to sell that land to a stranger. That will create tension between the brothers and her. But if she inherits property in her husband's family, everyone will be benefited because their daughters will likewise inherit their in-laws' property.

But the problem is that a young bride is never sure how she will be treated by her in-laws, whether or not she will even be allowed to live there?

If the law says that she will be co-owner in the property of her husband's family from the day of her marriage, they will not dare ill-treat her. You will see how she is pampered. (*Usde pairan thale hath rakhange.*).

She should be considered a co-owner automatically after her marriage. It should not even require the formality of registering the property in her name.

What if a girl does not get married?

A girl who does not get married should get a share of her father's property.

But since even today, girls do not normally claim their share of the father's property but sign it away to their brothers, why do you need to bother about a change in law?

Why should girls not be able to claim a share to property? That is also wrong. Why should they have to sign away their share and say they give up all right in their father's property? We want both women and men to have property.

What about the demand that a widow should marry her husband's brother?

She can marry whomsoever she likes. If she wants, she can marry her brother-in-law.

Even if he is married?

No. How can that be? A man is not allowed to have two wives, according to the law of our country. If he is unmarried, she can marry him. She can marry anyone she likes—our religion does not place any restriction on widow remarriage.

What do you have to say about the accusation which is repeatedly levelled against Akalis that they have weapons hidden in gurudwaras?

No illicit weapon has been recovered from any Akali worker. The Akali Dal has no weapons in any *gurudwara.*

But Bhindranwale had collected weapons . . .

Then he should have been asked where he got them from.

But the gurudwara is yours too?

The *gurudwara* is the whole world's. The *gurudwara* is not my property. Anyone can go there—Hindus, Muslims, Harijans,

Christians, all can go there. Everyone has a right to eat there, stay there. There is no restriction on anyone. We are responsible only for Akali Dal workers. And no illicit weapons have been recovered from Akali Dal workers. In any case, I say that the weapons found in the *gurudwara* belonged to the government.

The government wanted to defame the Sikhs, wanted to bring out a truckful of weapons to display to people. Bhindranwale used to openly move about in the country with sten guns, carbines, rifles. He went to Bombay, to Delhi and many other places. If those weapons were illicit, why did the government not stop him when he was moving about freely with them? Even after he was arrested, why was he released after the central government intervened on his behalf? He had licensed weapons. This recovery of weapons from the *gurudwara* was only to defame Sikhs, to destroy Sikhs.

But what did they get by defaming Sikhs?

The votes of Hindus. The whole massacre conducted by the Congress was only for votes. Whenever they have formented Hindu–Muslim violence, it has been for votes. The Hindu–Harijan conflict in Gujarat is also geared to getting votes.

But does it not prove very costly?

How is it costly for Congress? They got power. This newcomer has accumulated the kind of power that Nehru and Indira Gandhi never had.

The issue of the Sikhs *vis à vis* the central government is just like the issue of the Tamils *vis à vis* Sri Lanka government. Our government sides with the Tamils. We say: 'They are our brothers, do help them. But help us also. What you say about them should be applicable to us also. What you demand for them should be implemented by you in Punjab.'

What do you see as the solution to the problem?

The solution is oneness among the people. Until people understand their own strength and renew their unity, this problem cannot be solved. I am not speaking only of Hindu Sikh unity but of the whole of India.

What steps have you taken in this direction?

I can guarantee that if you go to any village in Punjab where Hindus are five percent of the population and ask them if Sikhs trouble them, you will not find one Hindu who will say that Sikhs trouble them in any way. All the troubles have been in cities where

Sikhs are in a minority and are being terrorized by the Congress. Their shops have burnt and looted. Then how can it be said that Sikhs want to kill Hindus? Have you heard of a single anti-Hindu riot in Punjab?

Hindus and Sikhs sit together at teashops and have tea, they eat together, they attend each others' weddings. The tension has been created by the government. The Akali Das has never at any stage raised any slogan against any other religion. But the government has control over the radio, over the television, over the press, they can spread their version throughout the country.

We are trying to the best of our ability to explain to the people the truth of the matter. Our helpers, honest Punjabis, both Sikhs and Hindus, are helping us in this task. We try to expose the guilty before the people. Unfortunately, the press gives more coverage to the government version. We are fewer in number but we are trying as hard as we can to present the facts.

Until the people understand the divide and rule policy of the ruling powers, they will continue to be divided amongst themselves. When they begin to understand the manipulative policies of the government, they will be able to think for themselves and will be able to see the truth for themselves.

We have been declared guilty. We, the Sikhs, the Akali Dal, have been declared guilty, have been called separatists and extremists throughout the country. But we are appealing to honest people to come and conduct an independent impartial enquiry here. The people of the country have passed a very wrong verdict in calling us extremists and separatists. Those who talk of terrorism should come here and see the reality for themselves before they decide who is responsible.

4

Need to Re-establish Links: Some Discussions with Sikh Communities in North America

The Indian government tries to attribute terrorism in Punjab to a mysterious 'foreign hand' that tirelessly conspires to destabilize India. The government wants us to believe that the main reason for Sikh terrorism is instigation by the governments of Pakistan, USA, Canada and Britain. Clearly, it does this to cover up its own mischievous role in generating and fomenting the conflict in Punjab.

Certainly, terrorists have been receiving moral and material support from outside the country. But the support is, in all likelihood, coming not so much from foreign governments as from elements in the Sikh community settled abroad, especially in North America and England. These elements can mobilize enormous reserves of money, weapons and people to enable the terrorists to continue and even deepen the conflict for an indefinitely long period. They can do this without the active support of foreign governments in the same way as the Irish community in the US has been able to provide support to the IRA for decades.

However, all Sikhs settled abroad do not support terrorist killings. There are also strong voices in favour of resolving the crisis through dialogue and consensus. These voices seldom reach us in India because the media oversimplifies and sensationalizes the situation, focusing exclusively on those who support terrorist politics.

Last year (1986), I had the opportunity to interact very widely with people of the Sikh community living in North America where I had initially gone to attend a National Women's Studies Association Conference. While there, I was invited to speak in about 20 cities and nearly twice as many gurudwaras by groups of Indians living in

First published in *Manushi* No. 41 (Jul–Aug 1987).

North America. Many of these invitations came from various gurudwara-based Sikh organizations. This report is based on dialogues with various overseas Sikh groups and individuals.

Indians in North America constitute a very prosperous and upwardly mobile migrant community. Sikhs constitute a large proportion of these people. According to one estimate, there are about 1,25,000 sikhs living in the U.S. alone.

Broadly speaking, there were three major waves of Indian immigration to North America. The first small wave consisted of agriculturists, most of them Sikhs from Punjab, who migrated to Canada and the West Coast of the US in the early twentieth century. Slowly, some of them became prosperous farmers. Even today, many illegal immigrants from Punjab go to work as farm labourers on fairly low wages. The second wave of immigrants were professionals, going to the US after the mid 1960s. At this time, immigration laws were relaxed to encourage large numbers of doctors, scientists and engineers to migrate from underdeveloped countries in order to fill the deficit of skilled labour power in the US. This group too seems to have done remarkably well and is considered one of the most successful migrant groups, along with the Koreans and the Chinese. The third wave in the late 1970s comprised small-sector businessmen and shopkeepers. This group has also been fairly successful. Many of them are importers of handicraft, carpets and garments or wholesalers in goods like electronics. Today, the Sikhs in North America are not principally farmers or farm workers, but shopkeepers, tradesmen and professionals. Not all the migrant Sikhs are from Punjab. Many have migrated from other states of India where their families are settled.

Even though a large majority of overseas Indians have opted for or are seeking US or Canadian citizenship, most of them retain active links with their families in India. It is fairly common for Sikhs in North America to come to India to find spouses for their children. They also constantly help relatives to migrate. Many frequently visit their families in India. Some even invest in property or business back home. Their connection with Punjab and the rest of India is a real and live one, not just defined through religion.

Given the fact that a certain amount of moral and financial support for the various forms of Sikh resistance in India, including the Khalistani factions, probably comes from some sections of the overseas community, it is important to understand their reactions, grievances and modes of expression.

We have failed to realize that the responses of the Sikh community abroad are varied and complex, tending to believe in the stereotype of all non-resident Sikhs as fanatically separatist. No doubt, terrorist groups are trying to establish hegemony, but there are strong voices in favour of a more responsible politics. They desire:

- an honourable settlement of the Punjab dispute;
- the right of states to more autonomy;
- an end of repression and false encounter killings in Punjab;
- punishment of those guilty of the November 1984 massacre.
- release of Jodhpur detenues and others against whom no charges have been framed.

The Sikhs feel aggrieved not just due to government policies, but also the fact that the official opposition parties have not been sufficiently impartial in their responses. The Sikhs have been condemned and isolated as a community. Many told me that the Longowal accord was possible because groups of concerned citizens like the People's Union for Civil Liberties, People's Union for Democratic Rights, and Citizens for Democracy, had protested against anti-Sikh violence, and had brought it to public attention. They feel that a settlement can be reached if more people intervene impartially.

The Indian government does not realize that it cannot afford to treat overseas Sikhs with contempt. It is foolish and unnecessary to alienate this influential and well-knit community. If we do not make an attempt at this critical juncture to establish a dialogue and reach an amicable settlement, the situation has the potential to worsen in the years to come.

In the absence of a dialogue, and with the growth of the anti-minority wave in India, exemplified in the rise of organizations which stand by such slogans as 'Hindi, Hindu, Hindustan', the more responsible Sikh leadership gets demoralized, and the small section that is not open to dialogue gains ascendancy in the community. Every time an Arwal, Meerut or Ahmedabad massacre takes place, fear and uneasiness amongst Sikhs grow.

Just as Hindus are often blinded by the rhetoric of national unity into justifying such massacres, so also Sikhs get carried away by the rhetoric of Khalistan as an ideally just state, and end up legitimizing the murders of Sikhs and Hindus that are committed in its name.

The breakdown of communication between Hindus and Sikhs living abroad is far more complete than it is anywhere in India. Many

Sikhs there told me how, when they went to attend condolence meetings for Mrs Gandhi, Hindus forced them to leave, saying: 'How dare you come here after having murdered her?' Thus, while news of some Sikhs having celebrated Mrs Gandhi's death was displayed prominently in the Indian media, other more responsible reactions were not acknowledged.

Following Mrs Gandhi's assassination, most overseas Hindus unilaterally and suddenly snapped all links with Sikhs. They behaved as if each Sikh was personally responsible for the killing. Many Sikhs narrated with anguish how Hindus, with whom they had extremely close family friendships which had been formed over decades, had stopped associating with them altogether. This was at times carried to absurd lengths. A Hindu family, whose child had been 'adopted' by a Sikh friend, the latter having performed the naming ceremony, stopped talking to her and her family. Several Sikhs were in tears while recounting such experiences.

The Sikhs were deeply hurt that their close friends who happened to be Hindus had not even bothered to call them to ask if their families in India were safe during the army rule in Punjab and the massacre that took place in north India following Indira Gandhi's assassination. As one old woman put it: 'Our Indian culture teaches us to bury all anger and enmity when there is a death. Somehow, even this little courtesy was not extended when the Sikhs were in mourning.' Another said: 'My biggest complaint is that most Hindus want us to stop feeling altogether. They want us not to feel hurt when innocent Sikhs are massacred, when the Golden Temple is attacked by the army or when all Sikhs are treated as criminals for the actions of a few.'

While some Sikhs also behaved as irrationally, it is significant that no Hindu complained of Sikhs shunning them. It seems that the initiative for a virtual boycott came from the Hindus. This was evident even during my visit. Several times Sikhs went out of their way to invite local Hindus to meetings. A few Hindus did attend some of the public meetings. But if the meeting was held in a Sikh home, Hindus would not come.

The few exceptions to this rule have had to face hostility from other Hindus. For instance, in New York, a couple of young Hindus suggested at the condolence meeting for Mrs Gandhi that a resolution also be passed condemning the massacre of innocent Sikhs. They faced such extreme hostility from fellow Hindus that they had to leave the meeting. At one place, a South Indian Hindu who informed

Sikhs about a condolence meeting for Indira Gandhi was subsequently boycotted by other Hindus who threatened to stop their business dealings with him if he continued his association with the Sikhs.

South Indian Hindus do not seem as involved in the hate-Sikh campaign. But, since interaction between Sikhs and South Indian Hindus has always been minimal, their lack of hostility has not acted as a bridge. As a result, when overseas North Indian Hindus stopped interacting with the Sikhs, the latter felt that the entire Hindu community had turned against them.

This attitude of the Hindus seems to spring from their feeling that India belongs to them, and the minorities are somehow less Indian than Hindus are. Thus, if some Hindus criticize the Indian government, they see themselves as being anti (a particular) government or party, but if some Sikhs do the same they are dubbed anti-national. Most non-resident Indians are usually full of stories about how their talent went unrewarded in India but is now recognized abroad. I found that many overseas Hindus talk with great passion about how they were compelled to leave India because the callousness and corruption of the government make it impossible for any decent person to survive with dignity in India. But these same people furiously oppose any criticism of the government policies by the Sikhs. Thus, many Hindus who condemn Sikhs for being anti-national do not realize that by considering the country and the government as the exclusive property of the majority community, they contribute to making minorities feel unwanted and alien.

I began accepting invitations to gurudwara meetings with some trepidation because I felt the Sikh leaders might be inviting me to speak with a limited agenda in mind. In North America, as in India, different political factions are trying to wrest control over gurudwaras. Some of these factions are committed to terrorist politics. I was not sure a dialogue would be possible under such circumstances.

The Sikh leaders said they wanted to honour *Manushi* for what they considered an impartial report on the November 1984 massacre. They were right in their assumption that I would support the Sikh community in its protest against the violation of its human rights and the government's failure to prosecute the culprits of the November 1984 riots. However, I was not sure whether they were prepared for the fact that I firmly oppose the terrorist politics being pursued by some Sikh groups. But, in fact, wherever I went, I was treated with typical Punjabi hospitality and made to feel completely at home, no matter how serious my political differences with my hosts. The openness and generosity with which the community argued and discussed these volatile issues were really impressive. Normally, when even minor political differences surface between groups, the dialogue freezes into hostility. In that respect, this was a unique political experience.

Though I openly voiced fundamental differences with the politics of many of the local leaders, they took pains to make space for open discussion, even when they could have easily avoided doing so. For instance, when I reached Vancouver, there was a preliminary meeting with about 30 active members of the local Sikh organization. Expecting this city to be a hotbed of separatist politics, I clarified my stand at this initial meeting so that the leaders could, if they so desired, cancel my public speech to the congregation at the gurudwara, scheduled for the next day. I did not want to speak from their platform under false pretences. When a group of them hinted that it might be better for me to avoid 'controversial' topics, I explained that I did not think it right to censor my opinions for fear of offending some people. They did not seem unduly perturbed at this.

The next day, a Sunday, there were thousands in the gurudwara. Far from wanting to cut short my speech, the leaders asked me to speak for at least 45 minutes. After I spoke, I was honoured with a *saropa* and a plaque, and then the secretary of the gurudwara took over the mike. There had been absolute silence while I spoke, but the gentleman who spoke next was interrupted by a young man who said aggressively: 'We don't want too much talk. We want to know whether or not you are for Khalistan.' The speaker clarified that he was, and also tried to interpret my stand as favourable to Khalistan. At this point, a few persons in the audience suggested that I had better speak for myself.

I reiterated my opposition to the politics of creating a Khalsitan by killing innocent people and forcing the Hindus to leave Punjab. Afterwards, many Sikhs came and congratulated me saying, 'Just as well you said what you did. If any one of us had said what you said, we would have been intimidated into silence.' I kept expecting the leaders to clamp down at any moment, because they might see me as spreading confusion among their followers. But, on the contrary, after the langar, they arranged an open forum at which anyone could ask me questions. This turned into an exciting exchange lasting over three hours. A couple of people from the audience gave fiery speeches defending terrorist politics, but others continued, undaunted, with their questions to me in the spirit of a genuine dialogue rather than confrontation.

Next day, the organizers arranged another big public meeting open to everybody—Hindus, Sikhs, Muslims and non-Indians. Again, the speech was followed by a two-hour question and answer session. It was followed by another discussion at someone's house, where people continued to talk and argue in good faith and without cynicism. They arranged for press conferences even though I had told them I would speak against terrorist politics. This experience, which was fairly typical, indicated the community's hunger for communication. Often, discussions went on late into the night. Many people came from long distances to attend these meetings. The intensity with which they participated showed that many of them were seeking answers, rather than taking rigidly fixed positions. They were eager for information.

No matter how forcefully I spoke against the terrorist politics of certain Khalistani elements, I continued getting invitations to speak at gurudwaras. When I asked some organizers why they allowed me to question their politics from their own platforms, they invariably replied: 'You spoke the truth at a time when few non-Sikhs were willing to do so. Therefore, we honour your right to speak the truth as you see it today, even if it differs from our view.'

After our discussions I found many more Sikhs willing to acknowledge the need for efforts on their part to end their isolation. Some realized that ever since Operation Bluestar, the Sikhs themselves have contributed in some measure to building walls of mistrust and hostility. This has prevented them from reaching out to more responsible and responsive sections of the Hindu community, both in India and abroad. They repeatedly asked me to inform them when any civil liberties activists from India visited America so that the dialogue could continue. However, they seemed diffident about extending direct invitations. They feared that invitees might consider it unsafe and that the government might obstruct them from attending such discussions.

Some groups among Sikhs are beginning to take more interest in international struggles for human rights such as that against apartheid in South Africa. They are trying to raise the question of atrocities on

Sikhs as part of a larger human rights platform. They realize that if terrorism continues, they will not be able to convince anyone of their human rights credentials. If this trend of supporting human rights struggles in India—not just human rights of the Sikhs but of all other minorities and disadvantaged groups (including the Hindus in Punjab)—can gather strength, it will be a positive break through in Sikh politics.

A good example was the meeting organized by a New York-based Sikh women's organization. They worked hard to ensure that representatives of different Indian community associations in New York, such as Gujaratis, Maharashtrians, Dalits, Muslims and many others, attended the meeting. The meeting was remarkably free from hostility between people of different communities. The Sikh women organizers spoke openly against terrorism as well as State violence.

After November 1984, certain US-based Sikh organizations had come together with the organizations of Dalits and other disadvantaged minorities in India on a common platform to discuss issues relating to the status of minorities in India. Some pro-Congress (I) Hindus went in a delegation to the Indian Embassy to request that such 'ganging up' of 'anti-national elements' be stopped. It is unfortunate that this positive development of the Sikhs getting sensitized to issues of discrimination against disadvantaged sections of Indian society should be viewed by Hindus as a threat.

The Indian government has been discriminating against overseas Sikhs in many ways. The introduction of stringent visa regulations to prevent Sikhs from freely visiting India seems to have had disastrous results. Even in normal times, the Indian bureaucracy is notorious for its high-handed functioning. With the new pretext of controlling terrorism, some bureaucrats seem to have found it easy to disregard even the minimal restraints that operated earlier. I was told by several people that they were not allowed to visit India to attend the funerals of close relatives such as parents.

The few who managed to get visas somehow were harassed no end when they reached India. For the Indian police and bureaucracy, 'curbing terrorism' seems to have become a lucrative business. People told me they had to pay bribes to avoid being arrested on trumped up charges. One person narrated how, while he was going to Punjab from Palam Airport in Delhi by a taxi, he was stopped every 20 minutes by the police, ostensibly to check his baggage for weapons, but actually to extort bribes. During the four-hour journey through Haryana, he had to pay bribes more than 20 times.

I was told that there were a few instances of Hindus and Sikhs getting together to collect relief for the victims of the November 1984 riots. But the Indian Embassy officials insisted that it be channelled through the Prime Minister's relief fund. None of the donors, Hindu or Sikh, wanted this as they did not feel confident that the money would reach the victims.

Embassy officials have also been shunning Sikhs. Many Sikhs complained that while the Embassy officials are often present at and involved with the functions organized by the Hindu community, they now refuse to attend functions organized by the Sikhs. Thus, there is considerable substance in the allegation that by treating every Sikh as a real or potential terrorist, the government has further alienated the community.

Unfortunately, many North American Hindus have fallen prey to the politics of mistrusting minorities. They feel that the Sikhs are getting what they deserve when the Indian government unleashes anti-Sikh propaganda in North America. They do not realize that in an atmosphere already vitiated by racism and anti-Asian sentiment, any hatred stirred up against Sikhs will soon spill over into suspicion of all Indians.

Very few Sikhs among those I met in North America dared speak openly against terrorism. This is because the chief targets of terrorists in North America are Sikhs themselves. The Hindus there cannot be intimidated so easily. Both Hindus and Sikhs believe the myth that terrorism is directed against Hindus alone. But many Sikhs confessed to me that in several places the *sangat* (congregation) is a hostage to the self-styled militants.

This fits in with the logic of terrorist politics. The first aim of terrorists is always to force their own community into silence. Then they can claim to speak on behalf of the community. Terrorism is the politics of a brutal minority within a community imposing its will on the silent majority. In India, Akalis and other Sikh leaders who refuse to succumb to terrorist politics are the primary targets of violence. Similarly, in America, the Sikh community is in a state of siege at the hands of terrorists. It needs to be known that as many Sikhs as Hindus have been killed in Punjab by terrorists.

Most Sikhs see terrorism as a Congress-inspired conspiracy to defame the Sikh community. They recount instances of certain terrorists in India who were liquidated in police custody after they confessed to being Congress(I) agents. They give examples of certain Sikh groups and gurudwaras in North America which are known to be receiving funds from the Indian government, which wants to control and instigate gurudwara politics by these means. These Sikhs were very critical of the Congress (I)'s role in gurudwara elections and politics, particularly since the party pretends to decry mixing of religion with politics.

However, I found that they had no satisfactory answer to my question: 'Why is it that even some of those who think terrorism is a Congress inspired game to defame and destroy the Sikhs, end up apologizing for it as the legitimate response of aggrieved Sikhs to the misdoings of the Congress government?'

Terrorism cannot be both a legitimate response of certain Sikhs as well as a Congress-inspired game. Those Sikhs who are convinced it is the latter should be the most determined in its condemnation. If some of them justify and support it as the response of aggrieved members of a community, then they have to assume full responsibility for the mad and self-destructive actions of the terrorists. These groups act under the guise of being the defenders of Sikhism. But they have been killing not just Hindus but also as many Sikhs, not sparing even little children.

Among the militants in North America there are many factions fighting for control over gurudwaras. Some Sikhs alleged that millions of dollars had been extorted and no one dared demand any accounting of gurudwara funds, even though they suspected misappropriation of these funds. Another complication is the widespread infiltration of Congress (I) agent provocateurs into gurudwara committees. Everyone suspects everyone else of being a government agent. In order to prove that they are not agents but are committed to the cause of the community, leaders try to outdo one another in militant rhetoric. People mistrust this rhetoric because they know the agent provocateurs indulge in it to provoke trouble. However, the leaders dare not stop using it, for fear of being called traitors to the community or worse still, Congress agents.

One prominent leader explained the dilemma. In a public meeting he presented himself as a staunch Khalistani. But when I met him informally later, he admitted that Khalistan was not a viable proposition. He said the demand for it was just a way of expressing anger against the Central Government. His reason for using a language in which he does not believe was: 'If I don't use this language, the militants will snatch the leadership from people like me. So we have to use this language to keep the militants at bay. Internally, we are trying to restrain them from doing crazy things.' It is important to realize that for many Sikhs abroad, Khalistan is a tactical position, a slogan raised in the hope that pressure of this kind will make the Centre concede the genuine demands of Punjab.

There is also a distinction between being a Khalistani and supporting terrorism or violence. Some combine the two positions. But there are also many pious Sikhs who oppose the killing of unarmed people while supporting Khalistan because they sincerely envisage it as a place where a peaceful, self-reliant and dignified human life will be possible. This trend is also visible in some sections of the World Sikh Organization which, in its Constitution, commits itself to fighting for Khalistan by non-violent means. Within this organization, different people speak in different voices, and the character of its local branches is decided by the inclinations of local leaders. Some are trying to organize a lobby to put pressure on the Indian government by mobilizing support from the Canadian and US governments. This seems to be a foolish strategy unlikely to yield the results they desire. Also, none of the WSO leaders is able to explain how Khalistan can be created without forcing Hindus out of Punjab and Sikhs out of the rest of India or without resorting to violence.

Many Sikhs harbour the illusion that by presenting their support for terrorism as being a simple consequence of the violation of their community's human rights they will be able to mobilize support in North America. However, this is not happening. On the contrary, given the already existing atmosphere of racial prejudice against Asian immigrants, their political activity is further strengthening the discrimination against Indians in general, and Sikhs in particular.

It is impossible for the Sikh community to appear as defenders of human rights while important segments of the community continue to be involved in supporting the politics of blowing up planes, massacring innocent people and creating an atmosphere of fear and intimidation in the gurudwaras. The blowing up of the Air India plane provoked as strong a reaction in Canada against the Sikh community as it did in India. Most Canadians are extremely resentful of the violence resulting from the activities of certain Sikh groups, not out of a concern for India but because they are genuinely afraid that the politics of violence will have an inevitable spillover in Canada. The fear is not misplaced. There have been instances of inter-group rivalries taking on a violent form as various Sikh groups compete with each other for hegemony. The forcible take-over of certain gurudwaras by terrorist groups has created an atmosphere of fear and tension with threats of violence constantly hanging in the air. They may not have dared go on a killing spree as in Punjab but incidents like the near fatal, murderous attack on Ujjal Dosanjh in Vancouver for his open and fearless criticism of Khalistani politics succeeds in frightening the entire community into silence.

The fear and resentment of Canadians against terrorist politics is reflected in the tightening of immigration laws in Canada and the repeated demands that they be made even more stringent for Asians. Indians were never particularly welcome in the Western countries but now there is a definite hostility to allowing Sikhs into these countries, whether as refugees or as immigrants, legal or illegal. Recently, when 174 Sikhs landed on Canadian shores illegally, there was a massive furore, demanding that they be denied refugee status. So far, Sikhs have been very successful immigrants wherever they went. But now, because of the indiscriminate violence the terrorist groups have unleashed, they seem to be jeopardizing their economic and political future.

North American Sikhs are more prone to exaggerated militant rhetoric than Indian Sikhs. One reason is inadequate information. The credibility of the Indian press has been badly tarnished in the eyes of North American Sikhs, because of its surrender to censorship with regard to the army rule in Punjab and slavish justification of certain government actions such as Operation Bluestar. Most North American Sikhs believe that what they read in Indian newspapers is censored information. So they rely more on rumours and have a distorted picture of what is happening in India. Many of them believed that the issues of *Manushi* which carried the report on the November 1984 massacre, and the PUCL–PUDR report on the same event had been banned in India. This was not the case. Similarly, many were convinced that anyone who spoke against the government would invariably end up in jail.

Many also believe that no community in India has been persecuted the way the Sikhs have been and that Indians do not sympathize with them. This belief also results from lack of information. The fact is that several communities and regions of India have suffered more brutal oppression for longer periods and received much less sympathy from other Indians, including Sikhs. Large parts of the North-East have suffered massacres and desecration of places of worship and been subjected to military rule and mass arrests. They have received a far less sympathetic hearing than the Sikhs in Punjab. The role of the Congress government in organizing the massacre of Sikhs in November 1984 was condemned openly by many more people than are willing to condemn the much more regular violence inflicted on the Muslims in different parts of India. Many more non-Sikhs also actively organized relief for the victims of the 1984 massacre than the number of non-Muslims usually do for Muslim victims of similar violence.

It is easy to give moral and other support to terrorist politics if one is sitting at a comfortable distance of 12,000 miles from the battleground. It is much harder to pick up a gun oneself when one knows that the consequences of being caught are brutal torture and death Anyone who espouses terrorist politics in India does so at some personal risk, but the risk element is much reduced for supporters abroad. A few people expressed open recognition of this fact. The wife of a committed Khalistani told me:

I ask all these people (including my husband) who are talking of Khalistan: 'Are even your own sons willing to go and live in that Khalistan? All of you want comfortable lives in America. Then why do you jeopardize the safety of millions of people in Punjab and other parts of India?'

Another woman, a doctor, was even more outspoken. She said:

I will believe in the sincerity of those demanding Khalistan if they are willing to send one son each to go and fight for it or, better still, if they go themselves and spend one year implementing their militant politics in Punjab. It is all very well to talk so militantly, sitting comfortably here, and make others, most of them from poor families, shed their blood. Sikhs have always prided themselves on their bravery. Where is the bravery in applauding the murders of innocent people, encouraging others to take to violence, and risking the lives of millions of people of your own community, while you sit safe and comfortable so far away?

Many Sikhs admitted that usually young men from poorer families are the ones who actually execute the terrorist politics in India even though the money bags are those who have made their fortunes and are taking no personal risk.

It is ironical that even though most North American Sikhs keep asserting that they have little or no faith in the Central government, they keep waiting for the same government to provide a solution to the Punjab problem. They themselves make no attempt to work out more people-oriented solutions. I found them resistant to openly acknowledging that though the militants claim they are fighting the Central government, their politics and rhetoric are actually leading their community not only into a deadly conflict with non-Sikh Punjabis but also into a bitter internal war within the Sikh community itself.

The desire for peace is not lacking. In Baltimore, a Sikh gentleman tried hard to persuade me to help organize a peace march of Sikh and Hindu women to the Indian embassy to appeal for an end to terrorist killings and state repression. Many others were keen that I address meetings in every gurudwara of North America and help initiate a dialogue between the Hindus and the Sikhs. My assessment is that even many of those who talk of Khalistan would in fact be satisfied with other honourable solutions. Many stated that the Congress party had deliberately destroyed the goodwill between the Sikhs and the Hindus, and that replacement of the Congress at the Centre by a more reasonable government would automatically ease the situation. Even the devout worshippers of Bhindranwale acknowledge that he was originally a puppet set up by Mrs Gandhi to divide the Akali Dal. The main reason they revere him is that they see him as a martyr who died defending the Golden Temple. Dynasty change at the Centre and decentralization of decision-making are two major issues. Many said what they really want is the kind of federal structure that exists in the USA.

Most Sikhs do realize the dangers and pitfalls of Khalistani politics. I heard many saying: 'How can we be desirous of massacring Hindus, so many of our relations are Hindus?' One leader who uses Khalistani rhetoric commented: 'If this bloodshed does not stop now, it will never stop—not even if Khalistan comes into existence. Sikhs will give birth to not just one Khomeini but many Khomeinis—because they won't put up with any one dictator.'

Once they feel reassured that it is possible for Sikhs to live in India as equal citizens, with honour and dignity, many would reconsider their stand on Khalistan. At present, they feel deeply hurt at being completely boycotted by the Hindus. The attack on the Golden Temple, the massacre of thousands of innocents in November 1984 for which not a single person has been brought to book, and the hostility almost every individual has suffered at the hands of the Indian government machinery simply because of being Sikh, have become symbols to them of the injustice meted out to them as a community.

The overseas Sikhs have the ability and the means to turn the Punjab conflict into a prolonged bloody civil war by lending moral and material support to terrorist groups in Punjab, just as some of the descendants of Irish immigrants in America have done in northern Ireland.

All those who wish to avoid further advances towards a situation of civil war in Punjab need to make the effort to understand the mood, the viewpoints and the grievances of the Sikh community overseas. The Hindus living in India and abroad urgently need to rebuild the numerous earlier bridges of communication, to end the isolation of the overseas Sikh community. We need to demonstrate to them that we in India are capable of resolving the conflict by sensible negotiation within a democratic framework and that in this country minorities can live with dignity. To demonstrate this, we need to:

1. unconditionally support Sikhs when their human rights are violated and fight to end government participation in such violations;

2. vigorously demand punishment of those guilty of the November 1984 massacre of the Sikhs;

3. ensure that no person is detained without legal and constitutional procedures, and end torture in police detention and killings in staged police encounters. Every detained person should be entitled to a speedy, fair and open trial, following due legal processes;

4. take the issue of regional autonomy seriously, instead of just assuming that all those who ask for decentralization of power are out to weaken the nation. We need to realize the dangers of the myth created by the Congress (I) that any opposition to its authoritarian rule at the Centre is automatically anti-national;

5. demand the abrogation of all legislation which places vast arbitrary powers in the hands of the government, for example, the National Security Act, Anti-Terrorist and the Disturbed Areas Acts;

6. bring together all Punjabis—Hindus, Sikhs and others—to negotiate among themselves, through their own chosen leaders, a mutually acceptable solution to the present crisis. They could then jointly press this solution upon the Central government with the support of all those searching for a peaceful and just resolution; and

7. demand an end to President's rule in Punjab because Central rule is the biggest obstacle in the way of solving the Punjab conflict.

Sikhs need to stop acting as the owners of Punjab; Hindus need to stop acting as the owners of India. Only then can a peaceful settlement be reached. Instead of waiting for the Central government to come up with a 'national' solution, an initiative should first be taken in Punjab to reach a regional solution acceptable both to Sikh and Hindu Punjabis living in Punjab.

At the same time, it is crucial that the overseas Sikhs should take an uncompromising stand against terrorist torture and killing of innocent people. Since a large part of the funds, weapons and support for terrorist activities is allegedly coming from the overseas community, a decisive shift of their support away from the terrorists would help a more credible Sikh leadership to emerge in India as well as overseas. This new leadership would then be in a better position to press for an honourable solution. The terrorists are only providing legitimacy to the Congress (I) government's policy of indiscriminate repression and further authoritarian centralization.

The overseas Sikhs have a special responsibility in ensuring that they do not, by their ill-informed actions, jeopardize the well-being of Sikhs living in India. It is easier for them to confront terrorist politics in North America, because even terrorists are aware that they cannot as easily go on a rampage in America as in Punjab. Therefore, it is relatively easier to isolate them there and deny them legitimacy. If they can at least neutralize them there, they will more credibly be able to mobilize general opinion abroad against the violation of human rights of Sikhs in India. This will also help bring into focus the real issues in Punjab, such as the need for decentralization of power. Finally, they need to inform themselves better of the situation in India, and to base their political thinking on facts instead of hearsay.

5

In Defence of Our Dharma

The ostensible success of the Ram Mandir Movement led by
the BJP–RSS–VHP Combine is proof that the Nehruvian brand
of secularism hitherto propagated in India has a very limited
support base, confined mainly to sections of the English educated
elite. Its appeal has remained limited for good reasons. The liberal,
secular intelligentsia is rooted more in the western liberal tradition.
It is, therefore, unable to comprehend, leave alone appreciate, the
sentiments and cherished beliefs of the majority of India's diverse
peoples. Their attitude is often similar to that of the erstwhile colonial
rulers who contemptuously dismissed the social, religious and cultural
beliefs of the Indian people as superstitions and proof of their
'backwardness'.

Today, a large body of Hindu opinion seems tired of the
thoughtless and disrespectful critique of India's indigenous traditions
and culture which has led to the brutal neglect of indigenous learning
and knowledge systems. The deadening system of education designed
by the colonial rulers was meant to destroy the self-respect of Indians.
Yet the self same contempt is perpetuated in the modern education
system that has produced generations of people alienated from and
ignorant of India's traditions of culture and learning. The people
who are joining the Ram Mandir movement in large numbers do so
in the mistaken belief that they are thereby reviving the glory of
India's cultural heritage. Their ignorance of their own heritage has
made them vulnerable targets for unscrupulous politicians who are
using their genuine resentment for very harmful purposes.

The real agenda of the BJP is to capture state power for the
purpose of implementing the politics of revenge. Even though they

First published in *Manushi* No. 60 (Sept–Oct 1990).

use the rhetoric of protecting the 'Hindu way of life', the BJP–RSS–VHP Combine has kept its followers deliberately ignorant of their cultural heritage. Like all fascists, they know that the politics of hate and revenge needs to emphasize whatever will aggravate the Hindu's low self-esteem. Among my students and in my own neighbourhood I have asked some of the most enthusiastic supporters of the Ram Mandir campaign which version of the Ramayan they had read; I drew a blank. All these educated young people are familiar with nothing other than Ramanand Sagar's TV serial *Ramayan*. Though they have heard of Tulsi's *Ramayan*, almost none of them has read it. They are not even aware of the existence of different regional and community versions of the *Ramayan*. It is almost impossible to get them into a discussion on the great epic. There is only one aspect of the Ram Mandir movement that excites them—taking revenge on the Muslims. The Ram Mandir movement is grounded not in the love of Ram or the *Ramayan* but in the hatred of Muslims.

The BJP–RSS–VHP Combine pretends to be outraged at the lack of respect for indigenous culture shown by the secularists among the English educated elite. However, they themselves are assiduously cultivating ignorance of India's cultural and religious traditions with their deliberate distortions. This Combine is not rooted in any tradition of learning, Indian or foreign. For example, the University of Chicago has much better facilities for acquiring scholarship on the *Ramayan* than all the educational or religious institutions associated with the BJP–RSS–VHP Combine. The latter has not even striven to ensure that Indians need not go to foreign universities to study ancient Indian literature. They display much greater fascination with Hitler's ideas and campaigns than with the *Ramayan* or other Hindu religious texts. The Combine's only connection with the Hindu texts seems to be to extract a few phrases out of context as tools for political propaganda. Therefore, they have never concerned themselves with the task of making such learning valued and respected in our universities.

I have vivid memories of the sense of outrage I experienced as an 18 year old student of English Honours at Miranda House when I was rudely ridiculed by some of my fellow students who saw a copy of the *Tulsi Ramayan* published by the Geeta Press in my hostel room. For them it was a symbol of backward-looking religiosity fit only for semi-literate grandmothers. Had it been an English rendering of the *Ramayan* brought out by some foreign university press, my interest would have been seen as somewhat more respectable. Reading Milton's *Paradise Lost* or even the English mystery and morality plays was considered a perfectly legitimate modern, secular activity. Only the *behenjis* of the Sanskrit or Hindi Department, a supposedly backward lot, were expected to read the *Ramayan*. These two departments were treated with visible contempt by both the students and the faculty.

I was even more disappointed when I found that even the Hindi-speaking behenjis held the study of the *Ramayan* and the *Mahabharat* in similar disdain and preferred to read pulp romance novels and film magazines except those doing Hindi and Sanskrit Honours who were compelled to study some of these texts as part of their curriculum. It slowly became clear that the dominant elite in any society sets the norm for what is considered worth learning and respecting. That is why the few western-educated elite who gravitate towards a serious study of Indian literature, art and culture usually do so during stints at foreign universities and at times and places where such study is in fashion among western intellectuals.

It is due to this ignorance that the BJP–RSS–VHP Combine can be so successful in manipulating Hindu sentiment. For example, in Ayodhya, there are several other temples that claim the honoured status of being built on the *Ram Janmasthan*. Yet this Combine insists that the controversial Babri Masjid site is the exact location of Ram's birth. Ram is a revered, religious figure, not a historical character. Ram's date or place of birth cannot possibly be ascertained with accuracy. But the BJP Combine insists on reducing him to the status of someone who lived at a specific time at a specific place because they are desperate to model their belief system on Islam and Christianity, religions that emphasize the significance of assigning a place and time of birth for their founders, Prophet Mohammad and Jesus Christ. They want Ayodhya to become a Jerusalem.

The following account is a fairly typical conversation I have had with a young English language journalist, who claims to be a BJP supporter; it demonstrates how even among certain sections of the English-educated elite, the uneasiness with their rootlessness is making them easy prey to the machinations of hate-mongering politicians. In response to his allegation that the Janta Dal government, personified by V.P. Singh, was out to destroy India, I asked him:

Who would you like to see as the next P.M. of India?
(Without a moment's hesitation) L.K.Advani.

What are your reasons for this choice?
The BJP is the only party that openly talks of establishing a Hindu rashtra and putting the minorities in their place. The Muslims have been pampered too long and have become a threat to this nation.

What will the Hindu rashtra do for Hindus? In other words, what is it that you wish to have for the Hindus with the establishment of BJP's Hindu rashtra which they can't have now?
Hindus are not allowed to have their way of life in India, the land of their birth.

By whom?
The government.

What is it that as a Hindu you would like to do which you can't do without BJP's Hindu rashtra?
All the traditional knowledge of Hindus is being undermined. Even those branches of knowledge which are being hailed by the scientifically superior West are not getting their due attention in India. For example, look at the neglect in our country of *yoga* and *ayurveda* as health care systems.

What prevents the Hindus from pursuing these two branches of knowledge? I practise an hour of yoga every day. No Muslim comes to obstruct me. If I read the Ramayan, no Muslim or government insults me for it. If anyone prefers to go to an Ayurvedic centre as opposed to an allopathic clinic, no government penalizes you.
[He admitted he had never tried to learn yoga or ayurveda.] But there is no government support for these things. Therefore, they can't flourish. Under a Hindu rashtra there will be government support.

But the great vaids of this land did not emerge from government laboratories. The great sages and gurus did not need to chase government patronage, to ask the kings to allow them to tutor their children. The kings went to the gurus begging that their children be taught by them. If the BJP and RSS believe in promoting these branches of knowledge why don't they promote ayurveda research centres, promote a sound health care system in the country, rather than jeopardize the lives of people and promote bloodshed?
I will have to think about it. You are asking too many questions. (Then, after a long pause) But I think state power is very important.

Political leaders, not religious organizations, dominate the Ram Mandir campaign. I include the VHP in the category of political organizations, as they are not even remotely concerned with the religious and spiritual well-being of the Hindus. Rather, they are obsessed with mobilizing Hindus as a political force to subordinate and terrorize non-Hindus in India. Their *dharma* is nationalism, not Hinduism. Their inspiration comes from Hitler, not from Ram. Their cloak of piety notwithstanding, the real agenda of the BJP–RSS–VHP Combine is to breed more and more mistrust and hatred against Muslims. One hears their cadres openly proclaim: 'We should do to Muslims what Hitler did to Jews.' Slogans like 'Pakistan *ya kabristan*' are meant seriously, as is evident from the increasing incidents of massacres of Muslims such as in Bhagalpur, Meerut, Ahmedabad and now, Gonda. An essential first phase in their campaign is to convince the people that Muslims should not be Indian citizens unless they undermine their faith and slavishly support whatever the Combine requires.

BJP's Ramayan

Nothing brings this out more clearly than the speeches of Uma Bharti and Rithambra, two women who have emerged as the chief rabble rousers of the Sangh Parivar. Their speeches are being sold commercially in the form of recorded cassettes. They are being used extensively by the BJP propaganda machine in many parts of the country. Of the two Rithambra is openly vicious and hysterical. The shrill, bloodthirsty tone of her hysterical voice pouring out hatred is strikingly similar to that which we can still hear in the recordings of Nazi leaders at mass propaganda rallies.

Their salient theme is that the only way Hindus can prove that they are not cowards is by initiating violent and murderous attacks on Muslims. These acts of aggression are presented as justified by the cruelties inflicted earlier, by some Muslim invaders who conquered parts of India.

The cassette is sold with a cover photo depicting Ramanand Sagar's Ram and Sita. Here is an extract from one of her hit speeches:

30 October will decide your fate. On this day it will become clear whether the Hindus or Muslims will live in this country. You must be concerned about your future... .

Throw off the cloak of cowardice and impotence. Learn to sing songs of valour and courage. Whoever wanted to rob, you let him. Your silence, decency and magnanimity were interpreted as cowardice... .

Your strength has been divided. Unite across caste, province, language, breaking these three artificial walls... .

Those who severed both the arms of Mother India... . For those hypocrites there is no place here. They should leave this Bharat. This Hindustan is not theirs... .

On 30 October, by beginning the construction of the temple, our holy men will be laying the foundations of making Hindustan a Hindu *rashtra*.

Bharat Mata Ki Jai... . Glory to Mahadev!

Destroy the tyrant in the same way that Ravana was vanquished. Do not display any love (nij preet). This is the order of Ram. Announce it boldly to the world that anyone who opposes Ram cannot be an Indian... .

Muslims, remember Rahim who longed for the dust of Lord Ram's feet... .

Songs of Hindu-Muslim brotherhood were sung by Mahatma Gandhi. We got ready to hear the Azaan alongwith the temple bells, but they can't do this, nor does their heritage permit them to do so. It exhorts them to organize themselves quietly in those places where they are in a minority. Where they are equal to those in other religions, they instigate riots. If Islam *rashtra* requires sacrifices, then they do not have to wait for the tomb or doomsday to reach heaven. The Koran exhorts them to lie in wait for idol worshippers, to skin them alive, to stuff them in animal skins and torture them until they ask for forgiveness. Our heritage enjoins repentance even if an ant is killed underfoot. The two cultures are polar opposites. But still we preached brotherhood, replaced *Vande Mataram* with *Jana Gana Mana*.

...How much have we sacrificed so that Hindu-Muslim brotherhood would continue! We even dismembered Mother India. Instead of Ram *dhwaj*, the symbol of Hindu martyrdom and sacrifice, we unfurled the tricolour, but this brotherhood eluded us... .

Those [Muslims] who value their religion more than their nation, they can never be nationalists. And those who treat religion as a personal matter [Hindus] can never be communalists. Hindus cannot be communalists because those who give pride of place to their nation over their religion cannot be communalists.

The PAC youth tell me they are looking forward to 30 October. They say when they were unemployed, they prayed to Bajrang Bali [another name for Hanuman, known for his devotion to Ram] for a job. Even after retirement they know they have to seek the protection of Ram. If the government orders them to fire, they will shoot, but it remains to be seen whether the bullets will hit Ram *bhakts* or pierce the chests of traitors of Ram. Though they are in uniform, the heart that beats in them is that of a Hindu. Though they are doing a job, the blood coursing in their veins is of a Hindu father.

Let this fire blaze magnificently. It was this feat of bloodshed that led to the dismemberment of the country, the death of so many Hindus... . Let there be a conflagration rather than this slow torturous simmering... .

We could not teach them with words, now let us teach them with kicks... . Let there be bloodshed once and for all.

We have come out to strengthen the immense Hindu *shakti* into a fist... .

You kept saying you will offer sacrifices. We will take thousands of sacrifices. Now we will not only shed our own blood, but the blood of others, too... . That Mahatma Gandhi led you to ruin... .

Tie up your religiosity and kindness into a bundle and throw it in the Jamuna *maiya*... .

Leftists and communists ask me if we desire to turn this land into a Hindu *rashtra*. I say it was declared one at the time of Partition in 1947—Hindustan, a nation of Hindus and Pakistan, a nation of the Muslims. Those Muslims who stayed behind could do so because of the tolerance and large heartedness of the Hindus. Any non-Hindu who lives here does so at our mercy (*kirpa pe jee rahaa hai*). Declare without hesitation that this is a Hindu *rashtra*, a nation of Hindus. In future we have to prove that only those who honour Hindu womenfolk and holy men, believe in Hindu culture, Hindu history and gods and goddesses can stay in Hindustan.

The resolution passed by eminent leaders in Haridwar will remain unchanged. There will be no change, no compromise, on these issues:
a) the date of the construction of the Temple, 30 October;
b) the blueprint of the Temple; we will not tolerate any changes in it... .
c) the site of the Temple, which will be raised where the present image of Sri Ram stands... .

A senior journalist asked us: 'If we remain firm and uncompromising on these three issues, then what is there left to discuss?' We answered that there is the issue of whether these wishes will be granted gracefully or wrested by force... .

Hindustan is foolish, it refuses to give up its foolish course, it gets beaten and forgives its opponent. Why? Because this is the land of Buddha and the Mahatma, Guru Nanak Dev and other Sants who sacrificed their lives, offered their necks but could not break the neck of others... .

This hate propaganda in verse is widely distributed at BJP–RSS–VHP rallies. In English the lines read:

Say with Pride, We are Hindus
Change the Constitution of India, remember 1947 when India was divided
Boycott Mussalmans
Now no one will be allowed to live here as an Aurangzeb or Babar
Now only those who can become Rahims can stay in India.
Now under the Constitution they will not cast a vote
They will bring up their children in India at the mercy of the Hindus
Just as we brought our brothers from Kuwait
So also send off the Muslims in shiploads
Only those who talk of Hindus' welfare will come to power... .
Hindus should become of one mind and make India prosper... .

Since the BJP–RSS–VHP Combine would find it hard to get endorsement among the vast majority of the people of India for this brand of murderous nationalism, they have hijacked Ram and are using him as a political cover. Ram has been converted into a vote-getter in much the same way as some parties use film stars. Newspapers tell us that Rs 700 crores have already been collected by this Combine. Much of the election expenses of the BJP are said to have been met by the money raised in Ram's name. Their *rath yatra* was conducted on the lines of an election campaign, with Mr Advani presented as the prime ministerial candidate.

It is a matter of shame that most Muslims are reported to have felt the need to lock themselves up in their homes as the rath yatra travelled from town to town. Many, even in Delhi, fled their homes and sought shelter elsewhere, far from the yatra route. This is making a Ravan of Ram, instead of promoting reverence for him. The blood-soaked temple they intend to build at Ayodhya on the rubble of a mosque would stand as a symbol of destruction of all the cherished ideals and norms of Hindu civilization.

We need to redeem Ram as a religious figure, religious in the sense of representing a revered moral and ethical code, and as an embodiment of rare spiritual ideals which have inspired generations of people in this land to lead upright lives. This appropriation of Ram by sectarian politicians to perpetuate communal massacres pours contempt on Ram. In popular imagination, he stands as a symbol of love and compassion (*patitpavan kripanidhan*), self-sacrifice and steadfastness to duty (*kartavynishtha*). The Ram we imbibed as children from our parents bears no resemblance to the BJP–RSS incarnation. He bore no malice even to those who did him wrong. He continued to love and respect Kaikeyi as his own mother even though she had him banished for fourteen years. We were taught that he triumphed over Ravan with moral force rather than through his superior skills as a warrior. His victory was foreshadowed when many of those close to Ravan, including Ravan's wife and brother, came to stand by Ram, for he represented righteousness. Today, the Combine leaders, though acting in Ram's name, are compelling many Hindus by their unworthy actions to oppose their politics, much as some of Ravan's well-wishers were compelled to oppose Ravan.

The BJP projects Ram as a national warrior hero, as opposed to a Hindu god, in the mistaken belief that they are thus elevating him to a superior status. The reclaiming of what they call the Ram Janmasthan is not being justified on religious grounds but presented as a case of struggle between nationalist and anti-national forces. Babri Masjid is to be demolished because it was built by an invading outsider on the site of a Ram temple—with Ram presented as a national hero. Muslims are expected to join the Hindus in devotion to Ram to prove that they are not anti-national. The Sangh Parivar deliberately overlook the fact that even among Hindus there are innumerable sects whose chosen deities are other than Ram and who would feel no less offended if compelled to forsake their own form of worship, as is being demanded of the Muslims.

Many secularists see the BJP politics as promoting unhealthy religiosity. Nothing could be further from the truth. The BJP–RSS–VHP game is to selectively use gods from the Hindu pantheon to practise their brand of murderous nationalism. Mr Advani and company are destroying all that is morally and spiritually elevating in the rich diversity of Hindu culture and forging from it a hate-filled ideology of nationalism.

In our time, far more murders have been committed in the name of nationalism than for the sake of any religion. The two world wars are a prime example. The war between Iran and Iraq, both Muslim countries, which has killed millions of people, is its most recent manifestation. Chauvinist nationalism is invariably targeted against some other group; it cannot sustain itself without the notion of a hated other. It thrives on the language of power and violence, and has little respect for the human rights of even those people it seeks to unify as a nation. These types of nationalists are forever endangering the lives and well-being of their fellow nationals in the pursuit of power games as, for instance, Hitler and Khomeini did, and Mr Advani is now seeking to do.

By systematically building an atmosphere of hysteria among the Hindus they have caused frenzied clashes between the *kar sewaks* and the police, resulting in firing and deaths. The peaceful town of Ayodhya has been turned into a virtual battlefield. Instead of mourning those they mislead, those whose blood is on their hands, they are glorifying their victims as martyrs, encouraging more and more Hindus to a frenzied do-or-die mood.

Their politics will make the lives of Hindus even more precarious where they are a minority as in Punjab and Kashmir by providing greater legitimacy to the separatist politics of fundamentalist groups in the two states. The lives of Hindus in other countries, where they are in small numbers, are also being seriously jeopardized. There are already many reports that Hindus are being attacked in Bangladesh and Pakistan. They may become even more vulnerable in the Gulf countries. In western countries, the prejudice against Indians may be further strengthened as reports of murderous strife in India reach those countries.

The respectability accorded to nationalism is due to its mistaken association with anti-colonial movements in third world countries. The vast difference between the two becomes evident if one compares Mahatma Gandhi's politics with that of Mr Advani and his friends in the RSS. The nationalism of the RSS asserted itself by actually murdering Gandhi then, and today it is as zealously trying to destroy all that Gandhi stood for. Gandhi's nationalism was based on his opposition to oppression of any group by another. He was essentially anti-statist. He stood for the rights of all the disadvantaged and oppressed groups (no matter what their religion) and against their exploitation by those who controlled state power. Mr Advani's nationalism, on the other hand, consists of trying to grab hold of state power in order to subordinate all those within the country to his tyranny and to wreak vengeance on the already vulnerable groups.

To achieve that end the nationalists build upon a culture of resentment, fear and hatred. The BJP Combine is encouraging Hindus to view Muslims and other minorities as betrayers of the nation. One of their chief arguments is that Muslims had no right to stay in India after the creation of Pakistan. As someone whose family was among the millions forcibly driven out of their homes in 1947, and had to migrate as refugees from the land that is now Pakistan, I share the anguish of the BJP–RSS at the criminal manipulations that led to the Partition of India. However, the chauvinist nationalism of the RSS and Hindu Mahasabha, which found support among large sections of the Congress as well, was a key reason for the success of Jinnah. It is ironical that the BJP–RSS Combine wish to fashion their politics in the Jinnah mould, a man they hate so much. In fact, the politics of both Jinnah and the BJP–RSS are merely two sides of the same coin.

Those who hold that Muslims had no right to stay on in India with the creation of Pakistan are seeking to model their politics on the pattern of the Muslim League. This amounts to vindicating Jinnah in a way that history did not. The groups who most actively sought the creation of Pakistan, the Mohajirs, find themselves treated like unwanted aliens in the nation state of their own making. Their language (Urdu), their culture, their connections with relatives in India, their lingering emotional attachment to the land of their birth and ancestors, are all suspect and under attack from the Muslim Punjabis, Sindhis, Pathans, Baluchis and others who exist so uneasily together in today's Pakistan. Despite the desperate attempts of the Muslim League and the army generals to weld the various groups in Pakistan into one nation based on religion, the ethnic strife in Pakistan is far more virulent today than before Partition. The Baluchis, the Pathans, Sindhis, Punjabis and Mohajirs all seem to be locked in more deadly battles than those that raged on the continent in 1947. Human rights violations are even more severe in Pakistan than in India. The ruling elite of Pakistan has taken much longer to even begin to allow some weight to the political rights of their fellow Muslims, for example, the right to vote—something that the people of India have always enjoyed. The spectre of military dictatorship is forever haunting Pakistan. Their democracy is far more fragile than is India's. Pakistan's *mullah* politicians have not yet learnt to accept even women from elite families as equals in public life. For example, Benazir's prime ministership was hotly disputed whereas in India, Indira Gandhi was easily accepted as Prime Minister. No religious leader cast aspersions on her solely on the grounds of her being a woman. All this is inextricably linked to the politics of intolerance upon which the Islamic nation laid its foundation—the politics of driving people out of their homes through bloodshed in order to force a Partition. Since the Pakistani nation was based on a lie, it made the Pakistan ruling elite far more neurotic and insecure in their politics. On the other hand, despite serious problems and conflicts, India has retained a democratic polity and—except in some of the border states, and despite fiery controversies, as over the Mandal Commission Report—ethnic strife does not threaten to tear Indian society asunder. This might well happen in Pakistan. It is even possible that if India opened its borders with

Pakistan and allowed a free flow of people, Pakistan would soon cease to exist.

Thus both Hindus and Muslims in India gained enormously, both politically and morally, by taking the stand, represented by Gandhi and others, of insisting that Muslims would not be pushed out of India despite the disastrous Partition. Those who talk of driving the Muslims out, or of letting them live here only as second-class citizens, in the same way that Hindus live in Pakistan, are asking us to surrender all our advantages and strengths and commit political and moral suicide. Those who wish to hold up Pakistan as a role model display their low self-esteem and lack of confidence in their own faith.

The second related argument of the BJP led Combine against Muslims is that Hindus have been wronged historically by Muslim invaders. Therefore, Hindus have the right to settle those historical wrongs. Indian Muslims are blamed not just for the Partition but also for the crimes, including destruction of temples, committed by waves of invaders who happened to have been Muslims by religion. In most cases, foreign invasions resulted in mass destruction, loot and plunder, as inevitably happens in all wars of conquest, including many of those fought among Hindu local rulers within India. Even so the RSS–BJP version of Islamic invasion is biased, for it presents an oversimplified picture of this period of our history and relies a great deal on hysterical exaggerations. However, even if one were to accept totally their view of our history, it would be self-destructive to come to the political conclusions they derive from it.

The present-day Muslims are no more foreign to this soil than those of us who claim to be Hindus. They cannot be used as scapegoats for the atrocities committed by the likes of Ghazni or Aurangzeb. The same logic that demands the reclaiming of all those places where mosques were built on destroyed temples can be extended further. Should we demolish many of the present-day Hindu temples which were built on the remains of the destroyed Buddhist religious centres? This is a never-ending deadly game which, if taken seriously, will leave India as devastated as was Germany during World War II. Most important of all, do the BJP–RSS leaders want to be remembered as the twentieth century

Aurangzebs among Hindus by their insistence on demolishing their entire hit list of mosques? The Hinduism being propagated by the RSS–BJP Combine resembles the many brutal periods in the history of Christianity and Islam when they wreaked destruction and massacred many people in proselytizing and conquering, all over the world.

Hinduism unites the animate with the inanimate. There are strong voices within the Hindu tradition which forbid violence even to animals and plants, leave alone human beings. God is seen as all-pervasive rather than as a formidable creature dwelling in some distant heaven. *Kan kan mein Ram basey hain* is a living faith with most Hindus. The word *dharm* in Hindu civilization has always been used in a more expansive sense, denoting a code of ethics and moral imperatives and in that sense 'the law of one's being' rather than in the narrow sense of a particular religion.

This is illustrated by a story that my mother often repeated to us while I was growing up. Whenever as a child I wanted to retaliate against someone who I thought had wronged me, she would patiently dissuade me from doing so, using the following story to illustrate the harmfulness of making a virtue of feelings of revenge.

Once a *mahatma* was bathing in a river. Suddenly he saw a drowning scorpion and tried to bring it to safety. As soon as he lifted the scorpion in his hand, the latter stung him. The pain of the sting jerked the mahatma's hand and the scorpion fell back into the water and began drowning again. The mahatma picked up the scorpion again, and again the same thing happened. This sequence of action was repeated several times. Some onlookers were very puzzled by what appeared to them as the mahatma's foolishness. They asked him: 'Why do you persist in saving the scorpion when you know he will sting you?' The mahatma replied: 'The scorpion's dharm is to sting, my dharm as a human is compassion. I have to be true to my dharm, not adopt the dharm of the scorpion. How can I forego my dharm and return injury for injury, when even the scorpion is not willing to leave his own?'

The BJP–RSS–VHP Combine seems determined to destroy the dharm of the Hindus.

Unlike the gods of Semitic religions—Judaism, Christianity and

Islam—the gods of the Hindus are not jealous gods. We Hindus have an easy relationship with our gods. We laugh and joke with them as one would with one's friends. We play games with them and even take the liberty of getting annoyed with them. The Hindu gods rarely order their worshippers to attack other people's gods and religions. A whole pantheon of them coexist with each other and with various goddesses as well. None of them claim absolute supremacy or demand absolute loyalty. Our gods are not known for wreaking vengeance on their devotees if they go and pray to other gods, or in mosques, gurudwaras or churches. They are forever able to accommodate new gods in deference to the wishes of their worshippers—be they recent creations within the Hindu fold like a Santoshi Maa, or the gods of other religions who are prepared for mutual accommodation. Most Hindu gods do not get upset if a Hindu family hangs up a picture of Jesus Christ along with that of Shiv and Parvati. They wouldn't be annoyed if anyone sits and reads verses from the Koran or Bible in front of them. Most importantly, they do not claim exclusive obedience. Even today in many rural areas a *baba*, a *fakir* or a *sadhu* will be received with reverence by both Hindus and Muslims. Shrines of *bhakts* and tombs of *sufis* and dervishes are visited by both Hindus and Muslims. One can even be an atheist without being any the less a Hindu. A Hindu is free to create his or her own gods or goddesses. Almost every village in India worships its own local deity without interference, as well as treasuring the stories of Ram and other pan-Indian gods, without requiring permission from any centralized religious authority. The god/goddess one creates can be named according to the devotees' wishes. The bhakt also has the freedom to make the god look and act in diverse ways. Devotees are free to credit their chosen gods with the attributes they consider important. For example, Meera's Krishna seems to be her own special being, different from the Krishna of the *Geeta* or the *Mahabharat*.

All this and more has provided a good deal of space for dissent and diversity within the Hindu religious and cultural tradition which counteracts some of its oppressive aspects. Hinduism also has the unique tradition of worshippers being allowed to judge the actions of their gods as they would those of ordinary human beings. Krishna's goading of Yudhishthir to tell a lie during the battle of Kurukshetra is not condoned by all Hindus. Likewise, Ram's *Shambhuk vaddh* and his unfair treatment of Sita in subjecting her to *agnipariksha* hang heavily on the collective consciousness of the Hindus. This discomfort of the Hindus with the agnipariksha came out very clearly when, during the making of Ramanand Sagar's television serial *Ramayana* a spate of protest letters against making Sita go through the agnipariksha compelled Sagar to deviate from his text and make it a different, symbolic act. Many folk-songs depict Sita as defiantly protesting Ram's injustice.

Since Hindus do not hesitate to pass judgement on the wrongdoings of their gods, it is unlikely that Mr Advani and company will manage to get away with their manipulations for too long. Much stronger voices will rise against this Combine's machination from among the Hindu fold than from among Muslims.

The Combine seeks to portray Muslims as a group which considers itself above the law of the land. Among the proofs of special privileges supposedly enjoyed by the Muslim community are cited instances such as the enactment of the retrogressive Muslim Women's Protection Act in violation of the Constitution, the appointment of a couple of governors and vice-chancellors from among Muslims, installing a couple of token ministers in the cabinet, getting the government to indulge in mindlessly extravagant pro-Arab and anti-Israel foreign policy rhetoric and getting this or that book banned through protest.

Undoubtedly, the politics of the current dominant leadership among the Muslims often does live up to the pernicious stereotype that the BJP–RSS Combine assert is characteristic of Muslims. They often give the impression of being religious fanatics incapable of adhering to secular norms even though they demand that Hindus practise secular politics. The virulence with which too many Muslim leaders oppose the human rights of Muslim women, crush dissenting voices within their own community and promote religious intolerance has contributed to destroying some of the moral and social strength of their own community. Their politics has strengthened the voices of intolerance among the Hindus.

However, government policy has played a major role in keeping

Muslim leadership addicted to the politics of crumb gathering. It has also given Hindus an excuse to believe that the government is pampering the Muslim minority. The dominant political parties, especially the Congress, have not moved away from knee-jerk responses calculated to consolidate the Muslim vote bank and aggravate the communal divide rather than to work out a coherent, just policy of majority–minority relations. Far from enjoying special privileges, the vast majority of Muslims are denied even the fundamental rights promised by the Constitution. Most of them are poor and despised and are compelled to live in ghettos. They are not given equality of opportunity in employment, housing or education and show all signs of being a marginalized minority.

Mr Advani and the BJP are feeling extremely heady with the large crowds they have been able to gather for their meetings on the Ram Mandir issue. Girilal Jain approvingly calls this the largest mobilization of the Hindus after Gandhi. It is the most absurd comparison ever made. Gandhi's Hinduism was rooted in the bhakti tradition which stood for the oneness of all human beings. Worship of god was to be expressed through love and respect for human beings irrespective of their caste, creed, religion or gender. Violence was not permissible even against the aggression of an enemy.

Gandhi tried to liberate the minds of all those Indians who joined him from fear of all kinds. This included fear of physical torture and deprivation. He tried to fill the hearts of his followers with real self-respect, which included respect for others, no matter how different they may be. The BJP–RSS, through manipulation and lies, are making even Hindus feel insecure and unsafe in their own land. Such is the power of relentless propaganda that the endangered Muslim minority is made out to be a grave threat to Hindus. The Muslims who are experiencing more and more difficulties in providing for their own minimal security are accused of jeopardizing the security of India. Hitler, too, succeeded in getting large crowds to cheer him even more enthusiastically than those who have attended the BJP–RSS rallies cheer Advani. But, often, mobilization of mass hysteria around hatred and fear has no less disastrous consequences for those who are thus mobilized than for those who are oppressed.

The most serious negative consequence of this current campaign to consolidate Hindus against minorities—by teaching Hindus to feel persecuted, filling their minds with lies and misinformation—is that many Hindus have come to believe that getting rid of Muslims is their national duty, that when they indulge in pogroms against Muslims they are doing it to defend their religion and their *rashtra*. Murder and mayhem are thus being made respectable, leading to a large-scale criminalization of many sections of the Hindu community. This, in my view, is the biggest danger. We must desist before the Hindu community is criminalized, as Hitler once criminalized the entire German people. This aspect of BJP–RSS ideology and work becomes evident in any city which has witnessed large-scale communal violence.

Among the few cases I have personally been exposed to, I would like to describe our experience in Meerut and Maliana after the great massacre of May 1987. An all-women's team of *Manushi* volunteers spent about a week in Meerut collecting information soon after the killings. The officially released figures, as usual, seemed to have very little relationship to the reality of the violence and destruction. Even a casual visit confirmed that in Meerut and Maliana many more Muslim than Hindu neighbourhoods had been targets of attack and looting. The pattern of violence was similar to the one reported in other such incidents in Ahmedabad, Bhagalpur and Gonda.

In Meerut, wherever Muslims lived together in large numbers, as in Hashimpura, Gaddha or Maliana, Hindus were usually accompanied by the Provincial Armed Constabulary (PAC) in their locting, killing and murdering spree. No real resistance or retaliation was possible in such a situation. Therefore, loss of life and property was extremely one-sided. It is well documented and well known that the Provincial Armed Constabulary (PAC) dumped dozens of bodies of Muslims from the Hashimpura area into a canal, and forced a mass burial of scores of Muslims they had massacred in Maliana village.

On the whole, among the shops, houses and commercial establishments attacked or burnt down, about 90 to 95 per cent belonged to Muslims. However, the death and injury toll was even more unbalanced. Despite intensive efforts, we could not identify more than five Hindus who had been killed by Muslims in Meerut. We met hardly any injured Hindus, despite conscious efforts to get to them. In contrast, hundreds of Muslims had been killed and hundreds injured.

Yet such is the power of communal propaganda that most Hindus we met were convinced that they were the main sufferers. They went so far as to believe that Muslims had not only instigated the violence but also burnt down their own homes in order to claim compensation from the government. The paltry relief measures announced (such as Rs 10,000 for each person killed) were said to be a form of pampering the Muslim minority. We were astonished to find that the Hindus were in some ways more nervous and frightened than the Muslims. Though four out of five in our investigating team were Hindus, we had greater difficulty in getting Hindus to talk to us. Invariably their first question was: 'Are you a Muslim or a Hindu?', putting on the defensive anyone who was not identified as a Hindu. Among the few Hindus who talked to us, a large number warned us against visiting Muslim neighbourhoods. The Hindus fed us with gory stories about how some women journalists who ventured into Muslim areas were brutally raped and murdered, how even PAC men were dragged into mohallas and butchered, whereas the authorities confirmed that nothing even remotely resembling these incidents had occurred. Their fear of those they had helped butcher bordered on the bizarre. They felt unsafe in their own city. The loss of confidence of the Hindu community was alarming considering they were a majority actually able to get away with murder, since the police and the administration were on their side. They were afraid to talk to any strangers, including harmless-looking women like us. This was contrary to the normal warmth, hospitality and openness one encounters in visiting most neighbourhoods in India—urban or rural. In contrast, the Muslims, despite having suffered greater loss of life and property, received us without reservations, grateful that someone cared to at least listen to their anguished stories.

It took a while for us to understand why those who had looted, plundered and murdered had reason to fear. The PAC had joined them and instigated them to violence. But they lived in fear lest they be implicated and tried for the crimes they had committed. Even though so many Muslims had suffered violence, the PAC stood guard only over the Harijans and the other Hindu households, many of whom had been the attackers, shielding them from journalists and outsiders, lest they inadvertently let out some damaging facts. Many of these people were only too aware that they had the blood of their neighbours on their hands, and could not hide the fear typical of criminals—the fear of being caught. They had been tutored by the PAC to allege that they had been attacked. They indulged in pathetic attempts to show evidence of damage to their homes. This usually amounted to showing us no more than a small mound of garbage carefully burnt in a corner of their compound resulting in a small token loss, leaving the rest of the house untouched. Among the tutored answers, a common one was: 'We don't know what happened, we were busy in our household work and did not want to look out' or 'The Muslims burnt their own homes down to claim compensation, pampered cheats as they are'. The most bizarre response was the answer we got from two women in Maliana, in the house directly opposite to that of an eleven-member Muslim family, all of whom had been killed. The highly decomposed bodies of the Muslims were recovered from the well in their compound. 'How did it happen?' we asked. 'We don't know, we were busy in our house,' the women told us. 'Did someone come to attack them?' 'No, we did not see anyone. They burnt down their house themselves to get compensation.' 'But then how did they get killed?' 'The bombs they brought to attack us must have exploded in their own house by mistake.' 'But how could their bodies end up in the well on their own without someone throwing them in there?' 'You don't know how *fasadi* these Muslims are, they can manage almost anything,' was the unashamed answer, after which the women of the family closed the door and refused to make any further conversation. Later we learnt that this lone Muslim family in a street full of Hindu houses had been attacked and killed by their own neighbours.

In a number of Hindu middle-class areas, the fear was based on ignorance fuelled by rumours. After the imposition of curfew, most people here had stayed confined to their neighbourhoods and not witnessed any of the violence. They were fed on hysterical rumours which they were in no position to confirm from Muslims, as they had scarcely any Muslim acquaintances and had a stereotyped impression of all Muslims as violent riff-raff.

There were dozens of similar incidents and the same conspiracy of silence and evasiveness that characterizes people when they have terrible crimes to hide. I was reminded of what a German friend had told me about a similar veil of silence in post World War II Germany. What happened during Hitler's regime became a tabooed topic. Parents would not answer even their own children's queries about their involvement in the Nazi crimes except with an evasive 'We did not know what was happening, we just did our job'.

Reports of communal massacres from Bhagalpur, Ahmedabad, Biharshariff and elsewhere all testify to a pattern of fearful silence or aggressive evasiveness typical of criminals. While there is some mention of the terrible consequences on the lives of Muslims as a result of being constantly made to live in fear of violence, and the resulting ghettoization and anxiety among them, we have altogether ignored the disastrous effects of the BJP–RSS–VHP incitements of the Hindu community. The latter is being systematically criminalized. Not just the poor but also young men from so-called respectable middle- and upper-class homes are being encouraged to become leaders of looting and murdering brigades. When the whole community learns to cover up these crimes, to try and wash off the stink of blood from their conscience, it is a sure sign of the advancing ruin of the community. Those of us who value the well-being of our community must not only feel ashamed of the bloodshed being committed in the name of Hinduism but must also take determined steps to halt it.

The irresponsible politics of most of the Muslim leaders does not absolve us of this responsibility. If the Hindu community continues to use the follies of the Muslim leadership to legitimize discrimination and violence against Muslims, we will be doing so at our own peril. The continuing pogroms against the Muslims marginalizes an already impoverished and politically vulnerable community even further. If they are denied legitimate means of earning their livelihood, even more of them are bound to be forced into a life of petty crimes and violence. Thus the marginalization, insecurity and ghettoization of the Muslim community has harmful consequences for all of us and for the health of Indian society. It is foolish to insist on treating Indian Muslims unjustly on the specious plea that Hindus are treated badly in some of the Islamic countries. Even enlightened self-interest demands that we work out a just policy for dealing with the minorities.

1. First and foremost, we need to restore the sanctity of our religious places and rid them of politicians. The distortions brought about in the system of temple management during British colonial rule, need to be rectified. Traditionally, religious places in India were not subservient to a distant political authority. Most temples were supported by the local community, which also exercised control over its affairs. The BJP–RSS–VHP attempt to take over the controversial Ram Mandir at Ayodhya from the hands of the local priests is not the only example of politicians usurping religious sites. Even the communists in Kerala are known to have fought fierce battles to try to wrest control over certain temples in the state. We need to work out clear rules about the governance of religious places and property, preventing politicians from taking over religious places, and ensuring they remain in the hands of the worshippers.

2. We also need to work out institutional safeguards so that the enormous wealth generated by the temples is used for social and spiritual well-being rather than for power games. Provision of free food and shelter for all who come for it, as gurudwaras do even today, could take care of many who suffer from hunger and destitution, probably better than some government-run programmes. The tradition of kar seva should be extended to improve the community's physical environment, for example, in the provision of sanitation, clean water supply and pukka roads. The government has failed miserably in all these areas. Provision of these basic necessities would be better taken care of if the local community, with the temples and

gurudwaras as one source of support, took over all these public tasks.

3. An equally important task for those who wish to restore lustre to their faith would involve reviving the tradition of temples as places of learning, of religious studies, of theology, and as centres of art and culture.

4. It is vital that we counter with carefully collected facts the hate campaigns of the BJP–RSS–VHP that are based on deliberate misreporting and lies. We should insist that the press and the government agencies give an accurate description of the losses suffered by different communities during communal violence. An accurate knowledge of facts may help to counter the mistaken sense of persecution being inculcated among Hindus and to restrain the irresponsible rhetoric of some Muslim leaders.

5. We need to work out concrete ways of making large-scale social interaction possible between the two communities. Such efforts should not be confined to *Iftar* parties hosted by ministers. The increasing ghettoization of the Muslim community is leading to an even greater communication gap than existed previously.

6. We need to work out ways of resolving communal conflicts without resorting to needless government interventions. For example, an important reason for the success of the BJP–RSS–VHP campaign is that, as always, the secularists continue to oppose them by relying mainly on the power of the state. Few attempts were made to oppose them in ways other than appealing to the government to use force to prevent them from performing the kar seva. The ham-handed way in which the police and the paramilitary forces were used to prevent the demolition of the mosque led to unnecessary bloodshed and killings, providing a halo of martyrdom to this murderous Combine. If we do not give up our slavish dependence on the state machinery to solve such problems, we will never move towards more lasting solutions to social conflicts.

7. We need to recognize that the vast diversity of India is a source

of strength and vigour and has been crucial for the survival of democracy in India. Instead of treating this diversity as a liability to be got rid of, as the Hindu *rashtravadis* do, we need to work to protect minorities from attack and discrimination. A consensus on this will not be difficult to attain. Every community is a minority in some part of the country (e.g. Hindus in Kashmir, Muslims in Jammu) and, therefore, can be convinced to accept a uniform policy for the protection of the minority rights in India.

8. The Hindu community can be mobilized to save its culture and religion from being distorted beyond recognition only if they are aware of it. In the name of promoting secular education, the western-educated elite has deliberately promoted ignorance about India's rich heritage. The task of promoting respect and creating adequate facilities for the learning of our varied religious and cultural traditions cannot and should not be left to the government. It is best undertaken by social and cultural organizations functioning outside the government patronage system.

9. A very vigorous effort is also required to preserve our ancient monuments, including temples, as these are repositories of our cultural heritage. Many of them have been destroyed beyond repair due to systematic neglect. The looting and plundering of ancient temples by unscrupulous smugglers is perhaps more serious than the depredations of Mughal invaders. Yet the Hindu rashtravadis have maintained a studious silence on this. They could have performed a greater service if they had started a campaign to protect these endangered temples. The Archaeological Survey of India (ASI) and other government departments are incapable of dealing with this task. The job of restoration has to be organized on a larger scale by ensuring the people's concerned participation.

10. No less, perhaps even more important, is the task of saving and restoring whatever is left of those historical, religious and other texts that shed greater light on our past. It is a matter of shame that, even for recent history, one finds records much better preserved in the British Museum and other foreign libraries than in Indian libraries. White ants are merrily feeding on our precious

texts and manuscripts. This process of destruction needs to be immediately halted. Much is already lost. We cannot afford to lose any more. For a people without a sense of its past is a people without a sense of self, and can more easily be manipulated into self-destruction.

6

Criminalization of Politics

T he Sangh Parivar poses a grave threat to the Indian polity and society, not so much because it mixes religion and politics, but because it resorts to criminal acts. For instance, had the BJP–RSS–VHP, Bajrang Dal and company stopped at the demolition of the Babri mosque in Ayodhya and proceeded to celebrate their victory through *aarti* and *bhajans* (devotional songs), more people might have accepted their claim that they were motivated by religious sentiment.

The deposed and recently murdered *mahant* of the Ram Janamsthan Mandir, Baba Lal Das, openly stated in various interviews that none of the VHP leaders ever came to pray or made any offerings at the Ram temple during this period. Lal Das alleged that after demolishing the Babri Masjid, the VHP cadres barged into the Ram Lalla mandir, looted the cash box containing a month's offerings and stole ancient idols worth several crores. According to the late Lal Das, they even stole the original, ancient Ram Lalla idol and replaced it with a fake one.

While some were looting the Ram Lalla temple, others went on a murderous spree. Between nightfall on 6 December and mid-afternoon the next day, these supposed kar sevaks killed and burnt 13 Muslim men and children. They could not lay their hands on more because the majority of Muslims in Ayodhya had fled before 6 December, and the rest on hearing the news that the Babri Masjid had fallen. The rioting in Ayodhya began in the early morning of 7 December; for nearly twelve hours Sangh Parivar gangsters roamed the streets, plundering and torching every single one of the 134 Muslim homes and business establishments in the city. First they

First published in *Manushi* No. 79 (Nov–Dec 1993).

looted all the valuables and currency they could lay their hands on. Then they smashed to pieces everything that was in the houses. What couldn't be broken, whether it was motorcycles, clothes or books, went into huge bonfires. After this the Muslim houses were set on fire. Barring two, all the masjids and *idgahs* of Ayodhya were either destroyed or damaged.

This was not just a euphoric mindless reaction of the Sangh Parivar to their success in razing the Babri masjid to the ground, but part of a well-prepared plan. The Sangh Parivar had made prior lists of the locations of all Muslim homes. So careful was the planned targeting of Muslim homes that, where a Muslim house was situated too close to a Hindu house, they only looted and destroyed whatever they found within, but refrained from setting the place on fire, lest the neighbouring Hindu houses catch fire. They could do all this openly, in broad daylight, because both the police and the Provincial Armed Constabulary (PAC) brazenly assisted them in the mayhem.

This pattern of targeted killings of the Muslims with the open help of the police and paramilitary forces, and often with government support, has been witnessed in all recent massacres and riots such as those in Meerut and Malliana in 1987, in Bhiwandi, Bhagalpur, Ahmedabad and more recently in Surat and Bombay. In many of these riots, women have been stripped and paraded naked in the streets before being gang-raped and brutally put to death.

These acts are not as much due to mixing religion with politics as they are a consequence of the brazen use of criminal means to win political battles. The issue is, therefore, not so much the survival of secularism as it is the increasing criminalization of our political life, and the active protection criminals receive from the political machinery. It is this nexus which needs to be broken.

Just as the *Hindutva* of the Sangh Parivar relies heavily on murder, mayhem, loot, rape and arson, so does the 'secular nationalism' of the Congress party. In recent years this party has been increasingly using riots and pogroms as a means of winning over vote banks. The anti–Sikh massacres of November 1984 were organized with a view to consolidating their Hindu vote bank. Anti–Muslim violence has been a regular feature of several Congress-ruled states. The Congress party has openly patronized the anti-social politics of Shiv Sena hoodlums and has joined the Sangh Parivar in legitimizing the politics of hatred and bloodshed. This increasing criminalization of the political and social fabric is the main danger, not the mixing of religion with politics.

Unlike in Europe, where religious authority, especially the Roman Catholic Church, has a long history of intervening in the secular domain, India has no such comparable tradition. Religion has never sought to dictate politics in India because there has been no consensual centralized religious authority which could claim to speak on behalf of the entire Hindu or Muslim population. Modern India is witnessing the very opposite of the battles fought in Europe to free politics from encroachments by religion.

In our country, there are hardly any instances of religious leaders insisting that politics be subservient to them. On the contrary, it is politicians who have in recent history attempted to take over religious institutions and destroy their sanctity. In Punjab, it was the battle between the Akali Dal and the Congress Party over who was to have exclusive control over gurudwaras, so as to be able to use them as a political base, that caused so much bloodshed and strife. This tradition was started by the British who tried to prop up corrupt mahants in gurudwaras leading to a long struggle by the Akalis to free the gurudwaras from British influence. There have been similar intrusions by the Congress government into the affairs of the mosques through control over Waqf Boards.

Since Hindu temples do not have a centralized body, they could not be taken over by politicians staging a coup from above. But in recent decades there has been a systematic attempt by politically affiliated criminals to forcibly take over temples. This is one of the reasons for the success of the BJP–RSS–VHP Combine in politicizing the Ram Mandir issue in such a murderous fashion.

In India, it is not politics which needs saving from religion but religion which needs to be protected from political hoodlums. Temples, gurudwaras and Waqf Boards provide criminals with vast amounts of economic resources and a ready-made political base. They have converted these religious institutions into battlegrounds for gang warfare.

Even this politicization of religion would be a relatively harmless affair if the parties concerned vowed not to use criminal means to secure their political ends. This is what made Jinnah so dangerous. He could secure the partition of the country not on the strength of religious fervour, but by instigating riots and bloodshed in the name of mass action for the purpose of polarizing Hindu and Muslims. That is what began the process of forcible Hindu exodus from certain Muslim majority areas, leading to retaliation by Hindus in areas where they were numerically dominant. Thus the foundation of Pakistan was laid through bloodshed and criminal acts of politicians rather than by religion dominating politics.

Advani, Bal Thackeray, Singhal of the Sangh Parivar and many in the Congress party insist on following the path chosen by Jinnah. In city after city where Hindu–Muslim riots have been politically engineered, we are witnessing the increasing polarization of the two communities. The Muslims of the subcontinent, especially the Mohajirs of Pakistan and those left in India, are paying a heavy price for not opposing 'Jinnahism' with vigour and determination. If we Hindus allow our own Jinnahs to get the better of us, we too will be following the path of self-destruction.

Calling the Sangh Parivar politics communal amounts to giving them undue respectability. To be communal-minded involves a strong devotion to the interests of one's own ethnic group rather than to those of society as a whole. On the other hand, the politics of the Sangh Parivar lies in instigating a large-scale criminalization of the Hindu community.

For years both the Congress and the Sangh Parivar used poor Dalit men to launch attacks on Muslim *bastis* while the middle and upper classes could feign ignorance of what was going on in their city. In recent years, however, young people from the so-called respectable middle and upper-class homes have also been encouraged to become the leaders of loot and murder brigades. Their success in mobilizing large numbers of women to join in the violence, as well as to abet and encourage the rape of Muslim women, as in Bombay and Surat during January–March 1993, is a cause for serious alarm.

This criminalization of the Hindus by the Sangh Parivar shows that these groups are no well-wishers of the Hindu community. Like the Khalistani terrorists, they too resort to murder to silence the voices of dissent within the Hindu community, as the murder of Baba Lal Das proves.

I reproduce extracts from a tape-recorded interview with Baba Lal Das when he came to Delhi in July 1993 to give testimony before the Citizens' Tribunal on Ayodhya:

My name is Lal Das. I was appointed by the court as the chief priest of Ramjanmabhoomi temple in 1983 and continued in that position until 1 March, 1992. Before that I used to oversee the work of the Ramjanmabhoomi Seva Samiti. I was attending to the court case [relating to the disputed site] from 1969 to 1983, before being appointed the chief priest. On paper I am still the chief priest. This appointment was made by the Government Receiver. Earlier, a magistrate or a judge used to be the Receiver. In 1992 the BJP government removed me and appointed their own supporters as the priest there.

Why did they do such a thing? Why did they feel that you would not work in their interest?

The question of working in anyone's interests did not arise. I was not under them. I was appointed by the court and the courts appoint an impartial person. Whatever they wanted from me and whatever expectations they had that I would work for them were not possible.

What expectations did they have from you? How did they want you to work in their favour?

They had two expectations, one that I should issue statements to the press in their favour and second, that I should tell everyone that all income the Ramjanmabhoomi *pujari* receives belongs to the VHP.

How much was received annually as offerings?

Initially it was not much. After the locks were opened, the amount of offerings increased to between Rs 5 to 10 lakhs a year.

How much was received before the locks were opened?

Before that, whatever used to come used to be at the *chabutra* of the *akhara*. People did not go inside the mandir. When we opened the donation box after five or six months, we would get about Rs 10,000 to Rs 12,000. On an average, we received about Rs 30,000 to RS 35,000 a year. This was used for our expenses.

Did they want whatever money that came to go to them?

No, they were interested in propaganda. What they wanted was that we should tell all the visitors that the VHP owned the mandir because they had already announced all over India that they had rights over the mandir.

Since when did the VHP start coming to Ayodhya?

From 1984 onwards.

Before that there was no interference from them in Ayodhya?

All the rioting and violence started in 1984. Before that there was no dispute or trouble. There was a small dispute in 1949 and both sides went to court to argue out their case. There was no fighting or slogan shouting on the roads, neither was there any violence.

What happened in 1984 to cause them to suddenly remember this place?

It all started at Sitamarhi in Bihar. There they took out a rath yatra to generate propaganda to get the locks on the Ramjanmabhoomi opened. They got popular support and also a lot of money. They realized that they could make a lot of money out of this and also get publicity. So, with more money flowing in, their programmes also went on increasing.

How did they remove you?

I was forcibly removed. It's like having dacoits enter your home and take away everything.

What about the police?

What about them? The police was on their side and the state government was theirs.

Did the other mahants of Ayodhya not protest about this?

What can the mahants do? Those who are on our side cannot come out on the streets to fight. But they did raise moral objections.

How did they do it? There have not been many statements from them.

There are nearly 8,500 big and small mandirs in Ayodhya. The press people come and meet a few people, generally those who are in the limelight. The Sadhu Samaj gave us moral support and protested against the VHP action, so did many members of the public and political parties.

Which political parties supported you?

We received support from the SJP, Janata Dal, Janata(S) and the Bahujan Samaj Party. Only the Congress and the BJP were silent.

How come the Congress party did not support you even though you were appointed by their government?

The Congress and the BJP have similar policies. What one does is supported by the other. All the troubles have been created by the Congress. Right throughout till the demolition, the Congress has fully supported the BJP. Today also the BJP has the full support of the Congress. They have an internal arrangement—whatever the BJP does the Congress supports. But to show the public that they do not support the BJP they make a big drama like in Ramlila. In the Ramlila you bring Meghnad, Ravan and Sita on the stage to show the public a good drama. But behind the curtain the actors are neither Ravan nor Sita. Just in that manner, all this drama is meant for public consumption. Behind the scenes both BJP and Congress are one and the same.

Supposing you were asked to resolve the dispute in your personal capacity, what steps would you have taken to settle the dispute?

Since the Muslims have never fought over it, the problem resolves itself. The Muslims had not used the Babri Masjid since 1949. The Muslims of Faizabad did not even know where Babri Masjid was situated, leave alone the Muslims from the rest of India. The older generation of Faizabad may have known where the Babri Masjid was but the younger generations did not know anything about it. The Sangh Parivar started propaganda supposedly to take revenge on the descendants of Babar and to send them to Pakistan. Their propaganda drew attention to the fact that Babri Masjid existed in Ayodhya. It is they who united all the Muslims in India. Thereafter, the Muslims gave the expected reaction—that it was a royal masjid and that it should not be touched while there was a case going on in the courts over it. The Muslims did not come out in the streets to fight over it till they were attacked openly.

On 1 February 1986, the district court ordered the locks opened. The BJP–VHP rath yatra processions had to be cancelled. They were silent till 7 February, wondering what to do, as their source of income had dried up. They used to collect a lot of money through the rath yatra; the villagers used to pay for getting the mandir opened. Now that the mandir was unlocked, what should they do?

Did the Muslims not create any trouble in all this time?

No, they were mourning, but they did not come out on the streets. They were fighting a legal battle in the courts.

There was a meeting in Lucknow on 6 February 1986. At this meeting, the VHP decided that the establishment of a mandir on the disputed site was the basis of their movement. They had already got a lot of money and political mileage out of the dispute. They now called for the construction of a mandir, and announced that their struggle would continue as long as the mandir was not constructed. Their slogans changed from that point onwards. They held processions all over India announcing that they would continue their fight as long as they could not rebuild a mandir there. They also used a slogan: 'This is just for starters—Mathura and Kashi are yet to come' (*Abhi to yeh jhanki hai, Mathura Kashi baki hai*). After this they started taking out processions in the Muslim-dominated areas and started abusing them. The Muslims, who were in mourning, became upset at these attacks. From 7 February 1986, riots started.

One result of these riots was that many Hindus were attacked in Kashmir. The state government was dismissed in Kashmir as a result of the riots. Elections have not been held in Kashmir ever since then. Even now there is governor's rule in Kashmir.

When the riots broke out on 7 February and continued till 20–22 February, the rath yatras were stopped by the then chief minister Vir Bahadur Singh. It was a Congress government then. When the locks were opened on the orders of the Central government, Vir Bahadur stopped the processions. Otherwise there would have been more violence. After the locks had been opened, the VHP started a campaign to lay the foundation stone for the construction of the mandir at the disputed spot.

They never betrayed their real intentions. In their affidavit to the government they announced that they would only lay the foundation stone of the mandir on three feet of land. They claimed they would not disturb anything else; they would not destroy or cause any harm to the disputed structure; there would be no violence of any kind. But their real intentions were different. Their thinking was that after they laid the foundation stone there would be more violence. Then construction would be halted. After construction was halted, the Hindus would get angry and join their side in the dispute.

They started construction work after they laid the foundation stone. Vir Bahadur Singh stopped the construction work. Then the VHP announced that they had been prevented from building a mandir. After that Rajiv Gandhi was killed. Then the elections were held. The Congress formed the government at the Centre and the BJP in Uttar Pradesh. That the Congress and BJP have a common programme was not known to the common man. The Indian public could not see through the BJP–Congress deceptions as they would alternately blow hot and cold.

The lock was not put on because of anyone's order. The lock was put on in 1971. It was not locked in 1949. The legal aspect of this situation was that the place was in charge of a 'Receiver'. The food was cooked in the kitchen of the Ram Chabutra. The sentry would open the lock for the *bhog* (food offering to deities).

In 1971, Priya Dutt Ram, who was the Receiver, expired. There was a dispute between the new Receiver and the Nirmohi Akhara. The police intervened, put their own lock on, and kept the key. The sentry on duty was changed; he handed over the key to the new sentry. There were two doors. One door used to remain open for *bhog* offering and prayers. This system was continuing. The BJP and the VHP found a very good opportunity in this to publicize and propagate their ideas and then the other lock was taken off. So it was not that the place was completely locked. Only from the point of view of security was the place locked at times.

It could have been opened without fanfare and all the propaganda on TV.

It was all done for political gains. They have no love for Ram, these people from the RSS, Bajrang Dal, Vidhyarthi Parishad, Shiv Sena and so on. These people are of the Arya Samaji faith, they do not believe in idol worship. But because they were getting a lot of money and political gain, they whipped up Hindu sentiments. In the entire history of the RSS, they have not constructed a single mandir anywhere in India.

Our flag of the Devi is hexagonal and flags over the mandirs of Ram or Krishna have the symbol of Hanuman. Their saffron colour flag is not a symbol of the Vaishnav's but of the Arya Samajis. *Om* is part of our *mantras* also, but they have made Om the basis of everything, setting aside all the mantras. Thus the way we pray has no similarity with the way they pray. They consider Ram to be human while we think of him as Brahm (God). We consider Krishna to be God, they think of him as a man.

Dr Golwalkar has written in his book that the biggest mistake of the Hindus is that they think of Ram and Krishna as gods. If according to him, this is the Hindu's biggest mistake, then it is clear that they think of Ram and Krishna as ordinary mortals.

Whenever they talk of Ram, they always say Bhagwan Ram.

All that is just play-acting, as I have already told you.

If you say that Ram is God, how can he have a birthplace?

Whether this is so or not is a subject of intellectual debate, I do not want to go into that. It is a matter of belief; we treat them as gods and they treat them as ordinary mortals.

You said earlier that there was no dispute about the mandir at all. When I asked you how you would resolve the crisis, you said that this dispute is an artificial crisis. Are you in favour of this campaign that has been started to construct the Ram Mandir there?

I think that a grand Ram Mandir must be constructed. Ayodhya is a city of mandirs. In Ayodha, Ram Mandirs are everywhere.

Is there need for one more mandir when there are already over 8,000 mandirs there?

The question is that of a Ramjanmabhoomi Mandir. Ayodhya is a city of 8,500 mandirs. The Muslims have never objected to the construction of a new Ram Mandir although 42 acres of land adjacent to the disputed site are even now recorded as a Muslim graveyard (*kabristan*) in the books of the revenue department.

But the Babri Masjid also comes in the disputed area.

That is part of the dispute. But the whole area is recorded as a graveyard. Eight mandirs were constructed in the graveyard after 1949. They were demolished by the BJP, who wanted to show the people that they were doing something.

Demolishing a mandir is not considered to be a good thing.

That is, only if they believe in Ram. But as they do not believe in Ram . . .

Was there no protest in Ayodhya?

There was a lot of protest. They demolished eight mandirs, including the ancient Sakshi Gopal Mandir, Hanuman Mandir and Keshavdas Mandir. The historic mandir, Sita ki Rasoi, was destroyed by them during the kar seva on 6 December.

The Muslims never objected to the construction of mandirs in their graveyard; rather, they had willingly handed over the land to the *maths* in Ayodhya. In that area behind the Janambhoomi there is a Shanti Bhavan and next to it a temple. The area was given willingly by the Muslims to the Hindus to construct their temples. They may have received some compensation but the fact remains that the land was given willingly by the Muslims to the Hindus. There was no dispute at all between the two communities over the construction of these mandirs in the graveyard. Whatever dispute existed was being sorted out in court. They never objected to our praying at the disputed site.

How many Muslims are there in this area?

In Faizabad and Ayodhya the total population would be around 1.25 to 1.3 lakh. In Faizabad, the Muslims would be 25 to 30 per cent. In Ayodhya there would be around 5,000 Muslims. There has never been any dispute or quarrel with the Muslims. In fact, there was a great deal of co-operation from the Muslims in the maintenance of the mandir. They owned flower gardens and they sold flowers to the mandirs. Other ingredients required for prayers were also provided by the Muslims. Things were going on smoothly; there was no discrimination. In fact, for the last 40 years the manager of one of the mandirs (Mangal Bhavan) is a Muslim.

In Ayodhya there was peace between the Hindus and the Muslims. People from outside have created the rift. For them it was an opportunity to unite the Hindu votes behind them—they wanted to form their own government even though it meant creating a holocaust which may ruin the country. They were not concerned about the consequences. They had only one aim—votes.

This money that they have collected in the name of the Ramjanmabhoomi Mandir, some say it is Rs 800 crores. Is there any account of that?

I have all the documents and proofs. The VHP had an office near the Bharat Sadhu Samaj. They received Rs 21 million from West Germany. Apart from that they received bricks of gold and silver. Hindu families all over India donated money to them. They have collected hundreds of crores of rupees, divided the money before the 1991 elections . . .

What would be the total amount?

I know about the money received from Germany and I know that Ramchandra Paramhansa took Rs 30 lakh as commission. Then only did he sign an authorization to let the BJP withdraw the money before the elections. They withdrew the money from here and deposited it in other banks.

The money collected for the Ramjanmabhoomi was withdrawn and deposited in banks in Delhi and used for the elections.

How much annual income are they getting now?

They have no income from the Ramjanmabhoomi at the moment as it is under the control of the government.

But aren't they still collecting money all over the country in the name of the Ramjanmabhoomi?

All the capitalists like Tata, Birla, Dalmia are giving them a lot of money. They give them money because they want the problem to continue so that public attention is diverted from the real issues and they can keep making money the way they want to.

In the film Ram Ke Naam *in the interview with you, you were told that you sound like a communist.*

Is speaking the truth speaking like a communist? I am just saying what is actually happening.

The VHP has removed you and forcibly taken over the mandir; similarly, it is said that they have removed many mahants from the mandirs in Ayodhya and installed their goons in their place. Is it true?

This is true. Not only in Ayodhya, but their idea was that everywhere in India, whenever there is a big mandir or math, they intend to send their men to take over the mandirs and maths so that their writ runs everywhere.

How did they take over the mandirs?

First of all the VHP and RSS people asked for place to stay. They said they were working for Hindu society. People here are not so shrewd or clever, so they gave them a room to stay. After that one by one they started bringing in more of their workers into the mandirs and maths. Since we don't have family dynasitics but a guru tradition, they chose one of their own disciples, made him the mahant and threw out the original mahant.

This could have been done only if the guru agreed.

There is no consent of the guru; it's all happening on the basis of force. The gurus have been thrown out on the streets; no one is concerned about them. For these people there is neither God nor guru (*na guru, na Gobind*). What can the gurus do? The police will not listen to them; they can't get justice.

Out of the 8,500 mandirs, how many have they taken over?

I know of eight mandirs they took over just as they took over the janamsthan.

There was no internal resistance over this?

Who will protest? Lakhs are protesting against Khalistanis but what is happening? These people are another incarnation of the Khalistanis.

What similarity do you see between them and the Khalistanis?

There is no difference between them and the Khalistanis. The Khalistanis want total control over Punjab. The RSS wants total dictatorial control over Hindu society. They want people to agree to whatever they say.

What would be the solution to this problem according to you?

Both Congress and the BJP should keep quiet and stay out of this. We the people of Ayodhya and Faizabad together will resolve the matter. The mandir will be constructed and the Muslims will not object.

Were you in favour of demolishing the Babri Masjid?
No, not at all.

You felt that without demolishing it a mandir could have been constructed?
The mandir was already there. Prayers were being offered while the court case was going on which was dragged on by the government. They wanted to keep the issue alive because at any time they could raise it and start riots.

Is it true that murders are routinely taking place in Ayodhya?
This is all their doing. They have goons and murderers on their side. Any mahant who does not obey them or toe their line is murdered.

In the last two years how many mahants have been murdered?
At least 50 to 60 mahants have been murdered, such as the mahant of the big cantonment, Ram Pratap Das, Maithli Sharan of Janaki Ghat. Bajrangdas at Hanumangarhi was murdered some time ago. Recently many people have been murdered. How many people can one name?

There should be some list somewhere.
I have a list. I cannot remember the names without the list. Every week there are murders—if not every week, every month. I wonder how a person like me is still alive.

Yes, it is a wonder that they have left you alive after what you said about them in public.
I am alive by the grace of God. They have tried to do everything to kill me. They have attacked my home, taken away my land and house. They have thrown bombs at my house and tried to burn it. They have tried all methods to destroy me. Vinay Katiyar of the VHP even organized a *yagna* to kill me.

Was this agricultural land?
No, it was land to build a house on. I am staying in someone else's house.

What are you doing these days?
I am looking after the mandir of the *riyasat.*

You mean the government?
No, not the government, the erstwhile king.

Do you have a leaning towards any political party?
I have no leaning towards any political party. I hate all political parties because they are the root of all our problems.

In your eyes is there any party that would reduce tensions?
I don't see any such party.

Not even the communists?
The communists have also become corrupt.

I had read in the newspapers that the communist MP from Faizabad had done a lot of good in Ayodhya.
He is a sinner. In this moment of crisis he never issued a statement that what is happening is wrong. He did not even go to the Muslims. He did not go to anyone—neither the Hindus nor the Muslims. He is MP only of the Ahirs and Yadavs, not of the whole region.

Have the Muslims whose houses were burnt down returned to Ayodhya?
Most of them have returned.

How is the situation now?
The situation is still not good. They are still unprotected. They will remain insecure as long there is Congress rule.

Will they be unprotected even under the BJP?
Yes, even then they will be unprotected.

What should be done? Should we banish the Congress and BJP for a hundred years?
If the Congress and BJP are not removed by their roots from this country, if the system does not change fully, if the Indian Administrative Service and Provincial Civil Service people remain here, the total revolution that Jai Prakash Narayan had spoken about cannot occur; India cannot change without these things happening first.

Why do you want to abolish the IAS and the PCS?
Because the IAS and PCS think they rule the country. The thinking amongst them is: 'While we are in service, we rule the country, and after we retire, we should get a ticket from the BJP or Congress so we can rule again'. Their wish is that from their childhood to death they should be the rulers. They want money and power. Both the Congress and the BJP have money and power. The capitalists are providing the money to these parties. The common man, the worker, the peasant has still not been able to understand why we have the vote. It is fools like me who have understood this.

Did the Mulayam Singh government do any good, in your opinion?

The Mulayam Singh government did its duty well. If I had been in his place I would have done more. By more I mean that I would have had so many bullets fired that people would not have dared to raise their eyes. He was a fool—he got scared. If I had been the chief minister in his place, I would have had thousands of people killed so that they would not have dared to look towards Ayodhya during their lifetimes.

Do you see any chance of Mulayam Singh coming back to power?
It is possible.

What about the hatred the Hindus have towards him?
Where was the hatred among the Hindus? It was all a creation of propaganda. Even today the people of Uttar Pradesh realize that Mulayam Singh is a good person. He worked for the interests of the poor and the farmers. He did a lot—like waiving agricultural loans upto Rs 11,000 and removing octroi. The things that farmers needed were made available at cheap rates.

In case he comes back to power, will this problem be solved?
Until a different government is formed at the Centre, how can the problem be solved? The condition of the mandirs depends on the people who control them. If they are corrupt, the mandirs will perish; if they are honest, mandirs will improve.

What do you feel about the politicization of the mandirs in the last 50 years or so?
Earlier thoughtful people used to come to the Sadhu Samaj, good people who had become tired of this material world and wanted to devote their thoughts to prayers. They stayed away from jealousy and hatred. Today society has become such that on the one hand there are these so-called followers of BJP who want to bring about Ramrajya through bloodshed and on the other hand you have the Sadhu Samaj which is becoming the home of criminals. Until the time there are good people in them there is no chance for improving political parties or mandirs.

How will people improve?
When there is change in society, when there is a total revolution, when the system changes, only then will people change.

7

Safety is Indivisible:
The Warning from Bombay Riots

I t is unfortunate that our political leaders, industrialists and opinion makers have responded to the tragedy of the Bombay bomb blasts and earlier riots of 1992 and 1993 in their usual irresponsible manner. Instead of mourning the dead, our political and business leaders are mostly concerned about the negative impact the bomb blasts and the riots will have on foreign investments. They do not care if the lives of the people are not safe or hundreds of thousands of people lose their source of livelihood in the repeated riots and massacres instigated by our political leaders. All they seem concerned about is whether the investments and profits of the elite who enter into collaborations with foreign corporations are safe.

So far there is no definite evidence of who is behind the blasts. Even if we were to accept the fact that the bomb blasts were the result of a conspiracy between the Pakistani intelligence and a few Muslims in the Bombay underworld, the self-righteous indignation of our political leaders is rather misplaced because the Indian government has been involved in somewhat similar activities over the last couple of decades. It has been injecting terrorism into the politics of Punjab and Kashmir to destroy the ruling parties' political opponents. The Research and Analysis Wing (RAW), the Indian government's own intelligence agency, has also been training the terrorist outfit, Liberation Tigers of Tamil Eelam (LTTE), for insurgency operations in Sri Lanka.

However, even more important than finding the culprits is the necessity to recognize the various serious flaws in our security system. The incompetence of the intelligence agencies is revealed in the ease with which huge quantities of sophisticated, powerful explosives

First published in *Manushi* No. 74–75 (Jan– Apr 1995).

are smuggled into the country. The intelligence agencies are either unaware of this fact or are unable to intercept their flow. Their failure to do their job might well be due to the involvement of top political leaders and police officials with weapons smuggling. The smuggling of drugs and guns has for a long time been carried out under powerful political patronage. Men like Dawood Ibrahim, who is being accused of involvement in the bomb blasts, are known to be proteges of powerful Congress politicians and are very 'secular' in their criminal and political alliances.

The bomb blasts highlight one simple fact: when the state machinery is hijacked by criminals, it loses its ability to perform the most elementary of tasks expected of it; i.e., to provide security of life to its citizens. They also give us a message of warning that safety, like health, is indivisible. Just as the elite of India cannot hope to stay healthy on the strength of Bisleri water bottles and air-conditioners as long as the general water and air are not clean for all, likewise the Hindus cannot hope to be safe as long as their leaders encourage violence against the Muslims, with active participation of the police and paramilitary forces.

It is unlikely that we will ever know the real truth behind the bomb blasts. The tendency of our government is to shroud everything in secrecy and tell the citizens half-truths and lies to suit the interests of those in power. The anxiety and fear generated by the bomb blasts are likely to be exploited by our rulers for further dividing Hindus from Muslims, and to cover up what happened during the Bombay riots of December 1992 and January 1993, following the demolition of Babri Masjid on 6 December. It would be suicidal not to realize the full implications of that violence because it demonstrates how large sections of the government became indistinguishable from criminals. The police joined hoodlum brigades and murdered and raped many hapless victims, looted thousands of Muslim homes and shops, and burnt houses, driving thousands out of their homes.

At first sight there is nothing dramatically new about these massacres. They are part of a continuing process, similar to the riots in Bhiwandi, Sitamarhi, Meerut, Ahmedabad and Bhagalpur. However, there are some new and noteworthy developments :

- The scale of violence and the extent of brutality is escalating with every new outbreak.
- The politicians who instigate these massacres are becoming increasingly brazen about their participation in it.
- The police and paramilitary forces do not feel the need to maintain

even a facade of neutrality concerning their expected role as keepers of law and order.

- The riots are not carried out by *goondas* and anti-social elements alone. The middle classes and other supposedly respectable sections of society are actively supporting and even joining the murder brigades.
- The violence is no longer confined to poor *bastis*. It is beginning to engulf elite areas as well.
- Women, and even young girls, are taking an active part in violence and hate campaigns.
- In recent years Hindu–Muslim riots are acquiring overtones of ethnic cleansing, similar to that attempted in parts of India at the time of the Partition—that is, hounding hundreds of thousands out of their homes, forcing them to flee as refugees from their own land. According to one estimate, during the outbreak of violence in January, 2,15,000 people fled the city of Bombay for their villages or wherever they could find shelter. Most of those who fled were Muslims.

Almost all the shops and business establishments belonging to Muslims in the Hindu majority areas were destroyed. So well planned was the targeting of Muslim homes and shops that in almost all cases the neighbouring Hindu homes and shops stayed intact.

This essay concentrates on the nature of violence in Bombay even though riots took place in several other cities as well. The reason for choosing Bombay for somewhat detailed reporting is that the violence was most ferocious here despite the fact that there has been no history of Hindu–Muslim tension in this city.

My report could not cover the entire city. A comprehensive account detailing what happened in each area of this sprawling city would require a much bigger and longer investigation than I could manage with my limited means. I have focused on a certain select area of Bombay and conversations with a fairly large cross section of people.

I have relied mainly on eyewitness accounts of Hindus in different parts of the city and accounts of the victims of violence, some of them in refugee camps. I have also used the narratives of accounts by social and political workers who are doing relief and rehabilitation work among the victims and, therefore, have good knowledge of what happened. All this does not constitute a systematic study of the Bombay riots but only an attempt to delineate the patterns of violence and some characteristic features of the riots in Bombay.

The impression created by the press, including supposedly secular papers, is that the riots that followed 6 December were caused by Muslim mobs getting violent as they came out to protest against the Babri Masjid demolition. But if one closely follows the pattern of violence in different cities, one finds these were not really Hindu–Muslim riots.

Bombay witnessed two rounds of violence—the first one happened soon after the demolition of Babri Masjid, starting 7 December, and the second one in early January. As far as the December killings are concerned, there is a widespread agreement about their nature. When the news of the demolition of Babri Masjid reached Bombay, Muslims in some areas came out on the streets to mourn and protest. In Muslim majority areas they called for a closure of shops as well. Their anger was targeted against the government for having failed to protect Babri Masjid after repeated assurances to the Muslim community that the structure would not be allowed to be demolished. To demonstrate their anger against their 'betrayal' by the Congress government, they burnt or attacked some government property such as bus-stops and stoned buses. They also burnt an effigy of Narasimha Rao.

This form of protest—that is, burning and damaging buses, though no doubt stupid, is a standard practice of all protesting groups in India. Students routinely burn and damage buses every time they have a real or imagined grievance. During the anti-reservation agitation hundreds of buses were burnt in Delhi and elsewhere while the police looked on. Even in agitations led by trade unions and political parties, bus burning is considered a 'normal' form of protest because state transport buses are the most visible and easily accessible government property. In this case, because the protesters happened to be Muslims, police responded with brutality and a determination to kill.

For instance, on the morning of 7 December, about 25 young Muslim boys came out on the streets in Delhi's Jaffrabad area, asking people to close their shops and the neighbourhood school. The police stationed outside the school beat up these boys. In retaliation, these boys burnt two buses, a scooter and some old tyres. They first asked all the passengers to get off the bus so there was no loss of life. Yet the police responded with firing—no lathi charge, no tear gas, not even *hawai* fire to disperse the protesting mobs. They fired to kill. The local Congress (I) leader, Jamal, rushed out to ask the police who had given them the order to fire. The DCP aimed his gun at him. A young Muslim boy thought the DCP was going to fire at Jamal and pushed aside his gun. This boy was immediately shot dead. The DCP hit Jamal on the head, saying: 'Who are you, a *dada* of this area?' At this point a Muslim boy snatched a wireless set from one of the policemen and threw it into the nearby *nallah* (gutter). That gave the police the excuse they needed to go berserk.

Three Muslims were killed in the firing and several injured. The police let loose a misinformation campaign saying that the Muslims had attacked the police and killed a policeman as well as snatched a police gun, forcing them to fire at the mob. Subsequent enquiries by various independent groups have revealed that no policeman was killed in Jaffrabad. Nor is there any record of the supposedly missing gun. Yet the recovery of this gun became the pretext for the police to conduct large-scale 'search' operations in Muslim homes. Under this pretence, the police looted Muslim property, beat up and arrested any number of Muslim men and young boys and subjected them to regular beatings and torture in custody. Dozens of homes were set on fire in neighbouring Seelampur where Muslims live as a minority in predominantly Hindu neighbourhoods. The police led the riotous mobs in looting Muslim property and setting their homes and shops on fire.

In Bombay, too, the murder of four policemen, supposedly by Muslim mobs in Deonar, was used to justify large-scale violence against the Muslim community as a whole.

However, physical attacks on policemen by Muslims was not a large-scale occurrence. The general pattern was that young Muslim boys, mostly in the age range of 16 to 25, came out to protest, burnt some bus-stops and tyres, stoned buses and shouted anti-government, anti-police slogans. The police retaliated with bullets.

It is noteworthy that in most places the Muslims did not attack or kill any Hindus. Nor was Hindu property destroyed. In fact, they did not even raise slogans against the BJP or Shiv Sena, as they were protesting primarily against the government.

According to official figures, about 300 Muslims were shot dead by the Bombay police as a response to the anti-demolition protests by Muslims on 7 December. The actual figure is likely to be much higher. At this time the violence was police versus Muslims, and in some areas Muslims stoned the police in retaliation against the firing.

Even though many Muslim lives had been lost and they were angry at the police, yet things quietened down after the first round of killings in December till a fresh wave of violence engulfed the entire city of Bombay. This was very different in character from the first one, and was more like a series of planned pogroms led by the Shiv Sena, the Congress and the Sangh Parivar and assisted by the police.

Around 2 January, the Shiv Sena started a citywide campaign, declaring: 'Till such time as the Muslims do not stop the use of loudspeakers in mosques for azaan, and squatting on streets outside the mosques for the Friday *namaaz*, we will also do *maha aartis* on the streets with loudspeakers.' Many people in Bombay say: 'When that happened, we knew they were preparing for a big riot.'

The issue of namaaz on the streets, which has been projected by the Hindutvavadis as an instance of continued 'provocation' by the Muslims, has two dimensions. It is not as if every street in Bombay is blocked all Friday by Muslims for their namaaz, as is often made out to be. Nor is it a deliberate act of the Muslims to annoy the Hindus. The people saying namaaz file out on the streets because most mosques, especially in crowded areas like Bhendi Bazar, are very small and cannot hold all those who come for prayers. In recent years the growing divide between Hindus and Muslims and the consequent siege mentality has led to an increasing religious fervour among the Muslims. Thus, many more turn up for the Friday namaaz than was the case some years ago. Hence, a larger part of the congregation spills over onto the streets, causing temporary inconvenience to fellow citizens. However, the namaaz is no more than a 15-minute affair and the Muslims do nothing other than offer prayers at these gatherings. There have been no instances of Muslims abusing Hindus during the namaaz. But the maha aartis started by the Shiv Sena are a different fare altogether. Firstly, their purpose is not religious at all. The maha aarti is more like a political meeting in which local Shiv Sena leaders give provocative speeches with slogans like: 'Send these *landias* (a pejorative term for a circumcized male) to Pakistan'. The idea is to mobilize anti-Muslim sentiment and have an abuse-hurling session against the Muslims.

The Shiv Sainiks arbitrarily decide which area is to have maha aartis on a particular day of the week without any reference to religious significance whatsoever. Everywhere it would be a two-hour long affair. In the months of January and February it was common for Shiv Sainiks and their Hindu supporters to pelt stones at Muslim homes and shops as they dispersed after the supposed aartis. In some instances, there were full-fledged attacks on the Muslims including stabbings. The maha aartis started in south Bombay, spread to central Bombay and then moved towards the suburbs. Every single day of the week, Shiv Sainiks would have their maha aarti in some area or the other, even during curfew times. In non-curfew areas, traffic would be diverted with full cooperation of the police for the long duration of the aarti.

After the start of the maha aartis in the first week of January, a spurt of stabbing incidents were reported from different parts of the cities in which both Hindus and Muslims died. This was a hidden riot on a relatively small scale with both Hindus and Muslims indulging in stray murders of the other community. Suddenly a well-organized wave of anti-Muslim violence swept virtually through every locality of Bombay. The government releases as well as press reports made it out that it was triggered off by three incidents attributed to the Muslims. These were:

- An alleged attack on the night of 6 January on a roadside Hindu temple near the Muslim majority area of Behrampada in Bandra East, causing damage to the Ganesh idol.
- The burning down of a *chawl* inhabited by four or five Hindu families in a Muslim-dominated area of Jogeshwari on 7 January, leading to the death of one Hindu family.
- Stabbing of two Hindu porters working at the Bombay docks on 7 January.

When these incidents first occurred, the mass media—both private and government-owned, including the secular 'liberal' press—projected and presented the ensuing violence as a natural reaction to the provocative acts by the Muslims. The entire Bombay press, especially Marathi papers, went hysterical in their coverage of these three incidents, making the work of the Shiv Sena, Sangh Parivar and their allies only too easy.

However, a few days later some sections of the liberal press themselves came up with an expose that the Jogeshwari incident was not exactly a communal attack by Muslims and that it had other dimensions. A Hindu builder called Shetty had purchased that property and was interested in getting the tenant families of that *chawl* evacuated. They happened to be Hindus surrounded mostly by Muslim families. Shetty is supposed to have offered *supari* (in Bombay parlance it means money offered to criminals for getting illegal work done) to some miscreants and got the chawl burnt down.

There were no eyewitnesses to say who had set fire to the chawl because it had happened at night. Yet even before the police carried out a proper investigation, they supplied the story to the press that some Muslims had burnt down the chawl. Since this was a Muslim majority area, this story was assumed to be authentic. Initially, all newspapers carried the police version as a prominent front page story, thus creating the impression that the Muslims were responsible for instigating the wave of violence that swept Bombay.

The story told by Muslims and confirmed by some Hindus of Jogeshwari is as follows: On the night of 7 January (*jumma* day), a young Muslim boy was shot dead by the police in a nearby area He had gone to enquire about his aunt after news of riots in that area. While returning home, he was killed by a police bullet. People came running from that neighbourhood into the Muslim majority area of Jogeshwari, shouting, 'Irfan has been shot dead.' Lots of Muslims from Jogeshwari ran in panic to find out what had happened. This was after 11.30 p.m. In the meantime this chawl was set on fire. Children from Jogeshwari went screaming to inform their parents about it. Given how closely built these houses are, there was great panic because it would not take long for the entire settlement to be engulfed by fire. So the neighbouring Muslim families ran back to put out the fire and rescued some of those trapped inside. But seven people (some reports say four) were burnt to death. They were all in one room and someone had bolted the door from outside. The police arrived after the fire had been extinguished by the local people. Only one room out of six was burnt down completely, while one was partially damaged. Others were left largely untouched. But all the surviving families abandoned the chawl and fled the area.

This incident was used to justify large-scale violence against Muslims all over Bombay in which a few thousand people, including women and children, were brutally killed. Thousands were also rendered homeless and destitute. According to government figures, about 600 people were killed in the January round of violence. But independent witnesses say the number could be anything between 2000 and 4000. Muslim homes and shops all over the city were systematically looted and burnt. Many women were gang-raped and several of them brutally done to death later. The accompanying stories describe the horror of the manner in which Muslims were systematically targeted.

In the hysteria whipped up by newspapers and the Shiv Sena–Sangh Parivar propaganda following the Jogeshwari incident, hardly any newspaper thought it worthwhile to notice or bring to the attention of its readers that this was a solitary instance of violence on a Hindu family. Even those who had established the connection between the builders and the incident did not care to print that most Hindus continued to live in that area and run their shops in a normal fashion. I met half a dozen Hindu families living right near that chawl who testified that they were safe and had not faced any threats to leave. I also saw a number of Hindu-owned shops continuing with their business. This is in sharp contrast to how Muslims were treated in predominantly Hindu areas where they were beaten and torched out of their homes. In January and February when I visited Bombay twice, only a microscopic number of Muslims had been able to continue staying in their own homes. Even well-known film stars and artists like M.F. Hussain were forced to leave their homes.

Parvati Shankar Dhanavade, who stays near the burnt chawl and has lived in that area for about 55 years, said: 'Barring a couple of Hindu families which left this area following riots in the city, all Hindu families continue to stay here, including in our own mohalla where there are six–seven Hindu families. When the riots were going on in the city, our children would go and sleep in our Muslim neighbours' house and Hindus and Muslims together would keep all-night vigil.' Another old woman who lives alone, said: 'We were very afraid that riots would spread out to the Jogeshwari area. I used to spend nights in the house of our Muslim neighbours. We are somehow able to pull on through the day. But we keep awake all night because the police always comes in at night and drags out and arrests young Muslims boys. So we are petrified at night.'

I asked her why she, a Hindu, was petrified of police arrests? Had they arrested any Hindus? She said:

So what if Hindus are not being arrested? They are our neighbours after all. There is no man in my house. So I feel especially afraid and also feel very bad when Muslims are arrested. We keep awake till about 4 a.m. and then I come back to my house and go to work to clean utensils and wash clothes in people's homes in Prabhavati. They recently arrested a Muslim woman of my neighbourhood in the middle of the night simply because she lives near the burnt chawl. Her husband is a very fine man (*seedha aadmi hai*). He never gets involved in quarrels. She is the mother of five small kids and her arrest is really unfair (*najaiz*).

This sentiment was echoed by several other Hindus. In a few Muslim majority areas like Nagpada, Hindus were attacked. But these were stray incidents. By and large, Muslims did not try to drive Hindus out of their neighbourhood. The more responsible Muslim community leaders probably realized that violence against them would be worse if they drove out Hindus from their areas. In Muslim-dominated areas, Hindus and Muslims seemed to intermingle freely. Muslims would insist I go and see for myself and talk in private to Hindu families to verify that Hindus were indeed safe in their neighbourhoods. But in Hindu-dominated, areas there were usually no Muslims left; the Hindus, instead of feeling any regret about the hounding out of Muslims, mostly had vicious things to say against them. Most of them were determined not to allow Muslims back into their neighbourhood.

The Muslim families of Jogeshwari say:

If a crime has been committed, we are not opposed to the police doing a thorough investigation and arresting the real culprits and punishing them whether they are Hindus or Muslims. No one who is *shahrparast* and *sakunparast* (has a sense of citizenship and desire for peace) will want that the guilty should remain unpunished because a criminal or terrorist has no respect for human life and will not care for the well-being of his own community either. But the police have no business to arrest innocent people and terrorize all Muslims by supporting the killings of Muslims. They always come in the dead of night, beat up and drag people out of their homes. They have arrested innocent people, including heart patients and young boys whose exams are very close. If Muslims of Jogeshwari wanted to burn Hindu homes, why did we not burn the hundreds of those homes of Hindus which would catch fire far more easily than that one chawl? That house was made of bricks and, therefore, far more difficult to burn. Even at midnight you can see Hindus of our area stroll around without fear. We continued to mix with each other and also helped each other during this time of crisis.

When the state machinery itself gets into the act of systematic misinformation, it is difficult, even for the supposedly secular press, to stay non-partisan and ferret out the truth. Even in normal times, the press is used to accepting government and police information hand-outs as news, and publishes them mostly without any attempt at confirming and evaluating facts independently. In abnormal times, such as widespread riot situations, newspapers are so overwhelmed by having to keep track of events that they end up carrying biased reports routinely and promptly provided by police authorities. Even papers having the best intentions of carrying out independent investigation end up recycling official information.

One key feature of the misinformation campaign was to project

Muslim-dominated areas as mini-Pakistans, as dens of Muslim fundamentalists and anti-national forces. Reports accentuated the misconception that these areas had regular factories for manufacturing arms and warehouses where huge quantities of sophisticated weapons smuggled in from other Muslim countries, notably Pakistan, had been stocked for the purpose of destabilizing India.

Throughout this period, the police was routinely raiding Muslim bastis and commercial establishments but they never claimed to have recovered anything other than crude weapons and petrol bombs. During the entire December and January violence, there was only one instance where Muslims used an AK-47 gun.

My first exposure to the full implications of this misinformation campaign came when I had gone to Meerut as part of a team of *Manushi* women volunteers, to put together a report of what had happened during the Meerut–Malliana anti-Muslim riots of 1987. We were repeatedly warned by both the jawans of the Provincial Armed Constabulary (PAC) and the Hindu residents of Meerut not to enter Muslim majority areas such as Hashimpura or Gadda, saying that no Hindu ever came out alive from there. We were told in graphic detail how, only a few days ago, some women journalists who had been 'foolish' enough to venture in, were gang-raped and hacked to pieces.

Having gone through the sinister experience of anti-Sikh propaganda during and after the riots of 1984, we did not heed their advice and went to Hashimpura or Islampur. We were deeply moved by the openness and the warmth of the welcome extended to us by the Muslim residents because we came to listen to their version as well. In sharp contrast to this, Hindus were aggressively hostile to us if they got to know we had visited or talked to Muslim families. The motive behind this rumour campaign was obvious: to completely cut-off all communication channels between Hindus and Muslims— by drawing out Muslims from Hindu majority areas, and by making Hindus fear to go anywhere near a Muslim majority area or where they are in large clusters. Thus they succeed in making large sections of the press avoid talking to Muslims, thereby making their own anti-Muslim propaganda appear as facts. This has been a common experience of anyone trying to do an impartial investigation into any of the recent anti-Muslim riots.

I interviewed several families in Behrampada and managed to talk to a few Hindu families as well in buildings of Bandra East bordering Behrampada. It was pathetic to see how frightened and paranoid the Hindus had become even though none of their homes had been damaged. The families living in those buildings had not suffered any loss of life by attacks from Behrampada residents. Yet, they were petrified of talking, not just to strangers but even to people they knew. I remember vividly how when Shama Dalwai, who has lived in one of the buildings neighbouring Behrampada for years, rang the doorbell of a neighbour's house in order to introduce me to them, the young daughter who came to the door only peeped out and wouldn't open the door to Shama, even though Shama knows the family well and this young girl is a friend of Shama's daughter. Apart from not wanting to let me, a stranger, into the house, she was visibly afraid of Shama, presumably because Shama is married to a Muslim. Some other families too were extremely reluctant to talk, and gave evasive replies when they did speak to us.

In contrast, the Muslims seemed more than willing to talk to any Hindu who was ready to listen to their version. They also insisted on my meeting Hindus and Christians who live in Behrampada. Both the Hindus and Christians seemed relaxed with their Muslim neighbours, but seemed as worried about their future as the Muslims if the plan to get the basti removed succeeded. Muslims showed me with great pride the Hindu mandirs within Behrampada which had stayed perfectly safe during this period of crisis.

When a petrol bomb thrown from the Bandra side landed on the roof of one of the temples, it was young Muslims who rushed to extinguish the fire and save the temple from being damaged. The account of the basti people was corroborated by two Hindu families who had been witness to the violence but wanted to remain anonymous for fear of reprisals. To quote Madan Bajaj (not his real name), a businessman living in a building directly facing Behrampada:

What I saw the police do here is of the greatest danger to an independent nation. The local Shiv Sena MLA Sarpotdar went to one of our neighbouring buildings and told the residents there that one Inspector Jhende would be coming and they should give him permission to fire at Behrampada from the top of their building.

They say that the Muslims gathered together at the time of namaaz and attacked the police. That is not what happened. The police needed an excuse to fire at Muslims. My daughter phoned a Hindu friend of hers living in that particular building from which the attack was carried out. This friend said the Muslims were doing namaaz when the Shiv Sainiks threw bombs and stones on them from above. As a result of this attack, the Muslims ran helter-skelter. There was general panic. The police gave out that the Muslims had attacked the police. I saw the next incident with my own eyes. About 8–10 Muslims were hiding in the *galli*. After all, if you harass someone too much, then he will retaliate to some extent. These few Muslims retaliated by throwing stones and soda water bottles. It is possible that one or two petrol bombs were also thrown. One of them had a country-made revolver. But on the other side there were 150 Shiv Sainiks. And they were holding the policemen by the hand and saying 'Fire here, fire there.' Is the police under Shiv Sena control? Can we afford to have the police protect one community and kill the other? Then what is the point of having a government? The government machinery is so huge, the military was also called. Did the government not have 25 intelligence people who were impartial and could have reported correctly who is attacking whom?

In my view, anyone who can throw a bomb on someone while he is doing namaaz, must be a devil. None of our gods have ever said that one should throw bomb on a person of a different religion while he is praying. In the *Ramayan* there is the story of the rishis who asked Ram and Lakshman to protect them from rakshasas who were obstructing their yagna and prayers. But here the Hindus throw stones and bombs on people doing namaaz. I want to keep away from such a Hindu. For me he is no Hindu . . .

I personally witnessed this. On 6 December, after the mosque was demolished, the Hindus of nearby localities were throwing petrol bombs etcetera on houses in Behrampada. That would lead to confusion and Muslims would come out in the gallis. After this the police would sound a whistle and start firing on the Muslims in Behrampada from three or four different firing points. They were firing on women and children. I myself saw a woman die in the police firing. Did that woman have a machine-gun? In the whole of Bombay, only one machine gun was used by the Muslims from a mosque. And yet people say that Muslims got modern weapons from outside! It is well known that smugglers, both Hindus and Muslims, have acquired machine guns and AK-47 rifles. So one out of these reached somewhere and was used for the attack. But for the rest, *desi* revolvers, acid bombs and soda water bottles were used by the Muslims . . .

After firing at the Muslim basti, the police would go to Behrampada on the pretext of searching Muslim homes—but actually to beat, kill, arrest and terrorize them further. Even if one were to accept for a minute the argument that the Muslims were attacking, one has to concede that Hindus were attacking as well because so many Muslims could not have died otherwise. Then why were Hindu houses never searched? After this riot planning by Shiv Sena MLA Sarpotdar, the military arrived here and arrested him because they found him moving around with lots of weapons in his car during curfew time. But the police released him soon after. The farce of apprehending him was repeated a second time. But even though it was curfew time, the Shiv Sainiks brought hundreds of women along who shouted slogans and gathered outside the police station to get him released. Following

Sarpotdar's release, for one whole hour, crackers were burst and a victory procession organized to celebrate his release . . .

The curfew was only for the Muslims. Not for the Hindus. We could go out in our car . . .

My wife and I go daily for a morning walk. Very recently we saw a *pau* seller come into our locality on a cycle. He had come to see if these scoundrels needed bread since the supply was not available here due to the destruction of local bakeries. Right in front of my eyes, they broke his cycle and beat him up. The poor fellow ran for his life in that injured condition. Though I wanted to, I could not help him. There were just four or five hoodlums, but if I had intervened they might have broken my head as well, because I am no Bhim. I had two choices—either get beaten up along with him or kill my conscience and quietly return home . . .

There are 28 families in this building. I found only one man among them who seemed to agree with my views. For the rest, most people think otherwise, including well-educated people—architects, engineers. They keep repeating that 4000 to 5000 Muslims came to attack the Hindus with AK-47s and machine-guns when they could see from their houses that there were 10 Muslims with no more than soda water bottles and at least 150 Shiv Sainiks attacking them with police help from above during curfew time . . .

If I say all this to them openly, they will simply ostracize me and do everything more secretly. Already, I have seen that when I return from my morning walk and my neighbours are standing around the building talking to each other, they keep quiet when they see me . . .

One of our neighbouring bakery owners, who is a Muslim, calls me uncle. He came to our house at 11 p.m. some days ago. He said, 'They have burnt my shop. I'm going back to my village.' I told him, 'Wait for a few days. Humanity may return.' But if I was in his place, I would have also left out of fear. They had pre-planned it all. They selected Muslim shops and the Muslim *jhopadpattis* and burnt them. It may well be that they want builders of their community to benefit from this exodus. Hundreds of thousands of people have fled their homes in Bombay. In a jhopadpatti, how can one survive the police bullet?

There is just one Muslim family in this building. They are still here. We told them: 'You stay here. Someone will have to walk over our dead body to make you leave.'

At this point his daughter, Ramani (not her real name), intervened to tell me the pressures on this particular Muslim family:

An educated and very well-placed man who is supposed to be a good friend of this Muslim family said to their grown-up daughter: 'Is there no one in Behrampada (the neighbouring Muslim slum) who can protect you? Can't you go away and stay for a few days in someone's house?'

Ramani narrated some more of what she had witnessed in her neighbourhood:

On Sunday 10 January, two Muslim boys were murdered openly at 11 o'clock in the morning in a nearby building. They were doing some painting/whitewashing job in a Hindu home. First the Shiv Sainiks went and discussed something with the police. Sometime later the police blew their whistle. Hearing this, about 150 Shiv Sena boys came down. They carried swords, rods, tubelights and so on. Just imagine—two of those Muslim boys versus 150 of these Shiv Sainiks. They beat them so badly that there was blood all over the floor. After that they hurled their bodies down on the road. One of them died immediately. The other one was bleeding. And what the police did was to position itself, aiming its guns at the two boys who had been battered and said nothing to the Shiv Sainiks. They washed the bloodied floor with water and cleaned it. After this, police car came and took away the Muslim boys—one dead, the other dying. Shiv Sainiks went back home as if nothing had happened. After this the curfew was imposed. But the curfew has no meaning. The police in this area eat, bathe and sleep at the homes of the Shiv Sena *wallahs*. They know the entire planning, confer with each other and decide the timing. They have a signal. That is, they blow one whistle to announce 'action'. Then a second for readiness. And at the third whistle, they attack. And if the military is about to come around, the police tells these Shiv Sainiks to go home quietly.

A Muslim family has been living for many years in the building opposite ours. One day a lone woman was at home with her daughter. The Shiv Sena men came and forcefully began to kick the door. The poor woman was obviously scared, but being spirited she screamed loudly from inside and did not open the door. The building people came and said: 'She is our neighbour, don't kill her.' So those people went away. But they told the whole colony that they won't let any Muslim stay here. So all the Muslims in the buildings in this colony have gone away . . .'

One Sunday morning, one poor fellow who used to supply chickens had come to our colony. There were about 150-200 chickens in his van. The Shiv Sainiks stopped and ordered him to take out all the chickens. After this they beat him mercilessly and took away his chickens and had a feast. Later it turned out that the chicken seller was a Hindu. They thought he was a Muslim. Who is to check them even if they attack other Hindus?

One neighbourhood boy active in the Shiv Sena came and told me one day: 'You are not at all cooperative. We are ready to die for Hindus but you don't protect us. You don't let us pass through your compound in order to attack the Muslims.' I kept quiet. He then asked me to buy a ticket for Rs 100 towards *Nirdhaar Nidhi* (protection fund). I said, 'No, I don't believe in all this.' 'Why not?' he asked. 'We are ready to fight and die for Hindus and you are not even supporting us.' Maybe I am putting myself in danger by refusing to pay up. But this was something I couldn't accept . . .

Some days ago at about 8 p.m., one or two Shiv Sena boys came. They lit a fire on the road. They lit one piece of wood from that—it was not a petrol bomb—the wood was wrapped in cloth and dipped in kerosene. There is a Hindu building, No. 30, at the corner here facing Behrampada. The Shiv Sainiks threw the burning wood towards it and started shouting loudly. The police was standing there while this was happening. They shouted loudly and the police went running. What did they try to show? That Muslims of Behrampada had attacked and tried to set that Hindu building on fire. After this the police fired on the Muslims.

Then, at 11.30 p.m. these people raised an outcry again and converged from all directions. They threw petrol bombs at Behrampada. The police fired on Muslims again, so that they could not even douse the fire destroying their jhuggis. But they managed somehow to douse the fire. Then a third time, at 2.30 a.m., these people enacted the same drama all over again. We were trying desperately to contact the fire brigade but could not get the number. Later around 3.30 a.m., the fire brigade and the military arrived. The police misguided the military that the Muslims had fired from Behrampada and thrown the petrol bombs and tried to set No. 30 building on fire, when the truth was that the Shiv Sainiks had attacked. And you won't believe the theatricals and *hungama* done by Shiv Sena people. We were trembling. The spectacle was frightening. And it seemed these Muslims would be finished that day. Their cries were coming from inside their homes: 'Throw water here, we have been attacked, save us.' You could actually sense these people's suffering inside that jhopadpatti. If they made any attempts to douse the fire, the police would open fire at those who came out to do so. If they did not douse the fire, they would burn to death inside. I have a small daughter who woke up from her sleep and was crying and screaming hearing the commotion. She could sense that something terrible was happening. All the people at home were trembling. Mummy started getting loose motions.

From the way our neighbours reacted it seems their hearts are closed, their eyes too are shut. Here, in this building, everyone says, 'Behrampada should be removed. We don't need Behrampada.' The truth is they have never troubled us.

We have a common compound wall. The wall between Behrampada and our building No. 3, is common. All our cars stand here. Those people did not throw a stone here. If the Muslims wanted, they could have burnt our cars to ashes. They did not even touch them. They have never troubled us.

In fact, there would have been a fire in our compound because petrol bombs were thrown by Shiv Sainiks which fell in our compound. It was hell, you know. That day we couldn't sleep. Couldn't eat. But that building No. 30 was never searched. No person in that building was interrogated.

My sister-in-law had delivered and we were all at the hospital. A young woman from Behrampada was also admitted. Because of all this tension and fear she delivered in five months. And both her twins were born dead. There was so much fear in these poor people.

I found the Hindus far more terrified though their houses had not been attacked. Savita, a young housewife in her 30s, says that their entire life is hedged in by fear. 'Even if kitchen utensils fall and make a noise, we jump with fear. I can't go out of the house leaving our children alone.' She is one of the few who admits that none of the Hindus living in buildings bordering Behrampada have been physically harmed. She realizes that houses in Behrampada have been destroyed. That is precisely what makes her terrified. What if the Muslims decided to take revenge? I ask her: 'Have they threatened you or done anything menacing to you so far?' She says: 'No. In fact, they have been surprisingly nice. The other day a stone came and hit our window. I looked out and shouted to people in the basti, saying, 'Please don't throw stones at our house'. They said: 'Sister, rest assured, no stone will come to you from our side. It must be some mischiefmonger elsewhere. We won't let any harm come to you.' But Savita's fear is how long will they stay restrained if the attacks by the Hindus continue on the basti.

This is not to argue that Behrampada is an idyllic basti. Like all other slums in Bombay, this basti too has its own quota of criminals as well as people involved in trading drugs etcetera. But their proportion is perhaps smaller than the number of people involved in criminal activities among our MPs, MLAs and ministers. The internal politics of Behrampada is as messy as anywhere else in the country.

The residents of Behrampada behaved with restraint because they realized they couldn't afford to retaliate when Shiv Sena had the police on its side. Among others, an elderly Muslim, popularly known as 'Uncle' in the basti, played an important role in keeping tempers cool within the basti. He is president of the local Congress district committee but was unable to get any help from the party bosses.

He kept the excitable Muslim youth under control, saying:

Look, the Shiv Sainiks can run away after throwing stones or petrol bombs at you. Their purpose is only to provoke you. But as soon as you come rushing out, they are gone and the police takes over and kills you with bullets. So why let them bait you like this? Their petrol bombs will burn at the most four–five *jhopdas* at a time if we quickly extinguish the fire. But if you retaliate, they will not hesitate to reduce the entire basti to ashes.

The point worth emphasizing is that the violence done by the Hindus against the Muslims outdid the violence from the Muslim side. However, this is not to suggest that the Muslims refrained from retaliation out of choice. Muslims are an easily excitable community. Had it been a direct battle between Hindus and Muslims, the outcome for Hindus would have been very different. In Dharavi, for instance, where there is a sizeable Muslim population, the retaliation was fierce and many Hindu homes and shops were destroyed. They did not lag behind in the stabbing spree either. Given the fact that Muslims comprise a disproportionately large proportion of the Bombay underworld, their ability to wreak havoc is indeed enormous.

However, criminals normally tend to be 'secular' and thrive only with the protection of the police which happens to be Hindu-dominated. When that protection was withdrawn from the Muslim criminals and the police came to play an openly partisan role on the side of Hindu criminals mobilized by the Shiv Sena, even Muslim *goondas* became fairly helpless. Men like Dawood Ibrahim could not even protect their own business establishments from Hindu mobs. In such a situation, providing protection to fellow Muslims was out of the question. That is perhaps what lies behind their trying to settle scores through bomb blasts; for this requires surreptitious movement and not an open confrontation of the kind Hindu mobs could undertake.

Even in places where the Muslims did riot and retaliate to begin with, they had to give up their adventurism soon enough. Squatters Colony with about 2000 tenements was one such Muslim basti. Since Muslims living in this area are economically much better off than in most other parts of the city, this colony carries a lot of influence among the city Muslims and acts as a political centre for the community. That is why the eyes of the Shiv Sena were trained on this area.

After the police killings of Muslims on 7 December, there was a real communal riot in this colony, with Hindus and Muslims both attacking each other. A Hindu temple was burnt and the pujari was stabbed. There were numerous clashes leading to injuries on both sides. But by January, this colony of Muslims had been 'taught a proper lesson' and was completely immobilized. I visited this area with social workers Sanobar Kishwar and Tommy at the end of January. This small basti of Muslims, surrounded by Hindu areas, had been sealed off completely by a strict curfew imposed by the army. Oddly enough, the curfew seemed to have been imposed on the Muslims alone while life went on as normal in the Hindu areas across the street. When we tried to enter the basti, the soldiers trained their guns at us and ordered us to leave immediately and literally chased us out.

The Shiv Sena had engineered a riot in the Squatters Colony on 26 January by organizing a maha aarti. I quote from Sanobar's and Tommy's account since they had kept regular contact with this area:

There is a road which separates Squatters Colony from Govindnagar, which are the Muslim and Hindu areas respectively. Govindnagar is situated on a hill. If the road between the two colonies had been policed and patrolled well, it is unlikely that anything would have happened. The maha aarti finished at about 8.30 p.m. on 26 January and soon after a group from among the people at the maha aarti started raining stones from atop, since Govindnagar is situated at a height. First came the stones, followed by acid bulbs and petrol bombs. And then this gang started coming down the hill. The militant youths among the Muslims were well prepared. They retaliated and drove the Shiv Sainiks back up the hill. This went on for 15-20 minutes and then the police came and repeated the same pattern as elsewhere in Bombay.

The policemen did not come from the centre of the road. They came along with the Hindu crowd and were also hit by stones. But throwing stones is not enough protection. The police moved into the Muslim basti, firing into the *gullis* at point-blank range. A man by the name of Faqir Mohammad, a 66-year-old heart patient, was sitting at home on a *chatai*. Inspector Patil came down and tried to open the door of his house. The door did not open. He broke the window and shot this old man where he was sitting on the *chatai*. In this way, 36 rounds were fired. That is the official statement. Nine people were seriously injured, two were killed. All of those killed and injured were Muslims. Not one Hindu went to the hospital. These figures speak for themselves. But they will say that Muslims attacked Hindus. Before people like us could persuade one or two non-partisan reporters to come and see things for themselves, the police had made hand-outs that said that as one section of people at the maha aarti was going home, a 500-strong mob from the Squatters Colony attacked the former and after this the police had to intervene. Firing occurred in the melee and in that two people died.

The firing was followed by continuous intimidation, indiscriminate arrests and search operations. Thus the police had succeeded in taming this otherwise volatile basti.

As in all other riots and pogroms, women's agony went far beyond the physical hurt or bodily injury. The attempt was to inflict unforgettable humiliation and to destroy the sense of self-worth not just of the women but the entire community, of making men feel helpless and unable to defend their women from being publicly raped and mauled. Seema Hakim's story typifies the experience of those women who fell into the hands of the mob.

Seema, a 35-year-old Muslim woman, is the mother of three children. She used to live with her husband, Shahid Hakim, in Charkop Ashiana Cooperative society, Plot no. 435, Sector IV, Room 3, Kandivilli (west) Bombay. Shahid Hakim had a small business exporting readymade garments and costume jewellery to African countries.

Seema's husband was battered to death in front of her eyes, their house looted and destroyed and she herself was gangraped after being dragged and paraded naked in the entire neighbourhood. I met her at the Dombivilli police station along with some social workers of Bombay who were involved in relief and rehabilitation work. Before we reached, Seema had been subjected to several hours of interrogation and had been asked to identify her attackers. She came out looking as if she had been through a torture chamber. When we saw the statement that the police had recorded on Seema's behalf, we were not really surprised to find the FIR was rather wishy washy. It neither mentioned all those people who Seema said she had named as her attackers, nor her gangrape.

The police had not got Seema medically examined either. The three social workers insisted that Seema be allowed to make a fresh statement in their presence. I took down her account almost verbatim while she was making her second statement to the police.

In Seema's words:

On 10 January, between 8-9 p.m., rioting broke out in Charkop. On 11 February, Wasim, our landlord, told us that some young men were standing around our house saying *'Yahan aaj angaar lagaana hai.'* (We are going to put this house on fire today) So Wasim advised us to leave the house. There were no more than four or five Muslim families in that area. All of them had left their homes and had gone away. My husband was the president of the local Janata Dal unit. I was also a Janata Dal member. He said: 'Wasim is not an educated man. That is why he talks like that. Nobody is going to come and burn our chawl.' On the night of the 11th, my husband and I, along with our children, left Charkop to visit my mother-in-law's house in Malad. The next day, the ground floor of my mother-in-law's building was set on fire. So we stayed on with her. On January 14, my husband and I enquired from a local autorickshaw man about the situation in Charkop. We were given to understand that the trouble had subsided.

We left our children with my mother-in-law and went to Charkop around 4 p.m. by autorickshaw so that we could see our home. Shahid was carrying a lot of money because we had planned to go shopping for his Nairobi trip, after checking on our house. We saw that our one-room house was bolted from outside, but the lock we had put on before leaving on the 12th, was broken. We opened the door and fornd all our valuables missing. These included a Sony TV, VCR, mixer, Rs 75,000 in cash and eight *tolas* of gold, some wrist-watches, imported clothes and other valuables. The fridge was broken, so was all the crockery. The house had been ransacked. Old clothes were lying scattered all around.

Even the fan had been stolen. My husband said to me: 'Seema, forget our valuables, Let's go back.' As soon as we came out of the door, we were surrounded by a group of 25–50 men. They began to hit us. We pleaded with our neighbours to give us shelter, but no one let us find refuge in their house. They said: 'You are a Muslim and ours is a Hindu neighbourhood, *Mussalmanon ke saath aisa hi hona chahiye.*' (Muslims deserve to be treated like this).

The houses of other Muslim families had also been broken. Even the roof had been blasted. Hindu women from our neighbourhood said to the gangsters: 'Beat them up, pierce their eyes.'

There is a man called Rocky in our neighbourhood who is very friendly with the police. Policemen are forever visiting his house. He said: 'Muslims should be killed. *Bahut charbi hai inke upar.* (They have too much fat on them). What Saddam does, we should do to them.' After this our neighbouring women closed their doors.

The men first attacked Shahid. I stood next to him and said, 'Hit me, don't hit him.' They said, 'You Muslims come with weapons.' We pleaded, 'We have no weapons. We only came to see our house.'

They had various weapons in their hands such as *guftis*, knives and *trishuls*. One of them started the attack by hitting Shahid with a *saria* (iron rod). After that they all joined in the hitting. They were not our immediate neighbours. But they came out of the houses of our neighbours and had their support. The neighbours were watching. The people of our *chawl* were saying: 'We will not let Muslims live here.

Then they started hitting me as well. Shahid fell down when one of the mob hit him with a *gufti* and broke his head. Then they pierced two *guftis* into his stomach. One of them got hold of a little fire and began to burn my husband's face. The fellow who runs a cigarette shop in the neighbourhood was helping these fellows and even providing them with cigarettes to smoke through all this.

They then hit me with a *saria*. My eyes got blinded. At this point I heard them say, 'Strip her naked and then beat her,' With a knife they tore up my jumper (shirt) completely. Even the *salwar* got torn and it had half fallen off. My *dupatta* was also tattered. They again hit me with a *saria* and took off all the valuables. I was wearing a gold chain, two gold rings, four gold bangles, gold eartops and a watch. My husband was carrying Rs 15,000 in cash and a heavy gold ring. They took away all this as well. He was carrying all this money because he wanted to go shopping after checking the house. He was to return to Nairobi on the 17th, just three days later.

One of those men was being called Mama by the others. I don't know him personally but I can recognize him. He caught hold of my hair and dragged me all around the street. They paraded and dragged me naked around the neighbourhood for a couple of hours and then brought me back to our house. I looked around for my husband but I could not see him anywhere. They pushed me into our room and threw me down where our clothes were lying torn and scattered. I was hurt by the fall. They boxed me on my eyes and I passed out. They had fully removed my shirt while they were dragging me around the streets but my bra was still on me and the *salwar* was half down while they were parading me. While I was still conscious I had heard the man, who was being addressed by those men as Mama, say, 'Now you see what all we are going to do with you. We will do *zeenakhori* (rape) with you. Take off what remains of your clothes.' After which they boxed me on my eyes and hit me on my head with an iron rod. They boxed me on my chest, kicked me in my belly. That is when I fainted.

When I regained consciousness, I found that there was not a shred of clothing on my body. My body was filthy. I was bleeding from my private parts. Even now the whole place is swollen and full of wounds. It hurts both inside and outside. I was in great pain when I regained consciousness. It was already dark. I found and wore a *salwar* and shirt from among the clothes lying scattered around. Very slowly I dragged myself out and saw a white car standing on the road. It had a Maharashtra number plate. I crawled along the walls and somehow reached this car. A man was standing outside it and another sitting inside. I explained my predicament to them and pleaded with them to drop me to the nearby police *chowki*. They said, 'No, no, go away from here.' There was another aged man standing nearby. He told them, 'Take her to the main road and drop her off there.' These two men then took me and dropped me off some distance from the police station of Charkop. I saw a police jeep and another big vehicle and four constables standing outside the police post. I screamed, *Bhai saheb*, see what a condition I have been reduced to. My husband has been killed.'

An elderly policeman had responded to my plea for help by saying, 'Why did you go back to your house? You people deserve to be treated thus. (*Tum logon ke saath to aisa hona mangta hai*). You have too much *charbi* (fat) on you. Why did you go there to do *fasaad* (rioting)? They refused me help, saying: 'We know nothing. Whatever you want to say go report to Kandiville *thana*. Here is an autorickshaw. Take this and go.' They hailed an auto standing nearby and asked one of their men to go along with me. I came to this very police station. Here I was put in a police van with two-three policemen who took a round of that area. I was half-conscious. They took me back to the area of rioting. They saw a dead body on the way. Then they took me to our neighbourhood. I kept sitting in the van. The policemen went and saw our house. One of the constables offered me tea. I refused. I was lying down. He too misbehaved with me. [Earlier Seema had indicated that she was raped by some policemen as well.] But while in the police station she seemed reluctant to talk about it and talked on of 'misbehaviour'. 'He pressed my belly, he squeezed my hand and my breasts and insisted I should drink the tea saying, 'It will make you feel better.' So I drank the tea. I was conscious enough to know what was happening but had no strength to protest or do anything about it because I was feeling dizzy.

Then the policemen took me to Bhagwati Hospital (a public hospital). I stayed in that hospital for three days. But for two days no one from my family could visit me. I was constantly passing out. (*Hosh mein aati behosh hoti*). In that condition, even if I asked for water, they would not put a few drops of water in my mouth. On the third day, I screamed at the hospital staff, saying 'You do not even care to give me some water.'

They gave me two injections for sleeping and gave me a prescription but since none of my relatives were around, no medicines could be brought. They did not give me an internal examination [to check for evidence of rape]. They simply looked at the wound on my chest, put me through some X-rays and wrote out a prescription. I said to them, 'Please change my pyjama. This one is filthy and it hurts me to sit or move in it.' But they said: 'Keep quiet. If you need something call you family members.'

I was released on the 16th morning when my family arrived and they admitted me to Holy Cross Hospital in Bandra. Even during my stay in the Holy Cross Hospital, they did not conduct any internal examination. I asked my *devars* (brothers-in-law) but they said: 'It is eight-ten days now since it happened. What is the point of a check up now? We have to go for our brother's burial and you are worried about your medical check up.'

I stayed two three days in Holy Cross Hospital. They had said two weeks' rest but I insisted on being released because I used to feel very nervous in the hospital. (*Mera dil ghabrata tha.*)

I had given all these details to the police the very first time, mentioning all those attackers whom I could recognize. But today when the police brought in people for identification, they did not produce either Mama or the cigarette vendor who was helping them and seemed to know every one of them well.

She said that the policemen kept calling her repeatedly to the police station and detaining her there for hours; pressurizing her to withdraw her case of molestation against the police.

Most Hindus justify their anti-Muslim sentiment by pointing to irresponsible acts of Muslim leaders like Shahabuddin and other rabid fundamentalists. Ironically, this is precisely the time when Muslims are themselves turning away from their fanatic leadership because they see how their interests have been harmed by them. A government official involved with relief work, said:

In many of the Muslim refugee camps, Muslim men have come and told me, 'Sahib, such and such is a goonda. He instigated trouble in our area. Please have him arrested.' If they were as communal as Hindus make them out to be, they wouldn't be giving evidence against the criminal elements of their own community. But the Hindus today are demanding more and more stringent loyalty tests from the Muslims. They are making them agree to humiliating conditions as the price for being allowed to return to their original homes. Many were made to give written promises that they won't keep Muslim tenants or sell their homes to any Muslims when they quit.

Muslims are expected to submit to prove that they are not 'traitors' to this nation. They are expected to give unconditional loyalty to the Indian state and revere its totems and symbols with a fervour not expected from Hindus.

Shaila Satpute of Svadhar poignantly describes the implications of what is being demanded of the Muslims:

The whole atmosphere is so vitiated that this year we have had to go to Muslim areas and encourage them to celebrate the Republic Day because they need to get a certificate of loyalty to this country and 'prove' that they are not 'traitors'. Compare it to those days when in my youth, as members of Yuva Kranti Dal, we used to commemorate it as a Black Day saying the dalits and other downtrodden had not got their due rights in this Republic. I vividly remember the Independence Day of 15 August 1971. Our organization was as usual observing it as a Black Day. That night we had planned a *mashaal morcha* (torchlight procession). I was barely 15 days away from childbirth and I fought with my husband that I was going to join the Black Day march. He was worried for me because the police was expected to stop the procession and that could lead to a violent situation. He said, 'If violence breaks out, I'm not going to be able to protect you and bring you back home safely. I will want to stay with the processionists.' Such was our spirit and enthusiasm in those days.

But this year we had to go from area to area to tell Muslims: 'You must hoist the tricolour. You will then be taken as *deshbhakts* (patriots). Nobody will then abuse you.' See how much our own politics is diluted. In our area, the Hindu localities had *sannata* (total quiet) but in Muslim areas, the Republic Day was being celebrated like Id. They had put on music, children were wearing new clothes and carrying the national flag in their hands.

The Muslims of Bombay have become very defensive. By celebrating

26 January they wanted to assert this is as much their country as it is of the Hindus. I felt really sad that they are having to celebrate this despite all that has happened. What must they be feeling in their hearts! But they are not expressing it because they know if they mourn at this time, they will be called traitors.

Let me tell you of another incident this morning. Early in the morning I went for the Republic Day preparation to a slum area called Golibar. This was around 7.45 a.m. They were in a good mood as though to say, 'We will show you how loyal we are to the country.' At the outskirts of Golibar, where the Muslim majority area ends and the neighbouring Hindu majority area begins, there is a row of toilets separating the two localities. A 16-year-old Muslim boy who is a cripple had gone to use the toilet. His sight is so poor, he cannot even see properly. Some Hindu boys of the neighbouring area caught hold of him near the toilet and wounded him with knives and a sword. They broke both his hands and legs and injured him on the head as well.

He fell down right there. This happened just as I reached. The police which was stationed all around had done nothing to stop this attack. After it was all over, they came, looked around and took away the injured boy to the hospital. When I reached the spot, I found that a big crowd had gathered there. Their mood of celebration of a while ago had changed to anger and violence. They were very agitated at this stabbing and began to abuse. Seeing me there they said: '*Tai*, you don't believe us? Go up on the roof of this nearby house and see for yourself.' I quickly climbed a ladder and saw a bunch of Shiv Sena boys running with weapons in their hands. Seeing me, an obviously middle-class Hindu woman, climb up like that they were really taken aback. I had my *bindi* on and my manner of dress indicated that I was not one of the slum dwellers. They quickly tried to hide their weapons and stood in a corner and started watching me. On the other side, there is some railway land with a wall around it. Behind this wall the railway policemen were standing merrily watching the whole show.

They were at a height so they could see how the young Muslim boy was cut up. I remember that scene vividly. Their guns were pointed at the Muslim basti, in my direction—not towards the attackers though they had been witness to the attack. Their calculation obviously was that the Muslims will get provoked by the stabbing. There will be chaos. Some will climb on to the roof tops and throw stones at the Hindu basti. That will give the police an excuse to fire at the Muslims. But my coming on the scene had upset their calculation. I yelled at them and said: 'Why don't you fire your guns? You have aimed them at me and the basti. If you have the courage, fire at me!'

They did not fire but neither did they stop those boys. If they had wanted, they could have arrested them or stopped them from running away by firing at their legs. But they did nothing. When I challenged them to fire at me, they put down their guns and began talking among themselves and laughing at me.

I climbed down and explained and begged the Muslims not to get provoked saying, 'Please do not make *fasad* today. This is all being done deliberately to malign you. Don't retaliate in any way.' They agreed. What else could they do? They are defeated and helpless. Their anger can only be suicidal. They said to me, 'Tai, we want *aman* (peace). But if these people go on acting like this, how can we have peace?' But on my request, they restrained themselves and avoided any further incidents.

Even in normal times Muslims are despised and discriminated against and are consequently poor and ghettoized. Repeated spells of violence have led to greater destitution and marginalization of the Muslim community. This is facilitating large-scale criminalization of the community. If they are not allowed normal decent channels of livelihood, many of them will have no option but to turn to crime as a survival strategy. This will spell disaster not just for the Muslims but for the rest of the society as well.

During these riots various factors came into play. The role of goondas, anti-social elements, the builders' lobby and political rivalries have often been mentioned as the causes of violence. Yes, they were all active. But only up to a point did they determine the course of events. No society can be taken over by hoodlums and builders' lobbies unless society gives its sanction to such a take-over by criminal elements.

In the earlier riots, it was the goondas who used to participate and indulge in killing and looting. And it would be easy to curb their activity by arresting them under the anti-goonda laws and put them under preventive detention for disturbing peace. Only those with a crime record needed to be picked up and everything would become normal. But in recent years, rioting is not confined to such elements even though they are no doubt active as well. Large sections of the middle and upper classes are participating in and actively instigating violence. As a senior government officer narrated:

People, who in normal times are afraid to have a large-sized knife in their house, were throwing petrol bombs at the Muslims, burning people alive and taking a lot of perverse joy in it . . .

For instance, in Dadar, a middle-class area, I saw a young Muslim *gheraoed* by a lot of respectable-looking people, many of them bank employees. He was asked to do sit-ups and told: 'When you sit down you say *Jai Shri Ram* and when you get up, you say *Vande Mataram.*' And on the hundredth Jai Shri Ram he was knifed in front of everybody. I've never before seen such perverted joy in killing. It has often been said that unemployed youth join in these riots to give vent to their frustration, but this time most of those who participated in rioting were employed people from the better-off organized sector, including government employees and professional trade unionists. There was nothing chaotic about the violence. It was all done in an organized manner . . .

It is amazing how even the city elite are not only condoning but also encouraging such behaviour. In Bombay there is a colony called Kalanagar where artists, writers, painters, intellectuals and the upper middle-class— the supposedly sophisticated elite—live. They organize prestigious lectures on intellectual matters and *sangeet sabhas* and get a big audience. On January 12, I was driving in my car in this area. A little ahead of me was a tourist taxi with two women sitting in the back seat. The taxi was asked to stop by two-three young men. They asked the taxi man his name. He probably uttered some Hindu name and they let him pass. The moment the taxi man had gone a little distance, they signalled, waving their hands to another group. Suddenly, about 25 men emerged from the other side with stones, lathis and knives in their hands and they blocked the road so that the taxi had to halt.

This gang of men asked him his name again and without paying heed to what answer he gave, they asked for his licence. From his licence papers they confirmed that he was a Muslim trying to pass himself off as a Hindu. Before he could say anything, someone pulled his pants down. And they started hitting him all over. He dropped down vomiting blood. Then some of them approached the two Hindu Gujarati women (one middle-aged and the other a young girl) who were sitting in the back seat of the taxi and said to them; '*Mataji/behenji, Bambai ki haalat bahut kharab hai, aap aage mat jayiye. Abhi yahaan hamara ghar hai.*' A man who looked visibly upper middle-class came from a nearby building, opened the taxi dickey, took out the bags of these two women and said to them: 'You can sit in our house safely. He's a Muslim, don't worry about him.' He escorted these two women to a nearby building.

After this, they overturned the taxi. It fell on its side. One man came with a small can of petrol from a nearby petrol pump right around the corner. While he was pouring petrol, another man came with a torch in hand, singing that famous national unity song that comes on TV, '*Mile sur tumhara hamaara*' (May your and my tune become one). They burnt the taxi. The injured Muslim boy tried in vain to get up and run, but when he got up, his pants fell down. While trying to pull his pants up, he was grabbed hold of by this gang who started battering him all over again. And as he fell down again, they picked a big stone slab lying on the pavement where some repair work was on, and with a shout of '*Jai Shri Ram*' they dropped it down on his chest with a bang. All this while several upper middle-class men were witnessing the scene from their balconies, as though they were watching a film. Not only that, there were several policemen standing not too far away from this scene who made not the feeblest attempt to stop this brutal murder in broad daylight.

Had I intervened, they would have said 'We will kill you first and him later.' Remember, I too have a beard. That alone would have been enough to get them provoked, to make them assume that I was Muslim. They forgot that even Shivaji sported a full, long beard. In those days of frenzy, they wouldn't have spared Shivaji himself, for what they now consider a Muslim symbol.

Near Dadar station, there is a famous store called Dawood Shoe Mart owned by a Muslim. After this was looted, expensive shoes were being sold openly for Rs 15 to 20 on the pavement. The middle class happily came and bought those and other looted goods at throw-away prices. Many even joined in the looting. They took whatever they could lay their hands on and later shamelessly went around exchanging these looted shoes with their friends in case they had picked the wrong sizes. This was an open acknowledgement of their crime, yet no one seemed to feel ashamed.

In some middle-class and elite areas, the Muslims were hounded due to threats from the Shiv Sena. A section of the city elite were indeed somewhat shaken by the brazenness of the mobsters who came even to posh areas threatening to burn down the multi-storey buildings where Muslim families also stayed. In such cases they had to organize heavy security around their buildings for their own self-protection because they knew that once the Shiv Sainiks came in, their arson and looting could not possibly stay confined to Muslim apartments. Many rich Muslims paid heavy sums as protection money to Shiv Sena (just as Hindus did) but even that did not often save the Muslims. In almost all multi-storey buildings people had removed all name-plates so that the Shiv Sainiks could not easily identify the buildings where some Muslim families lived. In many such buildings, even Hindus asked their Muslim neighbours to move out, at least temporarily, in order not to jeopardize the safety of the entire building. Many, including famous Muslim film stars, had to go and stay in hotels for those days of frenzy.

In many instances, middle-class families actively worked to make their Muslim neighbours feel insecure. For instance, in the Reserve Bank Colony situated behind Maratha Mandir, officers' families forced fellow Muslim officers to leave the colony. Even the little children of officers played an active role—they would stone the windows of Muslim homes, abuse, threaten and beat up Muslim children.

In many areas, residents have passed resolutions that Muslims would not be allowed to stay there. Those involved with rehabilitation work have heard many Hindus declare openly: 'We don't want Pakistan in our area—*Hamare area mein Pakistan nahin chahiye.*'

The popularity of Shiv Sena among the middle and upper classes during this phase can be gauged by the sudden increase in the circulation of the Shiv Sena paper *Saamna*. For the first time it reached the homes of the elite which till now prided themselves on reading only the likes of *India Today* and *Time* magazine. All of a sudden, *Saamna* and Sharad Pawar's *Navakaal* were eagerly sought after. In some places *Saamna* would be read publicly and displayed prominently at various street corners. On certain days the premium price of *Saamna* has been quoted at Rs 16 to Rs 25. Thackeray had succeeded in convincing even the upper-class Hindus that he was their saviour.

Around 18 January, a rumour was spread that Bal Thackeray was going to be arrested. Personnel managers of public sector undertakings started telephoning the police to find out if it was really true. They were saying that their employees were spontaneously walking out of their offices. Bazaars started closing down, offices were deserted and shops looted and burnt just on the basis of that rumour. As a result, the government had to make repeated announcements on radio and television as well as through the use of microphones in public places, saying, 'Rest assured. Bal Thackeray is not arrested.'

Murders were being committed in broad daylight—not just in slums but also in middle-class and upper-class colonies, and those who watched, by and large, applauded this violence rather than demand action against the culprits. School children and college-going boys of middle-class families carried knives and took pride in stabbing fellow Muslim students. Similarly, thousands of middle-class people, including women, children and teenagers, would collect for the so-called maha aartis even at curfew times, even though they knew the aartis were only an excuse for starting more violence, thus providing legitimacy to criminal acts. The police joined them as well.

However, some sections of the city elite demonstrated their concern by spontaneously coming together in a broad-based forum called Citizens for Peace (CFP). It was started by some people living in the posh Carmichael Road area witnessing with their own eyes the mayhem organized by the Shiv Sainiks. About 150 Muslim families who had been torched out of their homes came and sought shelter in one of the high-rise buildings. They were followed by Shiv Sainiks with weapons in hand, demanding that these Muslims be handed back to them. The residents resisted, called the police and handed over the Muslims to them. This triggered off the setting up of CFP which not only tried to raise resources for relief work but also set up a round-the-clock hotline so that trapped families could call for help and CFP would try to pressure the police or army to take note of that complaint. Their success in putting together a number of volunteers and collecting a substantial amount of relief supplies at a time when the majority of people in Bombay, including middle-class intellectuals, felt Muslims deserved what happened to them was a remarkable achievement. Their letting the administration know that they were monitoring government actions worked to some extent. In addition, a number of people from the civil liberties and left-oriented organizations organized a number of relief camps. Among the city's elite, the Jain community was in the forefront of raising funds and other resources for relief work.

One of the most disturbing features of this riot was the large-scale, enthusiastic participation of women and young girls in the acts of violence. The fascination of the women for the Sangh Parivar politics is especially noteworthy considering that their politics is brazenly macho, so much so that they have even obliterated Sita from Ram's world.

For centuries '*Jai Siya Ram*' has been a common form of greeting used by ordinary Hindus in the villages of North India. Even the unfair banishment of Sita by Ram could not separate the two in the minds of those people for whom the *Ramayana* presented a revered *dharmic* text. Just as Shiv cannot be conceived of without his Shakti, so is Ram inconceivable without Sita. It is noteworthy that Sita's name always comes before Ram's in the popular chant: 'Jai Siya Ram'.

But the BJP–RSS–VHP combine has consciously tried to obliterate Sita's name by amending the traditional greeting to 'Jai Shri Ram'. This obviously fits in with the martial Rambo type of Ram that it is trying to recreate in order to preach its politics of hatred and bloodshed. It has no use for the gentle and caring Ram of Valmiki, Tulsi and a host of other versions of the *Ramayana*—Ram who cries like a child in *viyog* when Sita is abducted, Ram who is a loving and caring husband, brother and son.

Those who are actively involved in instigating riots and killings, burning people's homes, killing their near and dear ones brutally in front of their eyes, not even sparing little children, can have no use for a non-macho Ram. *'Logon ke ghar jalane wale, Ram ki grisasthi kaise basi rehne denge?'* (Those who are destroying people's homes cannot let Ram's household stay intact).

The aversion of the Sangh Parivar to Sita is understandable. Sita's presence next to Ram poses a real threat to the hate-soaked ideology of the Sangh Parivar because Sita is the one who preached pacifism to Ram. The *Aranya Kand* records a very moving interaction between Sita and Ram—one of those rare occasions when Sita presumes to advise and correct Ram:

There evils are born of desire: speaking untruth—a great sin indeed; but worse still are: coveting another's wife and harming those against whom one has no quarrel. O Ram, you have never uttered a lie, nor will you ever be found to have that failing. And the vice of guilty love has never been yours—not even in thought, always true that you are to your wedded wife.
And this third great evil, thirst of blood where there is no enmity, to which the ignorant are prone, seems to be alarmingly near you.
O hero, my prayer is that when, armed with the bow, you are engaged in waging war against the rakshasas who have this forest for their home, you may never allow yourself to slay indiscriminately those who are not to blame... .

A Sita who exhorts Ram that he should never allow himself to slay indiscriminately those who are not to blame cannot be allowed to be one with Ram. The Sangh Parivar's idea of an appropriate consort for Ram would be a venom-spewing Rithambara type of woman who delights in sowing hatred and violence among the Hindus. Contrast Sita's words with some extracts from Rithambara's speeches:

We could not teach them [Muslims] with words, now let us teach them with kicks... . Let there be bloodshed once and for all... ,
Throw off the cloak of cowardice and impotence. Learn to sing songs of valour and courage. Do not display any love (*preet*). Let this fire blaze magnificently. Let there be a conflagration rather that this slow tortuous simmering... . We have come out to strengthen the immense Hindu shakti into a fist... . You kept saying you will offer sacrifices. We will take thousands of sacrifices. Now we will not only shed our own blood, but the blood of others, too... . That Mahatma Gandhi led you to ruin... . Tie up your religiosity and kindness into a bundle and throw it in the *Jamuna maiya* [river Yamuna]... . Hindustan is foolish, it refuses to give up its foolish

course, it gets beaten and forgives it opponent. Why? Because this is the land of Buddha and the Mahatma, Guru Nanak Dev and other Sants who sacrificed their lives, offered their necks but could not break the neck of others... .

Unfortunately, the Sangh Parivar has been avidly accepted by many women.

So far, women in India have mostly entered politics as wives, mothers and daughters of powerful male politicians. The Sangh Parivar has changed this by making space for two young women— Uma Bharti and Rithambara—in leading roles, both of whom came into politics on their own strength rather than through family connection. They have been surprisingly successful in mobilizing women in outfits like Durga Vahini, thus making a distorted use of another traditional Hindu symbol. *Durga* is supposed to have destroyed evil; but the Sangh Parivar's Durgas lead riotous mobs to burn homes and kill innocent people.

Several people in Bombay told me that for the first time in their lives they had witnessed women enthusiastically supporting violence. Normally, women do not applaud rape. But this time many Hindu women in Bombay were openly justifying the rape of Muslim women. They would argue: 'Why not? What is wrong with it? For hundreds and thousands of years, Muslims have done the same to Hindus. We are settling those old scores because now we are powerful and united. They have invited it on themselves.'

In Bombay, a woman corporator was killed by a police bullet while she was leading a riotous mob in an attack on Muslim homes and shops. This is one of the rare cases of a riotous mob being fired upon by the police. So confident was this woman corporator of police support that when a police officer ordered her to stop, she did not pay any heed and continued leading the violence. She had not calculated that there were still a few policemen who wanted to stop the rioting. It is alleged that she was involved in all kinds of illicit activities, including running of liquor dens. She belonged to that faction of the Republican Party which has an alliance with the Congress (I).

Likewise, another woman 'social worker' of the Congress (I), called Malsa, is supposed to have led the mob which burnt and looted a big commercial complex of ready-made garments and leather goods in Dharavi. Women and young girls avidly looting shops along with men was a common sight in Bombay during the January riots.

I heard accounts of how Hindu women dragged Muslim women and children out of their homes and joined the men in stoning them and setting them on fire.

When Madhukar Sarpotdar, the Shiv Sena MLA who played a very prominent role in instigating riots, was arrested by an army officer for carrying a carload of weapons during curfew hours, hundreds of women (some say several thousand) came and lay down on the road in front of the army vehicles, saying they could take away Sarpotdar only over the women's dead bodies. They went and demonstrated outside the police station and got Sarpotdar released. During the same period, when in Behrampada several Muslim jhuggis were set on fire by Shiv Sainiks, women of Shiv Sena families came and sat on the streets to prevent the fire brigade from reaching Behrampada.

However, many Hindu women who were mobilized by the Shiv Sena joined out of fear rather than conviction. The women of jhopadpattis who were taken to protest against Sarpotdar's arrest were told that the government was planning to arrest all able-bodied Hindus, along with Sarpotdar, under pressure from the Muslims: 'If you don't protest now, Shiv Sainiks won't help you when your husband or son gets arrested,' they were warned.

But there were at least a few courageous women who dared to go against the tide and intervened openly and sometimes even effectively in saving precious lives. While many might not have been able to intervene at the time of the violence, they joined the relief work. A few of them belonged to women's organizations, some others had been active in civil liberties organizations and a few were grassroot level political workers of the Janata Dal as well as the Congress. Such people were isolated within their own parties and worked mostly on their individual strength because no party or mass organization could put its act together and combat the violence in an organized way. Their efforts were sporadic and/or isolated. Yet sometimes they succeeded.

I quote from the account of Shaila Satpute, of the Janata Dal and one of the founders of a women's organization called Svadhar:

During the height of rioting in January, a mob of about 10,000 people had gathered near where we live. We came down to find out what had happened and were told that the nearby marble shop-owners, who are Muslims, had hoarded weapons inside their shop godowns. Behind these Muslim shops live a few Muslim families. The rest of the neighbourhood is inhabited by Hindus. We went to the local police station and asked the man in charge why he had let a mob gather at a time of such tension. The police repeated the same allegation about Muslims having stored weapons in those shops. The Hindus were all ready to attack and burn those shops after stoning them. But we managed to persuade the police to come with us, along with three-four such Muslims who are trusted and respected by their community. In addition, I prevailed upon the BJP MLA, Abhiram Singh, and the local corporator belonging to the Shiv Sena to come with us and conduct a thorough search of those Muslim shops. Nothing was found except marble slabs and the marble stones that are left over when slabs are cut. In addition, we found a few fused tubelights. In an establishment which uses 50 tubelights, finding four or five fused ones is not unusual. But there were no weapons there whatsoever. Yet had I not gone and intervened, those shops would have been destroyed that day and the owners physically attacked. Luckily, our local Shiv Sena corporator is a relatively mild man but in other places such rumours have led to brutal destruction.

However, Shaila did not succeed all the time. She could not even save the homes of her own party workers.

In my own area, each one of our Muslim party workers had their homes destroyed. There is a man called Khursheed who was to be elected our local unit president. When I heard that a 5000-strong mob had gathered to attack his house, I rushed there. But one of our senior party workers told me, 'Tai, you should go back. Don't stop here a minute. They will strip you and attack you as well.' Khursheed's house was looted and destroyed. He somehow managed to run away and save his life.

Likewise, Sushobha Barve's work in Dharavi is supposed to have saved many caught in a potentially explosive situation. Another name that was gratefully mentioned by the Muslims was that of Shirley Pawar, a woman corporator belonging to the Congress (I). She is supposed to have escorted more than a hundred Muslims to safety. Among others who described her courage and compassion were 20-year-old Parveen and her husband, Mohammad Hussain, who used to live in Tardeo. Their house was reduced to rubble right in front of their eyes and all the Muslim families of the area were asked to leave. Hussain says:

It was Shirley Pawar (he calls her Sarli Pawar), a local Congress woman leader, who helped all the surviving Muslims to escape from that area. If she had not helped us, all of us would have fallen as corpses. The police *chowki* did not help us at all. She escorted all of us Muslims out of that area. She brought some families to Bombay Central, some others to Madanpura and went back after seeing us off safely. But when she returned to that area, she too was threatened for protecting the Muslims. But she did whatever was in within reach. She was able to bring out 100-150 people.

But on the whole, women's enthusiastic endorsement of and participation in the riots shattered the popular stereotype of women as being innately more peace-loving and compassionate.

The biggest gainer from this violence was the Shiv Sena because their leaders were the only ones who dared play an open role in it and boast of their doings. The other parties had to perforce pretend that they were not happy with it, even when their leaders and cadres played an active part in fomenting the bloodshed.

Before the riots the Shiv Sena's political fortunes were sinking due to infighting in the party leading to continuing defections. In the last municipal elections they were badly defeated. The post of the opposition leader also went out of their hands and passed on to the BJP. Therefore, the Shiv Sena decided to capitalize on the Hindutva wave created due to the Ram Mandir campaign and outdo the BJP in rioting as well as in boasting of their role in the Babri Masjid demolition.

A young Shiv Sainik named Jais provided a fairly lucid statement explaining the logic behind Shiv Sena's targeting of Muslims. He works with his father who runs a furniture business in Bandra East. He narrated how after four days of mayhem, Bal Thackeray reportedly told Shiv Sainiks to halt the violence for a while because the Shiv Sena would need another anti-Muslim wave at election time. Jais boasted that had they been allowed another week of rioting, not a single Muslim would be alive in Bombay. In response to our question: 'Would you like to kill all Muslims?' his answer was: 'No, all Muslims should not be killed at once. Otherwise, what issue would we Hindus have left to fight for? Whenever there is an election, we need to kill a few Muslims to revive the anti-Muslim sentiment. If all the Muslims go away, we will have no enemy left and the Hindus will start fighting among themselves.' He added by way of an explanation: 'Whenever among our friends, young boys get angry and start a fight, we say, "*Bhai*, don't fight with another Hindu. Go and beat up or kill a Mussalman and cool your anger." If we fight among ourselves, we will become weak. We want some Muslims to stay in India, otherwise Hindus will have no issue to unite them politically'.

We asked him whether after collecting protection money from

Hindus in the name of Nirdhaar Nidhi, Hindus will actually get security or the money would be embezzled. His answer was: '*Khayenge to hamare log khayenge.*' (If the money is embezzled, it will be by one own people). Bal Thackeray also said in response to allegations of corruption among Shiv Sainiks, '*Apne logon ko khane do.*' (Let our own people embezzle).

Jais, who prides himself for being one of the few who became a Shiv Sainik much before it became fashionable among young boys to join the organization, seemed unhappy at the way the new breed of Shiv Sainiks were getting out of control. He narrated an incident in which his fellow Sainiks caught hold of a young boy, poured kerosene over him and lit a fire. The boy cried out, saying, 'Don't kill me. I am a Hindu. My name is Shankar.' But the Sainiks yelled back, 'You don't know Marathi. What kind of a Hindu are you?' and burnt him to death.

Jais's explanation was: '*Aur kya hoga,* madam? *Jo ladkon ki patthar marne ki bhi aukat nahin hai, unke haath mein bandook pakda denge, to aise hi hoga na phir.*' (Such things are bound to happen if you put guns in the hands of boys who have not yet learnt to pelt stones properly.) This was in the context of Bal Thackeray apparently calling all the Shiv Sena *pramukhs* to a meeting and saying, 'It is a shame on Hindu dharma that you are not teaching Muslims a lesson. Take whatever weapons you want. I'll open our stores and give you as many guns and weapons as you ask for. But you must do a good job.'

He admits to Shiv Sena having given them weapons and that all their *shakhas* have a big stock. Most Sainiks keep their weapons in the Sena office instead of taking them home so that they don't get caught in the eventuality of a police raid. But during the entire period of December and January riots, the police did not once raid any of the Shiv Sena offices even while they were daily raiding Muslim bastis.

He also narrated how for the first time he felt bad over anti-Muslim violence when an old Muslim friend of his, who used to join them whenever they went on a looting spree, became a victim of the current phase of violence. This friend's small shop of cassettes was burnt by his own friends. Jais says, 'I was very upset when my friend said to us, 'You people have burnt my shop, how will I live now? Throw me also into the fire".' Jais told us that this time Sainiks did not even spare the few Muslims who had joined the Shiv Sena.

There is general consensus in Bombay that the enormous clout that the Shiv Sena has acquired over the years is primarily due to the political patronage Bal Thackeray and his hoodlum brigade has received from the ruling Congress party. Bal Thackeray is often referred to as the *paltu kutta* (pet dog) of successive chief ministers, starting with Vasantrao Naik, who patronized him along with leading industrialists, to break the powerful trade union movement led by Dutta Samant in Bombay. Vasantdada Patil encouraged him to spread to rural areas to destroy the influence of Shetkari Sangathana among the peasantry. Sharad Pawar, the present chief minister, has been hand in glove with him and used the Sainiks to settle scores with political rivals of all kinds. As a result, Thackeray has become so powerful that no one dare take action against him.

Someone who has worked closely with various politicians summed up the reason for Thackeray's clout succinctly:

People say that Bal Thackeray was able to get politically so powerful because Shiv Sainiks are able to extort huge sums of money from industrialists and everybody else. I don't think money makes that much of a difference. If I give you Rs 100 crore tomorrow you will not be able to become a big political leader with that alone. But the moment I give you political power and moral legitimacy, things start changing. When successive chief ministers themselves invite Bal Thackeray and let him interfere in and influence police functioning and general government policy, all because they can use his hoodlum brigades to settle scores with political rivals or combat the challenge posed by various movements, such as the farmer's or the trade union movement, that amounts to actually building Thackeray's political clout. On his own he is a cipher. But the backing of all these powerful politicians makes him the invincible monster he has become.

Day after day, during the riots, Shiv Sena's mouthpiece, *Saamna*, came out with the most provocative lies, openly instigating violence against the Muslims. Despite their having violated every possible law of the land, their leaders were neither arrested nor their papers censored or banned. Shiv Sainiks openly talked about Congress MP Sunil Dutt and a senior police officer, among others, being on their hit list, for having played a supposedly anti-Hindu role. Sunil Dutt is the only national-level political figure who risked his very life to save Muslims and got actively involved in relief work. He even resigned in protest against his own party's role in the violence; but his resignation was not accepted.

Even as rehabilitation work started, Shiv Sainiks were openly threatening that Muslims would not be allowed to return to their old neighbourhoods. It was another way of either grabbing the deserted homes and shops or demanding a pay off. A political worker involved with relief work said that when efforts were made to encourage the Muslims to go back to their homes, the Shiv Sainiks would say openly: 'Give us such and such amount per jhuggi or shop or give us your *madrasa* or some other property as a fee for letting you come back.'

Shiv Sena trade unions were not letting Muslims come back to their jobs. In February, there were a number of instances of Muslim workers being physically attacked or even killed by Shiv Sainiks when they came to rejoin their jobs. Muslim street vendors and hawkers were likewise being prevented from plying their trade in Hindu or mixed areas. Muslim school children weren't allowed to come back to schools.

The winning over of a large number of Dalits to the cause of the Shiv Sena played an important role in making the riots so widespread as most poor Muslim bastis are surrounded by Dalit bastis. By successfully creating a fear psychosis among the Hindus, the Shiv Sena managed to persuade Hindus across the spectrum that they had saved them from the Muslims.

At the height of the anti-Muslim violence, the *Indian Express* published a news item which said that a Pakistani ship carrying a huge arsenal of weapons was intercepted by the Indian coast guard. The news report implied that the weapons were meant for the Muslims to help them fight against the Hindus. Shiv Sena's *Saamna* went much further in fuelling such rumours and said that 400–500 Muslims would come in black uniforms and attack Hindu houses and buildings. The Shiv Sena made a careful plan, as a result of which from Cuffe Parade to Boriviii, every Hindu stayed awake and kept guard over his respective building at night.

A businessman who requested anonymity, described thus the madness that had gripped Bombay:

In my own building I saw my neighbours collecting chilli powder and soda bottles. I asked them: 'The police is sitting downstairs. The military is all around. If their bullets cannot protect you, how will you protect yourself with soda bottles? The rumour is 400–500 men with modern weapons are going to come to attack you. Will you be able to protect yourself from them with chilli powder?'

But when sanity is lost, a person's capacity to think and understand also goes. The result was that the Shiv Sena was successful. When some Muslim goondas were raided, all that was discovered was swords and petrol bombs. In Andheri, the Shiv Sena corporator himself lied that 400–500 Muslims came to attack him, and the Shiv Sainiks went and burnt the huts of the poor and the small shops owned by Muslims. But the Hindus do not pause to ask, 'How is it that if Muslims have all these modern weapons, how come they are the ones to get killed most? It's mostly their homes which got burnt. Very few Hindus were killed.'

The Shiv Sena hoodlums are not content with terrorizing the Muslims alone. In fact, like all terrorists they have to first strike fear in the hearts of their own community in order that they can function without hindrance. Their targets too have kept changing. First it was all non-Maharashtrians, especially, South Indians, then rival trade unions, and for some years even Sikhs. Now it is the turn of Muslims and all those Hindus who dare oppose them.

Even at normal times, the people of Bombay have become used to paying whatever contributions Shiv Sainiks demand of them at festivals and other occasions. But following the riots, Shiv Sainiks were extorting huge sums of money from Hindus which no one dared refuse. Bal Thackeray gave an open call for collecting Rs 100 crores as election funds.

Even though Shiv Sainiks were committing violence in the name of safeguarding Hindus, yet the Hindus seemed far more petrified of Shiv Sena than even the Muslims. While Muslims would openly criticize the role of Shiv Sena and never once refused to be identified or photographed when they gave statements regarding the riots, very few Hindus were willing to talk about the violence. And the few who did, insisted on anonymity—such was the terror the Shiv Sena had struck in the minds of those whom they claimed to defend.

The Shiv Sena and the Sangh Parivar have been able to motivate large sections of Hindus towards criminal activities by playing on the negative stereotypes of the two communities and their views of each other as well as of themselves. Hindus harbour deep-seated fears of Muslims because they believe them to be innately cruel and violent. Their non-vegetarian food habits versus the vegetarianism of upper-caste Hindus and the fact that many of the butcher community people are Muslims, feeds the stereotype image of Muslims as *kasais* (killers). The presence of a large number of Muslims among the underworld dons confirms the stereotype of their being inherently violent. Hindus also believe that Muslims are more virile and circumcision helps them to 'perform' better. Thus, they are paranoid about Muslims being sexually attractive to Hindu women.

Interestingly, Muslims have come to accept some of this as their self-portrait, just as Hindus have accepted the Muslim portrayal of

Hindus being cowards. Shiv Sena cadres say openly that they will not allow the Muslims to have a monopoly on *dadagiri*. Bhisham Sahni's novel, *Tamas*, had a powerful scene in which a young Hindu boy recruited by the RSS is taught to overcome his revulsion of blood by killing a hen with his own hands, by way of an initiation rite. The Sangh Parivar and Shiv Sainiks are now taking these rites much further by encouraging Hindus to believe that by learning to kill and torture people and rape women, they are getting rid of the 'fatal flaw' of Hindus—namely, their propensity towards non-violence.

The large-scale criminalization of the Hindu community being fostered by the politics of Shiv Sena and Sangh Parivar by making young men feel 'brave' and righteous while looting and killing constitutes a grave threat for the well-being of the Hindu community.

The Sangh Parivar and Shiv Sena project themselves as the saviour of the Hindu dharma. In actual fact they are destroying both the social and moral fabric of the Hindu community as well as its dharma. For Hindus, the word dharma symbolizes far more than what the West understands by the word religion. Dharma stands for varied ethical codes of conduct for different roles and situations that a person has to deal with in life. It also means the essence or the inner law of one's being. Thus there is *matra dharma, putra dharma, pitra dharma, raj dharma, guru dharma, manav dharma, kshatriya dharma*, and so on. These refer to the ethical codes of conduct expected of a person as a mother, son, father, as a ruler, as a guru, as a human being, as a warrior. The list is endless and includes virtually every aspect of human life and every social relationship.

A person is enjoined to follow a specific moral code for each of the different roles he/she performs in society as well as in family life. The dharmic world view does not make allowances like, 'All is fair in love and war.' Warriors have to follow a strict code and enemies have to be dealt with honourably. Even gods are not forgiven for violating that code. For instance, Krishna persuading Yudhisthir to lie in order to win the Mahabharat war or telling Duryodhana that he should not go naked in front of his mother, Gandhari, when she had asked him to appear thus in order to make his body invincible are seen as violations of the code of conduct expected in warfare.

A Hindu is enjoined to treat the entire universe as one's family. *Vasudhaiva Kutumbakam* is the philosophical ideal. This gets translated into a concrete, everyday code of conduct in the popular culture as *padosi* dharma, or *mohalledari*. Neighbours are supposed to come to each other's help in times of need, share each other's joys and sorrows, protect each other from harm by outsiders, forget their grievances in times of illness or death in the house of a neighbour and share their sorrow and offer to help. This ensures mutual cooperation and provides valuable social security which is not available to people living in atomized societies, where there is no such sense of mutual obligations. So strong is the hold of this ideology of duty to one's neighbours that in many stable neighbourhoods even goondas are made to honour it by keeping their nefarious activities outside the neighbourhood and avoid teasing and misbehaving with the women of their neighbourhood, no matter how badly they may behave outside. The ideology demands that all the women of one's neighbourhood or village are to be treated as sisters or mothers.

In our own neighbourhood in Lajpat Nagar, I have never witnessed young boys indulging in sexual harassment of the young girls of the neighbourhood, though I am sure many of them do so outside. During the anti-Sikh riots of 1984 many neighbourhoods organized night-long vigils together and successfully repelled attackers. In all those areas in Delhi where neighbours came to protect the Sikhs, the latter were saved from the mob violence. Most of the violence was done by goonda brigades brought in from 'outside'. Even in those areas, where joint Hindu–Sikh defence of the neighbourhood was not organized, such as the poorer localities in trans-Yamuna areas, many Sikh families testified how even though their homes were destroyed, they were able to save their lives because of shelter provided by their neighbours. In the part of Delhi where my parents live, when a group of hoodlums came to burn a house belonging to Sikhs, just two unarmed old people—my father along with an 80-year-old woman—were able to prevail upon the rioters to go away without burning that house. In most of the earlier riots, including those involving Muslims, neighbours mostly provided protection and did not join in the loot and arson. The rioters often retreated from arson and looting even when a handful of determined people stood guard to protect their neighbours.

It used to be rare for people to be killed or have their own houses burnt for daring to save their neighbours. But things have changed fast. This time neighbours joined in the rioting against people they had lived close to for years. Most simply watched. The few who dared offer shelter were attacked if the Shiv Sainiks found out.

Several Muslims who had been saved by their Hindu neighbours narrated how they were punished for doing so. Bhamabai, who works as a part-time domestic servant, lives in a slum of Tulsiwadi all by herself. This old woman sheltered her neighbour Kehkashah, her six children and husband in her jhuggi. As a result, Bhamabai's own house was broken into and the pitiful little she had was looted. When I met her in March, she told me she had nothing left. Even the sari she was wearing belonged to one of her neighbours. Many others succumbed to the threats of the Shiv Sainiks that they would destroy the homes of all those Hindus who dared hide Muslims. Consequently, those who had been given shelter were asked to leave. In such an atmosphere very few people dared to protect their neighbours.

The sense of mohalledari or village solidarity, apart from being rooted in natural human compassion, is based on the pragmatic consideration that one's own safety lies in the safety of one's neighbourhood.

For some people, like Mahatma Gandhi, total and unconditional commitment to non-violence and peace was a moral, dharmic resolve. Most ordinary people keep away from blatant forms of violence such as murder and arson for more practical reasons—that is, their realization that killing or hurting someone, especially in one's neighbourhood, is a risky proposition, because violence inevitably leads to counter-violence which then becomes an unending, deadly game. On this premise of enlightened self-interest is based the code of mohalledari, of joining together to make at least one's immediate social environment safe. Almost every mohalla in the cities and towns of India follows the practice of appointing a chowkidar to ensure the common security of all residents. This is outside the police system as the latter is not trusted to ensure safety.

However, through their relentless hate propaganda, the Sangh Parivar and Shiv Sena Combine have succeeded in a large measure in tearing asunder these neighbourhood ties. Over the years they have engineered to divide neighbourhoods into warring camps. Earlier it was primarily due to a tussle between the Congress and the BJP (or its earlier incarnations) for political control over mohalla associations and traditional panchayats, thus bringing the ugly aspects of party politics into organizations which were meant to act on a consensual basis. In the process, they have also attempted to polarize neighbourhoods on communal lines. The process was started at the time of the Partition by the Muslim League and the believers in the ideology of the Sangh Parivar. But at that time the trouble was engineered at the national level and implemented at the local level mostly through outside goondas. Moreover, it stayed confined to select parts of India. But today the Hindu-Muslim divide has become widespread and has destroyed neighbourhood ties.

The Sangh Parivar is out to destroy the dharma of Hindus where it matters most, that is, in their day-to-day relationships with people with whom they have the closest interaction apart from their immediate family. By sowing the seeds of mistrust and hatred among neighbours, by encouraging Hindus to view their Muslim neighbours as enemies to be destroyed, they are actually making the lives of Hindus insecure, thus endangering the well-being of the Hindu community as well. What meaning can national security have for people if they do not feel secure in their own mohallas and villages? What good is national unity if one's neighbourhood is torn asunder by hatred and mistrust?

Repeated bouts of Hindu–Muslim violence have led to increasing ghettoization of the Muslim community—a process that started with the Partition. Both Hindus and Muslims start leaving neighbourhoods that have a preponderance of the other community.

That is exactly what the believers in the ideology of the Sangh Parivar want—complete isolation of the Muslims and breaking of all communication channels between the two communities. As long as Hindus and Muslims continue to interact with each other as neighbours and colleagues or business partners, they will know them as individuals who are not particularly different from themselves despite some cultural and religious variations. But as soon as the two communities are physically distanced, it becomes much easier for hatemongers from both sides to present the other as a fearful stereotype and legitimize hatred and violence against the other.

The Bombay violence has been variously described as the result of inflamed religious sentiments among Muslims and Hindus; as the handiwork of underworld dons in league with the builders' lobby which is believed to have encouraged the burning of slums and chawls in order to grab prime pieces of land; and as the fall-out of political rivalry between warring factions of the Congress party led by Sharad Pawar and Sudhakar Naik respectively.

No doubt criminals and builders played a role in stirring up violence. But no society can be taken over by criminals unless influential sections of that society give their sanction to such a take-over. The participation of the middle class and the tacit or active support of the city elite gave crime an unprecedented boost. Apart from the Sangh Parivar, large sections of the Congress and Republican Party leadership and cadres joined and led the killing brigades. Even the left trade unions did not or could not organize any resistance. The organized working class too had either been won over by the Shiv Sena or stayed immobilized. Even those trade union leaders who disapproved of the violence did not dare take a clear public stand for fear of alienating and losing their supposed following. When Shiv Sainiks began brazenly to prevent Muslim workers from rejoining their duties after the massacres subsided, the trade union leaders did not intervene to protect Muslim workers from being hounded out of their jobs.

While a couple of stray instances were cited wherein Dalits joined the Muslims to defend their bastis, by and large, Dalits including those aligned to the Republican Party, joined and even led the rioting brigades. Ramdas Athavle, Minister of State for Social Welfare, who belongs to the Republican Party, actively lobbied for the release of Madhukar Sarpotdar of the Shiv Sena. After he was released on bail, Athavle shared the platform with him to address a victory rally organized by the Shiv Sena supporters to celebrate the release of Sarpotdar.

Criminals cannot function without powerful political patronage. The riots cannot be attributed to land grabbers because then violence should have remained confined to a few selected areas. But the way it spread all over Bombay shows that it was not due to a spontaneous outburst of inflamed religious sentiment. Powerful political forces were involved and the riots were well planned and well organized.

But even politicians, no matter how influential and powerful, cannot instigate large-scale violence so brazenly unless they are confident of being able to get the police and other arms of the state machinery to function at their behest without any fear of consequences. Criminals, even in ordinary times, cannot go beyond petty crime without the connivance, help and patronage of the police and politicians. Similarly, the builders' lobby dare not undertake large-scale criminal acts like paying off someone to burn chawls and slums if they are not used to doing such things routinely and buying protection by paying off the police, the bureaucrats and the politicians.

Likewise, no matter how much the Hindus hate the Muslims and vice versa, few among them are likely to have the courage to act out that hatred. Most ordinary people refrain from killing, even when they are angry, simply because they fear revenge. In today's world of powerful state machineries, only those groups or individuals dare kill with impunity who can rely on the protection of the state machinery.

Shiv Sainiks and other criminals could run amok because, barring a few exceptions, the government machinery, especially the police, gave them whole-hearted cooperation. By and large the policemen either turned a blind eye or they themselves joined the rioting brigades. What better proof of police complicity could there be than the fact that rioting was most fierce in areas where there are police housing colonies?

Shiv Sena has for years especially targeted policemen's sons as their recruits. That is why, in localities around police quarters, young Shiv Sainiks could wreak vengeance without the slightest obstruction because the policemen were giving free support and encouragement to their sons who went looting and killing.

In the midst of the riots, an Indian reporter was able to record radio transmissions—picked off the police radio band—of conversations between policemen and their control room. Indian newspapers imposed a form of self-censorship and did not publish these testimonies of police complicity in the violence. Extracts from these taped conversations were, however, published in *The New York Times* of 4 February 1993. They indicate that the officers at police headquarters were repeatedly telling policemen patrolling during the riots that Muslim homes were to be allowed to burn without interference, and that aid to Muslim victims was to be prevented.

According to one transcript quoted by this issue of *The New York Times*, the control room referred to the site of a fire, saying it must be a garage owned by a Muslim man. The Marathi speaker at the control room said, 'Let it burn.' Then he added, 'If it belongs to a Maharashtrian, don't burn anything that belongs to a Maharashtrian.' The control room went on to urge the policemen to burn everything belonging to Muslims.

In another conversation, the police in district Dongri inquired over their police radio what they should do about two army trucks filled with milk that had been sent as relief to a slum area where many Muslims had been burnt out of their homes. The police control room replied, 'Why are you distributing milk to them?' and added, 'Do not distribute milk to the landias. Have you understood?' The control room then ordered these policemen to 'Seize that vehicle.'

The most damning testimony about government inaction-cum-complicity came from a fairly senior officer of the Maharashtra government, someone who claims to have witnessed the governmental goings-on as an insider: 'I myself witnessed how on one occasion the police and Hindu mobs kept their looting, burning and killing spree going even while the home minister's motorcade was passing by. They did not think it necessary to halt their violence even temporarily and continue after letting the home minister pass because they were sure no action would be taken.'

An Exceptional Policeman

Even while a majority of policemen violated the norms of their own profession, there were a few courageous and fair-minded policemen, who at an enormous personal risk remained true to their duty. DCP Pandey, in-charge of Dharavi police station, played a positive role in keeping things under control by being non-partisan. But, instead of being rewarded, he was transferred from that job to a department which allowed no public dealing. Many view his transfer as a punishment posting. A few other names were mentioned as well.

Sanobar Kishwar, a Bombay-based social worker who was actively involved in relief and rehabilitation work, described how one particular Sikh policeman acted with remarkable courage in Habibpur of Pratikshanagar Area. On 11 January , the Shiv Sena had organized a *maha aarti* in the local Hanuman mandir, which became the starting point of an all-out attack on the Muslims. Firebombs were thrown at their homes and shops, which were reduced to ashes right in front of their eyes. A mob of about 500 was led by an ex-corporator of the Shiv Sena, called Satyaram Jamkar. They came and set fire to some Muslim flats. Those trapped in the burning flats were too petrified to come down because the mob was waiting for them below.

Sanobar was later told by those people that they—and especially the women decided—that they would choose being roasted alive rather than falling into the hands of the Shiv Sainiks. A police force was stationed there but did nothing to save the trapped people,

SAFETY IS INDIVISIBLE • 195

except for one policeman by the name of Pratap Singh. A Muslim social organization had sent an ambulance with a driver and another helper to rescue the victims but the two men, themselves Muslims, were too scared to go and evacuate the building, defying the mob. At this point, Pratap Singh is supposed to have held the mob at bay single-handedly, with just one gun in his hand. He himself went up to the building and shouted, saying: 'I'll protect you. Come down or else you will die.' Because they recognized the Muslim social worker who accompanied the ambulance, many of the trapped people came down. But they would have been killed by the mob had it not been for the great courage shown by Pratap Singh. He kept them at bay by firing into the air and thus saved nearly a hundred families single-handedly. While Pratap Singh was thus risking his life, the other policemen shot dead the driver of the ambulance, injured the social worker and punctured the ambulance tyres. The injured driver still tried to drive it away but they caught and shot him dead in front of everybody. Sanobar says Pratap Singh refuses to talk about the incident and fears that he would be transferred from the area as a punishment for doing his duty.

Even though normally such situations come under control as soon as the army is called in, this time even the army was forced to play a partisan role. It is well known how former Defence Minister Sharad Pawar had come and planted himself in Bombay during the riots allegedly with the purpose of deliberately paralyzing the administration; he supposedly wanted to teach the then Chief Minister, Naik, a lesson for having tried to clip the former's wings by arresting some of his well-known criminal colleagues such as Pappu Kalani and dismissing some pro-Pawar ministers from his Cabinet.

Many in the government allege that the police acted like Pawar's private army. He wanted to show Naik who really controlled Bombay and so in most cases the police joined the rioters at Pawar's encouragement. But he didn't stop at that. This time, he succeeded in politicizing the army as well. A government official, on condition of anonymity, gave a detailed account of how the army command refused to cooperate with the chief minister on one pretext or another:

They would make excuses like: 'We will only do flag marches, no firing. We don't want to alienate civilians,' or 'We won't fire without written orders given to us in each specific instance.' Now, how do you ensure that a magistrate is forever accompanying each of the army contingents, ready to sign an order to fire whenever they witness a riotous mob? Even so, Naik's government gave a large bunch of pre-signed orders into the hands of army officers in charge of patrolling riot-torn areas. But with continuous attempts at sabotage by the Defence Minister himself, the army was not allowed to discharge its duty properly. In fact, this time there have been allegations that in some cases they too joined in raping Muslim women.

Even those sections of the press that condemned the role of the police were not willing to mention similar lapses committed by the army. However, Pritish Nandy, the editor-in-chief of the Observer group of papers, wrote describing what he witnessed personally:

I live on the 24th floor of a high-rise building on Carmichael Road, which is one of the poshest areas of Bombay. I could see 30 major fires from my window and saw the slum outside my house being cleansed of all Muslims. I called the police and asked them to provide protection. First they refused to come. When they did come, they were callous and indifferent. Then I called the prime minister's office. Not being able to get him, I called the then Defence Minister, Sharad Pawar, and was able to prevail upon him to send the army. But they did no more than coolly amble in and quietly drive out in the name of patrolling. It was like they were romancing down the streets of fire. Most of the time they did not even offload the soldiers. This when the violence was in full view and even little children and infants were being tossed around and thrown into fires.

The partisan role that is played by our criminalized state machinery in favour of dominant groups whenever a conflict occurs between different communities is the key reason for increasing communal violence in our society. In a Hindu–Muslim conflict, where the Hindus are assured of police and other protection, they do not have to fear reprisals. This violence can be curtailed only by making the government machinery more accountable for its actions. This task cannot be performed by the vulnerable sections of the population without help from the middle-class intelligentsia.

So far we have tended to respond to each such crisis by demanding that the guilty be punished. But nothing happens because there are no institutional mechanisms to ensure that this happens automatically. Steps in that direction should include :
1. Accountability of the police to the people. This means that the police in each locality be in the service of the local residents. These personnel should be recruited, and the power of dismissing them should be held, by elected representatives of the local residents. This will make it harder for the police to subject the

local population to arbitrary excesses. At present they are only accountable, if at all, to their district hierarchical police superiors, and are immune from accountability to the local people.

2. The centrally controlled police force should only have jurisdiction over offences that operate on a national level. They should be permitted to intervene at the local level only on the specific request of a freely elected local government or where there has been a violation of fundamental human rights by the local police.

3. A special peace force be set up to deal with communal and anti-minority violence. In each area, this force should have an equitable representation of the particular minorities that are resident in that area. Thus the representation of minorities will not merely be proportional to their overall proportion in the all-India population, for example, 11 per cent Muslims or 7 per cent tribals, but will be commensurate with their proportion in the particular affected area, for example, an equitable percentage reflecting the population of Muslims in certain disturbed areas of UP, of tribals in south Bihar or in the North East, as well as in each area of a city.

4. Suitable changes in the legislatures to ensure that the political representatives, MLAs and MPs, have to take responsibility and make effective provisions for the prevention of communal killings. There should be legal provisions for the recall of MPs and MLAs and for disqualifying them from recontesting if massacres or riots take place in their constituency. We need to make it politically unrewarding for politicians to instigate riots with a view to strengthening vote banks.

5. Likewise it should be made mandatory for the deputy commissioner to give a detailed, community by community description of those killed, injured or maimed, as well as an account of property losses suffered by each community. If it can be shown that the deputy commissioner is providing wrong information, (s)he should be immediately dismissed from service.

6. Legal changes to ensure that the deputy commissioner and superintendent of police are investigated whenever such incidents take place in their area of jurisdiction.

If specific government functionaries and elected representatives could be held accountable for their acts of commission and omission in case of communal violence, the fearful nexus between criminals, politicians, fanatic hatemongers and the government functionaries might be broken.

8

Ways to Combat Communal Violence: Some Thoughts on International Women's Day

This year (1991) a large number of women's organizations in the country will be observing International Women's Day by highlighting the issue of growing communal strife and violence in our country. This decision was taken at a national conference held in Calicut in December 1990. It is indeed a welcome step.

The survival of democracy in India is crucially linked to a humane, peaceful and just resolution of ethnic conflicts. The well-being of women is also integrally involved in the process of conflict resolution because the position of women in society deteriorates as the level of violence increases. Thus what was formerly viewed with horror becomes a common occurrence and then becomes an acceptable norm in inter-community relations.

However, it is not enough to simply highlight the issue, for it is already receiving enough attention. What is far more urgently required is the articulation and planning of meaningful and effective strategies to combat the growing violence. Or else our work will stay at the level of mouthing platitudes on communal harmony which few take seriously. This exercise requires, among other things, an honest and critical re-evaluation of our own work and our political responses to the crisis.

Considering the scale of violence that broke out as a result of the Ram Mandir campaign by the BJP–RSS–VHP Combine, our responses to this situation have been woefully inadequate and even inappropriate.

First published in *Manushi*, No. 62 (Jan– Feb 1991).

Mostly they consisted of:
1. Issuing press statements condemning some incident.
2. Organizing occasional *dharnas* or protest marches that included a small number of women activists and a handful of sympathizers.
3. Holding conferences and workshops for activists already committed to the cause of protecting human rights.
4. Occasional mass contact activities such as performing street plays, poster exhibitions and distributing leaflets.

All of these are valuable gestures. But they amount to virtually nothing in meeting the challenge posed by the large-scale mobilization of the BJP–RSS–VHP Combine for their politics of hatred and revenge. Apart from the platitudes and sermons exhorting people not to fall into the trap of communal politics, and emphasizing how women are special losers in such situations, we have had very little else to offer by way of political intervention. What is most disturbing is that we failed to organize even token relief work for the victims of riots and massacres. Why did we fail to make even token gestures of sharing the grief and anguish of those who were maimed and brutalized, those who their lost their dear ones, their houses and means of livelihood?

Relief work had spontaneously sprung up at the time of the anti-Sikh riots in November 1984, at least in Delhi. Even as the violence was raging in the city, a new forum called the Nagrik Ekta Manch (NEM) came into existence and brought together a large heterogeneous group of people, including many activists from women's organizations. It was heartening to see that there was no dearth of volunteers for the large-scale relief work undertaken by the Manch. Money and other resources poured in, in sufficient amounts to allow NEM to function effectively.

In addition to undertaking relief work on its own, NEM was also able to shame and pressurize the government into taking some responsibility for the rehabilitation of the victims of the 1984 riots. This included provision of alternate housing, pensions and jobs for widows and dependants, as well as other measures. Along with other organizations, NEM monitored these activities for several months. As a result, some aid finally reached the victims, unlike in instances of other catastrophes when relief measures are announced by the government but seldom reach the needy people. Even though no amount of relief or compensation could ever heal the trauma and scars of the victims, NEM played an important role in preventing the total estrangement of the Sikh community. It acted as a bridge of communication between Hindus and Sikhs at a time when powerful political forces intended to create a permanent schism between the two communities for electoral gains.

The detailed, eyewitness reports produced by some of the volunteers closely associated with NEM relief and rehabilitation work were also significant accomplishments. Because NEM had responded to the crisis instantaneously, these volunteers were able to gather information that would have been hard to get if they had reached the scene several days or weeks later. The NEM involvement with relief won the confidence of the victims as well as the Sikh community in general. As a result, the quality of information that was collected was far superior to the usual kind of riot reports. All this was combined with protest marches, petitions to the court, setting up of a Citizens' Commission and various other activities to mobilize public opinion for the indictment of those guilty of perpetrating the massacre.

The ruling party and the government managed to .thwart proceedings against the guilty because top-level politicians had themselves secured the connivance of the government machinery to unleash the massacre. Nevertheless the success of NEM lay in its multifaceted work which played a major part in changing social opinion and perceptions regarding the nature of violence in November 1984 decisively. Initially, large sections among the Hindu community were willing to condone the bloodshed and looting as a 'natural and inevitable' corollary to the public outrage at Mrs Gandhi's murder. They dismissed it as just one more riot, thereby implying that it was a spontaneous outburst of anger and a conflict between the Hindus and Sikhs. But the continuous determined efforts of the NEM in the years that followed showed that most people had begun to publicly acknowledge that the killings were a pre-planned massacre of the Sikhs by the Congress Party leaders with active help from the police and administration. Thus, it could well be said that the people's verdict has been passed against the killers even though the courts have failed to do their job. This was no mean achievement. Another notable achievement was that NEM was able to work closely throughout this period with community-based organizations of the Sikhs.

It is puzzling why the NEM example has not been replicated, given that it was amongst the most effective relief, rehabilitation, reporting, documentation and public opinion mobilizing exercises undertaken by human rights groups in recent years. We need to examine the NEM experience more closely to understand what were the factors that allowed such a large, heterogeneous group of people and organizations to come together on one platform and work efficiently and effectively for a considerable length of time; how it was able to draw support from the supposedly apolitical people, students, housewives, professionals. Above all, we need to find out why the present phase of more widespread violence has failed to evoke a similar response from us. Today, we are behaving like demoralized people, unable to think of anything more meaningful than issuing press statements, organizing conferences and occasional ineffective little protest marches and *dharnas*. The situation demands an urgent review of why we have been so politically paralysed.

This ineffectiveness may, in part, be due to the nature of the political space that most women's groups and human rights/civil liberties activists seek·to occupy .

In recent years there has been an increasing trend towards forming national and international networks, with much less attention being given to community-based work. Even the conferences, workshops, seminars and protest marches that we organize tend to be confined to a selected few areas and attended by the usual handful of like-minded people. In Delhi, for instance, the area between Mandi House, India Gate and Lodhi Estate complex witnesses most of the activity organized by women's rights and human rights groups. Sometimes, to make the point about our work being non-elitist, we take our protest marches, street plays, poster exhibitions, etcetera, to areas inhabited by the poorer sections. So we walk through Jama Masjid, Chandni Chowk or Mangolpuri distributing leaflets, singing songs or shouting slogans and end up with a small public meeting where a few curious onlookers from the area stand at the edges of our meetings listening to our speeches. But since this is seldom followed up by any consistent work in that particular area, the procession, meeting or the message is soon forgotten.

We have consistently shied away from organizing such activities in our own neighbourhood and community. This is where the mainstream political parties, especially the BJP and RSS, score over us. They invariably function through cadres who are encouraged to be active in their own neighbourhood and community, irrespective of whether or not they engage in state or national-level politics.

They take pride in being respected members of their own localities. Their larger political involvements are based on their influence in their community and locality. However poisonous their overall politics, the image of an RSS or BJP cadre within their own community is usually that of a dedicated social worker people can depend upon in moments of crisis. Their political life is integrally linked to their everyday social life and that is why their ideological work is able to acquire such deep roots. It gets woven into the very culture of the community.

In addition, they make it a point to work through the existing social and political institutions even while taking the initiative to set up new ones. A great deal of their political energy goes into exercising influence through control over mohalla associations, *biradari* panchayats and *gram* panchayats. This is not just for the purpose of having a vote-gathering machine at the time of elections, but equally for creating social hegemony in order to influence various types of decision-making processes at the local level. Their capacity for large-scale mobilization comes essentially from this day-to-day contact that their cadres are encouraged to consolidate systematically. This contact also provides them with a rich recruiting ground for new members as well as the ability to collect vast amounts of funds for their political work.

In contrast, most women's and human rights organizations are more inclined towards 'national networks'. Very few have attempted community-based work, starting work in our own neighbourhoods and communities. The few who attempt such work usually do so in communities other than their own; usually starting 'projects' among the poor in bastis, slums and villages on behalf of development agencies. The activists working in such projects are not considered an integral part of the community. They are viewed more as outsiders who have come to do a job; or sympathetic aliens who come and go as they please and shift from one project to another according to their own convenience.

Thus, they stay alienated not only from their own community and neighbourhood but also from those whom they try to help as outsiders. They have consistently avoided doing political work in our own neighbourhood or within their own community on the pretext that this would confine them to working with the middle-class and elite groups, whereas 'real' work is ostensibly only that which is done among the poor and the oppressed sections of the society.

A large number of women activists come from relatively privileged backgrounds. Like most who view themselves as 'radical', many women activists are prone to guilt—trapping themselves into believing that work among the middle class will discredit them as being pro-elitist. But since their work with the poor remains sporadic and fitful, they deny themselves the possibility of being considered 'insiders' anywhere. This, in large part, explains their marginalization and ineffectiveness. It also explains why many women's groups increasingly resort to becoming a part of national and international networks which distance them from the scene of social tension and conflict. Lack of a community base and local support also leads to a continual paucity of funds and cadres. Hence the increasing trend towards seeking financial support from funding agencies. That helps in making 'networks' abound, while workers become harder and harder to find. Most women's organizations find it hard to find enough volunteers for day-to-day sustained work. The kind of activists readily available are usually those who are provided paid jobs by social work or development organizations.

For effective work against violence, whether at the domestic level or of the kind witnessed during riots and massacres, we need to have localized, community-based workers. Voluntary defence committees should be formed to protect their own neighbourhood. At the time of the November 1984 massacre, it was evident that wherever neighbours got together to put up joint resistance, killings and burning were almost always prevented. Even a small number of determined people were able to act effectively in resisting killing and looting brigades.

Most women's organizations have not prepared the ground for such mobilization even in their own immediate neighourhood, let alone citywide. Yet they are constantly involved in holding 'national' level conferences and workshops. While the BJP–RSS–VHP Combine can mobilize hundreds of thousands across the country for their bloodstained politics, those who claim to be defenders of human rights are unable to put together ten people in each of their neighbourhoods to stand up and oppose rioting and killing. This imbalance needs to change and hopefully women's organizations will be among the leaders in this effort.

To begin with, neighbourhood-based work among the middle class may appear less urgent, or even redundant, given that outbreaks of communal violence take place most often in areas inhabited by the poor or in bazaars and shopping centres. However, considering that the middle-class intelligentsia provides the polemical weapons without which the communal forces could not keep up their steady barrage of hatred and self-righteousness, the power of the BJP–RSS–VHP Combine would be drastically curtailed if they failed to get endorsement from the ideologically and politically influential middle class. It is by winning over the middle class that they get their politics projected so favourably in the press and get to dominate important centres of ideological influence, such as universities, colleges and schools, and manipulate the government machinery to serve their political ends. For instance, the PAC jawans in Uttar Pradesh do not hesitate to unleash violence on Muslims because they are assured of protection from their bosses and other sections of the bureaucracy. They also thrive on the support of very large sections of the Hindu middle and upper classes, including most of the Uttar Pradesh press who have become vociferous defenders of the PAC's unlawful actions.

Once the middle classes turn fascist, they are usually successful in using the poorer, oppressed sections as instruments to carry out their hate campaigns. In riot after riot, it becomes clear that the middle-class-led pogroms have used sections of the poor and dalits to attack Muslims. The endorsement and participation of the middle class makes killing and rioting seem like respectable activities. Without this endorsement, the BJP–RSS–VHP Combine would find it much harder to recruit the poor and dalits to indulge in anti-Muslim violence by convincing them that they are acting as 'defenders of the nation' even while looting and killing their fellow citizens.

Thus we need to review our attitude of dismissive contempt towards the middle class. We need to get over our embarrassment and guilt about belonging to this group. Only then can we use our relatively privileged position to strengthen human rights politics. We cannot combat the ideology of communal hatred and violence without winning over large sections of the middle class and elite groups into endorsing a polity based on respect for human rights. Whether we like it or not, the middle class and elite groups play a hegemonic role in our society. In India, which has a very large and growing middle class, the ideological influence of this group is truly enormous. By totally ignoring the need for political work among this key segment of our society, we have failed to stop them from being partial towards authoritarian hate-soaked communal politics, rather than supporting humane and democratic-rights-oriented politics. Very effective challenges to the power of the establishment have often come from radical sections within elite groups. The middle class in particular have great propensity for being mobilized for causes not directly connected with their immediate material interests. It is important to ensure that this propensity does not seek destructive outlets, as is happening with the Ram Mandir campaign. Mahatma Gandhi's success, to a large extent, lay in his ability to channel the idealism of some of the privileged sections of the society into creative outlets. He could inspire them to rise above the politics of narrow self-seeking and support the cause of disadvantaged and hitherto despised groups. Gandhi's success in making upper castes and classes involved in the spinning and weaving of *khadi*, the removal of untouchability and promoting the cause of women's equality, accepting the right of Muslims to stay on in India even after so many Hindus had been driven out of Pakistan after the Partition, demonstrates how sections of the middle class and elite groups can act with some responsibility towards oppressed groups of society when sensitively approached. Our failure to take this potential seriously in post-Independence India has resulted in the successful winning over of the middle class to socially destructive causes led by the BJP–RSS–VHP Combine.

It is well known that rioters, killers and looters always get protection, patronage and encouragement from politicians and the government machinery. This has made the battle between Hindus and Muslims very unequal since the government and the political machinery are dominated and controlled by the Hindu majority. The rioters among the majority community are assured of police and other protection, they don't have to fear reprisals. This link can be broken only by making the government machinery more accountable for its actions. The task cannot be performed by the vulnerable sections of the population without help from the middle-class intelligentsia. The protests and demands of the oppressed groups are either ignored or met with further repression. However, if large sections among the elite groups were to get organized to oppose the increasing criminalization of the government and political machinery, they would be more likely to succeed in acting as a restraining influence.

9

Pro-Women or Anti-Muslim?
The Shah Bano Controversy

Anyone reading about the Shah Bano controversy in the newspapers would get the impression that:

1. Ex-Chief Justice Y.V. Chandrachud was the first judge ever to have granted maintenance to a Muslim woman under section 125 of the Criminal Procedure Code (Cr PC);
2. In doing so, he overruled the Muslim personal law.

The creation of such erroneous impressions by the media is an indicator of how much more dangerous ignorance can be when it is systematically disseminated by the press. In fact, while delivering this judgement, Chandrachud and his companions on the bench, Desai, Venkataramiah, Chinnappa Reddy and R. Misra, merely confirmed two existing Supreme Court precedents: Krishna Iyer's, Tulzapulkar's and R.S. Pathak's judgement in the case of Bai Tahira versus Ali Husain Fissalli, 1979, and Krishna Iyer's, Chinnappa Reddy's and A. P Sen's judgement in the case of Fuzlunbi versus K. Khader Vali, 1980. In both these cases, the right of the divorced woman to maintenance was upheld. No uproar was created by either judgement.

Why then such a furore over Chandrachud's judgement, which is not even a precedent? In order to answer this question, it is necessary to analyze the three judgements.

Justice Krishna Iyer, in the two judgements delivered by him, dwells upon social injustice to women. Not once in the Bai Tahira judgement does he even mention the word 'Muslim'. He emphasizes that under section 127, Cr PC, any amounts paid to a divorced woman under the Personal Law of the parties will be taken into consideration while settling the maintenance. If such amounts are sufficient to

First published in *Manushi* No. 32 (Jan–Feb 1986).

maintain the woman, no further maintenance need be granted to her. But if they are insufficient, then maintenance has to be granted to safeguard the woman from destitution.

In his judgement in the Fuzlunbi case, Krishna Iyer quotes Muslim authorities to show that *mehr** is a token of respect for the wife, a settlement upon her, and not a divorce payment. He makes no comments upon Muslim personal law in general. His emphasis throughout is on the need to curb what he refers to as 'masculine injustice' and to help 'a woman in distress'.

In contrast, every substantive paragraph of the judgement in the Shah Bano case obsessively dwells upon 'Muslims' and 'Muslim personal law'. Take, for instance, the following statement: 'Undoubtedly, the Muslim husband enjoys the privilege of being able to discard his wife whenever he chooses to do so, for reasons good, bad or indifferent. Indeed, for no reason at all.'

If the word 'Muslim' were deleted from this sentence, would it not hold equally true? Do not most husbands in our society exercise this privilege, regardless of their religion or lack of religion? By singling out Muslim men and Islam in this way, Justice Chandrachud converts what is essentially a women's rights issue into an occasion for a gratuitous attack upon a community. The entire tone of the judgement gives one the erroneous impression that other communities in India have a perfectly egalitarian and secular law. Of this, more later.

This is not to deny that Muslim personal law, as codified and practised in India, is heavily biased against women, and that Muslim politicians have so far resisted all attempts to introduce necessary changes, thus causing great harm to their own community, especially women. In this, however, they are no different from men of most communities anywhere in the world. Men have, throughout the centuries, managed to project their own sectarian interests as the

---

*Mehr, translated as 'dower', is somewhat similar to the marriage settlement that used to be prevalent in some European countries whereby the husband settled an estate on the wife as a security for her. The amount of mehr is of two kinds—prompt and deferred. Prompt mehr is that which the husband must give the wife any time she demands it. Deferred mehr is that which the wife agrees not to demand until the marriage is dissolved by death or divorce. The latter form is more prevalent in India. Justice Krishna Iyer, in the cases of Bai Tahira and Fuzlunbi, had cited Muslim authorities to show that mehr is not a compensatory payment to a divorced wife. It is a token of respect to every wife, and its payment is not necessarily linked with divorce.

interests of the entire community, thus denying women the possibility of asserting their interests, especially when these conflict with those of men.

Ever since the judgement was delivered, the issue, as framed by Chandrachud, has been picked up vociferously by various self-appointed reformers amongst the Hindus to whip up the most blatant kind of anti-Muslim hysteria, using the plight of Muslim women as a banner. Once again, women are being used by men of different communities to settle scores with each other.

The result is clear for all to see. Shah Bano spent ten long years fighting her case and stood firm in her demand. As soon as her case was picked up by the media and self-styled reformers, she withdrew for fear of being exploited by communalists, and requested the Supreme Court to rescind its judgement.

It is significant that when she was interviewed on television, she was very strong in asserting that injustice had been done to her by her husband. When asked to explain why she had appealed for the judgement in her favour to be withdrawn, she made a simple but revealing statement. She said this judgement seemed to be creating conditions for *danga phasad* (riots), and she did not want to be the cause of anti-Muslim riots. Thus, even while strongly acknowledging the injustice done to her as a woman, she felt compelled to give up her struggle in order to save her community from attack by Hindu communalists. She was made to feel as if by asserting her rights as a woman, she was exposing her already vulnerable community to further attack. As one M.Y. Kazi wrote to *The Times of India*:

... it is such a pity that the issue of Muslim personal law has been politicized by motivated people who have thus vitiated the atmosphere for a serious debate. As a Muslim, I am only too well aware of where the shoe pinches and what needs to be done. But let me make it very plain, I won't oblige those who regard any identity except their own as inferior, alien and unpatriotic, and who would shed copious tears on the 'plight' of Muslim women but have no sympathy to spare when those very women are made widows and orphans in the streets of Bhiwandi, Ahmedabad, Baroda, Meerut and innumerable other places ... As a Muslim, I would not mind having a common civil code provided that code incorporates the good points of all the existing codes.

It is not only women like Shah Bano who have been frightened by the nature of the 'support' extended to their cause. Even many of those Muslims who have all along favoured reform in Muslim personal law or advocated the need for a common civil code, are feeling rightly concerned. They are afraid that in the guise of sympathy for Muslim women, many non-Muslims, notably Hindus, may seize the occasion to spread even more hatred and contempt for the Muslims in an atmosphere already charged with anti-Muslim sentiment.

Before the stirring up of a storm over this judgement, a number of Muslim women were routinely granted maintenance by various courts under section 125, Cr PC. One example is that of Qaisar Jahan, who had approached *Manushi* for help. Her husband, Ghalib Husain, a reader at Jamia Milia University, Delhi, had divorced her and remarried. Qaisar, employed at Aligarh, was supporting their ten-year-old son, Feisal Ghalib.

Manushi lawyers filed a petition for maintenance under section 125 Cr PC, and in October 1984, a woman metropolitan magistrate, Deepa Sharma, awarded Rs 500 per month to Feisal, this being the maximum maintenance possible under this section for any person, regardless of religion. Separate maintenance would have been granted to Qaisar, too, had she been unemployed.

However, ever since the Supreme Court judgement in the Shah Bano case, the newspapers have been gleefully reporting each case of a Muslim woman getting maintenance in the lower courts as yet another 'victory'—in seeming ignorance of the fact that many such awards were made prior to the Shah Bano judgement.

The position under the Criminal Procedure Code and the Muslim personal law is stated by Daniel Latifi in his written arguments for an intervention in the Shah Bano versus Mohammed Ahmed Khan case:

Section 125, Cr PC, provides for maintenance up to a maximum amount of Rs 500 a month for a needy wife, child or parent. Section 127 (3) (b) provides that a maintenance order under Section 125 shall be cancelled where 'The woman has been divorced by her husband and . . . she has received, whether before or after the date of the said order, the whole of the sum which, under any customary or personal law, applicable to the parties, was payable on such divorce.'

Justice Krishna Iyer had interpreted this clause to mean that if the amount paid under personal law was sufficient to save the woman from destitution, the maintenance order under section 125 would be cancelled, but in case the amount paid under personal law was not sufficient to save her from destitution, then the order under section 125 would stand. He argued that section 125 exists to protect people from destitution, and to see that the state is not burdened with their upkeep if they have close relatives who should look after them.

However, Mohammed Ahmed Khan challenged this interpretation, pointing out that section 127 clearly states that if 'the whole' amount payable under personal law has been paid, the woman is not entitled to relief under section 125. Therefore, the Supreme Court had to decide whether Shah Bano had in fact received the whole amount payable to her under Muslim personal law.

Mohammed Ahmed Khan had paid the mehr of Rs 3,000 and also the maintenance during *iddat**. He claimed that under Muslim personal law, these are the only two payments due to a woman on divorce.

Shah Bano's counsel argued that apart from these two payments, another payment known as *mataa* is also due to a woman on divorce, under Ayat 241 of Sura II (Sura-al-Baqr) of the holy Koran: *'Wa lil motallaqatay mataa unbil maroofay haqqan allal muttaqeena'* which translated as 'And for divorced women let there be a fair provision. This is an obligation on those who are mindful of god.' (transd. Dr Syed Abdul Latif, 1969)

Shah Bano had not been paid mataa. Her husband's counsel argued that this provision is not obligatory on all Muslims but only on the muttaqeena or those who are specially pious, which he does not claim to be. Shah Bano's counsel replied that the Koran is addressed, right at its beginning, to the muttaqeena. So if all Muslims believe it is addressed to them, then all Muslims are muttaqeena and this verse applies to all of them.

Shah Bano's counsel also cited interpretations of this verse by several respected authorities:

Two reputed authorities who have dealt with this matter are Maulana Baizawi and Ibn Katheer. . . These commentators have declared that the obligation upon the husband of paying mataa-un-bil-maaroof (reasonable provision)

---

*Iddat is the period of three months following a divorce. During this period, the husband is supposed to keep the wife in his house and maintain her at his own standard of living. This period is provided for a possible reconciliation between husband and wife. At the end of iddat, the husband may either keep the wife 'with kindness and respect, or part from her with kindness and respect.'

to his divorced wife is imperative and binding and not merely optional. It may be noted that the opinion of Imam Shafei particularly is acceptable to all the schools of Sunni, including the Hanafi jurisprudence. . . The same view has been expressed perhaps with even greater force by Imam Jafar-al-Sadiq, the highest authority among all schools of Shia jurisprudence. Prof. Fyzee states: 'Imam Jafar-al-Sadiq held it (mataa-un-bil maaroof) to be obligatory (*farida wajiba*) and always decreed its payment.' He further states: 'The mataa should be a generous payment.'

Thus, according to several respected authorities, Muslim personal law is in favour of a generous payment to a woman at the time of divorce, apart from mehr and maintenance during iddat. Shah Bano's counsel appealed to the court to uphold the law in this matter, which they did. The interpretation of Ayat 241 relied upon by the Supreme Court judges was that of jurists like Imam Shafei and not the judges' own.

The spirit of the attack on Muslim law that is being carried on today has an interesting historical parallel. After the British succeeded in firmly establishing their rule in India in the nineteenth century, one of the main ideological weapons they used to justify their domination over Indians was to claim they had a mission to reform what they characterized as the 'uncivilized' and 'backward' state of Indian society. They arrogated to themselves a 'civilizing' role. Their favourite symbol of the 'uncivilized' state of Indian society was the plight of Indian women. Customs such as *sati*, child marriage, female seclusion, and ban on widow remarriage were used as proof of the backwardness of Hindu society, in much the same way as Hindus are today using *burkah*, *talaq*, and other discriminatory aspects of Muslim personal law and practice to 'prove' how barbaric and backward Muslims and Islam are.

In both cases, the issues picked up are indeed valid issues in their own right. However, in both cases, the motivation behind the ostensible concern is of greater importance than the issues picked up, because the motivation largely determines the actual outcome of the campaign undertaken. For instance, the British used instances of Indian women's oppression to demonstrate that Indian's as a race as were incapable of governing themselves. This became another justification for treating Indians with contempt. It also helped the British to distract attention from the economic, social and cultural subjugation of the entire Indian population.

Sensing this, many prominent nationalists ended up taking extremely defensive positions on the issue of social and religious reform. We would do well to remember that men like Lokmanya Tilak vociferously opposed the Age Of Consent bill which sought to raise the age of marriage for girls to fourteen. His arguments sound similar to those of many Muslim leaders today. He insisted that women's rights were an internal matter of the Hindu communities and the British had no right to encroach upon Hindu customs and personal law.

We would also do well to remember that even during the later phases of the national movement, Gandhi had continuously to struggle against prominent Congress leaders who opposed various social reform measures because they felt that internal disputes over these issues would weaken and divide the community in their struggle against the British.

A similar situation prevails among Muslims today. The manner in which concern for Muslim women is being expressed today appears to Muslims more like an attack. It seems to be born not out of sympathy for Muslim women but of antipathy towards all Muslims. Muslims, being a minority community, are constantly suspect in the eyes of Hindus, and are constantly expected to prove their patriotism and loyalty to this country. They are expected happily to agree to be 'reformed' as a test of their loyalty to the Indian nation. If a Hindu resists a particular social reform measure, he is merely seen as a 'conservative'. But if a Muslim does so, he is at once accused of being a foreign agent, propped up by petrodollars, or he is asked to quit and go to Pakistan. No wonder most Muslim women have also begun to demand that their law not be tampered with.

The manner in which the campaign for reform in Muslim personal law is being conducted has had the unfortunate effect of silencing the voices in favour of women's rights from within the Muslim community. Like the British attack on 'evil' customs of Hindu society, this attack is meant to divert attention from very basic issues:

1. Muslims are even today a heavily disadvantaged community, economically and socially.
2. They are constantly discriminated against in matters of employment and other opportunities.
3. Even today, despite much talk of secularism, most Hindus treat them as untouchables. They do not accept food cooked in a Muslim house or eating establishment.
4. Very few Hindu landlords will rent their houses to Muslims. As a result, Muslims end up living a ghettoized existence, and are then accused of creating 'mini Pakistans.'

5. Very little has been done to support literacy and education programmes for Muslim women of lower income groups.
6. Muslims are constantly subjected to brutal violence in the form of riots so that the community has no sense of security in their own country.
7. All Muslims are suspect as actual or potential Pakistani agents.

One could add many more grievances. However, instead of finding solutions to these basic problems there is a tendency to pursue red herrings. Just as the British, in their enthusiasm for pointing out the brutal treatment meted out to Indian women, almost always forgot that the situation of most English women in England was far from enviable, so the reformer enthusiasts of today are prone to overlook the fact that both the actual and legal rights of Hindu women are far from satisfactory.

Maintenance law in India is far from satisfactory, whether under Cr PC, Hindu law or Muslim law. The issue of maintenance and alimony needs to be re-examined and made more equitable in law.

Maintenance is available to Hindu women under the Hindu Adoption and Maintenance Act, 1955. A woman can claim a maximum of one-third of the joint incomes of her husband and herself. That means that if, for example, she is earning Rs 500 and her husband Rs 1,000, she cannot claim anything because she already has one-third of the joint income which is Rs 1500.

In practice, however, it is extremely difficult for a woman to claim and get her right under Hindu personal law, just as it is extremely difficult to get the 'generous payment' under Muslim personal law. The case is a civil one which means that the husband can employ all sorts of dilatory tactics to drag out the case for years. What a woman may finally get is a pittance, like the Rs 179 that Shah Bano got from the High Court and which the Supreme Court confirmed. She will have spent much more on court expenses by that time. And there is no way of ensuring that the husband will regularly make payments. If he stops paying, the woman has no redress but to go to court again. She cannot approach the police to compel the husband to pay her.

Therefore, most women prefer to plead under 125 Cr PC which is not really the relevant provision for maintenance of a divorced wife. Maintenance is the right of a divorced woman whereas 125 Cr PC exists to safeguard all destitute women, children and old parents.

Yet most divorced women have to sue for maintenance under this clause because it comes under criminal law and provides relief somewhat more quickly. But under this clause they can get a maximum of only Rs 500 which is much less than the amount many of them would be entitled to as maintenance after divorce. Also, the sum of Rs 500 is a fixed one and bears no relation to the income of the husband. Even if he is earning lakhs, she can claim a maximum of only Rs 500. Under the personal law, she may be able to claim more, but the procedures under the civil law are so cumbersome that it is hardly worth fighting for maintenance under those clauses. Thus, women are caught in a dilemma created by a biased system.

In practice, all the laws on maintenance are highly inadequate. It is not enough to state that a woman should get a 'fair' or 'generous' payment because the definition of generosity varies widely. Women have been too long dependent on the generosity of men. What is needed is an assertion that maintenance is a woman's right. She does not have to be a destitute to claim maintenance.

The procedures for claiming maintenance have to be such that a woman can get relief quickly, and the sum payable has to be in proportion to the husband's income. The society and the state too have a responsibility in this regard, not merely to safeguard women from dying of destitution, but to ensure a decent standard of living to a woman who is maltreated or abandoned by her husband.

Shah Bano's case is only one instance of the way most Indian women have to struggle for maintenance. She had to spend 10 years knocking at the doors of the secular legal system before she got a pitiful amount of maintenance—Rs 179 per month which is far less than the statutory minimum wage in even the poorest parts of the country. Earlier, she had been granted a sum of around Rs 25 by the lower courts, which is more of an insult than an award.

Can an ordinary woman, without the support of fairly well-off male family members (in this case, Shah Bano's sons) afford to carry on such a prolonged battle, after she has been abandoned by her husband, and to get so little in return?

Yet the media completely and deliberately ignored this aspect of the plight of women, whether Muslims, Hindus, Christians or Sikhs. Instead of sounding embarrassed or ashamed at this example of the failure of the legal system to offer any meaningful relief to a woman in distress, the judges made it seem as if they were bestowing a great boon on Shah Bano and, by implication, on all Muslim women. The media too have been mindlessly projecting the judgement as a great 'victory' for Muslim women.

Powerful members of any community, whether the majority or a minority, ought not to have the right to oppress vulnerable sections of the community in the name of religion or any other 'ism'. But Muslim men are certainly not unique in using religion as a shield for the purpose of exploiting women.

Most of the non-Muslims who are vigorously demanding scrapping of Muslim law seem to be under the erroneous impression that only minorities are governed by personal laws. Most Hindus seem to believe that their law is 'secular and Indian' and not 'religious' at all. But the fact is that Hindus continue to be governed by Hindu personal law in such matters as marriage, divorce and succession.

It is true that Hindu personal law has undergone some reform, and shed some of its blatantly discriminatory aspects. However, it continues to be heavily biased against women in many important ways. To give some notable examples:

A daughter's inheritance rights are severely circumscribed in comparison to a son's. A son, from the moment of his birth, is considered a coparcener, that is, an equal owner of the family's joint property, with other male members. A daughter cannot be a coparcener in a Hindu undivided family. She can only get a portion of what her father inherits if and when the property is divided. An unmarried daughter has a right to maintenance from the family property. But once she marries, she has no right to maintenance from her natal family's property, not even if she is divorced, abandoned or widowed.

In the father's self acquired property, a Hindu daughter is supposed to have an equal share if he dies without making a will. However, most Hindu fathers are averse to giving property rights to daughters so they usually make a will disinheriting their daughters. Even when a father dies without making a will, daughters are usually pressured into signing away their rights in favour of their brothers.

Under the Hindu Minority and Guardianship Act, 1955 (read in conjunction with the Guardians and Wards Act), a Hindu father is the 'natural guardian' of his legitimate child over the age of five. This means that if there is a conflict over child custody between separated spouses, the primary right over the child belongs to the father. The mother can get custody only by proving in court that he is unsuitable to be the child's guardian. This law is an important weapon in the hands of men who can keep blackmailing their wives into continuing a bad marriage by refusing to relinquish custody over the children.

Under the Hindu Adoption and Maintenance Act, 1955, a Hindu man or woman who is single can adopt a child in his or her name. But a married Hindu woman cannot adopt a child in her name. The child has to be adopted by her husband.

Further, there are many religious elements in the Hindu personal law which can and do cause serious problems for women. For instance, under the Hindu Marriage Act, 1955, a Hindu marriage is valid even if not registered. It is normally considered complete only if certain ceremonies like *saptapadi* are performed. Many men undergo a second marriage and deliberately omit certain parts of the ceremony. Since the second marriage takes place in public with pomp and show, it is recognized by society, but since a certain religious ceremony required by law was not performed, the court will not consider the marriage a valid Hindu marriage. This is one reason why it is almost impossible for a Hindu wife to get a husband punished for bigamy. So even though bigamy is prohibited for Hindus, in practice it continues to take place.

Of equal if not greater importance is that, though there are some differences between Hindu and Muslim law, there is very little difference between the practice of the two communities.

Most Hindus do not follow the codified Hindu law as represented by the Acts passed in 1955. Instead, they follow the customary laws prevalent in their own kinship group and region. For instance, a very large number of Hindu girls are still married and their marriages consummated before the girls attain the age of 18, despite laws to the contrary.

In some respects, the reformed Hindu law is worse than the unreformed Muslim law. For instance, a Muslim daughter cannot be disinherited by her father making a will. But a Hindu daughter can be and often is deliberately excluded by her father making a will exclusively in favour of his sons.

Even where Hindu law is better in words, it is usually not worth much more in practice. For instance, the Committee on the Status of Women in India stated in its 1975 Report that a census of India survey had revealed that the incidence of polygamy was 5.8 per cent among Hindu men and 5.7 per cent among Muslim men. That is, there is no meaningful difference in the incidence of polygamy amongst Hindus as compared to Muslims, even though polygamy is legal for Muslims and illegal for Hindus.

In practice, the law can be evaded or ignored by men, by virtue of their dominant position in society, the family and the community. A woman, whether Hindu or Muslim, can very often be compelled to accept her husband's bigamy if she is economically and socially dependent on him, or has no security against violence or threats of violence.

Much has been made of the injustice done to a Muslim woman by the provision which allows a man to divorce his wife by pronouncing the word 'Talaq' or 'I divorce you' three times. But, when a man walks out on an unemployed woman and refuses to maintain her or their children, it makes very little difference whether he says to her 'I divorce you' or omits to say this.

We have been approached for help by a very large number of deserted Hindu women who were no better off than deserted Muslim women. For example, a few days ago, a young woman with two small children who was living in a foreign country with her husband, a Brahmin priest there, was suddenly deserted by him. He had been maltreating her and having affairs with other women. Then he disappeared without giving her any warning. The temple authorities sent her back to India. Her parents are too poor to support her; her in-laws are hostile to her. She is uneducated and unskilled. She does not know where her husband is. It is no consolation to her that her husband did not say 'talaq, talaq, talaq' before he walked out.

In many other cases where the whereabouts of the husband are known, and the wife manages to sue him for maintenance, he simply disobeys the court order. The wife has to approach the court all over again. This process can continue indefinitely and the wife will spend more money on court expenses than she is likely to get as maintenance.

Thus, a key consideration is whether a woman has economic and social independence, so that if a husband walks out, she is materially no worse off than she was before. After all, if a wife walks out, a husband is rarely reduced to destitution. The present inequality is built into the economic and social condition of the husband and the wife, the man and the woman. Equality cannot be conferred by any law in the absence of substantial changes in the political, economic and social condition of women.

Unfortunately, the media has helped cloud the real issues. Instead of using this occasion to start a real debate on how to remove various disabilities imposed by the legal system on women of different communities, it has highlighted the issue of injustice to Muslim women in order to whip up anti-Muslim hysteria.

The newspapers are full of demands for a common civil code. This would mean scrapping not only Muslim and Christian personal law, but doing away with Hindu personal law as well. But scrapping Hindu personal law has not figured anywhere in the media debate. It is assumed that Hindu law is already the last word in secularism, and all that needs to be done is to extend a version of the so-called reformed Hindu law to all other communities.

As was stated earlier, while in some aspects Hindu law is somewhat better, in many other aspects it is much worse than Muslim personal law. But most people vociferously involved in the debate seem either to be ignorant of or are deliberately ignoring this fact.

A group of self-styled reformers in Uttar Pradesh has, in response to the Shah Bano judgement, prepared a cassette recording of arguments for scrapping Muslim personal law, a copy of which they sent to us. In this they wax eloquent about the agonies of a Muslim mother: 'What cruelty is inflicted upon a mother when her suckling child is snatched away because the Shariat gives the man the right over the child! The mother who kept the child in her womb for nine months, who suffered the pangs of childbirth, who starves so that she may feed the child, who remains sleepless that the child may sleep, who bears heat and cold but shelters the child in her lap, is told that on the authority of the Shariat this portion of her heart must be snatched from her! What kind of justice is this?'

What these ardent sympathizers of the Muslim mother forget is that under the Hindu Minority and Guardianship Act, a Hindu father is 'the natural guardian' of a child above the age of five. Under Muslim personal law, the father is considered the guardian of a child over seven years of age (although it has been held in certain cases that the mother is to be considered the guardian of a girl up to the age of puberty). What, then, is the intention of an outpouring like the one quoted above? Clearly, if it was inspired by sympathy for the divorced woman whose child is taken away from her, it would not focus exclusively on the Muslim woman, when other women too suffer the same lack of rights to custody of their children.

The cassette goes on to say: 'All social evils are built into the foundation of Muslim personal law.' There is no acknowledgement today that many features of Muslim personal law are in fact better than the features of other personal laws. To take only one example, a Muslim can dispose of only one third of his or her property by making a will. Two-thirds go to the heirs in fixed proportions. Thus, a Muslim father cannot disinherit his daughters by making a will in favour of the sons, as a Hindu father can.

When such facts are not acknowledged, and the Hindu personal law is assumed to be the only norm of 'reformed law' and secularism, the demand for a common civil code becomes suspect.

Hindu communalist bodies like the Shiv Sena and the RSS have issued statements demanding a common civil code in the interests of national unity. But what they mean by national unity is clear from their other statements. For instance, RSS chief Balsaheb Deoras said on 9 November, 1985, that the main purpose of the RSS is Hindu unity and it believes all citizens of India should have a 'Hindu culture.'

When confronted with such sympathizers, who are the very people that stir up anti-Muslim riots, small wonder that women like Shah Bano are compelled to retreat from the position they had taken.

It is indeed unfortunate that after the judgement went in her favour, several prominent Muslim leaders and many fundamentalist organizations began a pressure campaign against Shah Bano. They began to raise the bogey of 'Islam in danger' to frighten Muslim women into submission. This attitude is not unique to Muslim men. Men have tried throughout history to use religion to legitimize their unjust power over women.

When the Hindu Code Bill to reform Hindu law was introduced in Parliament, a similar campaign was launched against it by Hindus. It was not just known conservatives who opposed any reform of Hindu law in relation to women, but even eminent nationalists like Sardar Patel tried to thwart it.

The debate over the Hindu Code Bill waxed fast and furious in Parliament, in the media and amongst the public. Every time it was introduced in the Parliament the debate was inconclusive. The Bill was first introduced in 1944 but could not be passed until 1955.

The Congress was split over the issue, and stalwarts like Pattabhi Sitaramayya, president of the Congress Party, vociferously opposed it. Women members of Parliament were united across the party lines in demanding the reform. This was referred to by members in Parliament as a 'tyranny of women'. Sitaramayya regretted that 'half a dozen lady members can drag us by the heels and make us take up this bill.'

Every clause of the Bill was opposed, including the one that abolished polygamy. Members in Parliament called the Bill 'anti-Hindu and anti-Indian.' The cry of 'religion in danger' was raised. Massive demonstrations against the Bill were staged in different parts of the country and outside Parliament. This massive campaign delayed the passing of the Bill for many years. Various Congress members openly warned Nehru that the Bill would alienate people and could lead to Congress losing the elections.

The most vehemently opposed clause was the one that gave daughters a share in property. Because of this opposition, daughters were finally excluded from a share in ancestral property. Supporters of the bill regretted that by the time it was passed, it had been so amended as to be of very limited benefit to women.

In fact, even today any reform in Hindu law meets with a lot of opposition. For instance, the recent attempt by the Andhra Pradesh state legislature to amend the Hindu Succession Act and make daughters coparceners in joint family property came in for a lot of criticism and was delayed because of opposition by the ruling party at the Centre.

Perhaps we can better understand the implications of this logic if we compare the reactions of Muslims as a minority to a situation where Hindus are in a minority—say in Britain. What if the British government were to decide that Hindu marriage law and customs are backward and the cause of injustice to women and, therefore, declare that all those aspects of Hindu personal law which are contrary to contemporary British notions of justice for women are to be considered invalid? They could argue that since Hindu marriage ceremonies make women take vows which are contrary to the notion of equality between the sexes, therefore a Hindu ceremony would be invalid, thereby legislating that all marriages be performed in a secular way, that is, be registered in British courts. This would bring citizens of different faiths on a common platform and would remove their disparate loyalties to conflicting ideologies.

There is no denying that the British government could argue their case with some logic and that Hindu women in England would undoubtedly be better off in some ways. But it is very likely that the same people who are so strongly arguing in favour of scrapping Muslim personal law would react no differently from the way Muslim leadership is reacting today to what they call 'outside interference'.

Hindus in England are likely to see such a move as a racist attempt by the majority community to repress a minority's culture and religion.

Thus, a minority community's reactions have a logic of their own and cannot be lightly dismissed, especially if the minority has been a disadvantaged community. Both Muslims in India and Hindus in England can well be considered disadvantaged minorities.

In such a situation, the task of removing some of the real causes of their fears has to assume high priority in order to start a meaningful dialogue on the issue of reform within the community.

Even progressive Muslims are feeling nervous and insecure because of the way the community is today being held up for attack while liberal Hindus are taking increasingly aggressive postures. Many of those who have jumped into the fray on the basis of this case have stated that minorities must prove their loyalty to the Constitution by agreeing to a common civil code. Mr Ram Jethmalani is alleged to have even gone so far as to say that this is the price Muslims must pay for staying in India instead of going to Pakistan. In an article in *The Indian Express* of 26 October 1985 he wrote: 'Muslims of India owe loyalty to the Directive Principles of India's Constitution including Article 44. A newly added Article of 1976 (Article 51A) makes it the duty of every citizen to abide by the Constitution and respect its ideals and institutions, to develop the scientific temper, humanism and the spirit of inquiry and reform. The duty is declared to be fundamental and must, therefore, override all obligations arising from any source—secular or divine.'

A scientific temper and a spirit of inquiry can only be developed in an atmosphere of freedom from fear. It is absurd to imagine that a duty to be humane or scientific can be imposed on anyone and can be performed by anyone successfully when it is thus forced. All that can be done is to provide an atmosphere conducive to the development of such a temper, and hope that exposure and opportunity will lead people to develop the best in themselves. A scientific temper and a humane spirit are not commodities available for sale nor can they be obtained by filling out a form and paying a fee.

Further, to say that citizens must respect all the ideals of the Constitution is to convert the Constitution into a substitute for a holy book. If every word in the Constitution is to be taken as unquestionable truth and blindly obeyed, then how is it different from what many religions impose on their followers? It is most unscientific to advocate such slavish adherence to any set of ideals and institutions. It should be a fundamental right to criticize, comment upon and feel dissatisfied with aspects of the Constitution as of any book, holy or otherwise.

Is it possible or desirable to impose any one loyalty on people? Should loyalty to the state override loyalties to family, friends, community and to one's beliefs? If the state turns fascist, as it did in Germany under Hitler, would the citizens have an overriding duty to sacrifice their other loyalties at its altar?

This is precisely the logic used by fascists—one country, one religion (or lack of religion), one party, one leader—to crush all voices of dissent. Such oneness is achieved not by uniting people but by crushing out of existence those who do not fit into the ideal pattern imposed on them from above. A major reason why Jews were hated in Europe was because they were the main visible non-Christian group in Christian-dominated societies.

The Hindu community has to learn to enter debate and discussion about the affairs of the minority communities without engaging in physical and cultural aggression. Statements such as 'If the Muslims don't want this change, let them go to Pakistan' are based on the arrogant assumption that this country belongs only to Hindus and others can stay here only on their terms. Such an approach, far from bringing about 'national integration', will tear apart the country and its people. We have to understand that conservative Muslims and Christians have as much right to be citizens of this country as do conservative Hindus.

The most important task is to prevent Hindu communalists from using what is essentially a women's rights issue for the purpose of stirring up communal hatred against the Muslims and other minorities. This hatred campaign can only have the effect of strengthening Muslim fundamentalists and silencing the voice of reform within the Muslim community.

We should urgently proceed to draft a uniform secular code available to all in this country. However, while working in that direction we need to be extremely vigilant and remember that it is very easy for a dominant majority community to project its own customs and beliefs as the norm which ought to be followed by all others. That is why the idea of a uniform civil code like extending the Hindu personal law to other communities is inadequate and dangerous. We need to resist such a move with determination.

Many liberal-minded people have suggested that a common civil code be devised in such a way as to incorporate the best features of all the existing personal laws—including Hindu, Muslim, Christian and Parsi.

From the standpoint of women's equality, this stand is clearly not adequate. Even if we were to put together some of the best features of existing personal laws, they would still not help women obtain fair and equal treatment. Therefore, a uniform civil code needs to be devised keeping the principles of fairness and equality foremost in mind.

This common civil code should be available to any citizen of India on demand—man or woman. Equal rights for women should be an underlying principle of such a code.

Hindu, Muslim, Christian or other personal religious laws should be a matter for the believers to accept or not accept without being enforced by the state. The government should not be permitted to enforce or even participate in the administration of religious personal law nor should such law be incorporated in any way into the laws of the state, if it is to remain secular. Enforcement of religious law should be a private matter resting solely on the voluntary moral commitment of the parties to any dispute. The option of choosing the common civil code should always be available to all parties to any disagreement, and the government should only have the authority to enforce the common civil code, and not personal religious law. Implementation of religious law should occur solely as a consequence of the free assent of all parties to a dispute to the decision of the religious authority.

Instead of becoming the tail-end of controversies unleashed by men, women's organizations need to take the lead in working out the provisions of a common civil code. We need an intensive debate on this issue. We must also make sure that women of minority communities are fully involved in the debate and in working out a new code of women's rights.

Given the history of the actual functioning of the legal machinery in India, we need to give crucial attention to how these laws can actually be implemented.

Some important steps in that direction would be as follows:

1. The government should assume the responsibility for informing every citizen, especially women, of their basic rights and the options available to them. A manual of basic rights with special emphasis on women's legal rights should be provided free to every household by the government.

2. The new laws must be framed in simple language and available in all the regional languages.

However, even while making a strong plea for a common civil code, let us not have any illusions that this can have any rapid effect in substantially changing women's lives in this country.

The vast majority of women in this country cannot even dream of approaching courts of law for seeking justice. It is totally beyond the realm of possibility for them for various reasons. Most women do not have the right to take independent decisions in such matters. Just as marriage is decided by families, so is divorce and other related problems. In this country, divorce is not a matter of choice for most women, whether Hindu or Muslim. It is usually unilaterally thrust on them by their husbands. In such a situation, they are usually left without any means of their own so that they become dependent on their adult sons or their natal family's goodwill and support. Most women would not dare approach the courts against the wishes of their natal families. Most families in India settle these matters either by direct negotiation or by appealing to some biradari or kinship elders to act as intermediaries. Even though women don't manage to get justice very often through such interventions, the system has the advantage of being quick and inexpensive. Even among those who have adequate resources, few think of going to court. Even for them, the time and energy involved in legal procedures makes it a very unattractive proposition. Moreover, even women whose families have the required resources hesitate to take this recourse because the outcome is uncertain and unlikely to go in the woman's favour.

Given the remoteness of the legal system from most ordinary people, few women are even likely to be aware that such redress through the courts might be possible for them. Thus, the position of women within the family, most women's lack of resources to fight expensive legal battles, as well as the incredibly poor functioning of the legal machinery, make the legal system virtually inaccessible to all but a very few women in India.

Yet, this is not to suggest that attempts to change laws are a totally irrelevant exercise. Even if, in the foreseeable future, change in laws affect the lives of only a small minority, it does become a pointer in the direction from which overall changes need to come. One hopes that such changes will make the society publicly commit itself to more humane norms even if practice lags behind. It will make the task of extending equal rights to women somewhat easier.

10

Breaking the Stalemate:
Uniform Civil Code versus Personal Law

One of the most contentious political issues in India today is that of a uniform civil code versus personal laws of various minority communities. The bitter polarization of opinion around this question has played a big role in worsening relations among various communities in the country, especially between Hindus and Muslims.

The government policy on this issue has always been confused. Based as it has been on narrow and short-sighted electoral considerations, it appears to the majority community as proof of dangerous appeasement of the minorities, and has, therefore, come to be aggressively resented. In its attempt to placate sometimes one and sometimes another vote bank, the issue of a uniform civil code has been grievously mishandled by successive governments, thus sharpening the divide between the Hindus and the Muslims.

It is not often recognized that the controversy over the issue started with the methods by which the Hindu personal law was codified and reformed in the 1950s. The supporters of the Hindu Code Bill had described it as a major step towards 'social revolution', one that would 'eliminate . . . all disparity in the rights of men and women in matters of marriage, succession and adoption'. More important, the Bill was seen as a measure that would pave the way for a uniform civil code. It was also seen as an attempt to show that the Hindu Personal Law was superior to the laws of other minority communities and should therefore be emulated by them.

However, four decades later, most of these expectations have remained unfulfilled. Women governed by the reformed Hindu law continue to feel no less aggrieved than Muslim women, on account

First published in *Manushi* No. 77 (Jul–Aug 1991).

of the fact that at the ground level, especially in rural areas, things have not changed substantially despite the fancy promise of equality given to them at the time of the reform of the Hindu law. A good indicator is the continuing and growing disinheritance of women, especially with regard to property in land, housing and other income-generating forms of wealth. Despite the existence of the Hindu Succession Act since 1956 and its projection as the key to improving women's status, inheritance rights continue to elude most women. It is the same story with divorce, maintenance and custody laws.*

A close look at the reformed Hindu law exposes the following drawbacks:

1. The rights envisaged for women in the draft Hindu Code Bill were extremely limited and far from equal.
2. In the course of parliamentary debates even the limited provisions of the Hindu Code Bill were substantially diluted.
3. The new Acts set up an untenable and self-contradictory system that lent itself early to subversion.
4. The reformed law was a curious hybrid of Hindu law and British Victorian law, and in many cases, of the more irrational parts of the two systems of law.
5. Far from combining the most progressive elements of various branches of Hindu law, as was claimed by the pro-reform lobby in the government, the new Acts provided women with rights more restrictive that those laid down in many of the ancient texts or those sanctioned by some contemporary customs and practices. The actions of the reformers led to the decline of a number of functioning local customary systems, some of which provide better protection to women, not just in theory but in practice.
6. The flaws in the conception of the codified Hindu law were in large part owing to the fact that the Indian legislatures were hegemonized by certain north Indian castes and communities representing far more repressive social norms with regard to women than those prevailing in most other parts of India, especially in the South and the North-East. Their perceptions of what were and what ought to be the limits of women's rights came to dominate the codified Hindu law, thus causing a definite erosion of rights for women in many other parts of the country.
7. Even the limited rights conferred by the Acts remained illusory

*For a detailed analysis of reformed Hindu law see Madhu Kishwar, 'The codified Hindu Law', in *Economic and Political Weekly*, Vol. XXIV No. 33, 13 August 1994.

in the absence of an adequate implementation machinery. Even so, the use of an exaggerated rhetoric of reform created the misleading impression that the changes brought about were a radical move towards guaranteeing equality for women. Furthermore, the imposition of the legal reform on Hindus alone, leaving other religious communities to continue with their personal laws, created amongst the Hindus deep resentment against the minorities in general and Muslims in particular, thus aggravating the communal divide in the country.

What was meant to be a pace-setter for other communities ended up making the prospects of a meaningful, consensual uniform civil code even more bleak than was the case in the 1950s. The cause of a common civil code suffered a further set-back following the Shah Bano controversy This issue is now being used as a political weapon by the *Hindutvavadis* who insist that the minorities should show their patriotism by following the norms laid down by the majority communities. In the process, considerations of women's rights recede far into the background. The advocates of the common civil code seldom pause to ask themselves the basic question: if the reformed law could not adequately protect the rights of Hindu women nor protect them from domestic violence, what is the guarantee that a common civil code will prevent the violation of Muslim women's rights by the men of their own families?

However, even though the existing Hindu law is far from egalitarian, and its implementation inefficient, it has had substantial impact in changing social norms. The rhetoric of equality has encouraged Hindu women to believe that they are at par with men and given them confidence to demand further improvements in law whenever it does not pass the test of equality. Thus, Hindu law is constantly evolving, both through amendments and interpretation by judges, and provides space for hope, something presently denied to Muslim women. The refusal of certain sections of the Muslim leadership to consider urgently required changes in the Muslim Personal Law is extremely irresponsible and patently anti-women. Even if one were to gracefully concede the right of the Muslim community in India to be governed by their religious personal laws, one cannot overlook the following facts:

1. That there is a wide diversity in the manner in which Koranic injunctions are interpreted and implemented among diverse Muslim communities in various parts of the world. Saudi Arabia, Egypt, Malaysia, Pakistan and Sri Lanka are governed by different

interpretation of laws and different customary practices regarding inheritance and other rights for women. Even within India, there are enormous differences from one region to the other in the way community customs intermix with Muslim personal law and diverse practices observed, especially with regard to divorce and inheritance rights. For instance, Kashmiri, Malayali and Assamese Muslims have no tradition of purdah or burqa whereas Muslims of north India and Pakistan have treated it as an integral part of an Islamic religious code.

2. Many Islamic countries including Pakistan have introduced substantial changes in family laws. In Pakistan, a man cannot take a second wife without the permission of the court, which is supposed to allow bigamy only in rare circumstances, and that too with the consent of the first wife. Similarly, in Bangladesh, under the existing Muslim marriage law, a husband must have his wife's permission and a clearance in writing from the arbitration council, which is headed by a village-level political leader, before a valid second marriage can take place. Now, progressive sections are supporting a parliamentary Bill, moved by Farida Rahman of the ruling Bangladesh Nationalist Party, that seeks to make court permission mandatory for a husband seeking divorce or a second wife. However, the Muslim personal law in India imposes no such restrictions on a bigamous marriage. Even so, Indian Muslims continue to propagate the myth that the personal law they uphold for Muslims in India is part of a universal pure Koranic code. In actual fact, it deviates considerably from many of the Koranic injunctions as well as from Muslim law practised in many Islamic countries.

3. The Muslim religious leadership has failed to ensure that the rights sanctioned to women according to their own version of personal law or Koranic tenets are implemented. For instance, very few women inherit their legitimate share (half that of brothers) which they are entitled to get in their parental property. Likewise, divorced wives seldom manage to get the promised mehr from their husbands. Shah Bano herself came to the law courts only because her rights under the personal law were not protected and her husband refused to give her the amount due to her as mehr. The task of ensuring that the husband honoured some of his responsibilities and commitments had traditionally been performed at the community level. With the breakdown of those traditional safeguards, and the absence of alternative modern

safeguards, Muslim women's position has become very vulnerable.

There are long-term and formidable issues involved in introducing a uniform civil code in India. Their solution requires a delicate balance between the conflicting claims of minority rights of Muslims as a community and citizenship rights of Muslim women. This already difficult problem has been made almost intractable because the political thinking on this issue has presented it in absolutely dichotomous terms. The debate has consequently got hopelessly polarized. One is allowed no other position except being either 'for' or 'against' the common civil code. The Hindu chauvinists see the Muslim resistance to the common civil code as proof of their lacking national loyalty. The Muslim fundamentalists have made the retention of even the non-Koranic aspects of the Muslim personal law the ultimate test of the secular credentials of the Indian state.

The recent debate within the Muslim community on the issue of triple talaq is a welcome development and has been undertaken by people who clearly want to address themselves to two crucial tasks:

a) How to provide the requisite protection for Muslim women.
b) How to curb the growing hostility between the Hindus and the Muslims. Unfortunately, a section of the Muslim leadership is insisting on mere theological hair-splitting on the length of time required between the three pronouncements of the word 'talaq'. They refuse to face the fact that such arbitrary powers in the hands of men and the hapless dependence of women is not conducive to the well-being of their own community. Like the Hindu chauvinists, the Muslim fundamentalist leadership is also using the issue of personal law as a weapon with which to keep its own community ghettoized and in its political clutches.

Even those of us who oppose the politics of the Sangh Parivar in forcing the issue of a common civil code for political ends cannot overlook the manner in which the talaq provisions are being currently practised in India. It leaves the Muslim women totally defenceless in case their husbands choose to exercise certain arbitrary powers currently at their disposal. This needs to change.

One possible solution to the current stalemate is to forget the idea of imposing a common civil code on the Muslim community against its wishes. An optional but egalitarian common code should be made available to any person on demand, no matter what community he or she may belong to. This would mean that the state machinery is not made available for implementing any religious laws—Hindu, Muslim or Christian. Equal rights for women should be the underlying principle of such a code. The Muslim leadership cannot legitimately oppose the right of voluntary choice.

This also implies that the codified Hindu law as incorporated in the Hindu Marriage Act, the Hindu Succession Act and the Hindu Adoption and Guardianship Act will also cease to be administered by the secular courts. Those who wish to be governed by the Hindu, the Christian or the Muslim law will have to devise their own institutional arrangements for the purpose.

Hindu, Muslim, Christian or other personal religious laws should be a matter for the believers to accept without being enforced by the state. Enforcement of religious law should be a private matter, resting solely on the voluntary moral commitment of the parties involved. At the same time, the option of choosing a common code should always be available to all the concerned parties in any domestic dispute. For instance, if a man or a woman feels dissatisfied with the manner in which his/her community administered the personal law in his/her case, the person should be free to approach the civil courts and demand that the provisions of the egalitarian civil code be applicable in their case.

So far, the existing maintenance laws even for Hindu women are extremely unsatisfactory and unworkable. That is why most Hindu women seek maintenance under section 125 of the Criminal Procedure Code (Cr PC). Even Shah Bano approached the court to ask for maintenance under section 125A of the Cr PC. This section of the Cr PC is not really the relevant provision for the maintenance of a divorced wife. It exists to safeguard all destitute women, children and old parents. Yet most divorced women have to sue for maintenance under this clause because it comes under criminal law and provides relief somewhat more quickly. But under this clause, a wife can get a maximum maintenance of only Rs 500. This amount is about one-third to half the statutory minimum wage for unskilled labour. Shah Bano had approached the court under this provision of the Cr Pc and got a paltry sum of Rs 179 as maintenance allowance from the Supreme Court after a 10-year-long battle in the courts.

Unfortunately, even this pitiful relief has been denied to Muslim women after the Congress government passed the Muslim Women's Act of 1986. Thus, the state is behaving unconstitutionally by discriminating against Muslim women. Muslim women ought to be treated at par with other women if they come to government law courts.

An interesting proposal has been put forward by Dhirubhai Sheth, my colleague at the Centre for the Study of Developing Societies, in response to the recent debate on the triple talaq. According to him, we should start with the assumption that the right of unilateral talaq is available to Muslim men under Koranic law. It is futile debating on whether simultaneous pronouncement of the word 'talaq' is enough to make a divorce valid or a certain amount of time must elapse between the three pronouncements. We have to accept the fact that in reality the simultaneous triple pronouncement of talaq is the given practice and large sections of orthodox opinion are in favour of retaining the one time talaq. The traditional restraints imposed on making it an altogether whimsical affair have collapsed because of the rapid breakdown of community life and the accompanying social restraints. For instance, according to tradition, talaq was supposed to have been executed in the presence of others of the community, that is, an assembly of some kind. This at least ensured that the husband abided by the terms of the marriage contract. But now one hears of an increasing number of cases of gross abuse of this provision: a husband pronouncing triple talaq over a minor quarrel, without any witnesses or merely sending off a letter, or communicating divorce though a long-distance call, without any warning or preparation. The Muslim religious authorities have not shown themselves equal to the task of ensuring that the conditions laid down for the protection of women in the Muslim personal law are honoured. This leads to frequent irresponsible and whimsical use of the provisions of talaq.

Dhirubhai suggests that while the triple talaq may be allowed to stay as an integral part of the Muslim personal law, the entire procedure ought to be brought under the jurisdiction of the government law courts. Thus, a Muslim husband wishing to divorce his wife would be required to give a legal notice and pronounce 'talaq' in front of a judge in a full court. This would act as some kind of a modern substitute for the community assembly. The secular court would not challenge the validity of Muslim men's right to resort to unilateral talaq. Instead it would declare the talaq to be operative only after ensuring that all the other terms and conditions of the *nikahnaama*, Muslim marriage contract, have been honoured. Thus, the Muslim personal law would remain intact and the courts would merely ensure that it is not administered individually or capriciously and that it comes to be declared in the presence of legal witnesses.

This proposal is based on the premise that while the Muslim personal law may be considered sacred by the followers of Islam, the administering person does not enjoy any such status according to Islamic tenets. Since the Muslim marriage is in the nature of a contract, modern law courts are equipped to monitor and ensure that the terms and conditions of the contracted marriage are adhered to by the parties concerned in a satisfactory way.

11

Stimulating Reform, not Forcing it:
Uniform versus Optional Civil Code

T he recent Supreme Court judgement by Justice Kuldip Singh and Justice R. Sahai has strongly recommended that the Central Government enact a uniform civil code for all citizens irrespective of their religious faith. This judgement has received wide acclaim as an example of judicial activism. It is widely perceived as a laudable attempt to undo the harm done by the Muslim Women's Protection Act of 1986, passed by the Rajiv Gandhi government following the Supreme Court judgement by Chief Justice Y.V. Chandrachud in the Shah Bano case. Even though the Supreme Court decisions in both these cases were ostensibly meant to protect Muslim women against male tyranny and oppression, a close reading shows that the judges have let other considerations influence their concern for gender justice.

Justice Chandrachud and others had concluded the Shah Bano case judgement with the same kind of regret expressed by Justices Singh and Sahai that Article 44 of our Constitution (promising that the state shall endeavour to secure for the citizens a uniform civil code throughout the country) has remained a dead letter. They noted: 'A common civil code will help the cause of national integration by removing disparate loyalties to laws which have conflicting ideologies.'

The recent judgement by Justices Singh and Sahai goes much further. It has very little to say on the issue of gender justice. The judges seem more worried about Hindus converting to Islam than about the injustice done to wives whose husbands convert to Islam in order to enter into another marriage without obtaining a divorce. Even while discussing the illegality of a second marriage after such

First published in *Manushi* No. 89 (Jul–Aug 1995).

a conversion, Justice Singh concentrates mainly on denying legitimacy to the conversion. There is hardly any mention of the impact of bigamous marriages on the abandoned women and children. After that he goes on to devote disproportionate attention to the other supposed benefits of enacting a common civil code. In the opinion of the judges a unified code is imperative 'both for the protection of the oppressed and promotion of national unity and solidarity.'

The judges seem to be harbouring a curious misconception that 'the traditional Hindu law—the personal law of the Hindus—governing inheritance, succession and marriage was given a go-by as far back as 1955-56 codifying the same.' Therefore, they argue that there is no justification whatever in delaying indefinitely the introduction of a common civil code in the country: 'The Hindus, along with Sikhs, Buddhists, and Jains, have forsaken their sentiments in the cause of the national unity and integration, some other communities would not, though the Constitution enjoins the establishment of a "common civil code" for the whole of India.'

It needs to be understood that Hindu personal law was not secularized in 1955-56. It was merely codified and reformed—and not necessarily for the better as far as women's rights are concerned. The reformed Hindu law is a shabby, impractical piece of legislation and has failed to provide justice to women whose rights continue to be flouted by their own families.

The judges make it clear in their judgement that they have another agenda in recommending a uniform civil code:

Those who preferred to remain in India after the Partition fully knew that the Indian leaders did not believe in two-nation or three-nation theory, and that in the Indian Republic there was to be only one nation—Indian nation—and no community could claim to remain a separate entity on the basis of religion. It would be necessary to emphasize that the respective personal laws were permitted by the British to govern the matters relating to inheritance, marriages, etc., only under the Regulation of 1781 framed by Warren Hastings. The legislation—not religion—being the authority under which personal law was permitted to operate and is continuing to operate, the same can be superseded/supplemented by introducing a uniform civil code.

Two things stand out in this statement:
- That our administrators and judges define their relationship to the people they 'govern' in the same manner and form as did our erstwhile colonial rulers. The language used is haughty and imperial.

- Laws are not meant to reflect a social consensus as they strive in most cases to do in free and civilized societies. The laws are meant to reflect the will of the rulers—what they will 'permit' and what they will not.

No wonder no one heeds laws in our country and people go about their lives according to what their respective communities and biradaris consider appropriate.

It is surprising that even our Supreme Court judges are unaware of the fact that it is not just Muslims who follow their subgroup norms in working out their family affairs. Diverse Hindu subgroups do the same. One has only to compare the marriage, inheritance and divorce patterns among, say, the Hindu Jats of Haryana, with those of Kashmiri Pandits; or the Reddys in Andhra Pradesh and Nairs in Kerala, to observe that formal laws come into play only in those infrequent cases where families decide to go to court. By and large people settle these matters at the family and biradari level according to their respective customs and the relative bargaining power of the two sides, without reference to laws. Only a tiny proportion of marital dispute cases reach the courts. In a vast majority of these cases, the biradari elders work out the arrangements and the terms of separation. These vary from one community to another. Dowry, for example, is supposedly not permitted by law. Yet, by common consensus, large dowries are both given and taken by most people, including judges. In fact, our police and IAS officials command and demand the most exorbitant dowries in the marriage market. Clearly then it is not formal laws but social norms which govern social relations in our country. When Hindus themselves have failed to become law-abiding in such matters, why are they so enthusiastic about reforming Muslim personal law through a uniform civil code?

This is not exactly a legal judgement but more of a political sermon on how the Muslim minority should learn to behave and what ought to be its relationship to the Indian state. It is tempting to pick up cudgels against it as a case of judicial impropriety if one did not realize that the judges are echoing a very broad-based concern which cuts across the entire mainstream political spectrum in our country. The judges seem to believe and fear that the real reason for the Muslim community's insistence on their Islamic personal law is to reassert Jinnah's two-nation theory. This is a widely held fear; and parties like the BJP have been capitalizing on it most aggressively. Now the BJP has declared that it is going to enact a common civil code in all the states where it is in power. The insistence on a uniform civil code is a way of subjecting Muslims to a loyalty test. It is a way of asking them to prove that their allegiance to the Indian nation state and its laws (including the unjust as well as the stupid ones) stands above all other competing allegiances, especially to that of religion.

In the opinion of most Hindus, the offensive part of Muslim personal law are the provisions of triple *talaq* and and that allowing a Muslim man to have up to four wives simultaneously. In this their real concern is not the injustice it involves for Muslim women, but the absurd fear that through polygamous marriages the rate of population growth among Muslims will outstrip that of Hindus. Thus the Hindus will become a minority in India. In actual fact, Muslim men do exactly what a large number of Hindu men do—that is, beat and force the first wife out of the house or simply marry a second time without the bother of a formal divorce. They make it so difficult for the first wife that she is compelled to leave her marital home. Recently, we were approached for advice by a young woman who is the daughter-in-law of a well-known retired Delhi High Court judge. The only son of this judge has a relationship with another woman. He even brings her home and lives with her openly in the presence of his first wife. Do you think this High Court judge and his wife have assisted their daughter-in-law in suing her husband for cruelty because their son beats and abuses her in an attempt to drive her out of her marital home? Far from it. All they are doing is trying to bully her into giving their son a formal divorce so that he can remarry. Needless to say, the first wife will not be getting a divorce on grounds of cruelty because she has been prevailed upon to obtain a divorce by 'mutual consent'.

Bigamy may have been outlawed by the Hindus, but the law against it is invoked only in rare cases when the first or second wife decides to take the matter to court. Census statistics and various surveys have shown that the extent of polygamy among the Hindus is about the same as among the Muslims, even though the Hindus are not allowed bigamous marriage according to Hindu Code law. We even have several bigamous marriages among Hindu celebrities such as the one between film stars Hema Malini and Dhamendra. The courts could do nothing in the matter simply because Dharmendra's first wife did not approach the courts. My own domestic help, Sushila, has been deserted by a man who married four times without divorcing any of his wives. If the bigamous marriage of Dharmendra or Sushila's husband are not a threat to 'national unity', why are Muslim bigamous marriages perceived to be such? When Haryana or Punjab Jats continue the customary practice of *karewa* marriages(marrying a widow to her late husband's brother), sometimes involving bigamy in defiance of the Hindu Marriage Act, the state governments even support those measures. The Hindu and Sikh Jats are not assumed to be disloyal to the Indian nation by committing bigamy. But a Muslim defending polygamous marriages is seen as a threat to national unity—not as just another propagator of gender injustice.

This is not to justify bigamous marriages but only to point out that the problem is more complex than the uniform civil code enthusiasts are willing to concede. The problem can be solved only if we focus on the gender injustice dimension of it rather than let other political considerations derail the women's rights agenda. In fact, the present Hindu marriage law against bigamy is so hopelessly ineffective that even if a deserted wife wants to take action against her husband, there is not much that she can do. The onus of 'proving' the second relationship to be a bigamous marriage falls on the first wife. To prove the second marriage was bigamous, the first wife has to be able to procure witnesses willing to testify not only that the second marriage was solemnized but also that all rituals and ceremonies were duly performed. For example, a Hindu marriage is not legally valid until the ritual *saptapadi* (seven *feras* round the sacred fire) is completed. Thus, if a man can get a couple of witnesses to say that he took only six feras and not seven, he would not be considered legally married to the second wife. In such cases, the first wife cannot get him punished for bigamy but only for adultery— and that too only if she can prove to the satisfaction of the court that adultery occurred. There is no real punishment for adultery except that the wronged spouse can use it as grounds for divorce. Thus it only facilitates the process of a legal divorce, often in the man's favour, as opposed to punishing him for the crime of bigamy.

Manushi has had to deal with several cases where a woman approached us for help in getting her husband charged with the crime of entering into a second bigamous marriage without divorcing his first wife. But despite their best efforts, they could not establish the fact of a second marriage even though the husbands concerned were openly living with the second wives, and had even had children by them. A first wife is not likely to be invited to collect evidence at the time of a second marriage that was attended and managed by the man and his second wife's close friends and family. None of these people are likely to give evidence in favour of the first wife.

Since Hindu marriage law does not require all marriages to be compulsorily registered, for most people a marriage is valid if the families concerned and their relatives give social recognition to them as a married couple. A Hindu man may commit bigamy with impunity as long as his family recognizes his second marriage. His first wife needs superhuman clout to 'prove' bigamy in a court of law if she is to challenge the second marriage. Thus, the continuing practice of bigamy is clearly not the real worry of common code enthusiasts for otherwise they would have taken steps against maltreatment and unilateral desertion of wives by Hindu men. Their real worry is the insistence of Muslim leaders that allegiance to Shariat is more important to them than their allegiance to the Indian nation-state.

Instead of seeking assurance that Muslims are loyal to India in indirect ways, why don't the leaders of these campaigns struggle over this issue without using the well-being of Muslim women as a battering ram?

The Hindu fears spring from the fact that, especially in north India, they have neither forgotten nor forgiven the Muslim leadership of pre–Independence days for forcing a partition in the subcontinent. Most Hindus are convinced that, given the opportunity, Muslims will force more and more Partitions on India. The ongoing secessionist movement in Kashmir with the active help of Pakistan further fuels these fears.

For Pakistan, the secession of Bangladesh was no more than a political humiliation and loss of territory. That is why Pakistanis were able to get over the breakup of their country with relative ease. Most Pakistanis have no emotional attachment to the land and culture of Bangladesh. Nor did renouncing sovereignty in Bangladesh involve any uprooting from their homes for the people of West Pakistani. For Hindus, on the other hand, Partition meant very different things. To begin with, millions were uprooted from their homes and their culture. Even though the Hindu refugees have been fully absorbed into the social and political mainstream in India, unlike what has happened to the Mohajirs who went to Pakistan, the wounds of Partition remain and are, in fact, shared by even those who were not personally affected by it. This is because Hindus see India not just as a political territory but as a civilizational entity. They are imbued with a sense that its geography is sacred, that their country is *punyabhumi*. Bharat Mata has, in fact, become among the most revered Hindu goddesses. Muslims are portrayed as her disloyal sons who severed her arms. Moreover, many of the important religious and historical spots of Hindus and Sikhs are located in what is now Pakistan.

The inability of most Indian Muslims to feel hostile towards Pakistan and to consider Pakistanis as enemies makes many Hindus distrust them. The trauma of the Partition might perhaps have been easily forgotten had the two nation-states evolved more civilized polities and worked out sensible norms for mutual coexistence. The leadership in both countries did the very opposite and kept their mutual phobias alive.

On the Hindu side, there is some justification for feeling wronged because the fate of Hindus in Pakistan and in Bangladesh is even worse than the fate of Muslims in India. They are not even treated as second-class citizens. Both countries have declared themselves to be theocratic Islamic states. Though in the 1940s, the Hindus constituted a substantial percentage of the population in what is now Pakistan, there is only a minuscule community of Hindus left there today. Similarly, in recent days there has been a steady and continuing decline of the Hindu population in Bangladesh. This is mainly due to forced exodus and open persecution of Hindus in these two countries. Voices like that of Taslima Nasreen, exposing the plight of the Hindu minority in Bangladesh, are far more rare than are the voices of defenders of Muslim minority rights in India. These two governments are also far more brazen in pushing Hindus out by forcible expropriation of their properties, open religious persecution, denial of jobs and political rights, as well as destruction of Hindu religious shrines.

The separatist and pro-Pakistan secessionist movements in Kashmir have reinforced Hindu fears that wherever Muslims are in a majority, they tend to work towards the breakup of India, and that Muslim majority polities, be it in Pakistan or Kashmir, inevitably move towards driving the Hindu minorities out by sheer force. All Muslim majority *mohallas* like Behrampada in Bombay and Jama Masjid in Delhi tend to be labelled as mini-Pakistans and targeted for attack like enemy territory during periods of Hindu–Muslim conflict. In this matter, Hindu leaders display the nervousness of a besieged minority rather than behave like a self-assured majority. It is indeed important to sort out the various irritants and mistrust between the Hindus and the Muslims in India. This task needs to be undertaken even more urgently than reform of Muslim personal law or bringing justice to Muslim women. Our capacity to sort this out in a straightforward fashion and work out decent norms for Hindus and Muslims to live together will decide the fate of democracy in our country.

The growing mistrust between the Hindus and Muslims cannot be resolved by imposing a uniform civil code on an unwilling Muslim community. It will suffer the fate of the Anti-Dowry Act and become another joke in the name of reform. Most laws have a chance to work only if enough people see them as beneficial to them. Today, by and large, even Muslim women are not enthusiastic about their personal laws being superseded by a uniform civil code. If these women are unwilling to approach the courts to seek the application of new civil laws, what good will it do to have a uniform code on paper?

This is not at all to suggest that social opinion must be the only consideration, or that patently unjust or even criminal types of behaviour must be allowed in the name of respecting social opinion. However, we need to ensure that our laws are respected, not despised. They should be seen and perceived as a rational way of ordering our social relations (as ought to happen in truly civilized societies) rather than an offensive imposition from above as is typical of mentally colonized societies.

For centuries, Hindus and Muslims have been able to evolve fairly impressive norms for living together as neighbours on the basis of shared common interests and other identities that derive from their village, occupational, linguistic, cultural and regional characteristics. Today those traditional pacts are breaking down because the leaders of the two communities have stopped dealing with each other directly. Most of their communication is mediated through the instrumentalities of a venal and incompetent state. For example, if there is a Hindu–Muslim riot, the two communities expect the government to protect them from each other through the use of state police and other arms of the government. There is little attempt to independently and directly work out mutually acceptable arrangements between the two communities for their mutual safety at the local levels, removing the irritants by mutual accommodation. Similarly, those who are upset about the vulnerable position of Muslim women rarely take the trouble to initiate a dialogue with members of the Muslim community as concerned fellow citizens or neighbours. Instead, they begin to yell at the government and demand that *sarkari danda* be used to reform the Muslim community. This facilitates the rise of those politicians who seek power by playing a divide and rule game, leading to escalation of ill–will and conflict between the two communities, rather than any real improvement in the condition of women.

Voices for reform in Muslim law would have been much stronger by now had our lawmakers and lawcourts shown that they are capable of making just laws and implementing them honestly and competently. The majority of Hindu, Sikh and other women who have knocked at the doors of our courts for justice have come away feeling disillusioned and bitter. Not only are the marriage and inheritance laws governing Hindus patently unfair to them, but the way our courts malfunction only adds to the misery of the already aggrieved. A meaningful attempt at reform in any system of laws must first begin by making our legislators, courts and police behave lawfully, fairly, efficiently and competently. Had our courts been able to demonstrate their ability to effectively protect the rights of Hindu women there would have been a much bigger ferment among Muslim women for demanding a reform of Muslim personal law through judicial intervention.

Moreover, there is a real misunderstanding about the nature of personal laws in India. What goes by the name of Muslim personal law is not really based on Shariat, and conforming to it is not a religious requirement. Even triple talaq as practised in India has as little to do with Koranic injunctions as the present-day Hindu marriage laws have to do with the Code of Manu, or the diverse practices of various Hindu communities. The Muslim leaders' position is based on a misunderstanding that the Muslim personal law is founded on the teachings of the Koran and, therefore, any attempt to change it amounts to an attack on the religious identity of the Muslim community. In actual fact, what goes by the name of Muslim personal law is actually Anglo-Indian-Islamic law as it developed in the 19th and early 20th centuries under British rule, in British courts, administered not by Muslim Qazis but by Christian judges. It is now being administered by Indian (mostly Hindu) judges who slavishly hang on to this colonial legacy. The Anglo-Indian-Muslim (as also the Anglo-Hindu) personal laws are a confused interpretation of British court officials' records of customary practices. Similar is the case with the interpretations of the Koran and the Shariat by European judges who neither understood Islam nor the actual customs of Indian Muslims. Yet their judicial verdicts on these matters have come to acquire the force of law because British (and now Indian) jurisprudence allow court judgements to acquire the force of binding precedents, enforced first by the colonial and now by the post-Independence Indian state. Ironically enough, the Muslim leadership rallies around this Anglo-Indian-Islamic law and defends it as though its judgements conform to the words of Allah in the Koran. In actual fact, it is no more than the word and interpretation of British judges and their inheritors.

If we want India's diverse communities to feel a sense of loyalty and goodwill towards each other, if we want all our people to have a stake in building a well-knit society, we need to build a decent civilized polity based on consensus rather than confrontation. This task can be performed better if we build on the following premises:

Every person—Hindu, Muslim, Sikh, Christian, man or woman— ought to feel more secure about their citizenship rights and be able to count on them as their legitimate due in this society. The Indian state has so far failed to perform satisfactorily the task of protecting and safeguarding rights such as those enshrined as fundamental rights in the Constitution. This has led to a growing sense of alienation, especially among socially and economically vulnerable groups. We need to understand that in a democracy, only those states and governments evoke loyalty from their citizens which are able to provide people with a sense of security and safety and are known to behave in a lawful and non-partisan fashion. Thus, it is far more important to ensure that our lawcourts and police function lawfully and efficiently. They should be capable of delivering justice, so that people feel secure about their rights as citizens. This would be better than having one poorly devised and implemented uniform law for all citizens and communities for governing family relations. Meeting these requirements is the only effective route to genuine national unity.

Those of us concerned with women's well-being need to understand that social peace is an absolute precondition for strengthening the rights of women. Whenever violence and bloody conflicts come to dominate a society, women tend to get marginalized and their lives become more vulnerable. At such times they are less able to resist their oppression or effectively protest against abuse. As long as the Muslim community continues to face the brunt of riots, as long as they continue to be ghettoized and feel despised and mistrusted, voices of reform within the community will continue to be marginalized and silenced.

Muslim women can be strengthened to fight for their rights as women only when they stop feeling insecure about their rights as Muslims. They will assert their rights as women more vigorously when they do not feel victimized on account of threats to their religious identity. Therefore, all those interested in the welfare of Muslim women ought to focus their energies on building effective communication channels between Hindus and Muslims so that they can resolve their mutual differences directly and amicably and build an atmosphere of mutual trust and peace. This is as much in the interest of Hindus as of Muslims. Those societies where minorities feel unsafe finally end up being unsafe for all. Safety is indeed indivisible, as the example of Pakistan shows. By forcibly driving out the Hindu majority, the Pakistani politicians have not built a strong and united Pakistan but a nation-state which is dominated by criminalized politicians within various ethnic groups (Punjabis, Mohajirs, Sindhis, Baluchis) at war with each other.

A genuine democracy must have genuine safeguards against majoritarianism. Those who identify themselves as the majority community must not be allowed to tread over the sentiments of the minorities even when they are doing so ostensibly in the latter's interest. While one important component of a democracy is majority vote or opinion as the basis for determining policy, an equally important principle in well-functioning democracies is that majorities, no matter how they are constructed, no matter how preponderant, ought not to have the right to make certain decisions that affect minorities such as deciding whether the minority has the right to live within the boundaries of the territorial state, or to make decisions regarding curtailment of the latter's citizenship rights. Pakistani or Bangladeshi democracies are dysfunctional and authoritarian precisely because they do not provide respectful space for religious or other ethnic minorities. By imposing a uniform civil code on the unwilling Muslim minority, we would be legitimizing the majoritarian authoritarianism of Pakistani and Bangladeshi politics, as well as that of the Kashmiri Muslim separatists.

The ongoing secessionist movement in Kashmir is a good example of the dangers inherent in resorting to majoritarianism even when the majority has a legitimate grievance. The Kashmiri Muslims are undoubtedly right in complaining that the Central Government crushed their democratic rights by repeatedly denying them the right to freely elect their own governments. Instead the Congress party kept imposing puppet regimes or the Central Government's military rule on them. However, their struggle for self-determination is not presently taking a democratic route not only because they resort to terrorism, but also because their demand for secession is based on a majoritarian premise. They have disregarded the sentiments of the substantial Buddhist and Hindu minority (36 per cent) in the state of Jammu and Kashmir who do not share the aspirations of the Kashmiri Muslims and whose right to self-determination the Kashmiri Muslims do not respect.

By creating further disgruntlement in the Muslim minority in the rest of India, we will only strengthen the majoritarian politics of Muslim separatists in Kashmir. A secure and confident Muslim community in India is the best refutation of the poisonous legacy of Jinnah with his two-nation theory, both as practised in Pakistan and as being currently exported to Kashmir through Pakistan-trained terrorists. By resisting reform of many of its outdated social practices, the Muslim community is only harming itself. However, by insisting that the Muslim community be forcibly 'reformed', Hindu leaders are harming the entire Indian society because they are using this issue to whip up anti-Muslim hysteria and promoting social strife and violence in the country.

In reality, diverse Muslim communities follow variegated customary practices, depending on their regional, class and caste status. Just as Urdu is not the language of all Muslims in India, the customs of Kerala or Assamese Muslims, for instance, are substantially different from those of Punjabi or Uttar Pradesh Muslims. By demanding a uniform civil code, the Hindu chauvinist leaders are only facilitating the task of obscurantist Muslim leaders. These leaders can then mobilize the diverse Muslim subgroups using the cry of 'religion in danger', and pretend to lead them as an all-India monolith. Like the Hindu nationalists, the Muslim leaders are also averse to acknowledging that the Muslim community is as rich in cultural diversity as is the Hindu community.

It seems pretty certain that most uniform civil code enthusiasts would lose their enthusiasm for a common civil code if it was optional for all citizens, genuinely egalitarian, and actually implemented. If the Muslim leadership in our country were not as short-sighted as they presently are, they would take the lead in the matter and find that the nationalist chauvinists are not really serious about strengthening the rights of women.

In a country like India, where people do not live atomized lives, where community identity (based on caste, *jati*, religion, language, village and so on) matter a great deal, social opinion and customs determine social behaviour more effectively than government-enacted laws.

The anti-women cultural patterns among various communities need to be combated urgently and effectively. But this task can only be undertaken by those whose real concern is gender justice rather than by people interested in settling political scores with the Muslim community. The cause of gender justice can best be served by:

- Sustained dialogue and discussion within each community as well as among various communities.
- Providing viable options to women who feel they are being treated unjustly by their family or their community, as well as for those who simply do not wish to be governed by religious laws.

Our secular civil courts must not entertain or decide disputes involving personal laws such as the Hindu Marriage or Succession Act nor Muslim or Christian personal laws. The jurisdiction of the secular state starts when a citizen chooses to exercise her option to present her case to be judged under the common civil code. This option should especially be available to persons who feel dissatisfied with the dictates of their community's religious laws or customs.

Many people have responded to *Manushi*'s original proposal of a non-discriminatory optional code by saying that it is impractical and will only create further confusion. Far from it. Before clarifying the principles on which an optional civil code can function, let me explain some of its obvious advantages:

It starts with the realistic premise that in actual practice most people in India—Hindus, Muslims, Sikhs, or Christians—continue to govern their family affairs according to their prevailing community norms. The state can do nothing if the women concerned do not approach it for help. Thus, a common civil code, even if it is enacted, will come into effect only for those who seek its adjudication. However, by presenting it as an option available to any citizen—

man or woman—on demand, rather than something forced on unwilling communities the opponents of reform will have less legitimacy in opposing the enactment of an optional civil code.

Our courts will be freed of some of their backlog if all those desirous of being governed by their religious or customary laws have to make their own arrangements. This will make it more likely that those who come to seek protection under the non-discriminatory civil code get speedier justice and better attention from judges. While enacting such a code we need an in-built provision limiting the amount of time the court is allowed to take to reach a decision. Today, the money and time wasted in judicial delays and corruption keep women frightened of getting involved in legal battles.

If our civil courts actually begin to offer justice to those who opt for the non-discriminatory civil code, various communities will have an incentive to attempt to provide women with a better deal within customary religious laws. Otherwise they will find women opting for the non-discriminatory civil code.

The broad principles of the code would be as follows: when one argues that different communities should be allowed to retain the right to decide issues of personal law among believers who voluntarily accept their jurisdiction, one does not thereby imply that women should be left to the mercy of men in their respective communities who are allowed to tyrannize women into submission in the name of upholding community customs or religious traditions. No one giving a judgement regarding a case in customary or religious law will have the right to invoke sanctions using the power of the state, or enforce their personal laws through physical violence or even threats of violence. For example, issuing of death threats through *fatwas* would clearly not be allowed. Threatening or administering punishments by any other authority but the country's criminal courts is considered a criminal act and would be punishable as such. Similarly, the enforcement through violence of certain taboos among various Hindu communities regarding who one can or cannot marry would be impermissible. For example, there are a number of instances of daughters being killed by their fathers and other male relatives because they dare to marry a man of another caste or religion. This power to kill, maim, or cause bodily harm cannot be sanctioned to biradari panchayats. In case physical violence is used on a dissenting member to ensure submission, the state would treat it as a cognisable offence—even without the person concerned complaining about it.

The common civil code would have to rule out gender discrimination, starting with the rights of daughters, and not just focus on relationships between spouses. For example, a father's will disinheriting a daughter would be considered an invalid legal document under the common civil code. Nor would the secular law-courts be permitted to discriminate against women in the inheritance of joint family property—women will be equal co-sharers in their property and daughters have full coparcenary rights.

What happens if a wife seeking divorce and child maintenance comes to civil court and the husband chooses to turn to his religion's personal laws? When any party to such a dispute chooses the civil court, the case must be governed by that person's decision. For instance, if an adult daughter feels aggrieved at being excluded from Hindu joint family property, she would have the option to come to court and demand that property distribution be made according to a non-discriminatory civil code so that her interests are protected. However, if she voluntarily commits herself to some other system of inheritance, and does not approach the court, the courts cannot interfere.

Similarly, a Muslim woman could sue her husband for bigamy through the civil courts if she feels that the Muslim personal law will not give her justice and that, for her, it is more important to get justice than to submit to the decisions of her community's religious leaders. Thus, law would not be indiscriminately forced on all but will be applied only when the community is unable to satisfy both the parties in a dispute. This is bound to generate pressure within each community to adapt their personal laws to be less discriminatory and acceptable to resolution by consensus, rather than allowing women to be coerced into self-harming situations due to lack of real options.

12

Religion at the Service of Nationalism:
An Analysis of Sangh Parivar Politics

The obsession of the Sangh Parivar—a combination of the BJP, RSS, VHP, Bajrang Dal and other similar groups—with building a new Ram Mandir at Ayodhya is interpreted by secularists as the promotion of excessive religiosity. Nothing could be farther from the truth. The priest of the disputed Ram Mandir at Ayodhya accuses them of embezzling crores of rupees which they collected through donations in the name of Ram. He is reported to have said that none of the Hindutvavadi VHP–RSS leaders had ever 'made a single offering nor had they ever prayed in the temple.'

This is not surprising considering that many of the Parivar leaders belong to sects that did not confer the status of a divine god upon Ram. Moreover, the RSS-BJP support base of activists and leaders in the north comes largely from an Arya Samaj background. This nationalist reform movement, which began in the late nineteenth century, sought to purify Hinduism of 'evils' like idol worship. But today, many Arya Samajis are enthusiastic supporters of the campaign to instal one more idol of Ram Lalla at Ayodhya. This is not out of any religious feeling but with the view of using Ram as a symbol to unify all Hindus as a political community.

The present-day Hindu–Muslim conflict is not really a religious conflict, nor is it rooted in medieval history, as is often assumed. Political conflicts between the likes of Aurangzeb and Shivaji and religious persecution of the Hindus by certain Muslim rulers notwithstanding, India does not have a history of devastating, centuries-long religious denominational wars. Nor do we have a chronic history of Hindu–Muslim riots in pre-British India. Following the period of Islamic invasions, the conflict with the invading Afghani,

First published in *Manushi* No. 76 (May–June 1993).

Mughal, and Turkish Muslims came to be settled rather creatively in India.

Among the many other attempts at accommodation, the Bhakti movement, within the Hindu fold, and Sufism within the Muslim fold, built enduring bridges between the two contrary faiths and softened some of their confrontations on many theological issues. Kabir, Nanak, Rahim, Ravidas, Tukaram as well as many Sufi sants challenged the religious bigotry and tyranny of those claiming to speak in the name of God. They created a corpus of shared beliefs between the followers of Hinduism and Islam by preaching that a life of piety and love was the true religion—not sectarian rituals or following the priesthood blindly.

Almost all sants, bhakts and Sufis had common following among the Hindus, Muslims and the Sikhs. They influenced the language and belief system of popular religion and helped evolve humane norms for living together. Despite all the bloody Hindu–Muslim conflicts of the twentieth century, it is noteworthy that none of the prominent disputes are of a theological nature. The contemporary Hindu–Muslim conflict is primarily the product of late nineteenth and twentieth century politics.

The ideology of the Sangh Parivar is often described as an example of Hindu communalism or Hindu fundamentalism. Those who claim to believe in secularism, including Congressmen, socialists, and leftists, attempt to counter the Sangh Parivar's ideology by emphasizing the need to keep religion out of politics, presumably in order to inculcate the true spirit of nationalism.

The Sangh Parivar cannot be considered as Hindu fundamentalists because the Hindu faith does not base itself on any fundamentals. There is no one text or set of commandments which can be projected by any Hindu religious authority as representing the fundamentals of the Hindu religion for all the diverse communities that come within the Hindu fold. The vast multiplicity of gods and goddesses held sacred by different communities in India make it impossible for any one religious deity to be accepted as the chosen deity of all Hindus. For instance, most Shaivites do not worship Ram, an *avatar* of Vishnu, and Vaishnavites are not inclined to worship Shiv. The Ramayan itself has hundreds of living versions created during different historical periods by different communities. In some of these versions, Ram is not provided the halo of divinity and in some others, he is not even the hero of the epic. The existence of multitudinous sects among Hindus, each with its own set of do's and don'ts, as well as gods and goddesses, make it impossible to devise a set of fundamentals acceptable to all Hindus. In their attempt to unite all Hindus around the Ram Mandir issue, the Sangh Parivar is trying to semiticize Hinduism and make it resemble those aspects of Christianity and Islam which, in their view, helped these two religions become globally powerful and contributed to the evolution of strong nation-states.

Similarly, there is a problem in describing the Sangh Parivar as communalist. Outside of India, communalism is ordinarily defined in one of the following ways:

- A theory or system of government in which virtually autonomous local communities are loosely bound in a federation;
- Belief in or practice of communal ownership of goods and property;
- Strong devotion to the interests of one's own ethnic group rather than those of the society as a whole.

It is noteworthy that the word communal is mostly used in a positive sense in the West. But in India it is almost always used as a pejorative term to denote a person with a religious bias.

The Sangh Parivar is not communal even according to the Indian usage of the term because most of its members are not serious about religion. A religious person would want to retain the autonomy and sanctity of religious institutions. The manner in which the Parivar has brought politics into the religious sphere and hijacked religious symbols for electoral and other political purposes shows that their concern is not religious at all. Nor are the Parivar's leading lights well-versed in religious texts or theology.

Given the well-known bias of the Sangh Parivar for a centralized authoritarian polity, controlled by a strong Centre, it cannot be called communal according to the first definition of the term. Nor does it believe in the communal ownership of property. If one studies the Parivar's own literature seriously, it becomes clear that it cannot be called communal even by the third definition—that is, they do not believe in being devoted to the interests of one's own ethnic group as opposed to devotion to the interests of the nation as a whole.

The last thing the BJP–RSS–VHP Combine wants is that people remain committed to their respective ethnic identities based on caste, language, race or religion. The leaders of this Combine are not comfortable with the fact that different linguistic groups feel a ferocious sense of loyalty to their respective languages. These groups are not willing to accept the one *rashtra bhasha* the Parivar wishes to impose on them. Even while the Hindutvavadi leadership itself articulates the aspirations of certain upper caste groups far more than those of its new-found lower caste supporters, it is uncomfortable with caste-based loyalties because they come in the way of 'uniting' all Hindus. Likewise, regional identities are opposed by the Parivar, as for example, the Nagas demanding autonomy for Nagaland. The Parivar's agenda is to remould the people of this country into one monolith called 'Indians' (also called Hindus). The assumption behind the Sangh Parivar's homogenizing effort is that once people become 'proper Indians' they will have overcome other multilayered, contending loyalties and learnt to put the 'nation before self'.

The Parivaris are embarrassed about the people of India being as they are and want Indians to be 'modernized', that is, Europeanized. It is no coincidence that the uniform of the RSS is not a *dhoti* or any other local dress but khaki knickers which was the uniform of British Sergeant Majors. The Parivaris think that homogenizing the varied people of India is a precondition for building India into a strong modern nation-state modelled after twentieth-century west European nations. In their view, India has failed to become 'strong and mighty' because we are not a monocultural people. They consider the existing diversity of cultures, religions, regions and languages to be the prime cause of India's weakness. They want us to get over this fatal flaw by becoming 'one people' as they imagine Germans, Jews or Japanese are.

They apparently do not realize that truly monocultural states are only possible within tiny homogeneous areas like Denmark. Even west European nations could become only somewhat less multicultural after exterminating or driving out ethnic minorities like the Jews. But in India, even exterminating Muslims will not achieve the task the Parivaris have set themselves because we have inherited numerous other diversities. Pakistan's rulers drove out almost all Hindus but that did not succeed in uniting the wide diversity of peoples in Pakistan. East Pakistan revolted and finally seceded.

Being 'Indian' cannot be a communal identity. It is a political identity. In India there is no community called 'Indian' except perhaps a microscopic section of the English-educated elite. But even this national elite retains its separate communal identity for the purposes of marriage and social bonding. Unlike ethnic identities based on caste or language, political identity can be changed by political acts. For instance, many Muslims born in Uttar Pradesh became Pakistanis during the Partition merely by migrating across the newly created border and accepting the jurisdiction of the government of Pakistan. Similarly, all those who migrate and accept the citizenship of other countries lose their Indian citizenship.

The Parivar leaders clearly admit that for them *rashtra dharm* (that is, nationalism) stands above their religion. To quote a popular theme of the Parivar:

Muslims who value their religion more than their nation, they can never be nationalists. And Hindus who treat religion as a personal matter can never be communalists . . . because those who give pride of place to their nation over their religion cannot be communalists. (Extracted from one of Rithambara's recorded cassettes.)

The Sangh leadership is selectively using gods from the Hindu pantheon while destroying or undercutting the religious and spiritual core of Hindu dharma and forging out of it a hate-filled ideology of nationalism. The Advanis and Jinnahs are mistaken for religious fundamentalists simply because they draw on select religious symbols of the people they seek to mobilize. But that is because of the compulsion of all nationalists to present this alien western ideology in an indigenous garb.

Nationalism has caused more bloodshed and hatred than any other ideology in recent times. The two world wars, other devastating twentieth-century wars, the current bloodshed in East Europe and the war between Iran and Iraq have all been rooted in nationalism.

Before the fifteenth century, nation-states of the modern type were extremely rare. Nationalism as an ideology emerged as a major force in seventeenth-century Europe and achieved maturity in the late nineteenth and early twentieth centuries. Since then, it has become the most dominant ideological force the world over. In India the Sangh Parivar has succeeded in giving it a more virulent form in recent years.

Like all nationalists, this Combine manipulates history to serve its present political purposes. It wants us to believe that every notable Hindu god, king, intellectual figure or warrior in our history or mythology—from Ram, Krishna, Arjun, to Vikramaditya, Chanakya, Shivaji and Rana Pratap—was a nationalist, even though they all lived at a time when the geographical entity called India was not a nation state. The Muslim nationalists of Pakistan face a greater problem. They dare not encourage an honest study of the pre-1947 period, nor look into the early periods in the history of their land, before Muslim invaders came into the subcontinent. Such an inquiry would threaten the very foundation of Pakistan as a nation-state. A friend from Pakistan told me that the Archaeological Department of the Government of Pakistan has put a signboard at the entrance to Mohenjodaro, the famous excavated site of a very early settlement on the Indian subcontinent, saying something to this effect: 'This is what Allah does to infidels—reduces them to ruins.'

The excessive respectability accorded to nationalism in Third World countries is due to the legitimacy it enjoys in the hegemonic West, the homeland of this ideology as well as the original source of its association with the patriotism evoked by anti-colonial movements.

However, anti-colonialism (freedom from foreign rule) and patriotism (love of one's people and the land in which one is born) are not identical with nationalism. For instance, Gandhi's patriotism was very different from the nationalism of Jinnah and that of the RSS. Gandhi's politics focused on ending colonial rule as well as strengthening the rights of the poor and the vulnerable. Jinnah's politics was not anti-colonial. He was known to be pro-British and only too eager to make opportunistic deals with colonial rulers in order to weaken the Indian freedom movement. His politics was elitist and showed little concern for redistribution of power and wealth in favour of the poor within the Muslim community. He confined his battle to strengthening the power of the Muslim elite against the Hindu elite. Jinnah was not even remotely religious and did not observe basic Islamic religious tenets. He merely used and manipulated certain religious identities to mobilize Muslims to declare themselves a separate nation. He cannot be called a patriot for he voluntarily deserted the land of his birth in western India for a new nation-state. He jeopardized the safety and well-being of millions of his own people, by forcing a bloody Partition on the country. All those Muslims who remained in India after 1947 are living precarious lives because of the manner in which the Hindus were forcibly driven out of Pakistan by Muslim nationalists. Yet Jinnah succeeded in presenting himself as the sole spokesman of Muslim nationalism even though he harmed the interests of his Muslim as well as his Hindu countrymen.

On the other hand, Gandhi, despite being a devout believer in the Hindu faith, stood against the idea of a Hindu nation. He sacrificed his own life defending the rights of Muslims to stay in India as equal citizens even after the Muslim nationalists drove out almost all Hindus from Pakistan. Gandhi saw Indian Muslims as being his own people. He was a patriot because he believed that the well-being of his fellow countrymen was more important than the interests of the Indian state. He was not much of a nationalist even though he sometimes used the vocabulary of nationalism. It was Gandhi, not Jinnah, who was killed by a RSS member as a traitor to the nation because Gandhi insisted that India provide safety and equality to the Muslims living in India. He also wanted India to deal honourably with those living in the newly created state of Pakistan. The final provocation which cost him his life was his insistence that India honour its pledge of giving a certain agreed sum of money to the Pakistan government as part of the process of creating the two nation-states.

The nationalist credo is: 'My nation (meaning the nation-state) right or wrong.' Gandhi's credo was to insist on doing right and opposing wrong even if it went against the supposed interests of the nation-state. He put *manav dharm* above rashtra dharm— humaneness above nationalism— because he recognized that those who insist on putting the nation before everything ended up endangering and sacrificing the lives of their followers at the altar of mythical ideals and building societies based on violence and strife, as did Jinnah.

The Sangh Parivar ideology is secular insofar as its concerns are of this world and political rather than spiritual or religious. The Parivar wants to build a strong nation-state on the European model. This vision is shared even by most of those who oppose the Parivar, including the leftists, secularists and the liberal nationalists. They too keep harping on the primacy of the Indian nation-state and want people in this country to 'be Indians first and foremost'. The HIndutvavadi ideology has acquired unprecedented influence because we are witnessing a new and ferocious wave of nationalism the world over. Its agenda is an internationally respected agenda.

Barring the Combine's obsession with the demolition of certain mosques to rebuild the mandirs supposed to have been destroyed by Muslim invaders, their various grouses against the Muslims are unfortunately shared by most people in India today. Let us look closely at the grievances of the Sangh Parivar: the list given below was synthesized from themes frequently repeated in a variety of its media efforts, including its political organ, *The Organiser*, its propaganda leaflets, and the recorded cassettes of its celebrated *pracharaks*.

- Muslims are traitors because they forced the Partition of India. To quote a VHP propaganda cassette, 'Those who severed both the arms of Mother India . . . for those hypocrites there is no place here. This Hindustan is not theirs . . .'
- Since the vast majority of Hindus were driven out of Pakistan, and later even from Bangladesh, the Congress Party led by Mahatma Gandhi betrayed the nation by insisting that Muslims should not likewise be driven out of India.
- Muslims living in India are not loyal to this country and harbour pro-Pakistan sentiments.
- Muslims put their religion above the nation, and the Koran above the Constitution. The refusal of Muslims to accept a common civil code, and their insistence on being governed by their religious personal laws, are proofs of their lack of nationalist spirit.
- Muslims are inherently intolerant and obscurantist and do not allow even reasonable criticism of Islam.
- Pakistan is constantly attempting to destabilize India by fanning secessionist movements in Punjab and Kashmir. Muslims of India are willing pawns in the games played by Pakistani rulers.
- The Congress Party has followed a policy of appeasing the Muslims by submitting even to their unreasonable and anti-national demands. Muslims behave like 'a virtual nation within a nation' (*The Organiser*, April 1992); a people who assert their right to be above the law of the land. The passing of the Muslim Women's (Protection) Act under pressure from Muslim fundamentalists, thereby putting Muslims beyond the pale of some laws governing other citizens, is one of the examples of this appeasement. Other examples are the special status given to minority institutions and the rules allowing the Muslim majority state of Jammu and Kashmir separate provisions in the Constitution and a few separate personal laws.
- Muslim invaders and rulers who persecuted Hindus, such as Aurangzeb or Mahmud of Ghazni, are not condemned in the name of secularism while Hindus are constantly expected to

criticize and suppress their own heritage to prove that they are modern and secular. Muslims continue to honour even those rulers who persecuted Hindus. This is seen as another proof that Muslims are anti-national.

- The large-scale inflow of Muslim Bangladeshi illegal immigrants into India is jeopardizing the security of India and putting a great strain on the Indian economy, as well as upsetting the demographic balance. They accuse Muslims of using their electoral clout with the Congress in order to prevent strong steps from being taken to stop the continuing persecution of Hindus in Bangladesh which is forcing a large number of them to flee to India.

- The mullahs do not allow Muslims to accept birth-control measures. This, together with the right of Muslim men to have four wives encourages a higher birth rate creating the danger of the Hindus being swamped by the Muslims.

- Muslim leaders try to dictate on foreign policy matters to the Indian government. For example, they succeeded for a long time in keeping India from having full diplomatic relations with Israel and making it tilt in favour of Palestine and other Arab nations which are inherently hostile to India because they are Islamic countries.

- India is surrounded by hostile and troublesome Muslim nations like Pakistan, Bangladesh, Malaysia, Indonesia, Afghanistan, the Mid-East and the Gulf States, and the new Muslim states which have emerged after the breakdown of the Soviet Union. They are all threats to the country's security. The supposed extraterritorial loyalty of Indian Muslims adds to the threat as their presence amounts to having an enemy within.

A large number of these charges are based on half truths, outright lies and paranoid fantasies. For instance, the supposed Islamic invasion from Bangladesh is nothing more than the influx of economic refugees, both Hindus and Muslims. They are driven by poverty to cross a remote and poorly regulated international boundary line. As the poorest of the poor, they are providing services in Indian urban centres such as scavenging, collecting waste products and recycling them, and working as domestic servants and rickshaw pullers for low wages. There is no evidence that the birth rate among poor Muslims is higher than that of Hindus living in similar states of poverty. Except for Pakistan, no Islamic country is contemplating strife with India. Some Islamic countries have offered jobs and business opportunities to millions of Indians, including many Hindus.

However, even where the Sangh Parivar's grievances are based on facts rather than fantasies, such as those concerning the flow of Hindu refugees from Kashmir and Bangladesh, the political conclusions they derive from these facts are wrong. India cannot solve any of its problems by driving out the Muslims. That would amount to carrying forward the disastrous politics set into motion by Jinnah to its logical conclusion.

It is noteworthy that there are hardly any religious issues in this list of grievances. The Sangh Parivar adds the religious flavour when it brings in the demolition of temples and the persecution of Hindus by Muslim rulers in medieval times—but even that historical conflict has been given a new contemporary political colour. The obsession with building a Ram Mandir at the site of the Babri Masjid and reclaiming what the Parivar calls Ram Janmasthan is not being justified on religious grounds but is presented as a struggle between nationalist and anti-nationalist forces. In its view, the Babri Masjid had to be demolished because it was built by an invading outsider after he supposedly destroyed a Ram temple. Ram is presented as a national hero and not as a Hindu god. The propaganda speeches of its leaders forever emphasize: 'Anyone who opposes Ram cannot be an Indian.' The Sangh Parivar is not saying that a Ram opponent cannot be a Hindu. VHP propaganda insists that 'every person who lives here will have to flow with the tide. Ram-Krishna will have to be accepted as the national ideals,' not, it should again be noted, primarily as religious ideals. Shiv Sena leader Bal Thackeray congratulated his followers for playing a leading role in the Babri Masjid demolition for that proved their nationalist credentials. Likewise, he is reported to have justified the participation of his party cadres in large-scale anti-Muslim violence, saying: 'If nationalism is a crime, I will commit it a thousand times.'

Rithambara, the celebrated pracharak of the VHP, makes the point clear in all her speeches that the sadhu–sants who have joined the VHP bandwagon are not fighting a religious battle. They have not come to save the Hindu religion, but to 'save the nation' because the nation is in danger as it has fallen into the hands of traitors—that is, Congressmen willing to barter away the national interest in order to secure Muslim votes. I quote from a typical speech of Rithambara:

The job of a sadhu–sant is to help the seeker of joy to acquire the storehouse of happiness within. But today, India's sages have had to turn away from this to concentrate on the nation. It is not the duty of the sages to . . . worry about questions of nationalism, or the protection of India's borders, but today's compulsions have brought them amongst you . . . Merely to raise the cry of 'Jai Shri Ram' is no sign of awakening. How much do you worry about the good of your country, your own future? . . . India's sanyasis, sants have forsaken their spiritual practices and blown the bugle of Hindu rashtra and come to proclaim that India's youth, the aged and women need to be awakened. My brothers, get admitted to the Bajrang Dal. My mothers and sisters should join the Durga Vahini, so that the feeling of nationalism may awaken in you and we may be able to change India's condition, which is wretched today . . . We are truly secular because we have accepted the national religion. We removed the Jinnahs and we removed the Jaichands . . . We will do Bharat Mata's *archana* with our very lives which will burn like lamps.

That is the crux of the matter. The most sacred deity of the Sangh Parivar is Bharat Mata (Mother India). The Parivar insist that Muslims, Christians and people of other religions must learn to worship Bharat Mata and *Bharat bhumi* more than they worship their own gods. The Hindus are also encouraged to put her above their sectional beliefs and gods. Even Ram and Krishna or Kali or Durga are sacred only so far as they lend themselves to the service of Bharat Mata. The national flag is more sacred to them than any Ram *dhvaj* or temple. The national anthem and Vande Mataram are in their view more sacred than any religious bhajan. One of their oft-repeated threatening slogans aimed at the Muslims is: '*Hindustan mein rehna hai to Vande Matram kehna hoga*', that is, Muslims will have to say Vande Matram (salute to Mother India) if they want to stay in India. They are not insisting on Ram bhajans because they themselves do not care as much about the latter.

Unlike Christianity, Judaism and Islam, the Hindu religion does not have the tradition of being presided over by a jealous god. But the nationalist Hindus make very jealous devotees even though Bharat Mata herself is presented as giving and nurturing. Since the feelings of many Indian Muslims towards Pakistan are ambivalent, they can never be trusted to be loyal to Bharat Mata. The occasional bursting of firecrackers by a few Muslims in the event of Pakistan's victory in a cricket match between India and Pakistan becomes incontrovertible proof that Muslims in India are at heart Pakistanis and traitors to Mother India.

Bharat Mata is not a religious deity but a secular symbol. Loyalty to her requires that her devotees put her worship above that of all other deities and gods. She came into existence during India's struggle against British rule. Her origin derives from a benevolent primeval, nurturing mother goddess. Unlike goddesses such as Kali, Bharat Mata is benign. It is not she who punishes people for wrongdoings or betrayals. Instead, her worshipping sons mete out punishment to anyone lacking in their devotion to her. A worshipper would not need to fear Bharat Mata as would a worshipper of Kali, but would need to fear her sons who can easily become Hitlerian in their zeal to protect her honour. She remains mostly a vague idea to most, given concrete expression only in school plays in which an older girl in the school dresses up to resemble Lakshmi. She is positioned in such a way that her shadow is cast on an outline map of India. Her class-mates stand in a formation also resembling the map of India and sing songs of devotion and praise.

Only in recent years has the VHP tried to get Bharat Mata accepted as an all-India deity, as a part of their attempt to ritualize Hindu nationalism. In 1983, the VHP undertook an *Ektamata Yajna* (sacrifice for unity) which travelled throughout India performing sacrifices to Bharat Mata and Ganga Mata. They have also built a temple dedicated to Bharat Mata in Hardwar. It enshrines various deities, warriors, 'martyrs' and satis, gurus and sants, all of whom are interpreted through the Sangh Parivar's version of history, religion and culture within the framework of Hindu nationalism.

The fear of the Sangh Parivar that Muslims are loyal only to their religion and consider the Koran more sacred than the Indian Constitution or Mother India is, unfortunately, shared by many Hindus across the political spectrum, including those in the Left parties. In Bombay many secular-minded people who bravely went against the tide and condemned the killing of the Muslims, would confess that they were very hurt by the behaviour of those Muslims who celebrate a Pakistani victory in cricket matches. The Hindus can easily be more tolerant in the religious sphere because even their jealous gods know how to co-exist with each other. But when Hindus learn to give rashtra dharm primacy over all other dharms, they become as intolerant as any chauvinistic nationalist. In this paradigm Advani becomes indistinguishable from Jinnah, their contrary religious backgrounds notwithstanding. We forget that people of Indian descent who have taken the citizenship of Britain or other foreign countries frequently celebrate India's victory in an England–India match. The fact that many Indian Muslims have relatives across the border makes it harder for them to think of all Pakistanis as enemies, as many Hindus do. The ambivalence of many Indian Muslims toward Pakistan is comparable to the predicament of the Mohajirs, Indian Muslims who migrated to Pakistan in or after 1947. They find themselves treated as unwanted aliens in the nation-state of their own making. Their language (Urdu), their culture, their connections with relatives in India, their lingering emotional attachment to the land of their birth and ancestors, are all suspect and hence under attack from the dominant Punjabis, Sindhis, Baluchis and others in Pakistan. This is not a sign of their being traitors but rather a proof, if further proof were necessary, that the Partition of the subcontinent was unrealistic and unsound. Our prejudice does not allow us to realize that many Indian Muslims are anti-Pakistan because they feel that the makers of Pakistan jeopardized the safety of millions of Muslims who chose to live in India, and became a despised and mistrusted minority because of the Partition.

What makes the ideology of the Sangh Parivar so powerful today is that it is able to convince large sections of the population that it alone is serious about building a strong nation-state to defend national honour, unity and integrity. The genuine disgruntlement of the people with the unscrupulous politics of the Congress Party—playing group against group—is being used by the Sangh Parivar to present the Muslims as traitors within India.

At the time of the Partition the Hindus had reason to be hostile to the Muslims, yet leaders like Gandhi, and even Nehru, were able to prevail upon the people of India to concede that the Muslims had a right to stay in India even after the Partition. They thus successfully managed to marginalize the politics of the Sangh Parivar.

Why is it that the anti-Muslim nationalism of the Sangh Parivar has become so appealing to large sections of the Indian population four decades after Partition? The political support base of parties like the Jan Sangh (precursor of the BJP) remained extremely narrow in the years after Independence. It was confined to some regions in urban north India and appealed mainly to sections of the trading community and small sections of the urban middle and lower middle classes. Even those communities that were victims of the Partition, such as the Punjabis from the areas that went to Pakistan, did not support the Jan Sangh in overwhelming numbers. Hindu Bengalis who were pushed out of Bangladesh, in fact, remained indifferent to the politics of the Sangh Parivar.

But in recent years the Congress Party has witnessed a serious erosion in its support base which has now shifted to the BJP and Shiv Sena. This is particularly true among the urban educated elite, including the liberal intelligentsia. Even upto the late 1970s, when I was a student at the Jawaharlal Nehru University, it was considered extremely lowbrow to be associated with the RSS or any of its allied organizations. Their support base among students and teachers at that time was largely confined to the low-status institutions whose students were generally from lower middle-class backgrounds. However, in recent years large sections of the western-educated elite, including students, teachers, professionals and bureaucrats, have switched their allegiance to organizations associated with the Sangh Combine. What are the factors responsible for the appeal of their brand of nationalism whose chief component is a virulent anti-Muslim sentiment?

The Congress Party was able to marginalize the Sangh Parivar as long as it lived up to some of the expectations it had aroused during the freedom movement, and as long as it acted as a vehicle of patriotism. The fact that many RSS leaders were more often than not pro-British and had a history of opposing the anti-colonial movement led by the Congress Party, isolated them from mainstream Indian political life. They were known to be actively hostile to Gandhi who became synonymous with anti-colonialism in popular imagination. This kept the influence of the RSS limited at a time when the anti-colonial aspect of nationalism reflected the predominant mood of the country.

There are, no doubt, some differences between the liberal nationalism of Nehru and the chauvinist nationalism of the Sangh Parivar. But the liberal nationalism of the early years of Congress rule could not be sustained for long because a centralized, authoritarian state machinery emerged as the result of Nehru's policies. It was more appropriate for the governance of an empire rather than a democracy. This top-down machinery controlled from the Delhi *durbar* uses the national bureaucracy as a vehicle for imposing its version of national unity and the implementation of national policies. This bureaucracy further estranges itself by choosing to use the alien English language. The hallmark of this machinery is its lack of accountability to the people it is supposed to serve. It allows them no participation in devising or implementing policies. This makes the Centre incapable of dealing with grievances of both everyday life as well as those that emerge in special crisis situations.

The nation-state Nehru built destroyed whatever little was left of village, urban, and community-based institutions of self-governance after the depredations suffered during colonial rule. Democracy was reduced to a ritual of casting ballots enacted once every five years while all real power remained vested in a permanent bureaucracy controlled mainly by the rulers at the Centre. The national and, to a much lesser extent, the state capitals, became the all important nodes of power. The voices of ordinary people did not reach these capitals. Politics and administration became a matter of loot and plunder by those who ruled.

Politics in our country has come to revolve around who is to occupy those offices of power which allow opportunities for unbridled corruption and embezzlement. Most of the major confrontations between the Congress Party and the regional parties such as the Akalis, the DMK, the TDP, the CPI(M) and the National Conference, are the result of the Congress' desire to monopolize political power in order to plunder the country. The opponents of the Congress in these struggles often raise legitimate demands for reorganization and decentralization of Centre–State relations as a battle cry. However, they never consider the task as sufficiently important and are only too ready to abandon it when they are offered some share in the loot instead.

Those groups who find their grievances unattended in this system find that they must get shriller and shriller in order to be heard. The Congress Party has built no real mechanisms for political settlement of the grievances of disgruntled groups such as the Akalis in Punjab, Jharkhandis in Bihar, various movements in Assam and Kashmir, or the anti-Tehri and anti-Narmada dam agitations. It tries to deal with each crisis as either a law-and-order problem or as an occasion for a pay-off to as narrow a group of those in the opposition as possible. If the opposition leaders refuse the pay-off they are accused of destabilizing the security and integrity of the nation-state.

Repeated use of the nationalist rhetoric to stifle democratic demands has resulted in the practice of chauvinistic nationalism by the Congress Party. This is especially true in its dealings with movements in border regions such as Kashmir, Punjab, and Nagaland where a majority of the population is not Hindu and their demands can easily be misrepresented as being anti-Indian.

In addition, the Congress has come to be increasingly identified with factional fighting for personal advantages, widespread corruption, and patronage of antisocial elements. This transformation is symbolized by the way the Gandhi cap and khadi have been portrayed in Hindi cinema. In the films of the 1940s, 1950s and the early 1960s, a man in khadi wearing a Gandhi cap was a symbol of honest, selfless social work. However, in recent decades, the same dress is used to depict a corrupt and hypocritical goonda politician. The Congress Party's involvement in shady foreign defence and business deals that brought it huge kickbacks has made people cynical about its 'nationalist' credentials. The genuine disgruntlement of the people with the Congress Party has been used by the Sangh Parivar to present themselves as incorruptible militant nationalists. As the nationalism of the Congress Party got increasingly divorced from social justice and democracy, it came to rely more and more on the 'nation-in danger' gimmick, thus becoming indistinguishable from the chauvinism of the Sangh Parivar.

The unscrupulous manner in which the Congress Party cultivated Muslims as a vote bank has encouraged the growth of an equally unscrupulous leadership among this community. Dubious concessions, such as the enactment of the Muslim Women's Protection Act, and the banning of Salman Rushdie's book have strengthened the stereotype of Muslims as a dangerously intolerant community which is supposedly being pampered by the 'pseudo-secular' politics of the Congress Party. The policy of keeping certain obscurantist Muslim leaders happy by throwing them occasional crumbs in lieu of providing their vulnerable community real security or opportunity has created the misleading impression that the Muslim minority has unfair political advantages over the Hindu majority.

The Muslim leadership has failed to take up basic issues of anti-Muslim discrimination and terror. The excessive emphasis they have placed on their special rights as Muslims while failing to effectively claim many of their rights as citizens has contributed a great deal to the increasing estrangement and political vulnerability of the community. As a result, most other communities in India have come to view the Muslims with contempt, as backward obscurantists who hinder India's progress.

Since Indira Gandhi's time, the Congress Party has systematically destroyed the more rational and progressive leaders among Muslim politicians. It has done this in order to keep the captive Muslim vote bank as a ghettoized, fearful minority. Muslim politicians who have tried to take thoughtful forward-looking positions on various issues concerning the Muslim community have been systematically bypassed and neglected in favour of the more obscurantist leaders. At the time of the Shah Bano controversy, for example, certain prominent leaders within the Congress Party opposed the Muslim Women's Protection Bill. Nevertheless, the party yielded to the pressures from the Shahi Imam, Shahabuddin, and leaders of the Muslim League, thereby making it seem as if these were the genuine leaders of the Muslims.

The preference of large sections of the Muslim leadership and westernized Muslim intelligentsia for a Nehruvian brand of secularism has proved very harmful for Muslims in the long run. In the process they have rejected and ridiculed Gandhi's approach to inter-community harmony largely because they are uneasy with his use of certain Hindu symbols. This has strengthened the feeling that the Muslim leadership is innately hostile to the Hindus who are rooted in their own faith and is comfortable only with westernized Hindus like Nehru who are contemptuous of their own culture, religion and people.

Gandhi's approach to Hindu–Muslim amity was influenced by the Bhakti and Sufi traditions. He drew on centuries-old traditional bonds whereby people of various communities evolved humane norms of co-living. Such a life-style was based on the notion of enlightened self-interest and strove to attain mutual safety on the basis of neighbourhood or village solidarity (mohelledari and *gaon bhaichara*).

Gandhi mistrusted the use of the army and the police to guarantee the rights of minorities or other vulnerable groups. He saw the modern state machinery as rooted in violence and therefore incapable of ensuring safety for the local communities. In Gandhi's vision, decentralized traditional community-based organizations are better able to promote peace and security. He emphasized the importance of people taking responsibility for each other rather than depending on an external police force. He knew that enduring social peace could not come from the government-controlled police, but only from community-based vigilance.

Nehruvian secularism relied almost exclusively on the state machinery to provide protection to the minorities. One of the key limitations of this approach is that it assumes the state machinery is neutral, whereas, in actual practice, this is rarely the case. The Nehruvian brand of secularism misled the Muslims into believing that as long as they had a certain clout with the government and the latter mouthed secular slogans, their interests were safe. Just as Jinnah had bargained on the British government providing for the safety of the Muslims against the Hindus, post-Independence Muslim leadership focused exclusively on extracting 'concessions' from the government. Thus they allowed themselves to be continually estranged from the Hindu majority and other communities. The Congress Party encouraged this estrangement in order to cultivate them as a vote bank.

Even during normal times, ours is a fairly lawless government. The police and administrative machinery are often found protecting criminals rather than honest citizens. During communal riots, its brazen tilt in favour of the criminals and the rioters of the majority community is inevitable. Yet riot after riot, the Muslim leadership has focused all its energy and ire at the government for failure to provide it protection. It is making demands such as proportional representation of the Muslims in the police force, but has paid scant or no attention to the growing communication gap between the Muslim community and the rest of the people. This gap has made the task of the Sangh Parivar easier.

In their attempt to become the sole spokesmen for the Muslim community, leaders like Shahabuddin have tended to articulate the grievances of the Muslims in a Jinnah-like manner. They thus tend to evoke hysterical responses from the Hindus who fear more and more partitions of the country if the Muslims are allowed to have greater influence on national politics. They have created a misleading stereotype of the Muslims as a monolithic community with one standard set of interests no matter which region or occupation or linguistic group they belong to. This tendency has helped the Hindutvavadi's to get all Hindus to act like a monolith group in relation to the Muslims. The Hindus have become paranoid that the Muslim minority can veto everything that the majority wants to do in the same way as Jinnah came to have a veto during certain periods of the negotiations for Independence. Many see an urgent need to 'put the Muslims in their place'.

Even though leaders such as Gandhi and Nehru were able to prevail upon the people to let Muslims stay in India after the Partition, the ruling elite in both Pakistan and India have failed to make a definitive peace with each other. They have not worked out decent norms of coexistence as neighbours. Rather they have resorted to phobia-building among their respective populations, thus allowing the nightmarish memory of the Partition to remain alive, especially in the North. The political leaders in both countries have defined their nationalism largely in terms of uncompromising hostility to the other nation-state. There is a very thin dividing line in the two countries between being anti-Pakistani and being anti-Muslim or between being anti-Indian and anti-Hindu. The Pakistani rulers need to paint India as a monster because they are afraid of the Indian democracy. The Indian ruling elite allowed its phobias to get the better of them because of US support to the military dictators of Pakistan, just as the Pakistani government came increasingly to fear India's receipt of Soviet military support. These superpower interventions kept the two nations from a more realistic assessment of each other's capacities as the basis for negotiating terms for peaceful coexistence.

After the collapse of the Soviet Union the political perceptions of the US and other western powers have swung dramatically in a different direction. Now that Pakistan and certain other Muslim countries are not needed as buffers against communism, the West has created a new bogey. The very same Islamic fundamentalism that the US and its allies kept fanning and supporting in Pakistan, Afghanistan, Saudi Arabia and Iraq as a counter to communism is now being projected as the new evil to be fought and kept under check. Western intellectuals and politicians are now busy convincing the world that the genie of Muslim fundamentalism has become the chief threat to world security, in the same way as communism was during the cold war era. This has given a new moral high to anti-Muslim sentiment in India, especially since India is surrounded by Islamic nations and Indian Muslims can easily be portrayed as anti-national elements.

The open help and support being provided by Pakistan to secessionist movements in Punjab and Kashmir, as well as the sight of Hindu Kashmiris being pushed out as refugees because of threats from Kashmiri Muslim militants, confirm the deep-seated fears among Hindus. They believe the Muslims will continue the fragmentation of India unless they are 'taught a lesson'. In their bid to take over Kashmir, the Pakistani government is thus actively endangering the lives of Indian Muslims by funding those terrorist groups who wish Kashmir to secede to Pakistan.

Negative stereotypes about the Muslims became far more easy

to legitimize after the Partition because it was mostly the poorer Muslims who were left behind in India. Large sections of the elite and the middle classes migrated to Pakistan. Up to my parents' generation middle- and upper-class Hindus in many regions knew Muslims who they viewed as social equals; often they knew Muslims in superior status positions to them. They also had a great deal of everyday interaction with a cross-section of the Muslim community. In contrast, the upper- and middle-class Indian elite of the post-Independence generations either know no Muslims at all because many of them are poor and ghettoized, or know them only as menials. In such a situation it is far easier for unsavoury types to be offered as indisputable portrayals of the entire community, giving rise to unjust prejudices and phobias.

In recent years the growing prosperity among a section of the artisan groups within the Muslim community stemming from jobs in the Gulf countries and their inroads into small-scale family based industries have provided them with new avenues of upward mobility. The new-found wealth of some working-class Muslims, who were once easier targets of contempt due to their poverty, is an important factor in the new hostility that they face from poor Hindus. This attitude is especially seen amongst the Dalits, who have traditionally lived in close proximity to the Muslims. In riot after riot, Dalits living in adjacent bastis to the Muslims have been in the forefront of mobs attacking Muslim homes and looting their property. A common refrain of the attackers is '*In par bahut charbi chadh gayi hai.*' ('They have accumulated too much fat on their bodies'—fat being used as a symbol of prosperity.)

The post-Independence generation of young Muslims are beginning to get more assertive about their rights and are desirous of moving out of the ghettos. This assertiveness frightens many Hindus who then try to push them back through the use of violence. The Gulf connection has also brought in a new fervour for a more conservative version of Islam. The flow of Gulf money for mosques and other Islamic institutions has strengthened the fundamentalists among the Muslim leadership who are trying to wean the Muslims away from their Indianized Islam towards a more middle-Eastern version of the faith, removing from it practices which built cultural bonds with the neighbouring Hindus. Even the Urdu they advocate is heavily Persianized and Arabicized. Many Hindus have begun to fear the new religious fervour among the Muslims as a worldwide Islamic conspiracy to overrun India.

Earlier, politicians who instigated riots had to keep their involvement a secret. The increasing criminalization of politics, along with the willing endorsement of violence against the Muslims by the middle class and the elite sections of our society, have made the politician–goonda nexus brazen about engineering riots.

The criminalization of politics has given a further fillip to the criminalization of the government machinery. The open protection and support provided by the police and other government functionaries to rioting mobs of Hindus has made the confrontations between Muslims and Hindus more and more unequal. Traditionally, Hindus and Muslims evolved certain workable norms for living together despite their respective biases against each other based on the recognition that acting out their prejudices through aggressive acts was a risky proposition. The tradition of neighbourhood solidarity is in part founded on avoiding acts of violence through rational recognition of your own enlightened self-interest. However, the intrusion of external political forces with police and government protection provided to the majority community—i.e. Hindus in India and Muslims in Pakistan—makes the power balance hopelessly unequal for the minorities. The majority does not have to fear retaliation for the violence inflicted on the powerless minority, and therefore has escalated its attacks.

The increase in the incidents of the politically inspired ethnic violence have made every community, including Hindus, fearful and paranoid. The inefficient and corrupt law and order machinery makes even Hindus unable to rely on it to consistently act in their favour. This is because there are no established procedures and rules for ensuring a measure of social safety. In the years after Independence, vulnerable groups such as the Muslims and the Dalits tried to obtain a measure of safety through political alliances with ruling parties like the Congress. But as the Congress Party itself degenerated into a loose alliance of crooks and criminals rather than political leaders, stable political alliances could not be made and relied upon. The general breakdown of the political system and its enforcement agencies makes people believe that they have to join together with some gang or seek protection by supporting Mafia-type leaders to ensure their own safety and survival. This fear has resulted in increasing reliance on paramilitary forces and armed groups, such as the Shiv Sena and the Bajrang Dal, as well as Mafia dons like Haji Mastan and Dawood Ibrahim among the Muslims, and militant groups in Punjab and Kashmir.

All of these groups offer a measure of protection to their supporters, not only from the supposed threats from other groups and communities, but also against the fragmenting state machinery. These organizations teach martial arts to their followers and keep them in a state of readiness to engage in armed combat. Even the rich business elite now rely more and more on their personally hired security guards rather than the law and order machinery. Nevertheless, they are forever nervous that anarchic violence will come to dominate and, therefore, they seek protection from politicians like Bal Thackeray.

The Pakistani ruling elite were insecure from the start because the very foundation of Pakistan was based on a lie. In contrast, the Indian ruling elite started off on a far more self-confident note due to Mahatma Gandhi's influence and his vision of building a compassionate and just society. Hence, soon after Independence it was relatively easy to build a consensus for the equal rights of minorities. But the confidence of the Indian elite lies shattered now due to their own incompetence, mismanagement, and misgovernance of the country. Today they find themselves grovelling before the IMF, the World Bank, and other foreign investors . They know that the world views India with contempt for its failure to live up to its promises on the economic and political front. They hate themselves for it but do not have the courage to find a way out of this mess. This shame and self-contempt is being systematically manipulated by the Sangh Parivar. Even though the Parivaris themselves go about wooing Western governments, assuring them that foreign investments will be safe and welcome if they come to power. Yet they never tire of playing on the fear that India is being sold out to foreign powers and that it is in danger of breaking up like the erstwhile Soviet Union.

A sensible way of dealing with our past failures would be to face our mistakes courageously and resolve to improve things. But the self-hating ruling elite in India (as in Pakistan) lack the confidence to do so. They are only too willing to shift the blame elsewhere.

The case of the ruling middle classes is similar to that of a man who is ridden with anxieties about his 'manhood' and 'virility' and tends to be more aggressive and violent in his relationship with his wife, constantly blaming her for his inability to perform. Having failed to put their act together, they are looking for a scapegoat for their shameful performance. The Sangh Parivar's ideology of projecting the Muslims as the source of all problems caters to this need. One commonly hears their cadres and sympathizers say that India would have been as successful as Germany but for the Muslims who are dragging us down.

The Ram Mandir campaign was devised as a counter to the job reservation policy announced by the Janata Dal government. Fearing the joint electoral might of the highly mobilized lower and backward castes which endangers upper-caste dominance, the Sangh Parivar is trying to unite all Hindus into a single force by projecting the Muslims as the main common enemy.

In any multi-religious, multi-lingual and multi-ethnic entity such as the Indian subcontinent, where substantial differences exist among the cultures of various regional groups, people have overlapping identities. One cannot be an Indian without also being a Punjabi, Kashmiri, Malayali, Manipuri, Tamilian, and so on. A Punjabi would have several other identity layers—Punjabi from a specific region such as the Doab or Lahore, while also maintaining an identity as a Punjabi Sikh, Hindu or Muslim. A Punjabi Hindu would have other sub-religious identities, such as Arya Samaji, Sanatani or Radhasoami. Then there would be the layers of caste identity such as Hindu Khatri or Bania or Brahmin. Within each caste are the jatis, within them the *gotras*. Most important of all are the biradari and family ties and then, of course, age and gender.

A person may begin to assert one particular identity over others if that particular identity is threatened or conversely if any one of them begins to pay off politically or economically. For instance, the policy of job reservations for certain 'lower' castes makes it advantageous to assert one's caste for those who cannot otherwise gain access to those jobs. But an upper-caste boy who has studied in an elite institution such as St Stephen's College, tends to assert his identity as a Stephanian more often than his caste identity, because the former is more lucrative for professional advancement.

In the political sphere, the identity that gets to acquire primacy depends on the complex interaction between many factors. The rise of Sikh nationalism has very important lessons to teach. We can ignore them only at our own peril. The Sikhs of Punjab began asserting their separate identity in the nineteenth century in response to attacks on the Sikh *panth* by Dayanand and his Arya Samaji followers who initiated *shuddhi* campaigns to induct Sikhs into the Hindu fold. The next major wave of assertion came in the 1950s with the demand for Punjabi *Suba* because the Sikhs felt that they were being discriminated against, on account of the fact that the principle of linguistic recognition of states was not applied to Punjabi-speaking regions. The Punjabi Hindus felt threatened by the Akali demand for Punjabi Suba and went as far as disowning their linguistic identity and declaring Hindi as their mother tongue because they felt their Hindu identity would be politically threatened in a Sikh-dominated Punjabi Suba. The Akali Party, being gurudwara-based, provided little space for the political aspirations of non-Sikhs. The result was a truncated state of Punjab for the Sikhs, with several areas going to form the states of Himachal Pradesh and Haryana. The Sikhs were not the only ones to be checkmated. The Hindus too lost out in Punjab by becoming a permanent minority and, therefore, they began to look towards 'national' parties like the Jan Sangh and the Congress to safeguard their political interests.

When the Akalis launched a movement in the early 1970s demanding alteration in Centre–State relations in a way that provided for decentralization of political and economic power, they were asserting their regional identity as Punjabis and articulating the economic interests of the Jat farmers who constituted their political base. The Jat peasantry provided the thrust for decentralization because of the manner in which the Central government forced the Punjab peasantry to sell its wheat at artificially depressed government-controlled prices. The freedom to trade across Punjab's borders, including the export of farm produce, was one of the key demands in the Anandpur Sahib resolution. The Hindus of Punjab deliberately undermined their regional identity as Punjabis and opposed the demand for regional autonomy because they felt that their political interests would be further threatened if Akalis got more power in Punjab. The inability of the Akalis to carry the Hindus (who are over 40 per cent of the voters in Punjab) along in their struggle for the much needed decentralization of power was also responsible for the success of Mrs Gandhi in claiming that their legitimate demands were 'anti-national'. It also set her on the path of repression and confrontation with the Akalis, culminating in Operation Bluestar.

This army operation caused such an unprecedented schism between Hindus and Sikhs all over the country that many Punjabi Hindus, who have always worshipped the Granth Sahib, supported the desecration of the Golden Temple by the army. In November 1984, when thousands of Sikhs were brutally massacred by supporters of the Congress(I), many Hindus felt that the killings were justified and that the Sikhs needed to be 'taught a lesson'.

Sikh militants pushed the movement for decentralization of power in the direction of a demand for Khalistan with the help of the Congress(I), which propped up Bhindranwale to destroy the influence of the Sant Longowal-led Akali Dal. The Congress Party instigated and encouraged Bhindranwale to raise the slogan of Khalistan to discredit the movement for regional autonomy. Even though it was well known that Bhindranwale began as a Congress Party agent, many Sikhs began to identify with his demands for Khalistan after Operation Bluestar. They began to declare themselves to be a separate *quam* or nation, in the same way that some Muslim leaders did in the 1930s and the 1940s.

Communal differences or conflicts can be far more easily resolved by the concerned local communities on the basis of their several shared interests as cohabitants. In the 1950s and the 1960s, the Jan Sangh, the party representing urban Hindu interests, had no difficulty in forming a coalition government with the Akali Party, their political, religious, and other differences notwithstanding. However, the moment one or the other community decides to 'purify' itself and declares itself as a separate nationality, their interests appear almost irreconcilable and the conflict assumes the shape of warfare. Thus, the moment a section of the Sikhs began 'purifying' the Sikh religion of Hindu influences and declared Sikhs to be a separate nationality, Hindus, even of Punjab, not to speak of distantly situated areas, became willing to condone the worst atrocities against Sikhs, even though culturally and ethnically Sikhs are inseparable from Punjabi Hindus. Similarly, militant Khalistanis felt no compunction about selectively killing Hindus in order to force them to move out of Punjab so that Punjab would become a Sikh state.

If Sikhs, who have historically played the role of defenders of Hinduism, could be so alienated as to declare themselves as inherently different from and antagonistic to the Hindus, once they felt that their Sikh identity was in danger, and the Hindus were willing to avidly seek the massacre of their own erstwhile defenders when they felt their own survival threatened, we need to understand that any of the various cross-cutting identities can easily become the basis of separatist sentiments if not allowed an appropriate realm for legitimate assertion.

Viewed in retrospect, the reorganization of states on the basis of language in the 1950s was a very favourable political development. It allowed space for assertion of one's linguistic identity. Bangladesh seceded from Pakistan mainly as a reaction against the imposition of Urdu on Bengali-speaking Muslims by the ruling elite of West Pakistan—their common Muslim identity notwithstanding. When Hindi was sought to be imposed in India in a similar manner, the southern states revolted and the protest in Tamil Nadu assumed separatist overtones. Had a certain measure of linguistic autonomy not been granted, there would have been many more national separatist movements in India than there are today. And they could not possibly have been countered by demands for national unity.

There are similar issues involved in the assertion of other ethnic identities. In 1947, the Kashmiri Muslims did not oppose the merger of Kashmir with India when the local Maharaja opted for India over Pakistan; their Kashmiri identity prevailed over their Muslim identity. However, recurring spells of President's rule after dismissal of democratically elected state governments strengthened the demand for regional autonomy in Kashmir. Finally, it led to the call for the secession of Kashmir from India. Kashmiri nationalism, seen as Muslim nationalism, in turn, made the Hindus of Jammu and Kashmir and the Buddhists of Ladakh oppose regional autonomy and demand greater devolution of powers to their respective regions.

Just as the Kashmiris do not wish to be dictated to by Delhi, neither do the Dogras and other Hindus of Jammu, and the Buddhists of Ladakh, wish to have their region remote-controlled from Srinagar. Thus, a large portion of the state's population has come to oppose the demand for regional autonomy because they know that the rulers in Srinagar will not extend the principle to include a measure of autonomy for those regions like Ladakh or Jammu within the state where Muslims are a minority . The Congress Party could not have isolated and destroyed the National Conference Party so easily by projecting the latter as anti-national (as with the Akalis) had the leaders evolved a meaningful programme of decentralization of power within the state, so that varied overlapping identities and political aspirations of the various regional, linguistic and religious minorities in Jammu, Ladakh and Kashmir could find their legitimate space for assertion.

It is the same for individuals. When I am walking on the streets of Delhi, I do not think of myself as an Indian. I am more aware of my urban and gender identities because I have to constantly guard against sexual harassment. However, I have never needed to assert my gender identity in my family because I was not discriminated against as a daughter. But while travelling in crowded DTC buses, I do often feel tempted to claim the ladies' seat to avoid being pawed by men. When I go looking for rented accommodation, I become more acutely aware of my gender as well as Punjabi identity because of the prejudice in Delhi against renting houses to Punjabis and to women. I become aware of being an Indian when I am travelling outside the country, especially in the West, because the colour of my skin, dress and language mark me out from the majority. In addition, the prejudice I encounter on account of my being identified as an Indian makes me somewhat defensive and, therefore, enhances my awareness of being an Indian. One comes to aggressively assert whichever part of one's identity feels more threatened—both in inter-personal as well as in inter-community relations.

Many people think that the resolution of the Hindu–Muslim conflict in India is crucially dependent on an improvement in Indo-Pakistan and Indo-Bangladesh relations. They also argue that as long as Bangladesh keeps facilitating the migration of Hindus from Bangladesh, and Pakistan keeps supporting terrorist, secessionist politics in Kashmir and Punjab, Hindus will continue to target their hostility at Indian Muslims. This is true, to some extent. However, given our misfortune in having neighbours whose politics are far less democratic than ours, we cannot allow the incompetency and phobias of the Pakistani and Bangladeshi regimes to drive us towards suicidal politics. The way out of this conflict lies in refusing to give legitimacy to those who want India to follow the deadly path chosen by Pakistan, to refuse to support those whose dharm is not Hinduism, that is, those forces who argue that Muslims should be treated the same way as Hindus are treated in Pakistan or Bangladesh.

The Sangh Parivar's way of hating the politics of Pakistan is strange indeed—they want India to blindly emulate its theocratic politics. It is unfortunate that Advani aspires to be nothing better than another Jinnah. The essence of the Sangh Combine's politics implicitly amounts to a vindication of Jinnah, even though history has proved him wrong. Attempts to 'unify' the Hindus into being Indian *rashtravadis* are bound to produce similarly disastrous results, as we can see from the continuous ethnic strife in Pakistan.

The conflict between the Hindus and the Muslims, and between the Hindus and the Sikhs, cannot be resolved merely by chanting the mantra of national unity. Our traditional bonds acted as a better glue than has modern nationalism. Supra-nationalism is not an effective enough counter to various sub-nationalistic tendencies. It often fails to prevent the latter from assuming separatist undertones. The inherent logic of nationalism is to give rise to contending nationalisms; it is based on the supposed unity of one group, almost always against some other. It attempts to make diverse peoples 'become one' by accepting an arbitrarily chosen, real or mythical culture and history as a common bond. The all-inclusive nationalism advocated by the Congress in the twentieth century came to be challenged by various sub-nationalisms, especially the Muslim version, resulting in the Partition. Pakistani nationalism in turn came to be challenged by Bangladeshi nationalism (even though they both shared the same religion). Even after the breakaway of Bangladesh, Pakistan is facing an acute crisis on account of the Sindhis, Baluchis, Mohajirs, Punjabis and others asserting their right to separate national identities. Similarly, our 'secular' appeals demanding that religion be kept out of politics do not make much sense, for the Sangh Parivar is actually fighting a secular battle using carefully selected religious symbols to give their movement an ethnic flavour as an aid for mass mobilization for political purposes. That is why the leftist and secularist appeals for national unity are not able to counter the BJP's plank of Hindu *rashtravaad*. The Sangh leadership is saying essentially the same thing, 'Put the nation before religion.' In their view, all those who put religion above the nation are traitors.

The way out of this mess lies in ensuring that each individual, each group and community feels a measure of safety and basic security. Today, our government fails to protect people even against brutal forms of violence and exploitation. National security cannot mean much to people if their own lives are full of fear and insecurity, and their own survival threatened by open murderous attacks. Nor can people continue indefinitely to feel loyal to a nation if its government actively prevents them from retaining some shred of dignity. Only citizens confident of government protection from threats of harm and death can have a stake in supporting the stability of the state.

Loyal citizens are found more often in societies where nationalism is tempered by higher values such as respect for human life and freedom, where governments are made to act lawfully and with responsibility, where equality among different ethnic groups is accepted as a fundamental principle of social and political organization. Wherever these principles do not prevail, and nationalism is the sole substitute, there are tensions and strife, and governments face active disaffection endangering the health of the society and of the peoples that compose it. The very high crime rate in the US is linked to discrimination against and the consequent ghettoization of the Blacks and other despised minorities. In neighbouring Canada, there is much less social strife and crime because the minority groups are comparably less discriminated against. Nationalism becomes increasingly poisonous as it divorces itself further and further from social justice.

The only effective way to counter the belief in the permanent and irreconcilable enmity between one community and the other, being advocated by the Sangh Parivar, is to pre-empt the emergence of monolithic identities involving deadly 'purifying and cleansing' tendencies among various communities. For instance, it is only when political leaders try to insist that all Hindus, or all Muslims, have identical sets of interests—no matter whether they are from Kerala or Maharashtra, whether peasants or artisans, Urdu speaking or Tamil speaking, rich or poor, Sunni or Shia, lower caste or higher caste— that they can be pitched against each other as permanently hostile monoliths. But if Muslim and Hindu peasants can come together to safeguard their interests as farmers, or as Gujaratis or Kashmiris to assert their linguistic or their regional identity, or acknowledge bonds of commonality on account of being from the same village or neighbourhood, they cannot easily be pitched against each other as hostile warring groups on an all-India basis by letting religious identity overwhelm all other identities.

The problem is not one of Hindus having any inherent conflict with Muslims. The problem is due to not working out decent norms for majority–minority relations. All over the world we find that in the absence of proper procedures for working out majority–minority relationships, majoritarian community politics can easily become tyrannical. All groups begin to fear for their physical survival, until finally the only way out seems to be to exterminate or drive out the other group/groups. Thus the Hindus in Pakistan and Bangladesh are even more marginal than Muslims are in India.

Given India's heterogeneity, every community is a minority in some place and a majority elsewhere. For example, the Hindus are a minority in Kashmir, Ladakh, Punjab and Nagaland. The Muslims are a minority everywhere except in Kashmir. The Sikhs are a minority everywhere except in Punjab; the Christians are a minority elsewhere but not in Nagaland; the Tamils are a minority except in Tamil Nadu; the Brahmins are a minority everywhere except in certain government jobs and elite professions.

We need to define decent, workable norms for power sharing, be it with the Hindu minority in Kashmir or Punjab, with the Muslims in Madhya Pradesh, or with the Christians in Tamil Nadu. As of today, our country does not have a well-worked out policy framework for minority rights which will have safeguards for the Hindus as well as the Muslims, the Sikhs, the Christians and all others, wherever they are situated as a minority. Our government is only capable of making gimmicky gestures such as declaring Prophet Mohammad's birthday a national holiday or succumbing to fundamentalist pressure on issues of Muslim personal law or banning *Satanic Verses*.

A policy that actually provides a fair deal for minorities will work only if it is accompanied by a thorough overhaul of the government machinery to ensure that principles of accountability are introduced in such a way that these agencies become answerable to the people they cater to. Unless we succeed in making the law and order machinery behave lawfully so that individuals do not have to gang up as groups and groups do not have to seek the protection of mafias, we will continue to have more and more violence, on one pretext or another.

An effective law and order machinery calls for a rehauling of the political system to ensure effective and meaningful decentralization of power—not just between the Centre and the states, but also between different regions within a state, so that each village and each city is allowed a degree of autonomy. A village panchayat or a city corporation should not have to depend on the political bosses in state capitals or in Delhi for managing their day-to-day affairs.

Excessive centralization of power inevitably breeds corruption and tyranny and tends to foster greater conflicts among various ethnic groups, as the collapse of the Soviet Union demonstrates. Excessive homogenization of meaningful group identities, in favour of an all-powerful national state requiring sacrifices from all and benefits only to a small elite will inevitably promote more civil strife, as has happened in the erstwhile communist bloc.

If India has escaped going the way of Hitler's Germany or becoming another Yugoslavia, even though politicians of the Sangh Parivar are trying hard to take that route, it is because the country's heterogeneity makes attempts to unify all the people at the same time for a murderous purpose rather difficult. The diversity of our rich civilization is our best guarantee against a tyrannical dictatorship. If we allow politicians to destroy it, it would amount to destroying the very soul of India.

13

Kashmir and Kashmiriyat: The Politics of Language, Religion and Region

During my recent visit to Kashmir I was shocked to learn that hardly anyone in Kashmir can read or write the Kashmiri script. Kashmir would thus qualify as one of the few places in the world where almost everybody including the educated elite are illiterate in their mother tongue. Kashmiri is neither taught in schools nor in most colleges. Therefore, there is no question of it being used as the official language of the state. Urdu and English are the languages of teaching and official use in Kashmir.

This despite the fact that the Kashmiri language has a rich body of written literature. Moreover, unlike their western-educated counterparts in other regions of India, Kashmiris always speak to each other in Kashmiri. During my five-day stay in the Valley I almost never heard Kashmiris speak to each other in any language other than Kashmiri. Those fighting for *azadi* (freedom) never tire of stressing the uniqueness of Kashmiri culture and identity.

For people all over the world language is one of the key definers of identity. Most nation-states in the modern world are carved along linguistic lines. Not too long ago in the subcontinent, Bangladesh broke away from Pakistan because the Bangladeshis resented the imposition of Urdu on them leading to the subjugation of their mother tongue, Bengali. This repudiated the founding principle of Pakistan— that Muslims were a distinct and separate nationality on account of their religion. Even after the separation of Bangladesh from Pakistan, the domination of Urdu has caused deep resentment among other linguistic groups in Pakistan—the Sindhis, the Baluchis, the Pushtoons, the Punjabis and others. Yet Kashmiri Muslims accepted the replacement of their Mother tongue by Urdu.

First published in *Manushi* No. 82 (May–Jun 1994).

On the other hand, in India, Urdu is a suspect language and neglected even in the land of its birth—Uttar Pradesh. Hindus are extremely wary of giving Urdu official recognition because it has come to be stigmatized as the language which led to the partition of the country. The main momentum for the creation of Pakistan came from Urdu-speaking Muslims in India and not from those areas which today constitute Pakistan. As the proud creators of Pakistan, the Urdu-speaking Muslim migrants from north India tried to impose national unity among different linguistic groups in Pakistan by making Urdu the national language even though it was the mother tongue of a small minority which had migrated from Uttar Pradesh.

In its spoken version, Urdu is indistinguishable from Hindustani, the spoken language of most north Indian Hindus. The two sister languages were torn asunder despite their close kinship, because the scripts were different and they came to be identified with different religious traditions. Urdu uses the Persian script and is therefore identified with Islam. Hindustani, using the *Devanagari* script, is associated with Hindus.

The neglect in the study of Kashmiri language is also in large part due to a different history and ethos that is imposed on the language by the Muslims and Hindus of Kashmir. The Kashmiri Pandits tell you that real Kashmiri can only be written in the Sharada script whereas the Kashmiri Muslims believe that the Persian script can serve the Kashmiri language better since it has been in use for nearly four hundred years and has been suitably modified to meet the special requirements of Kashmiri. The controversy extends even to Lal Ded, the 14th century mystic poet of Kashmir, who is, by common consensus, regarded as the mother of modern Kashmiri language. The Hindus call her Lalleshwari and believe that she belonged to a Brahmin family and was a proponent of Shaivism. On the other hand, there are long-standing legends recorded in Persian chronicles that she accepted Islam and was influenced by the Sufi tradition. Thus, both communities claim her as their own and they both have a strong sense of attachment to the Kashmiri language.

Yet, despite a long history of popular upsurges asserting the Kashmiri identity to justify the demands of autonomy and separation from both India and Pakistan, there has been hardly any demand by the proponents of *Kashmiriyat* (Kashmiri identity) and the 'fighters' for azadi for the introduction of Kashmiri as part of school and college curricula and its adoption as the language of the administration.

Naseem Meharaj is a rare Kashmiri who can read and write the script in its Persian version. She teaches Kashmiri language and literature in one of the very few colleges which offer a diploma course in the language. In her opinion, it is a great misfortune that Kashmiris are illiterate in their mother tongue. In the 1970s, due to pressure from some Kashmiri writers, a decision was taken by the government that Kashmiri would be taught in schools up to class 5. But this decision could not be implemented and most children continued learning Urdu. Some writers and intellectuals then pressurized the government to introduce it from above. As a result, a nine-month diploma course was started at the university level. Since then some colleges have provided for elementary study of Kashmiri. But whatever little work is being done in Kashmiri is confined to two institutions, the state government-run Cultural Academy and the Kashmiri Department at the Kashmir University.

Naseem was among the first batch of students to take the diploma. She explains that the earlier manuscripts of Kashmiri were all in the Sharada script: 'Most of our words were originally Sanskrit-based. But later a lot of Persian words were absorbed into the language because of the influence of Muslim kings. It remained a living language because it absorbed outside influences. It is a sign of our slavish mentality that we have failed to give Kashmiri its due. Ever since the Mughals deposed the last Kashmiri king, Yusuf Shah Chak, by fraud, there has been a conspiracy to undermine the Kashmiri language.'

It is noteworthy that the Mughal ruler Akbar, held in high esteem in the rest of the country, is considered an enemy by the Kashmiris because he arrested and deposed Yusuf Shah Chak. Kashmiris believe that they have been enslaved ever since because Kashmir was ruled from then on to date by outsiders—Mughals, Afghans, Sikhs, Dogras and now 'Indians'!

How is it that there has been no political pressure for making the study of Kashmiri a matter of routine rather than giving it the status of a special course as is done with foreign languages? I asked this question of Naseem as well as several important political leaders of the Kashmiri movement for 'freedom'. Some leaders glibly blamed it all on the Indian government and its conspiracy to suppress the Kashmiri people. But they could not explain why the Kashmiris had not even raised it as an issue. Some like Zafar Meharaj, a Srinagar-based journalist, say that the continuing political instability in the state and the unresolved issue of Kashmir's right to self-determination overshadowed all other concerns. Others are satisfied that Kashmiri is used by them for their everyday oral communication. After all, you cannot get jobs by studying Kashmiri, was a common response. The Muslim students learn Urdu and the Kashmiri Pandits learn Hindi in schools.

Sonnaullah Butt, the forthright editor of *Aftab*, a Srinagar-based Urdu paper, explained it thus: 'Since the time of the Sikh rulers, Urdu has been the official language in Kashmir. Earlier the Mughals had introduced Persian. Even after Dogra rulers took over Kashmir, they continued using Urdu as the language of administration. After 1947, the Assembly resolved that Urdu would be the state language though most government offices used English. Moreover, the Muslim sentiment is attached to Urdu since a lot of Islamic literature is available in this language and not in Kashmiri. When Radio Kashmir started functioning in the 50s, it began to broadcast daily news in Kashmiri. Though the Pandits were keen to encourage the use of the Kashmiri language, the Muslims began to resent the fact that Kashmiri was being propagated at the cost of Urdu.' Thus, Urdu has come to play a divisive role between Kashmiri Pandits and Kashmiri Muslims on the one hand and Kashmiri-speaking Muslims and other ethnic groups living in Jammu and Ladakh, on the other.

Yasin Malik, the much lionized JKLF leader, answered this question on a more politically pragmatic note: 'The Kashmiri language is not the only language of the people of Jammu and Kashmir. Dozens of languages are spoken in this state—Punjabi, Dogri, Gaddi, Ladakhi and a host of others. You cannot concentrate on any one particular language even though there is no doubt that Kashmiri, the language of the Valley, has suffered a great deal. Yes, I am in favour of Kashmiri being taught in schools. The truth is that the moment you talk of Kashmiriyat, then one has to include the varied cultures of the entire state. It is not just the Kashmiri language, but the cultures of various regions of this state have also suffered. I am of the view that Urdu has been thrust on us. It was the language of Lucknow. But now it has become an integral part of the Muslim culture.'

The conflicting pressure to speak on behalf of Kashmiris while soliciting the support of non-Kashmiri speaking people explains the complex dilemma the JKLF faces. However, Ladakhi Buddhists, Hindu Dogras, Gaddis and various other non-Kashmiri speaking groups are not going to support the call for independence under an exclusively Kashmiri Muslim leadership because of their strong sub-regional sentiment. The Ladakhis and people of Jammu region also harbour a sense of being discriminated against and neglected by the Kashmiris in the same way as the Kashmiris feel ill-treated by the national leadership.

The azadi slogan can have credibility only if it carries a majority of people from Jammu and Laddakh along with it. The substantial Hindu minority in Jammu and Kashmir is, by and large, opposed to azadi because the symbolism of azadi has come to connote an Islamic rather than a Kashmiri identity.

The attempt of JKLF leaders to neutralize the sub-regional sentiment while defining their own politics in both regional and religious terms has created a vicious circle. The more they resort to Urdu and Islam, the more they get estranged from the non-Muslim people of Jammu, Ladakh and Kashmir. This takes the JKLF activists closer to the pro-Pakistan politics in Kashmir and away from their cherished dream of azadi for all Kashmiris. Their bottom line is to unify all Muslims in the Valley as well as in Jammu and Ladakh. Urdu and the symbolism of Islam come handy for this purpose as they have the potential to neutralize the sub-regional sentiment among Muslims. The result is that even for the JKLF, Kashmiriyat has become a subset of *Islamiyat*.

Does that mean that the religious identity of the Kashmiri Muslims has overshadowed their Kashmiri identity? Has azadi for Kashmiri Muslims come to mean cleansing all those elements of their culture which smack of Hindu or non-Muslim ethos, Kashmiri language being one of them? The answer is both yes and no.

Undoubtedly, a significant though small section of Muslim Kashmiris want to join Pakistan after dissociating from India. Outfits like Hizbul Mujahiddin have popular support in certain pockets like Sopore. Yet, even there the anti-India demonstrations end up more often with slogans for azadi than for joining Pakistan. Today the organization that enjoys the greatest popular support is the JKLF which is engaged in a life and death struggle against Pakistan-supported outfits like Hizbul Mujahiddin, Al Baker, Harkat ul Ansar and others.

Though initially Pakistan lent armed support to the JKLF, they soon withdrew it and began propping up their own captive organizations. This was done with the purpose of undermining and attacking the JKLF because the Pakistani rulers were determined to suppress the Kashmiri sentiment for azadi. Hence, the continuing neglect of the Kashmiri language and the promotion of Urdu are an integral part of the agenda of the pro-Pakistan groups in Kashmir.

Their agenda is to stifle the Kashmiri sentiment of azadi and to promote a pro-Pakistani sentiment. Yet, despite all this, a large majority of Muslims in Kashmir continue to give their Kashmiri identity precedence over the Muslim one. However, the growing religious fervour among the Kashmiris could tilt the balance in favour of the Pakistani or west Asian version of Islam being imported into Kashmir.

No community can sustain its cultural identity for long without being rooted in its own language. As the leading organization for Kashmiri rights, the JKLF will have to pay attention to keeping the Kashmiri language alive as an integral aspect of and their fight for azadi.

Likewise, the Kashmiri Pandits are seriously undermining the distinctness of Kashmiriyat by proudly adopting a syndicated version of Hinduism being peddled by the BJP. For centuries they had willingly learnt to read and write Urdu and Persian under Mughal, Afghan, Sikh or Dogra rule simply because Persian and Urdu were then the languages of opportunities and elite employment. But today, they would rather study Hindi—an alien language—than their own Kashmiri in the Arabic script.

However, the educated among both the Hindus and the Muslims are now gravitating towards English rather than Hindi, Urdu or Kashmiri because the best jobs and material opportunities are available only through learning English. The bearer in charge of my room in Ahdoo hotel in Srinagar told me that they were running an English medium school in his village through contributions from parents of school-going children because they did not want to send their children to the Urdu medium government school. Only the very poor, who could not afford better, send their children to Urdu medium schools.

So, for all the noise about Kashmiri identity, it is English education that is most sought after. And those who harbour the illusion that the English-knowing elite which will thus emerge is likely to be more 'secular' and rise above narrow ethnic divides ought to remember that the perpetrators of the Partition and the initiators of the most vicious Hindu-Muslim divide have almost all been over-educated in English. Had the political elite of our country, for instance, studied in local madarsas or *pathshalas*, we might never have experienced the nightmare of the Partition.

14

Voices from Kashmir

*D*uring the last week of May 1994, I visited Jammu & Kashmir
along with Mr. Kuldeep Nayar and Justice Tarkunde of
Citizens For Democracy. This was not an enquiry team out
to document cases of atrocities and human rights violations, even
though wherever we went, by and large, this is what most Kashmiris
wanted to talk about. Our purpose was mainly to assess for ourselves
whether instances of excesses by security forces had lessened and
whether there existed any scope for a negotiated solution to the
Kashmir issue. The focus in this report is mainly on Kashmiri Muslims
in the valley. We have not dealt with the point of view of people in
other regions of Jammu & Kashmir or of Kashmiri Pandits not because
their viewpoint is any the less important, but because a peaceful
solution to the problem cannot be found unless we build bridges of
communication with people in the valley.

We reached Srinagar on the afternoon of 25 May. The atmosphere
at the airport seemed relatively relaxed. As soon as we sat in the taxi
to take us to our hotel, the taxi driver asked us: '*Aap* press *wale*
hain?' (Are you press people?). We said 'yes' and added that we
were a human rights team. 'Then you must know my clients Tavleen
Singh and Harinder Baweja?' he asked. 'What do you think of their
reports?' was my counter question to him. '*Harinder theek, theek
likhti hai, par Tavleen, to baapre! Main to uske sath jane se bahut
darta hoon.* (Harinder's writing is alright, but Tavleen! My God! I am
scared of taking her in my taxi). The last time she came, I took her
to a distant village where some woman had been raped. The Border
Security Force (BSF) tried to stop us from proceeding to that village.
She really gave it to them. She is not afraid of anyone. I shudder to

First published in *Manushi* No. 25 (Nov–Dec 1984).

accompany her anywhere because if she picks up a fight with the security forces again while travelling in my taxi, I will be finished.'

That a Delhi-based woman journalist could get away with challenging the security forces, whereas a local Kashmiri would be afraid of even being her chauffeur gives one an insight into the relationship the security forces have with the ordinary people of Kashmir today.

'How are things now as compared to the last couple of years?' we asked. 'Much better. There are far fewer confrontations between the militants and security forces. But the number of people being killed has not gone down. Things are likely to improve now that Yasin Malik has been released. He is among the most respected leaders of Kashmir. The day he was released from jail and brought back to Srinagar, the entire route from the airport to his house was lined up with people who had come out to greet him. It took him nearly seven hours to reach home from the airport—a distance normally covered in half an hour.' Even though our driver was clearly sympathetic to the JKLF demand for *azadi* (freedom), he made no bones about his own priorities: 'My politics is my *rozi roti* (daily bread). The day I have no customers, no one is going to come and feed me and my family. There are ten people dependent on me, including my two younger brothers. One of my brothers was picked up for interrogation because one of his friends who was arrested had given his name to the security forces. He was detained for interrogation and then let off. But they left him in such a bad shape that he was confined to bed for 20 days. He was released as he was able to convince them that he was not a militant.'

One of the most noteworthy aspects of our interaction with Kashmiri Muslims was that every time we heard a tale of woe about arrest, torture or killing by the security forces, people did not try to hide the fact whether the person targeted was a militant or not. I got the impression that the information we got on this count was by and large reliable. They would even tell us whether the person concerned had given up militancy or was still a militant. For instance, we were told that one of the young boys arrested in Delhi on a charge of trying to plant a bomb in Plaza cinema had given up militancy and had gone to Delhi for *mazdoori* (working as a labourer)—but he was arrested and made out to be an active terrorist. The same group of people had no hesitation in telling us who were genuine terrorists. People's anger and indignation was much stronger wherever an innocent person was targeted. Arrests of actual militants did not evoke strong indignation. Most people agreed that though the situation was in some ways returning to 'normal', the feeling of alienation is stronger than before.

Even though on the surface things appeared more 'normal', yet it would be wrong to assume that normalcy has returned. There has been no let up in crackdowns, whose frequency has actually increased. For instance, one of the localities called Batwal in Srinagar had recently gone through it for the 125th time. However, there is a perceptible change in the pattern. Till recently, the security forces seemed not to be able to distinguish between ordinary people and militants; killings and arrests were totally indiscriminate. In recent months they seem to have focused more on rounding up the militants.

The word 'crackdown' refers to the security forces' cordoning off a city locality or an entire village with the purpose of conducting search operations. All the men, including young boys, of the area are asked to come out. Often the men are beaten, humiliated and many are even tortured. For instance, in a village near Anantnag the security forces asked the men including the very aged ones to come out and made them roll in mud and filth. The security forces then go from house to house ostensibly to search for arms or hiding places. But on most occasions they just loot the houses, vandalize and break up whatever comes into their view. Every now and then, they misbehave with women. There have been some instances of rape. We were provided details of only three cases and met one rape victim.

We reached Sopore on 27 May, a day after a major crackdown by the BSF. The town is supposed to be a stronghold of pro-Pakistan Hizbul Mujahideen. This was the only place where we were faced with a hostile demonstration. Within minutes of our reaching Sopore, a large group of women gathered outside the house where we were having a meeting with local residents. They were excited and kept shouting pro-Pakistan and anti-India slogans like: *'Yeh tamasha nahin hai, yeh matam sahi hai'* (This is not a farce, this mourning is for real) and *'Yahan kya chalega—Nizame Musalmeen'* What will apply here? the rule of Muslims)'. I could not tell whether it was a stage-managed show or a spontaneous demonstration. However, the mood was far more angry than at other places we visited. This was probably because Sopore had been subjected to a major crackdown on the previous day.

On the morning of 26 May, all the men and young boys were ordered to gather at one place around 7 a.m. and were subjected to an identification parade. A young boy sitting in a Gypsy van was acting as the informer. Twenty-three men were picked out and taken to a makeshift interrogation centre one by one. We met several of them in Sopore medical college hospital later in the day. The first one to be picked out was a 45-year-old man whose son was a militant but had been killed in cross-fire four years ago. They asked the father to hand over his dead son's gun. When he told them that he did not have the weapons used by his son, he was tortured.

Feyaz Ahmed Antoo, a 34-year-old shopkeeper, described his own ordeal thus:

I was the third one to be called in for interrogation. They wanted me to tell them the hiding places of militants. I told them that I didn't know of any hiding places and that the militants had stopped coming here ever since the BSF established its bunkers around Sopore. They then stripped me naked and tied my hands behind my back. One of them kicked me and I fell down. They then placed an iron rod on my thighs. Four of them climbed on top of it. They stuffed my mouth with my own banian (vest). One of them caught hold of my head with one hand and with the other he began to pour water into my nostrils. Another jawan was simultaneously giving me electric shocks. After fifteen minutes of this, they asked me to accompany them to our old house. There they began another torture session. After a while they took me to the third storey of our house asking me to show them the hiding places. When I said there were no hiding places to show, they tortured me a third time. When finally I was brought down, my mother was standing outside our new house. She had a bag containing Rs. 6,37,000 in cash, several fixed deposit receipts (FDRs) and jewellery. They snatched the bag from her. I protested saying that this was our hard earned money, our bank has all this in its record. My brother-in-law also tried arguing with them. Consequently, he too was taken for interrogation and tortured. Later they returned the jewellery but took away the cash and FDRs. But they gave the FDR numbers and a receipt for the cash. Our family runs a leather business. One of those they arrested was a young employee of ours. He was tortured the most. As he tried to run away they fired at him and injured him in the leg. Everybody we talked to agreed that this young man was totally unconnected with militancy. The next day's newspapers in Delhi carried the government version of this incident whereby they announced that the BSF had recovered Pakistani currency during a raid in Sopore town. Feroze Ahmed complained that the security forces not only looted their belongings but they drank liquor in their house, misbehaved with women, even bit their faces and threatened to kill all the young men of Kashmir.

Another one of those tortured was 35-year-old Mohammad Mubashir Naik who is employed as a work supervisor in the Rural Development Department of the state government. He admitted candidly that he was interrogated and tortured because his *saala* (brother-in-law) Tariz Ahmed Mitha is a Hizbul Mujahideen militant. Mubashir was stripped naked and given the roller treatment. A metal rod was inserted in his penis and his anal portion cut up with a knife. He had bled for three hours through his anus till he was brought to the Sopore hospital and stitched up. They had also given him electric shocks through his fingers.

Each one of those admitted to the hospital had a similar story to tell. Sopore has experienced nearly 30 to 40 such crackdowns in recent years. The area has pronounced Islamic fundamentalist politics because this is the constituency of the Jammat-e-Islami leader Sayed Ali Gilani. However, the crackdown on 26 May was not in retaliation against any provocation by the terrorists, though this time the BSF had targeted those families whose relatives were operating with the militants.

Back in Srinagar, Mohammad Jawad of Baghwanpura, Lal Bazar in Srinagar brought to us a whole case file pertaining to the continued detention of his son Mohammad Yusuf Lone, aged 25, who he insists has been wrongly implicated by the police. Yusuf was arrested in Delhi on 25 April 1992. His father was consumed by grief and kept asking us to look at the photos of his son saying: 'Does he look like a militant to you?' He told us that he had sent off his son to work in Delhi because he wanted him far away from the troubles of Kashmir. He was married on 26 October 1991 in Srinagar and returned to Delhi, just 15 days after his wedding. He was employed with Gulshan Carpets in Delhi since 1989, and lived at F-100, Lajpat Nagar. On 25 April 1992 there was a raid at the M-27 Lajpat Nagar office-cum-residence of the owner of Gulshan Carpets and Mohammad Yusuf was arrested along with six other people. He has been in police custody since then. Yusuf's father complained that his son's bail application has been rejected four times even though the police has not pressed any charges against him. In contrast, one of the seven arrested, Mohammad Akhtar Dar, who is the nephew of the owner of Gulshan Carpets, has been released even though there are serious charges against him. The implication was that the latter had bribed his way out. Yusuf's father also showed the many discrepancies in the paper work associated with his son's arrest. The desperation of the family unable to get a proper hearing against the high-handedness of the police, as avenues of redressal had been shut off, explained why even those who are unsympathetic to militants are turning against the Indian government.

It is not so much the brutality and torture which made people so despise the security forces. It is their utter lack of discipline and self-respect which had made the armed forces appear an object of contempt rather than fear. We saw one of the houses which had been converted into an interrogation centre. The BSF had vandalized everything that came into their sight. They broke the TV, crockery and whatever else they could lay their hands on. Even the wooden staircase had been chopped into pieces. One had to hang one's head in shame when we heard outbursts like:

Unka to haldi mirch khatam ho jaye to raid karne aa jaate hain. Jo khana pina dikha kha liya bachon ka doodh tak bhi. Purane joote tak hamare le jaate hain. Ghar mein aurton ke doodh ke liye bachaye paise bhi chura lete hain. Jo log ande tak chura lein aap soch sakte hain unki level kya hogi. Bade bahadur bante hain! Militants ko dekh kar to bhag jate hain, per innocents ko aakar maar jate hain. Jung lado, to jung ke usoolon ke sath.'
(They come to raid every time they run out of rations or even spices. They eat and drink whatever is in sight—even children's milk. They take away anything they can lay their hands on, even our old shoes. They even steal the little money women keep in the kitchen for the supply of daily milk. You can imagine the level of those who even steal eggs. They call themselves brave, but they run away at the sight of militants. And later they come and beat up the innocents. Fight a war if you will, but observe the rules of war.)

Such behaviour by the army and its attitude towards the general population has reduced the armed forces' efficacy in combating genuine terrorism. Men who behave like petty thieves and marauders are not likely to inspire awe or confidence. This is, unfortunately, not a new phenomenon for Kashmiris. Ever since Kashmir became a part of India, it has been denied free and fair elections barring once in 1977, and the state has repeatedly come under the rule of the Central Government. Moreover, it is a border state whose future was supposed to have been decided through plebiscite in both India and Pakistan-controlled Kashmir. Consequently, the state has experienced a heavy dose of army presence. The Indian army, like most armies in the world, has a tendency to treat civilians with contempt even in normal times. During the last few years it has become even more unrestrained. This has been the singlemost important factor for the alienation of Kashmiris who feel that they were never trusted with full citizenship rights and have been treated like a subject population under imperial rule.

Today it is not just ordinary citizens who are complaining against the behaviour of the security forces. Many senior bureaucrats feel no less aggrieved at being totally sidelined with the army taking over not only law and order from the police but also wanting control over day-to-day administration. Two officials based in Jammu narrated the following incident as an example of how the army men think that they are a law unto themselves.

Around mid-April on a Sunday, some army men had gone for a picnic to Mansal lake near Jammu. Though this is a popular picnic spot, there is a sanctity attached to this place, especially the lake. It is a known, popularly accepted taboo that no one will fish or drink liquor in that lake. However, these soldiers carried liquor bottles with them and they wanted to carry their drinks with them while they went boating. The local tourist officer tried to stop them from doing so. The army men got so annoyed that they took out their belts and started beating up the tourist officer. The local policemen at the spot tried to intervene and stop the violence. This further enraged the army men. They beat up the policemen, tied them up, and bundled them into their jeeps and took them to their base at Udhampur where the army men gave them another thrashing. Next day they brought them back to the *thana* (police station) these policemen were attached to and handed them over to the officer in charge. So confident were they of getting away with it that they even insisted on taking receipts that the abducted policemen had been handed over!'

When the complaint reached the civil administrator in charge of the area, he wanted to order an enquiry and sent the facts to the Governor asking for his permission to hold an enquiry into this incident. The Governor plainly refused. That is where the matter ended. According to a senior IAS officer (his name is purposely kept back), this is inevitable if you have a former army general heading the civil administration. 'He is not likely to accept that the army could be wrong. It gives the armed forces the feeling that they are supreme.'

Even though the army is supposed to aid the civil administration, in Kashmir, the army is actually running the show. A senior administrator complained: 'In Kashmir, the army has been given special powers ever since 1947. Consequently, army officers have come to consider themselves as special creatures, altogether above law.' The army has been entrusted with unified command. The BSF and all other security forces have been placed under them. According to some responsible senior officials, 'After the army was bestowed with unified command, both the number of casualties and militancy has gone up. Even very senior IAS officials have no say in the administration. In fact, they have been made answerable to the army. Given the total political vacuum, and the fact that even panchayat elections have not been held for so very long, people have no real channels of grievance redressal.'

The lack of discipline in the army has become a serious menace. We were told that even the officers seem afraid of their men, who have become used to running amok and getting away with it. Even senior police officials are kept in the dark about anti-insurgency operations not just in the Kashmir valley but also in the Jammu area. This, despite the fact that some of the recent 'successes' of the army in nabbing militants have been on the basis of information provided by the Jammu and Kashmir police. The army is hampered by the fact that, unlike the local police, they don't know the local languages. Their 'interrogation' often consists of no more than torture sessions interspersed with the standard questions: 'Where are the arms? Where are the militants hiding?'

The sidelining of the bulk of the local police is justified on the ground that they are sympathetic to militants. One of the senior government officials is known to have declared that all Jammu and Kashmir policemen are Pakistanis (agents of Pakistan). If there is truth in this, then they should have been put on trial and fired from their jobs. But that is not what has happened. The state police continue to draw their salaries while stripped of all responsibility. This has led to great demoralization and a sense of humiliation for being so mistrusted.

The existing political vacuum combined with the paralysis of the state government machinery has meant a total alienation between the army-run administration and the local people. Nothing symbolizes it better than the lifestyle of the Governor and other senior army officials. The Governor's residence is an old colonial mansion situated miles away from the city and its suburbs. Built on sprawling acres of land between two mountains, it provides an idyllic view of the Dal Lake. But no human beings or human habitation are visible from this palatial mansion. Sitting in the Governor's drawing room, listening to his monologue on the successes of the army and his plans for the state, one was reminded of the colonial days. His mannerisms, his style and thinking would have done any British Viceroy proud.

The Kashmiri people charge the army of repeatedly indulging in frequent and large-scale identification parades because it provides an avenue for making money. There is a rule that whenever people are gathered for an identification parade, they are to be provided refreshments at the rate of Rs 6 per head. In actual fact this is seldom done. This rule provides the incentive to gather as many men as possible so that the money meant for refreshments can be pocketed.

The methods used to nab militants are often counter-productive because the forces do not distinguish between collaborators and ordinary citizens. Jamshid, a lawyer practising at Anantag courts, gave the following account of a crackdown aimed at pure humiliation of the entire local population:

My house is situated a few kilometres outside Anantnag. Last year around 12 July 1993, some terrorists planted a mine on the road. When the news spread in our area, people began to flee their homes fearing an army crackdown. Only the elderly people were left behind. During the night there was a crackdown by the army. My old father was pulled out of the house at 3 a.m. along with the other elderly people of the village. They stripped them naked, made them lie down in a dirty pool of water and beat them up ruthlessly till they were unconscious. Then they dumped them into trucks, still naked, and took them to Khandura headquarters. When they were released in the evening because they were found innocent, my father and others were in such a state that they could not even talk.'

Because of such ham-handed operations, the security forces are completely alienated from the local population. Consequently, their intelligence sources have also dried up leading to still cruder methods of interrogation and crackdowns.

Far from telling exaggerated stories of rape, I found that the people were as cautious while narrating incidents of sexual violence as they were when describing whether the person killed was actually a militant or not. There were no wild allegations of large-scale rape of women. In the few places we held discussions, we were always given names and dates of specific incidents. For instance, the Anantnag lawyers mentioned only two recent cases of rape. One took place in early April. In a crackdown on village Vailnagbal of Anantnag tehsil, the daughter of an old freedom fighter, Mohammad Rajabwani, was raped by the army while she was alone in the house as the men had been dragged out. Another lawyer, M.Y. Shehardar, gave the following account:

In my village Sailia, there was a crackdown in the early hours of the morning. The BSF jawans ransacked a number of homes. My neighbour Ahmed was locked in a room and his wife Zainab was dragged into another room and gang raped. The husband pretended he had managed to save his wife, but the villagers knew he was merely putting on a brave face because she was bedridden for three days.

People alleged that though hundreds of women have been raped, only a handful of cases have been registered because of the social stigma attached to being identified as a rape victim. Mohammad Sultan Butt, another lawyer, testified to the following incident:

Some days ago a mine was planted by terrorists some 3 kms. from Anantnag which killed some soldiers. In retaliation, the RR9 army camp soldiers raided a house around 4 a.m. They did not find any militants there nor were any weapons recovered. They, however, took a ball of gunpowder and blew up the house, roasting seven people alive.

The lawyers were no less upset about the fact that their elite status got them no concessions.

'They force us to come out of our homes and work for them like coolies. They don't spare us even when we show our identity cards.'

In Anantnag, the Muslim fundamentalists' insistence on calling the city 'Islamabad' is a special bone of contention . The use of the Islamic name is seen as proof of their pro-Pakistan sympathies. The army personnel go around defacing sign boards which say Islamabad. The use of crude methods make people more firm in their defiance. A common refrain one heard was that militancy came on the heels of the BSF. People point to Bijbehara which was a fairly peaceful zone till not long ago. 'As soon as they established a BSF camp in the area, incidents of terrorism began cropping up. As soon as the army/BSF is posted anywhere, the area becomes a problem zone.' We were repeatedly told: 'Their very presence is a provocation and a humiliation.'

Armed with a whole range of draconian laws and estranged from the local people, the security forces feel no need to be discreet or discerning in their anti-terrorist operations. For every genuine terrorist they nab, there are dozens of innocent and unconnected people brutalized, tortured, maimed and killed. Despite the much publicized human rights abuses in the international fora, in most cases the 'excesses' go unchallenged. As inevitably happens in such situations, a lot of personal enmities are being avenged by the local people through the army.

In the Baramula courts, young Gulzara Bano narrated a harrowing tale of what appears to be a typical case of ham-handed anti-militancy operations by the army. Gulzara was married about two years ago to Bashir, a resident of Lacchhipura in Uri district bordering Pakistan Occupied Kashmir (POK). Bashir is the only son of his parents and has three sisters. His mother is dead. Apart from his own father's land, he has also inherited the land of two of his paternal uncles who died without leaving a direct heir. In addition, he runs a small business in Channawadi. He is considered one of the most well-off persons in his village where most families have very small landholdings. According to his wife, this has caused much jealousy and resentment. In particular he has had a long-standing enmity with a man called Lassa, a neighbour of Bashir's family. Lassa has inherited a very small piece of land because he has five other brothers to share the family property with. Since Bashir has had no child in the two years he has been married, Lassa and some other neighbours had threatened him openly that they were going to get rid of him and take over his land.

Instead of bloodying his own hands, Lassa apparently told the army that Bashir and his sister's husband were both militants. Consequently, both of them were arrested by the army and taken for interrogation, around the 9th of May. The wives of the two men were told nothing of their whereabouts, despite their best efforts to find out where their husbands were detained. On 27 May, the day before we met Gulzara, the dead body of her sister-in-law's husband, Ali Asghar, who had been arrested along with Bashir, was handed over to the family. According to Gulzara, there were visible marks of torture all over his body. As soon as she saw what had become of Ali, Gulzara fled her home in panic and sought shelter with her younger sister who lives in a students' hostel in Baramula. The next morning she went to the Deputy Commissioner of Baramula to plead for the release of her husband. She also sought help from local lawyers. That is how we chanced to meet her in the Baramula courts where we had gone to meet members of the local Bar Association. She was beside herself with grief and fear:

As soon as they went to bury Ali, I ran to Baramula. When I saw his dead body, I lost all sense. I only have an old father-in-law who is half blind.

There is no one to help or protect us among our neighbours because others too want my husband out of their way so that they can grab his land. Lassa had made a few attempts on my husband's life even earlier and would openly threaten to kill him. When that didn't work, they resorted to *mukhbari* (informing) and got my *nanad's* (sister-in-law's) and my husband arrested by the army.

Settling personal enmities, property disputes and fights over women through the army is becoming a frequent occurrence. Gulzara says:

Our area is not a militant stronghold. In fact, the militants mistrust the people of Uri accusing them to be *mukhbirs* (informers). We can't even come to Baramula openly. We have to keep hiding from the militants and their sympathizers. Otherwise they'd attack us for being mukhbirs. Once my husband and I came to this place together. My uncle's son who was studying in Srinagar had failed in class 10 exam. He asked us to accompany him to Srinagar so that he could get his paper re-checked. When we returned and reached the Baramula bus stand, the militants caught hold of my husband and beat him up because somebody told them we were Uri residents. The people of Uri have this reputation because we are near the border. Both sides suspect us of being informers.'

Dilshad's account seemed more garbled than Gulzara's and also less reliable. She used to live with her husband Mohammad Ashraf Khan in Srinagar. The family owns a bakery in Jawahar Nagar. He was arrested soon after Id in May this year. They have been married for 12 years and supply bread from their bakery to Srinagar's Medical Institute. She alleges that her husband has been burnt all over his body and face and the army is trying to get him to confess that his wife is also a mujahid (militant). 'I have small children to look after. What kind of *majahidgi* (militancy) can I do?' she asks vehemently. She says all this has befallen them because her husband divorced his first wife and married Dilshad.

The first wife is a Gujjar from Uri. These Uri people are all bad people. She took her revenge on me by giving my photo to the army saying that I am a militant and I have hidden lots of arms and ammunition. On the one hand they have implicated us with the army saying we are mujahids. Earlier they got us into trouble with the militants saying we are army informers. Before the army took away my husband, the militants had abducted us both and subjected us to physical torture at the behest of my husband's first wife.

She showed me a number of photographs of her body displaying torture marks. They had beaten and stubbed burning cigarettes all over her body. She was accused of informing on one of their comrades, Hamid Sheikh, leading to his arrest. According to Dilshad, the first wife felt let down by the fact that the militants did not torture her enough and let her off after a day or two. Therefore, she got them into trouble with the army as well. Dilshad's husband is in the army's custody and she says he is being badly tortured. I was not able to figure out how she herself has managed to escape arrest, though she says the army is on the look-out for her.

We met Gulzara, Dilshad and others at a meeting organized by the Baramula Bar Association where some victims' families came and gave details of family members arrested, tortured or killed. Most of the victims seemed to be present by chance as they had come to attend court that day. In the first round people were allowed a few minutes each to present their case. All we heard were standard stories of army atrocities. I then requested that I be allowed to talk privately with some women. They sent one of their women colleagues to sit with me. She became very uneasy because the stories that began unfolding seemed far less stereotyped. As soon as the organizers realized that when allowed a proper hearing these women had more complex stories to tell, stories that indicted the militants as much as the army, they began obstructing me on the pretext that I had to go for lunch. Despite my best efforts to say that lunch was not important, I was not allowed to talk to more than three or four women before I was whisked away for lunch. I requested the women to wait for us and promised that I would return soon after lunch. But I found our hosts had no intention of allowing me to go back. I had to struggle hard to come back to where the women were still waiting for me. But I was really surprised to find that some of the women had changed their version altogether. The very same Dilshad who earlier seemed desperate to talk to us began shouting and screaming that we Indians should leave Kashmiris alone. 'You only come to see whether we still have any fighting spirit left in us. Please don't come here.' I got the feeling she had in the meantime been tutored by some of the lawyers.

At Baramula we were feasted with a sumptuous lunch at the house of one of the lawyers—Khwaja Sarwar Shah. As we entered his prosperous-looking home, he pointed to a bullet hole in the glass pane of his drawing room window. He told us the story of how this bullet had been fired at their house about a year and a half ago from a nearby army bunker. They had preserved the bullet mark like a proud medal to be displayed to all important visitors even though the rest of the house was freshly painted and spruced up. This lawyer and his friends indulged in militant anti-India rhetoric which I found amusing because earlier he had proudly shown me pictures of his maternal uncle prominently displayed in his drawing room because his uncle was once a Member of Parliament and had also been appointed as an ambassador of the Government of India. When I asked him why he was proud of an uncle who had been a collaborator of a government which he said he hated, he pretended that he had not heard my question. But he could not evade the question of why he continued practising law in the Indian courts instead of taking up the gun since he was so enamoured with the politics of pro-Pakistan mujahidins. His answer was not convincing: 'When the time comes, I will also take up the gun. Right now I am serving the movement through the lawcourts.'

There was a distinct difference in the tenor of discussion in our meetings with Kashmiri lawyers, political leaders and those with ordinary Kashmiris. The anti-India sentiment of the latter was based on their personal suffering whereas some of the politicians and lawyers indulged in far more exaggerated rhetoric than their collaborationist past justified. Every mistake the Indian army made provided grist to their mill. These lawyers were far from willing to acknowledge the atrocities and human rights violations being committed by their supposed liberators. Ordinary Kashmiris seemed equally upset by both and did not overstate or dramatize their suffering. For instance, in a meeting held in the home of one of the victims of army killings in Dabrana village near Anantnag, people talked quietly and in measured tones as compared to the militant rhetoric of many lawyers. In the village there was no hysteria, no exaggerated political statements nor an inflated account of atrocities—just plain matter-of-fact description of how the army had been behaving with them. Describing a crackdown which took place on 25 April 1994, the villagers told us that at night they heard sounds of firing. The next morning at 8 a.m. the army told them that militants had fired at the army and they had come to search the village. All the men were ordered to come out for identification. Four men were taken out of the identification parade—Ali Mohammad, Feyaz Ahmed, Farooq Ahmed and Javed Ahmed Shah—and were shot dead. The villagers told us without any coaxing that Feyaz Ahmed and Farooq were indeed militants, but Ali Mohammad, a 35-year-old tailor by profession, was killed simply because they suspect every Muslim with a beard. Another villager Mohammad Amin told us that he shaved off his beard after that incident because the army specially picks on men with beards. Ali Mohammad's brother, Mohammad Ibrahim is employed in the BSF, but even that could not save him. As usual, during the crackdown, the army people looted a lot of stuff from people's homes, including used clothes, tape recorders, boots, and watches.

The people openly admitted that this village had produced three terrorists. Javed Ahmed was a first-class-first graduate in the mid 80s. He applied for admission in the engineering college. They asked him for one lakh rupees as a bribe for admission. He then began looking around for a job but could not find one. He ran away and became a terrorist. We were told that another militant of the village had left for some foreign country. The third one, Farooq, has given up militancy and just whiles away his time. With a laugh we were told 'Ab woh kabutar palta hai (Now he rears pigeons!) while his old and poor father does mazdoori (labours).' The young man was promptly produced before us when we expressed the desire to meet him.

Farooq was candid about his 3-4 year involvement with Al Jehad. 'I joined them in 1990 because I did not get a job even though I was a matric pass. Therefore, I picked up the gun. My parents are very poor and my father supports the family by mazdoori; reda chalata hai (pulls a cart). I left a year ago because my parents are old and very poor. They were being constantly harassed by the army. If they don't stop harassing us, I may pick up the gun again.' Would he give up militancy if he got a job, I asked. 'No, I will not take up a job. Now I want to throw out Hindustan from Kashmir (Hindustan ko bhagana hai).' What exactly does he mean when he refers to Hindustan? 'The army,' came the unhesitating reply.

That is essentially the tragedy of Kashmir. An average Kashmiri views his affiliation with India only in terms of army rule. Repeated spells of Central rule supported by a heavy and high-handed presence of the army has made them associate India with the arrogance and tyranny of the armed forces and near total suppression of democratic institutions.

However, despite the all pervasive hatred Kashmiris feel for the Indian government, many young men confess to having turned towards terrorist politics because they could not 'get a job'. The job refers not just to any employment but specifically to government service. For instance, the waiter in charge of my room at Aahdoo hotel told me that he had 'no job'. When I pointed out that he was employed as a waiter, he said *'Yeh to koi naukri nahin hai, yeh to aise hi thoda bahut kama lete hain.'* (This is no job. This is just a way to earn a little money). He gets a salary of Rs 800 and makes another Rs 1500 a month on an average by way of tips, but it is 'not really a job' like the ones his two brothers have with the government. It is probably because, as in the rest of the country, even a lowly government job implies not only a substantial, regular salary for no or little work but also unlimited avenues of money-making through corruption. Kashmir has been notorious for its corrupt governance because democratic checks and balances have been altogether missing. Kashmiris manning the government have made a lot of money. The army soldiers who go on a looting spree in towns and villages are often heard saying: 'You have amassed a lot of wealth from India. First we will get that out and then talk to you about azadi.'

The lack of professionalism is one of the most important reasons for the inability of security forces to isolate the terrorists and bring the situation under control. It is not just a matter of a certain number of mistakes or lapses that are inevitable in a counter-insurgency operation. Nor are the 'excesses' by security forces a result of provocations by militants because of the former having to work under extremely stressful conditions, as is often presented in our newspapers, magazines, television and now even popular cinema—such as in the film *Roja*.

The unprecedented success of *Roja* has been attributed to the realistic portrayal of the way in which security forces and government employees are risking their very lives out of sheer idealism, in order to protect the unity and integrity of India. Unfortunately, the ground reality is substantially different. Many people in Kashmir, including the respected editor of Jammu based *Kashmir Times*, Mr. Ved Bhasin, told us that the security forces and certain sections of the bureaucracy have acquired a vested interest in prolonging the disturbance rather than seeing an end to it. The reason is simple—the scope for corruption and amassing huge wealth gets enhanced manifold when there is army rule and the officers have been given unchecked powers. Since all democratic institutions which can mediate between the state and the people have been wiped out in Jammu and Kashmir and as the army enjoys unquestioned authority, security forces at all levels are indulging in open loot and extortion under the cover of anti-insurgency operations.

To begin with, despite the government propaganda about their trying at great risk to control the infiltration from across the border, people in Kashmir openly talk about the going rate paid to the BSF for crossing the border. Thus, the sharper and more jingoistic the rhetoric about stopping infiltration, the higher is the rate demanded by the BSF for letting militants go across the border or come back with arms. So is the case with the much publicized 'arrests of militants'. Often innocents are arrested solely for the purpose of extorting money out of their families. We were told that the minimum rate of letting an arrested person off is Rs. 20,000 and could be much higher depending on the paying capacity of the family. According to reliable persons, there have been numerous instances of the release of even known militants through bribes. Similarly the weapons seized are often sold back to the very same militants from whom they were captured. The process is simple. For example, the security forces capture ten guns, they show only three 'seized' in the records and the other seven are given back to the militants in exchange for some money. Even ordinary shopkeepers are constantly threatened with arrests if they do not pay bribes.

Apart from tyrannizing even the innocent people, the very large presence of security forces is causing unprecedented damage to the ecology of Kashmir. Forests are being cut and wood is being sold illegally on a large scale by the security forces. Barren mountains are a testimony to the rapacious theft of forest resources that has escalated in the last few years. We heard stories of how senior officials get the famous *akhrot* (walnut) trees cut illegally to get the renowned carved furniture of Kashmir made through local craftsmen, who mostly have to work free for the army. People talk of officers carrying back truckloads of such furniture when their term comes to an end in Kashmir. One of the most commonly cited instances of corruption and vested interest of the paramilitary forces is that of a Central Reserve Police Force (CRPF) commandant who had been posted in Kashmir upto 1991, after which he was sent to Punjab. There he received a bullet injury in an encounter with terrorists. After that he was told that he would be given a posting of his choice. Normally people are expected to opt for a peace station, but he asked to be reposted to Kashmir and manipulated his transfer in such a way that he was sent back to Padgaon. The reason was obvious; he had made a lot of money there.

The army is still considered relatively more disciplined than the BSF or the CRPF. But if the army is continuously used for crushing internal rebellions, it might become indistinguishable from the notorious BSF. To quote Ved Bhasin: 'Our experience in the past is that wherever BSF was posted, the situation deteriorated.' He feels that, though the area has been handed over to the security forces on the ground that there is a serious law and order problem created by the militants, the lawlessness of the security forces is adding fuel to the fire rather than quelling it. Even though India has so far avoided the fate of Pakistan where the army has got used to dominating the political life of the country, the situation in Kashmir is like an army-ruled state. The army generals and the top officials of the BSF are constantly making political statements. They are unable to work as a coordinated team with the BSF giving one version and the army or the CRPF giving an altogether different one about the same event. To put it very mildly, they all seem to be functioning at cross purposes in pretty much the same manner as the Home Minister Chavan and his junior Rajesh Pilot who are more often than not singing contrary songs on Kashmir and sabotaging each other. The situation at the ground level is not very different from the situation at the Home Ministry level—one hand does not know what the other is doing. And when it does know, the attempt is to pull down the other rather than work as a coherent team.

The corrupt among the bureaucrats also seem happy at the state of affairs. In the prevailing atmosphere, the crores that are pouring in as development funds can be more easily pocketed because even the minimal checks on their authority that operate under 'normal' conditions, are absent at the moment.

The militants too, are a sadly divided lot, especially since Pakistan began arming rival outfits of the JKLF. Apart from political rivalries between groups owing allegiance to different ideologies and political interests, there is a great deal of mutual mistrust and hostility towards each other. As inevitably happens with groups pursuing underground politics, these outfits have all been infiltrated by intelligence agents from both India and Pakistan. Consequently, the level of mutual suspicion is very high. No one, not even their most celebrated heroes, are spared. For instance, Yasin Malik has a very high level of credibility and respect at the popular level, for he was among the first to have crossed the border when he was a mere teenager and started this phase of the secessionist movement. Yet, when he was released from jail after four years and began publicly admitting that the solution to the Kashmir problem cannot come through guns alone, one heard several people including his colleagues in the Hurriyat Conference (a platform of diverse Kashmiri organizations) suggest that he had made a 'deal' with the Central Government. His open criticism of the criminal elements within the liberation movement and resolve to isolate and purge them seems to have caused further suspicion. In fact, some prominent people even hinted that the visit of our team was linked to a 'deal' made in Delhi to co-opt Yasin. Two attempts have already been made on his life and most people fear that his life is in serious danger from rival militant groups now that he is emphasizing the need for a negotiated settlement rather than continue with the earlier warlike confrontation.

Those resisting takeover of the movement by criminal elements, and those who wish to put an end to the mindless violence that has come to dominate in Kashmir, face the greatest threats to their lives. However, the Pakistan-backed outfits like Al-Jehad, Hizbul Mujahiddin, and Harkat-ul-Ansar have come to acquire disproportionate gun power and it has become almost impossible to restrain them just as it is impossible to restrain the provocative acts by government-planted agent provocateurs.

The situation reminded me of the atmosphere of mistrust in the movement for Khalistan during the heydays of Sikh separatism. In 1986, I was invited to address a series of meetings in gurudwaras in the U.S. and Canada at a time when the overseas Sikhs had become very active in supporting Khalistan. The North American gurudwaras were then almost completely under the sway of Sikh terrorists. In the meetings I addressed, some people would adopt very aggressive postures and use the most extremist rhetoric. After the discussion, I would have people sneak up to me and whisper in my ear, 'Madhuji, don't heed so and so who took such extremist views. He is actually a Congress agent.' There was a strong suspicion that many of those who were loudest in justifying bloodshed to achieve political ends were agent provocateurs. No one knew whom to trust. I found suspicion even between close relatives. People were afraid to talk sensibly because the militants would dub them as *sarkari* Sikhs. Thus, even those who had strong reservations about the path being pursued by Khalistanis would either keep quiet altogether or join in supporting militants for fear of being dubbed government agents.

In Kashmir too, I found it hard to figure out, especially when talking to elite sections like lawyers and journalists, as to who was speaking out of genuine conviction and who was just adopting a militant posture to remain above suspicion with the extremists, especially the pro-Pakistan elements whose gun power is as feared as that of the security forces, because neither of the two seem to be following any rules in their warfare. In all our meetings with lawyers' associations, for instance, the pro-Pakistan lobby was the most articulate. They were seldom challenged vigorously, though many people let it be known quietly that pro-azadi sentiment was far stronger than pro-Pakistan sentiment. Those in favour of merger with Pakistan are a small minority, but they seemed a determined lot. They successfully drowned the voices of those opposed to Pakistani interference because pro-Pakistan outfits are far better armed and far more determined to kill.

For instance Zafar Meharaj, a Srinagar-based journalist, who is very close to the JKLF politics today says that he was known for being pro-India till not very long ago but had now come to the conclusion that coexistence within India is neither possible nor desirable. From the manner in which he expressed his politics, I got the feeling that he was bitterly anti-India. I was, therefore, surprised when I was told by someone who knew him well that he was put on the hit list of terrorists a couple of years ago for taking a moderate line. Consequently, he had to leave Srinagar and move to Delhi for a few years. I could not tell, therefore, whether his supposedly moderate pro-India politics gave way to strong secessionist politics under threat, or whether the transition was due to progressive disenchantment with the Indian state, or both. In fact, during the course of an interview, when he told me that he had shifted to Delhi in 1991 looking for a job in a Delhi newspaper, I had expressed my surprise saying: Why would someone who strongly believed in seceding from India move to Delhi—the capital city of the nation with which Kashmiris were waging a virtual war? And that too at the height of the secessionist movement in Kashmir! Why did he not stay on and contribute actively to the cause he believed in?

His answer was: 'I want to propagate the cause of Kashmiris through the national press. That is why I left Srinagar.' The answer did not sound convincing, even at that time. But when I heard the story about his being on the hit list of militants at that point, things fell in place.

Despite the routine abuse of power by the army and the BSF, people are not afraid to talk against the Indian government. However, they are far more scared to talk against the high-handedness and atrocities being committed by the terrorists. Even men like Zafar

Meharaj do not dare to criticise them. In fact, they go out of their way to defend them in public. He goes no further than saying that militants have committed some 'mistakes'. 'They don't forcibly extort money from people, they merely ask us for help. Instances of extortion are very few.' When asked to give an instance of their 'mistakes', he says, 'Maybe they should not come to people with guns when asking for money. They should send some unarmed person.' Today, the fear of the terrorist's gun is far greater than that of government guns because the terrorist movement has been hijacked by Pakistan-trained mercenaries and some foreign elements. Those people are extremely intolerant of any dissensions and altogether unscrupulous about whom they kill. Therefore, only a handful of courageous men dare condemn them openly. Sannaulah Khan, editor of *Daily Aftab* in Srinagar, is amongst the few who admit that the people do not like the doings of terrorists but the behaviour of security forces is such that they still are unwilling to condemn and confront the terrorists openly. He admits that though he personally disapproves of their politics, even in his paper he dare not refuse to print the militants' hand-outs. It is in this context that Yasin Malik's open condemnation of criminal acts of terrorists, his resolve to purge such elements from the movement, and an open acknowledgement that guns alone will not provide a solution is a major breakthrough for resolving the Kashmir crisis. Sannaulah echoes a popular sentiment when he says that the government of India will be committing a blunder if it does not respond sensibly to his offer for unconditional negotiations. He has taken a big risk, both personally and politically in saying that we are not fighting a religious war. He has also declared that he has friends among human rights activists in India. His statement that the Dogras, Buddhists and Kashmiri Pandits are their brothers and that the problem can only be solved by taking their wishes into account has annoyed the Islamic fundamentalists no end. But since Yasin enjoys tremendous credibility and respect, he can change the political atmosphere provided the government of India acts sensibly. As in Punjab, there are many allegations that the government has unleashed its own criminals in the underground movement. Prior to separatist terrorism, criminals routinely got patronage from all political parties, money through anti-social activity and black-marketing. They used to be called the Rice-Brigade because many of them were involved in the broken rice trade. It is alleged that these political goondas are being injected into the terrorist movement to give a bad name to militancy.

Politicians—of both the Congress, the National Conference (NC) and other smaller parties are seen as having collectively created the mess. Sannaulah Butt gave a relatively non-partisan account of the Kashmir crisis:

In 1947, we Kashmiri Muslims drove out Pakistan invaders. Once again in 1965, we thwarted Pakistani moves by handing over Pakistani infiltrators to the Indian security forces. But the Indian rulers have let us down badly. They did not trust us nor allowed us to have any free and fair elections right from 1951, when elections to the Constituent Assembly were held. Sheikh Abdullah did not allow even one seat to be contested. People who dared stand against NC candidates were kidnapped, beaten and had their nomination papers rejected on bogus grounds. Sheikh Sahib never believed in democracy. He felt he was sent by God to rule Kashmir and felt outraged at the presumption that people should elect their own government.

In the subsequent elections, a similar story was repeated. Bakshi Gulam Muhammad and Sadiq behaved no different from Abdullah.

'Why do you then blame the Central Government for the doings of Kashmiri leaders?' I asked. 'Far from stopping such misdoings, the Central Government encouraged this fraud on Kashmiri people because it did not trust us. They should have openly expressed their disapproval and displeasure at this state of affairs and ensured that such corruption and rigging did not happen.'

As angry as they are with the Indian Government and the national political parties, one hears the same people talk of Morarji Desai with glowing respect because he was one politician who prevented his party and government from rigging the elections. To quote Sannaulah Butt:

In 1977, all the leaders of the Janata Party, which was then in power at the Centre, had agreed that that time too the election would be rigged in favour of the Janata Party. Morarji Desai, however, put his foot down and insisted on a fair election. However, he could not prevent Sheikh Abdullah from rigging the votes in favour of the National Conference which was totally needless because he would have won anyway.

Because the Centre was not involved in manipulating and forcing a government of its choice on Kashmiris, they felt secure and to this day remember that one election and Morarji Desai with respect and fondness. It is not too far fetched to say that if the Nehru-Gandhi dynasty had half the good sense and political integrity that Morarjibhai displayed, today the Pakistan-held Kashmir would be in rebellion and not Indian Kashmir.

After his release from jail, JKLF leader Yasin Malik has been reiterating that his outfit will initiate a dialogue with not only Kashmiri Pandits living in refugee camps but also with the people of Jammu and Ladakh, who cherish different ethnic identities than Kashmiri Muslims. He will try to carry them along in the movement for azadi , recognizing the fact that the demand for azadi is currently being supported only by Kashmiri Muslims. The Kashmir valley and Kashmiri Muslims have so far dominated the politics of Jammu & Kashmir. Their conflict with the Centre came to override all other political considerations. Those asking for plebiscite to decide the future of Kashmir cannot for long ignore the fact that Jammu and Ladakh occupy a larger territory and have a larger population than that of Kashmir valley and that people in these regions do not share the political aspirations of Kashmiri Muslims. Of the total area of 1.01 lakhs sq. kms. in Jammu & Kashmir state, Ladakh is the biggest division with in area of 59,146 sq. kms. Jammu division comes next in size with 28, 293 sq. kms. while the Kashmir valley covers only 15,948 sq. km.

As per the 1981 census, Muslims in all three divisions account for 64.2 per cent of the total population out of which Kashmir valley Muslims are 49.7 per cent of the state population. Hindus account for 32.3 per cent of the state population. Most of them are concentrated in the Jammu division where they constitute 66.3 per cent of the total population. Ladakh division has a majority of Buddhist who constitute 51.87 per cent of the population.

The Muslims in Jammu and Ladakh regions are of a different ethnic stock than the Kashmiri Muslims. JKLF leaders admit that Jammu & Kashmir is 'like a mini-India' in so far as its population is not ethnically or linguistically homogeneous. Even Kashmiri Muslims are politically divided, with only a small section supporting secession to Pakistan. The Ladakh and Jammu regions would want autonomy more from the control of Srinagar than from the Central Government. The separatist movement in Kashmir can easily trigger off counter separatisms in Jammu and Ladakh. In a free plebiscite, the majority are unlikely to vote for Pakistan. That is why the Pakistan government is ruling out azadi as an option available to Kashmiris. But when Kashmiri Muslims insist on azadi, they risk not only annoying the Pakistan rulers, but also unleashing a similar demand from the Jammu and Ladakh regions. Yasin Malik is one of the few leaders to acknowledge the dilemma inherent in the situation.

My impression was that the average Kashmiri's anger and hatred is focused on the Central Government and its armed forces. They display very little anti-Hindu feeling and would not be in favour of driving out Kashmiri Hindus. However, sections of the educated elite among the Kashmiri Muslims hate Kashmiri Pandits with a fair degree of gusto because in matters of education and employment it is they who come into direct conflict with the Pandits who are far better educated and, therefore, get jobs more easily. According to the 1981 census the literacy rate among the Pandits was 80 per cent in a state where the overall literacy rate was a mere 26.7 per cent. The resentment of educated Kashmiri Muslims is due to the fact that the Pandits had got used to dominating on account of being economically and educationally better off and never reconciled to the spread of education among Kashmiri Muslims. Whatever the reasons for their mutual antipathy, I got the impression that the educated sections among the Muslims would pose the real hurdles in the return of the Kashmiri Pandits to their homes. The matter is further complicated by the fact that Kashmiri Pandit leaders have followed self-harming politics at the behest of the Bharatiya Janta Party (BJP) and the Home Ministry. The Pannun Kashmir outfit, started at the instigation of the Home Ministry, have been demanding a separate homeland in the valley for Kashmiri Pandits. This has made them even more suspect in the eyes of the Kashmiri Muslims.

So far, only Yasin Malik is talking of making efforts to get the Pandits to return to the valley. He announced that he would visit the refugee camps and initiate a dialogue with them. However, he has not yet carried out this promise. It may well be due to the fact that if he were to do so the pro-Pakistan militants would intensify propaganda against him claiming that he has become a Government of India agent. Even erstwhile liberals like Zafar Meharaj say, 'This is no time for the return of Kashmiri Pandits. They dissociated with the 'Kashmiri cause' by siding with the former Governor, Jagmohan. They can return only if they publicly admit their mistake and apologize for it.' This statement gives an idea of how deep the communal divide has become. However, his wife Naseem spoke in a different tenor indicating that all is not yet lost. She described how passing through one of the Srinagar bazars recently, she saw a lone saree hanging from a balcony. She felt good at the sight and wished more such sarees would become visible. Since sarees symbolize Kashmiri Pandit households, more such sarees on the balconies would indicate that things have become normal and Hindus have returned to the valley.

I was reminded of our meeting with the Bar Association in

Anantnag, where several Muslim lawyers repeatedly pointed to Motilal
Bhatt, a Hindu lawyer, who continued to stay in Anantnag even
after all the other Hindu families had left. This was to 'prove' that
the Muslims had not driven the Pandits out of Kashmir. They kept
emphasizing that he was absolutely safe. Motilal Bhatt himself was
most unwilling to say whether the situation was indeed safe for
Hindus, though he said that his family had not been attacked. But
surprisingly enough, in a huge gathering of his Muslim colleagues,
he ventured to say: 'We cannot freely express what the militants do
because if we do, we will be killed the very same night.' Very few
Muslims were willing to say even this much openly, though in private
conversations they did indicate that the pro-Pakistan terrorists were
brazenly committing atrocities, including rape and abduction of
women.

As in the case of terrorist killings in Punjab, people outside Kashmir
are unable to recognize the fact that as with Khalistanis, Kashmiri
militants are killing more Muslims than Hindus. Of the nearly 5000
civilians killed by the terrorists, only 360 were Kashmiri Pandits.
The rest were all Muslims. The militants thus represent an even
greater danger to the Muslims than to the Hindus because the latter
can at least count on government support. The Muslims cannot expect
to be similarly protected.

Most people we met were extremely sceptical about the possibility
of an acceptable solution, though there was a widespread consensus
that the problem cannot be solved through guns. Even though very
few Kashmiri Muslims are willing to talk against terrorism as they
are afraid of terrorist guns, yet there is no doubt a growing
disenchantment with terrorism. A senior Muslim bureaucrat said it
all: 'While Kashmiris are fed up with militancy, the army excesses
are preventing the people from opposing the militants unequivocally.'
He thinks that though the alienation is deep, the situation is not
hopeless and that the Kashmiri leaders would be willing to settle for
genuine autonomy of the type envisaged in the arrangement worked
out under Article 370 plus a credible commitment that the Indian
Government will not behave as badly in the future. Many people
echoed sentiments like the following:

Even as we begin to tire of militancy, your forces come and instigate us to
come back to the battlefield. Our movement has not gained as much due to

the hard work of *mujahideens* as it has from the misdoings of the Indian army. They have succeeded in estranging us from India better than the propaganda of mujahideens.

However, even in the present polarized political situation, people were open and willing in their praise of a few army officers and bureaucrats who have behaved with responsibility. Several such persons were openly named during the course of our stay in Kashmir. The criminalization of the movement and the coming in of foreign mercenary terrorists trained by Pakistan to curb the influence of the pro-azadi JKLF has disillusioned even many of the die-hard supporters of azadi. The transformation of Yasin Malik from a gun-wielding militant to someone who is adopting Gandhian techniques of protest reflects a widespread recognition that violence will only breed more violence. Therefore, most leaders are beginning to talk of a negotiated settlement. However, there is a great deal of misapprehension that even if a settlement were reached, the Government of India would then start dragging its feet. To quote Maulana Ansari: 'Both sides will have to come without pre-conditions to the negotiation table. But we will have to set a time limit. Not like what happened with the Shimla Agreement.'

One of the biggest grievances Kashmiris have is that the Indian Government is unwilling to include the Kashmiris when negotiating a solution with Pakistan. Though most Indians are familiar with the term Pakistan occupied Kashmir (POK), it is not fully understood that the forced partition of Kashmir is something Kashmiri Muslims have not made peace with. There are enough political symbols to remind them that this is supposed to be a temporary phenomenon. For instance, the state assembly is supposed to have 100 seats out of which 25 are reserved for the POK region. Likewise, the migrants who came to the Jammu region after the forced partition have not been given citizenship rights nor allowed to own property, hold jobs, or vote in state elections under the specious plea that when Kashmir is finally united, they will go back to their homes. Likewise, the property of those who left for POK from the Jammu region has been reserved for them and not used for resettling refugees as in other parts of India. Moreover, many Muslim families are divided on both sides of the border, which is in any case an unnatural border and has, therefore, remained porous through the decades following partition. Thus for a Kashmiri Muslim, 'crossing the border' into POK does not have the same kind of connotation of illegality and anti-state activity that it has for the rest of mainland Indians.

Therefore, one major demand is that people from both sides, or at least political leaders, be allowed to interact with each other and find a mutually acceptable solution for unification of the two Kashmirs and to opt for a system of governance of their choice. Just as Indian Kashmiri Muslims are divided into three camps (those who favour azadi, those who wish to merge with Pakistan and those who wish to stay with India), likewise there is an equally serious conflict in POK. It is a mistake to think that allowing a free flow of people between the divided Kashmir valley will endanger India's security. Pakistan stands to lose much more. As Zafar Meharaj put it, 'Those who are now pro-Pakistan should be especially encouraged to visit that side so that they can see the reality for themselves.' If the Government of India were to make a unilateral declaration of this kind, it would put the Pakistan government on the defensive. The social and political scenario is far more bleak in Pakistan than in India and the ongoing conflict between various ethnic communities in Pakistan is far more murderous just as their democracy is far more fragile than India's.

If India tries to compete with Pakistan in authoritarian measures, as we seem to be doing with regard to Kashmir, we are bound to lose the battle. However, if we build and strengthen democratic institutions in Kashmir rather than act as an occupation force, Pakistan is not likely to win the Kashmir battle. The Kashmiri Muslims are beginning to gravitate towards the Muslim state of Pakistan not so much for religious reasons as because the Indian Government mistrusts them on account of their being Muslims. Otherwise there is very little in common between the Pakistani version of Islam and the benign Islam that the Kashmiris have evolved.

Various suggestions came up during our talks with different sections of Kashmiri leadership. Broadly speaking, there was a widespread consensus on the following:
- Release of imprisoned leaders like Abdul Ghani Lone, Shabir Shah, and Syed Ali Gilani as a precursor to starting a political process.
- Sending the army back to the barracks because it is legitimizing militancy. The army should be called only if a disturbance or incident takes place.
- Starting a dialogue for settling the Kashmir dispute without preconditions on either side.

- Allowing free flow of movement of people between the two Kashmirs.
- Including Kashmiri representatives in dialogues with Pakistan to settle the Kashmir dispute between the two countries.
- Allowing the various regional groups such as the Kashmiris, Dogras, Ladakhis, Buddhists, Punjabis, Kashmiri Pandits, Gujjars and so on to work out a mutually acceptable political settlement for the governance of Jammu & Kashmir.

All these are fairly reasonable demands and can easily pave the way for a solution provided the Central Government behaves responsibly and in a trustworthy manner.

15

To Sing or not to Sing:
The National Anthem Controversy

L ike most other people in this country, I had never given much thought to our national anthem until the recent controversy was triggered off following the expulsion of three Christian students from a school in Kerala for refusing to sing the national anthem. The vigorous debate carried on in newspapers and magazines could well have been dismissed as much ado about nothing.

But, then, the government and the Prime Minister stepped in to proclaim that they intended to make the singing of the national anthem obligatory. Not to sing it will be considered anti-national. Therefore, I now feel compelled to examine the issue seriously.

It is important to ask: Why this sudden enthusiasm for making everyone sing the national anthem? I say 'sudden', because I remember that, many years ago, when it was made compulsory to play the anthem in cinema halls after each show, the move had to be withdrawn because most people, especially adults, would either walk off or remain seated. Many grumbled openly and called this ritual an unwarranted nuisance. Many others openly made fun of it. At that time, no one mentioned taking disciplinary action against people who refused to stand in respect or to sing along.

Even in more recent years, whenever I have attended functions where the national anthem is played or sung, while most people stand up they do not sing, primarily because most people, including the educated, do not know how to sing it.

Why then this new wave of enthusiasm for the anthem? Can it be that more people have learnt the anthem and begun to appreciate its beauty?

First published in *The Illustrated Weekly of India*, March 8 1987.

To find out, I interviewed 50 people, most of whom I had never met before, in a few neighbourhoods of Delhi. I deliberately picked Hindus because the Hindu community seems the most agitated about the need to make anthem-singing compulsory—whatever that means. I also deliberately picked educated males because this section is the opinion-making section in urban India and has been in the forefront of the present controversy.

The sample included 5 postgraduates, 20 graduates, and 20 who had passed the higher secondary or matriculation examination. Several of these last were undergraduate students. Fourteen were under 25 years of age, twenty seven were 25 or above, and the age of nine men was unknown.

Of the people interviewed, only one person knew the national anthem and could actually sing it. Interestingly, he was the only one who was categorically against making the singing of the anthem compulsory, although he said he himself held it in respect. He sang it with great feeling , sitting at a dinner table in a restaurant.

His was the most humane response: 'It is not necessary to have a particular national anthem. What we need is to think about the country in the right spirit, develop socially responsible thinking on various issues such as child marriage, wife beating, wife abuse and so on.'

The other 49 out of the 50 interviewed could not recite the full national anthem. A majority could not get past the first two lines and the rest stumbled after reciting in a chaotic fashion the lines which list the provinces of India. It is noteworthy that not one person of the 50 interviewed knew the meaning of all the words in the anthem, not even the meaning of all the words in the first two lines.

One person insisted that *Sare jahan se acchha* is the national anthem. Three elderly Hindu gentlemen said that since they had studied in Urdu, they did not know what the national anthem was, yet they thought singing it should be 'compulsory'. Several others, most of them businessmen and shopkeepers, said they were so busy with their work that they had no time to think of or sing the anthem, but nevertheless they felt it should be compulsory.

The responses broadly fell into three categories. One category consisted of those who thought the national anthem was a unifying factor:

1. 'The national anthem would encourage you to be proud of your own country . . . Unity should become stronger. Today, unity is at peril . . . Unity can be generated by homogenizing; if Sikh and

Hindu and Muslim all sing the same song, then naturally there will be a sense of unity.' [Age 46, PhD, scientific officer]

2. 'It stands for national unity and national integration, so it should be made compulsory.' [Age 35, MA History, government service]

The second category, which was quite large, consisted of those who saw the anthem as under threat from the minority communities, and, therefore, wanted to protect it:

1. 'There are people who say they will not sing the anthem. Why shouldn't they sing it? They live in India, they will have to do everything in India. [*Bharat mein har cheez karni paregi*] . . . People who live in India have to respect India, acknowledge its importance. The Congress has been pampering minorities but once Hindus awaken, they will show that Hindus are everything [*Hindu hi sab kuch hai*]. Now the Congress has stopped pampering the minorities. Hinduism is coming. Gradually, Hindus will overshadow India, Hindu religion will overshadow India.'

'Do you mean this is a religious conflict'

'Yes.'

'Not concerning the country?'

'It concerns the country too. What does Hindustan mean? The country of Hindus.'

'So for you, the only meaning this has is to promote Hinduism?'

'Yes'

'It has no other significance?'

'No'

[Age 22, B.Com., businessman]

2. 'In every country there are certain things which nobody questions. Unfortunately, in India, some people think they are free to indulge in anything they like. This is possible only in India. Even the most free countries like the United States and England do not allow so much freedom as is available to people in India, particularly to some communities who are trying to exploit it, against the interests of the country. It should not be allowed. It should be stopped at the first instance.' [Age 52, MA Economics, government service]

A third, sizeable, category consisted of those who could not adduce any reason for their belief that anthem singing should be compulsory, not even when pressed:

1. 'It should be compulsory.'

'Of what use will that be?'

'It will be of some use or other.'

[Higher Secondary, businessman]

2. 'It should be compulsory. It has to be sung by every Indian.'
   'If someone does not sing, should he be punished?'
   'No'
   'Then what do you mean by compulsory?'
   'It has to be there. There is no reason for that. It has to be there.'
   [Age 20, Second year BA student]

However, most of those who wanted the anthem made compulsory singing did not want it made compulsory for themselves. When I asked whether singing the anthem should be made compulsory daily in all offices and business establishments, hardly anyone wanted this version of 'compulsory'. No one wanted it re-introduced as a compulsion in cinema halls and similar public places. Most felt it would become a joke there.

It is clear from such responses that the enthusiasm for the national anthem does not arise primarily from any love for the song itself, but rather from the following reasons:

1. A strong suspicion and mistrust of the minorities and a belief that the refusal to sing the anthem by two children of the Jehovah's Witness sect of the Christian religion is a reflection of the inherent anti-national character of the minorities.

2. A feeling that Hindus need to protect the nation and the national symbols from the minorities—that Hindus are the special guardians of the national honour.

3. An assumption that minorities can live in India only if they abide by the terms and conditions laid down by the majority community—that if they are allowed to dissent on some issues, they may become uncontrollable.

4. A forced association of the national anthem and other national symbols with Hinduism.

5. A willingness to advocate compulsion together with an underlying presumption that only minorities will need to be coerced, since it is assumed that Hindus are already in unanimous agreement on such issues.

6. A belief that if people are taught to respect the national symbols, it would promote national unity.

It is significant that the whole controversy over singing the anthem is confined to the educated elite. Most people in this country do not know what the anthem is nor do they care about it, one way or the other. Several uneducated and semi-literate people I spoke to said they knew nothing of the debate nor did it matter to them. On the whole, it is not the poor and uneducated but the educated in this country who are the root cause of the ideology and practices that result in the spread of communal hatred and violence.

The Hindu majority is increasingly being taught to believe that the country belongs to them and the minorities can live here only on the terms decided by the majority community. The slightest evidence of dissent by the minorities is taken as an affront to the self-appointed owners of the nation.

The attitude of the Hindu community towards the country thus resembles that of a property owner towards property, or of a husband towards his wife. The same man who mistreats, disrespects and beats his wife will feel justified and self-righteous in beating up anyone else who, he thinks, wants to define an independent relationship with her, which he considers an affront to his honour.

The moment one assumes special rights of use or abuse over something, whether it is a wife or a nation, and turns it into a symbol of one's honour, all others begin to be seen as hidden enemies who can only covet or disrespect what is 'ours' or 'mine'.

National unity seems to mean different things to different sections who are most vigorously talking of it today. For the ruling party and its lackeys, national unity means servility to the Congress(I). Any attempt to question its stranglehold is dubbed anti-national, whether it was JP's movement in Bihar in the late seventies, or the formation of non-Congress(I) governments in West Bengal, Kashmir, Nagaland, Karnataka or Punjab.

While the Congress(I) is ferociously turning different sections of the population against one another in order to grab hold of different vote banks in different regions, it continues to use the rhetoric of national unity to mask its anti-people doings.

Another section much taken with the national unity rhetoric is the educated, urban, Hindu middle and upper class which is vociferously advocating that national honour and national symbols be put above all else. But they do not mean to practise what they preach. For, if indeed they wish to subordinate their own personal interests to those of the national, no one is preventing them from doing so.

But very few people seem keen to live by this morality in their own lives. In concrete terms, their own jobs, considerations of social status, personal power and family loyalties determine their actions much more visibly than any considerations of national honour or unity.singing

318 • RELIGION AT THE SERVICE OF NATIONALISM AND OTHER ESSAYS

Clearly, then, they expect this test to be applied only to the minorities. Since 'national unity' has increasingly become synonymous with bowing before the will of the government and the Hindu majority, 'putting the nation above all else' in concrete terms means submitting silently to every dictate of the government, as these dictates increasingly coincide with the sentiments of the chauvinistic organizations which claim to speak for the Hindu majority.

The dictates of the government, which claim to stand for the nation, are beginning to supersede even such integral institutions of our democratic system as the Constitution and the Supreme Court. Thus, the Prime Minister openly declared that his government does not agree with the Supreme Court judgement which ruled that singing the national anthem cannot be enforced on citizens and it is enough if they stand up in respect.

A ruling party member tore a copy of this judgement on the floor of the Parliament, and was not censured. Even more openly undermining the authority of the Supreme Court and the principle of separation of judiciary and executive, the Prime Minister stated that if the government cannot legally enforce anthem singing as a fundamental duty of all citizens, they will break or bend the Constitution. 'We will use constitutional means for the purpose.'

The third section most enthusiastic about promoting national unity through preaching of compulsory respect for national symbols are the erstwhile radical intellectuals who in recent years have been turning into statists. They argue that an individual who opts to be a citizen of a country, entitled to all the rights and privileges of a citizen, has certain obligations, the primary one among them being respect for the national flag, the state emblem and the national anthem.

This group is vociferous about the virtues that singing of the anthem has the power to inculcate in people. They glory in its symbolic meaning and links with the freedom struggle. They seem to forget that first, most people do not opt to be citizens of any country and second, most of the promises made to the people of India during the freedom struggle and at the time of Independence have been betrayed by the national leaders, so that most citizens cannot boast of many rights or privileges.

It is time we asked ourselves what we mean by promoting national unity. If by unity is meant the curbing of dissent then attempts to promote such unity are likely to result in greater disunity. I, personally, feel no sense of unity with people who are chanting slogans like 'Send Muslims to Pakistan or Kabristan' (a slogan used during the riots in Ahmedabad). I feel no sense of unity with people in Ahmedabad who called for an economic boycott or even extermination of Muslims and openly cited the analogy of Hitler's attempted extermination of European Jews.

Likewise, I feel no sense of unity with those who were responsible for the murder of Harijans at Arwal or at Pipra. No amount of singing the anthem or saluting the flag in the company of such people will make me feel a sense of unity with them.

Does singing the anthem by and of itself teach one to respect the country and to feel proud of being an Indian? A country is essentially its people. Respect for them involves care for their well-being and I cannot and refuse to be proud of being an Indian as long as:

a. millions of people continue to die of malnutrition in India while food is rotting in government and private godowns;

b. millions die of diseases that could have been eliminated years ago by the launching of public health campaigns. India has, for example, one of the highest infant and maternal mortality rates in the world, higher than those of many countries whose people are just as poor;

c. millions are deprived of basic needs such as clean drinking water, housing, clothing, health care facilities, and literacy;

d. thousands of women are routinely burnt or beaten to death in their homes in the name of upholding 'Indian family tradition';

e. citizens have to grovel before arbitrary bureaucrats and beg for their elementary rights;

f. policemen behave like criminals in uniform;

g. politicians, especially those of the ruling party, behave like mafia leaders and gangsters;

h. periodic communal, caste and other riots are unleashed against the minorities, with the connivance of significant elements of the ruling party, the bureaucracy and the police.

The singing of the national anthem cannot wipe away the shame of all these injustices in our country. There is no guarantee that if Harijan women learn to sing the national anthem, the power elite in villages will stop exploiting and raping them, and will begin to consider them equals.

Nor can Muslims be assured by guardians of national unity that if they sing the national anthem with respect, the police will not wreak horrors on them as they have been doing in Ahmedabad, Bhiwandi, Hyderabad and many other places. Likewise, there is no guarantee that if Sikhs living outside Punjab sing the national anthem with respect, they will not be persecuted and held accountable for the misdeeds of mad terrorists in Punjab.

Will the singing of the national anthem teach the policemen of this country to treat citizens like human beings? Will it prevent husbands from battering or burning their wives and teach them to treat them as human beings? Clearly, it is not supposed to perform any such miracle. Then, what kind of unity are we talking about?

Today, the national anthem is being used as an excuse to persecute the minorities by all those who are 'united' in this one-point programme. It is significant that of all the millions of people in the country who neither know nor have cared to know how to sing the anthem, three Christian children were picked up to drive home the need for respect to the anthem, were expelled from school and deprived of their right to an education by a government which professes to be desirous of extending education to all children.

Today, those school children, whose religious sect has a long history of refusing to sing the national anthem of any country, are being accused of 'subverting the Constitution'. Many citizens are deeply agitated by the prospect of a rising tide of such subversion. Mohammed Yunus was sued for declaring that the Supreme Court judges in the national anthem case were 'neither Indian nor judges.'

However, on 12 September, when the Prime Minister announced that 'the government would suitably amend the Constitution to make singing of the national anthem compulsory if the Supreme Court did not correct its decision' regarding the singing of the anthem [*Times of India*, 13 September, 1986], there was no protest against the declared intention to flout the principles of the Constitution by interfering with the judiciary's functions.

The separation of the judiciary and the executive in order to preserve the impartiality of the judiciary is a basic premise of the Constitution. By arrogating to himself the right to decide that the Supreme Court decision is not 'correct', the Prime Minister is practically denying the legal supremacy of the Supreme Court. On 2 December, the Prime Minister again declared that his government did not accept the Supreme Court judgement in the national anthem case.

This cavalier attitude falls in line with the trend started by Mrs Gandhi of keeping the Constitution a virtual hostage and amending it to give legality to her illegal actions, as when she declared the Emergency and amended the Constitution to suit her purposes. The tragic difference is that at that time there was a viable Opposition which protested against such usurpation of powers. Today, Rajiv Gandhi is widely applauded when he subverts the remains of the institutions of democracy.

Today, the Constitution needs to be protected most of all from the government. The police, the bureaucracy and the ruling party have many more violations of the Constitution to their credit than all the criminals of the country put together.

Having failed to meet the basic needs of the people, our government has constantly sought to use gimmicks to distract their attention from important issues. Failing to provide food and employment to millions of rural and urban poor, the government began to offer them tubectomies and vasectomies in the name of building a strong nation with a controlled population. Now, the effects of that gimmick are wearing out, so new ones are being tried.

Having failed to provide security of life to people, having failed to curb the criminal activities of its own machinery, the government proposes to require that the hungry, the impoverished, the unemployed and the discriminated sing the national anthem, salute the flag and swear loyalty to the Constitution—a Constitution which is violated the most by the government.

Today, the government might want to protect 'national honour' but the honour of the people of India needs protection from the government. Today, the government might talk of upholding the Constitution but the Constitutional rights of the people need to be protected, first and foremost, from the government.

If our purpose is to inculcate love for India in our people, we would do well not to confuse this with servility to the tyranny of the government. It should mean an intrinsic love and respect for India's people and their integrity, and an ability to draw inspiration from the glorious tradition of our cultural heritage. One of its glories is its history, replete with examples of creative and humane dissent. Revolt against dogmatic ruling groups and religious authorities, diversity and certain important forms of tolerance have always had a legitimate part in our culture.

The most rich periods of Indian civilization have been periods when social protest and challenge to tyranny were expressed forcefully, humanely and creatively. The historical figures that we should be most proud of and remember most often should include those who represent this trend—Buddha, Nanak, Kabir, Mirabai, Mahadeviakka, Phule, Mahatma Gandhi. All of them represent a spirit of revolt against authoritarianism and social tyranny, and deep love for our people and compassion for their dilemmas.

These reformers opposed ritual worship of empty symbols, whether religious or otherwise, and stood for the right of the individual to live in a humane way, by the light of their own conscience. Today, when we insist that people will have to sing the national anthem under threat of punishment by the government, we are teaching people mindless servility rather than love for India's heritage and its people.

Among those who do not know the literal meaning of our national anthem is our honourable Prime Minister who is reported to have said: 'The words in the national anthem given by Guru Rabindranath Tagore give us the message of tolerance, equality and integration but unfortunately some have come to regard them as mere words.' For the Congress(I) and Rajiv Gandhi equality and tolerance are not even mere words; they are manipulative slogans.

Even if one were to forget the controversy about whether or not the anthem was written by Tagore to celebrate the visit of the British emperor, and whether the *'Bharat Bhagya Vidhata'* [arbiter of India's destiny] refers to the emperor or to god, one cannot escape the fact that the song does not mention the rights and aspirations of the Indian people.

The anthem consists of a list of provinces with a pronounced northern bias (the entire South being summed up as 'Dravida' and the North–East being conspicuous by its absence), and assigns to people the passive role of accepting a destiny defined by some powerful entity. It celebrates geography, albeit rather badly, and victory, not humanity. It was originally composed as a paean to the British emperor.

I know the words of the national anthem from beginning to end and know how to sing it. I am from a Hindu family whose religious and other sensibilities are not offended by the singing of the anthem. In fact, I am not embarrassed to admit that even today it moves me as deeply as when I first learnt to sing it as a child. This is not a learnt intellectual response but a deep emotional upsurge. Therefore even after the words stopped inspiring me, I still cannot help being moved beyond words everytime I hear it. Yet I cannot think of any conditions under which I would sing the anthem, if the government tries to impose the singing of it on any citizen. Such an imposition would be another violation of the human rights, freedom and dignity of the people of this country.